THE
HISTORY OF MEDICINE
IN IRELAND

To My Wife

THE
HISTORY OF MEDICINE
IN IRELAND

JOHN F. FLEETWOOD

THE SKELLIG PRESS
DUBLIN
1983

First edition published 1951
Second edition published 1983
Copyright © by John F. Fleetwood 1951, 1983

Published in Ireland by
The Skellig Press Ltd.,
28 Mount Merrion Avenue,
Blackrock,
Co. Dublin.

British Library Cataloguing in Publication Data

Fleetwood, John F.
  The History of Medicine in Ireland. — 2nd ed.
  1. Medicine — Ireland — History.
  I. Title
  610′.9415   R486
  ISBN 0-946241-02-3

Typeset by Grove Graphics, Tring, Hertfordshire
Printed and bound by Billing & Sons Ltd.,
Worcester and London

Contents

Illustrations

Foreword to the first edition

By

WILLIAM DOOLIN M.B., F.R.C.S.I., M.R.I.A.

It has become the fashion of recent years for novelist or playwright, script-writer or journalist, to use the medical practitioner as the central subject of his romantic creation. The task of the medical historian is a more sober and a more difficult one: it is to present the practitioner and the investigator in an accurate assessment of their impact upon our social development.

Our knowledge of the early growth of medical theory and practice in this country is sadly fragmentary. In other lands, in which the written records of bygone centuries have been better preserved, this task has been accomplished by many gifted writers. To those records Irish exiles made their several contributions which, in large part, remain as yet unrevealed to their compatriots at home. One thinks of O'Glacan, who left Donegal to fill the Chair of Physic in the university of Toulouse; of Bernard O'Connor, who looked back to his Kerry hills in his declining years as physician to a King of Poland; of John O'Higgins, who became physician to Philip of Spain; and of Georges Mareschal, son of an Irish officer in the armies of Louis, who lifted the trade of surgery to parity with the scornful physicians of Paris, thus pointing the way to the later establishment of our Royal Colleges of Surgeons in Edinburgh, in Dublin, and in London.

The assessment of these − and other − Irish contributions to the story of medicine is a task which still awaits the historian. Their records still lie *perdus* on the shelves of many libraries in the universities and monasteries of Western Europe, awaiting the attention of the translator who will have the leisure and the learning enabling him to fill in these gaps in our knowledge of the past.

Such a task − and it will be no easy labour − is not for the man whose days and nights are filled by the claims of busy practice. With commendable zeal and no small meed of industry, Dr Fleetwood has given us here within the covers of a single volume the outlines of the evolution of our schools of medicine as they stand to-day in the Four Fields of Irleand. He is, so far as I am aware, the first who has attempted so comprehensive a survey. The definitive history of Irish Medicine has yet to be written: that will be a task for the scholar equipped with the knowledge of Gaelic, Latin and English, middle and old, as well as of medicine. Dr Fleetwood's work has here

provided for the general and the medical reader interested in history
an admirable précis of the growth of our medical schools, and for
the future historian a valuable *mémoire pour servir*. I count it a high
privilege to have been asked to introduce his work to what, I hope,
will be an ever-growing number of readers.

WM. DOOLIN.

Foreword

What would Henry Ford, who said 'history is bunk', have thought of the history of medicine? He would probably have dismissed it as the esoteric and time-wasting indulgence of literary-minded doctors, as many of their colleagues do. They are mistaken. Although it is a hybrid, compact of the history of ideas, the history of science, biography, folklore and mythology, it is a challenging, rewarding, and above all an under-valued subject. It is an important branch of social history and as medicine, in some degree, mirrors human mores and increasingly influences economics — which Government Ministers now bitterly realise having offered a cornucopia of remedies — its pursuit could help to chart more rationally the future of medicine which at present includes the ministrations of 'bare-foot doctors' in the east and nuclear magnetic resonance in the west.

To admit that medical history lacks high academic patronage (the situation is different in American medical schools) is not to denigrate the efforts of a handful of authors whose publications have provided information about medicine in Ireland. Outstanding among our Irish medical historiographers were Sir Charles Cameron, John Knott, T. P. C. Kirkpatrick, 'Bill' Doolin and J. D. H. Widdess. More than thirty years ago the publication of Dr Fleetwood's *History of Medicine in Ireland*, a considerable achievement for a young man, placed him in line with his eminent predecessors. The passage of time has brought John Fleetwood into the senior ranks of the profession but his book, by now a standard reference work, has been long out-of-print. It is my pleasure to welcome its re-incarnation and to congratulate his publishers for their enterprise in making 'Fleetwood' available in a revised edition to a new generation of readers.

J. B. LYONS
Department of the History of Medicine,
The Royal College of Surgeons in Ireland,
St Stephen's Green, Dublin.

Preface

In the foreword to the first edition of this book the late William Doolin wrote that to write the definitive history of Irish Medicine would require a detailed knowledge of Latin, Gaelic and English with their many variations over the centuries as well as of ancient and modern medicine. Equally important would be the time and finance to visit libraries, medical schools, monasteries and national archives in many parts of Europe. This book falls far short of that high target but I hope this record of our medical past will demonstrate how old that past is and encourage us all to take some pride therein.

I have been helped by my many colleagues, librarians, secretaries of hospitals and medical societies both in Ireland and elsewhere. Amongst them my special thanks are due to, in alphabetical order:—

Miss A. Allen − Royal Belfast Hospital for Sick Children.
Dr M. Berber − Irish Institute of General Practice.
Dr M. J. Boland − R.C.G.P. (Southern Faculty).
Mr J. F. Browne − Mater Infirmorum Belfast.
Sʀ M. Butterley − Medical Missionaries of Mary.
Dr B. Coffey − R.C.G.P. (Southern Faculty).
Dr G. Crookes − Royal Victoria Eye and Ear Hospital.
Mr D. J. Dempsey − Federated Dublin Voluntary Hospitals.
Mr J. Donnelly − Berkely Court Hotel.
Prof P. Froggatt − Queen's University Belfast.
Mr I. R. Gault − Rotunda Hospital.
Mr P. Harnett − Barrington's Hospital Limerick.
Dr G. R. Henry − Rotunda Hospital.
Mr J. D. Kenny − Jervis St Hospital.
Mr M. B. McCann − Medical Union.
Dr D. MacDonald − National Maternity Hospital.
Prof P. J. Meehan − St Patrick's Hospital.
Dr F. O. Meenan − St Vincent's Hospital.
Prof P. N. Meenan − University College Dublin.
Dr S. Moore − R.C.G.P. (Northern Faculty).
Dr E. J. O'Brien − R.C.G.P. (Southern Faculty).
Mr J. O'Hanlon − Mater Misericordiae Hospital.
Mr J. B. Prendiville − Dr Steeven's Hospital.
Dr M. Rahill − Newcastle Hospital.
Miss M. Smithwick − Coombe Lying-in Hospital.
Mr S. K. Verna − Embassy of India, Dublin.
Dr and Mrs O. Wood − R.C.G.P. (Northern Faculty).

Two colleagues deserve my special thanks, Professor J. B. Lyons who kindly wrote the foreword to this second edition and Dr H. G. Calwell, Archivist of the Royal Victoria Hospital, Belfast, who gave me much information about the Belfast School and enabled me to correct what I now recognise were serious deficits in the first edition.

As well as taking the photographs for several illustrations Conor Fleetwood secured many useful pieces of information in the course of business visits to various hospitals and medical schools.

Our secretaries Ann Devine and Colette Ryan put in many hours of deciphering illegible handwriting and producing legible copy for the publishers and printers whose technical advice was invaluable.

My wife saw little of me during the writing of this new edition. Once again to her 'Thank you for your unfailing help and support in this as in so many other things'.

JOHN FLEETWOOD, M.B., F.R.C.G.P., D.P.H., D.P.A.

Blackrock
Co. Dublin
1983

A Thighearna, tabair gnosa dom an saothar so do deanamh cum do gloire-se, cum leasa m'anma agus do réir mar atá orduigte agat-sa.*

* An old Irish prayer said before commencing work.

CHAPTER ONE

THE PRE-CHRISTIAN ERA

The early history of Ireland, whether medical or general, is like that of most countries, a mixture of folk-lore, doubtful facts and mixed pagan and Christian superstitions. Ancient tales say that the Celts had to conquer the Tuatha de Danann, who had themselves wrested the country from the Firbolgs. The battle of Moytura, in which the Firbolgs were overthrown, is the background to one of the earliest references to surgery in Ireland although events of medical interest had been noted at an earlier date.

Many burial-places dating from very early times have been excavated throughout the country but, owing to the custom of cremating bodies, it has been difficult to secure evidence of surgical skill. In a few instances it has been possible to diagnose bone and joint conditions from which early inhabitants suffered.

Generally, the teeth of skeletons dug up in Ireland show poor resistance to wear. This may be due to the limestone soil. Pyorrhoea, caries and bone abscesses are constantly found.

In 1934, excavations were carried out at Kilgreany, Co. Waterford. Human bones were discovered, as well as metal and stone objects belonging to various archaeological periods. All the bones were very fragmentary but many of them, from the vertebrae and forearms, showed evidence of chronic arthritis. (See *Journal of Royal Society of Antiquaries of Ireland*, Vol. LXV, Dec. 1935.)

In Carrownacon, Co. Mayo, the Second Harvard Archaeological Expedition to Ireland excavated a cist containing Bronze Age and cremation burials. One skeleton was thoroughly examined, even to the extent of X-raying the skull. The X-ray picture showed that this woman, dead over 2,000 years, suffered in early life from an inflammation of the mastoid process on her right side.

In another skeleton dug up at this place there was chronic arthritis of the spine. The deceased suffered from a stiff neck during life, as the second and third cervical vertebrae are fused.

In Mac Firbis' genealogy we read:

Thus saith an ancient authority; the first doctor, the first builder and the first fisherman that ever were in Eirinn, were:

1

> Capa for the healing of the sick,
> In his time was all powerful,
> And Luasad, the cunning builder,
> And Laighne, the fisherman.

Eaba, the female physician who accompanied the lady Ceasair into Eirinn, was the second doctor; Slanga, the son of Partholan, was the third doctor that came into Eirinn; and Fergna, the grandson of Crithinbel, was the fourth doctor who came into Eirinn, with Neimhide. The doctors of the Firbolgs were Dubhda Dubhlosad, Codan Connchisnech and Finghin Fisiocdha, Maine the son of Greasach and Aongus Anternmach. The doctors of the Tuatha de Danann were Diancecht, Airmedh, Miach.

The first reference to an event of medical interest noted in the *Annals of the Four Masters* occurred about 940 B.C. We read that: 'Nine thousand of Parthalon's people died in one week on Sean-Mhagh-Ealta-Edair, namely, five thousand men and four thousand women. Whence it is (named) Taimhleacht Muintire Parthaloin—Ireland was thirty years waste until Neimhide's arrival.'

The word *Taimhleacht* signifies a communal burying-ground for plague victims. This place has been identified with Tallaght, Co. Dublin where some very ancient tumuli are still to be seen on the hills. The word *Taimhleacht*, according to Joyce, is of pagan origin and is a common appellation of burying-places throughout the country.

Further in the *Annals*, the Neimhide mentioned above, who was probably of Greek origin, died of 'a plague' with three thousand others on Great Island in Cork Harbour.

A.M. 3959 was remarkable for the death of Slanoll after seventeen years on the throne at Tara. The *Annals of Clonmacnoise* and other writings are silent on the cause of his death, but are agreed that during his reign the country was free from all sickness and that his body remained incorrupt for forty years after burial.

The chronicles of this period are a wearisome repetition of battles, slayings and woundings. No reference is made to healing in the work of the Four Masters, until the account of the first battle of Moytura, 487 B.C.

In that conflict, the rule of the Firbolgs was overthrown by the Tuatha de Danann, who brought with them the civilisation of the East. The leader of the de Danann, Nuadhat son of Eochaidh, had his hand cut off during the battle. This was sufficient to debar him from the kingship. The wound was the occasion for the earliest recorded co-operation between surgeon and artificial limb-maker. Credne Cerd made an artificial hand in silver. Diancecht, the Irish AEsculapius, fitted it to the stump. From this Nuadhat was ever afterwards known as *Airgetlamh* or Silver Hand.

It is stated in the *Leabhar-Gabhala* of the O'Cleary that Diancecht and Credne formed the hand with motion in every finger joint. Miach, son of Diancecht, to excel his father, took off the hand. He then infused feeling and motion into every joint and vein, as if the hand were a natural one. The story has a sad ending. Twenty-seven years later, in the second battle of Moytura where Nuadhat was killed, Diancecht, jealous of Miach's superior knowledge, murdered him.

Diancecht is the only one of the traditional physicians of whom we have any full record. Two translations of his name have been suggested, one, 'vehement power,' the other, in Cormac's Glossary, 'god of healing' from the Irish, *Dia na h-ice*. Tradition held that, in addition to his son mentioned above, he had a daughter, Airmedh, who inherited much of his medical skill.

As in all primitive races, the early Irish physicians were of the priestly or Druidic caste. Their traditions were handed down orally from remote antiquity and, unfortunately for the historian, allowed to die with the seers.

Probably the Druids belonged to the same body as the magic workers of the East and were sufficiently skilled in hypnotism to induce others to see and hear as they desired.

The most important instance of Diancecht's medical skill occurred at the second battle of Moytura where he prepared, in the rear of the army, a bath of medicinal herbs, into which wounded plunged for instantaneous healing.

'After a time,' continues the legend, 'there grew up from Miach's grave 365 herbs, from the 365 joints and sinews and members of his body, each herb with mighty virtues to cure the part of the body from which it grew. His sister, Airmedh, plucked the herbs and, carefully sorting them, wrapped them in her mantle. But, jealous old Diancecht came and mixed them up so that now no leech has knowledge of their distinctive qualities unless the Holy Spirit should teach him.'

The belief that there were 365 joints and members of the body was common up to historical times. A reference to this occurs in the religious treatise called *Na Arrada,* which Meyer dates as not later than the eighth century A.D.

The *Book of Lecan*, compiled in 1417, derives the name of Lus-magh, near Banagher in Co. Offaly, from the bath of herbs– 'the plain or field of herbs, so called, because it was out of it Diancecht brought every healing plant which could be brought to Slainge's well in Acadh Abba, at Magh Tuireadh, when the great battle was fought between the Tuatha de Danann and the Fomorians.'

The battle was fought along the north-eastern bank of Lough

Corrib, between the villages of Cross and Cong. There are still many remains of stone circles, cairns, tumuli and forts in this area.

Medicated baths were frequently mentioned in Irish historical tales. During the reign of Eremon, inhabitants of the east coast were attacked by British invaders who used poisoned weapons of such potency that the least scratch caused death. At last, the king, by the advice of a druid, prepared a bath, into which was poured the milk of 150 white hornless cows. The wounded were bathed here and suffered no ill-effects from the poison. In the epic of the Cattle Raid of Cooley, Conchubhar mac Nessa's physician, Fingin, used a bath of herbs medicated with the marrow of cows.

Although these are legends, it is certain that the ordinary bath was used for skin diseases, including leprosy. In Cormac's Glossary, the word *fothrucud*, a bath, is referred to as being applied to a medicinal bath, most often used for lepers. At the time leprosy might have been diagnosed in many cases which were really scabies or impetigo. Either of these complaints would respond favourably to bathing.

Several authorities record that, in the second century B.C. Josina, the ninth king of Scotland, was educated in Ireland by native physicians. He is credited with the authorship of a treatise on the use of herbs. The tradition at least shows that Irish physicians had a reputation abroad at the time. Josina's succession to the throne is dated as either 137 B.C. or 161 B.C.

About the beginning of the Christian era, Conchubhar mac Nessa, King of Ulster (died A.D. 37) was wounded in the head by a missile from a sling. At that time it was an Ulster custom to remove the brains from defeated enemies. These organs were then mixed with lime until they formed hard balls which were used in the place of stones in sling shots. It was such a weapon that wounded Conchubhar. O'Curry in his *Lectures on Manuscript Materials,* gives this translation of the account in the *Book of Leinster*:

In the meantime his physician was brought to Conchubhar namely Fingin. He it was that could know by the fume that rose from a house the number that was ill in the house, and every disease that prevailed in the house. 'Good,' said Fingin, 'if the stone be taken out of thy head, thou shalt be dead at once, if it is not taken out of it, however, I would cure thee, but it would be a blemish upon thee.' 'The blemish,' said the Ultonians, 'is better for us than his death.' His head was then healed, and it was stitched with thread of gold, because the colour of Conchubhar's hair was the same as the colour of gold. And the doctor said to Conchubhar that he should be cautious, that he should not allow his anger to come upon him, and that he should not go upon a horse and that he should not run.

He continued then in that doubtful state as long as he lived, namely, seven years, and was incapable of action but to remain sitting only, that is, until he heard that Christ was crucified by the Jews.

The death of Christ was marked by tempests, thunder and lightning, the appearance of which troubled Conchubhar.

Bacrach, a druid, explained the reason of the storms which arose. The king became enraged at the thought of an innocent Man's execution and rushed forth with his sword into the woods, where he began to cut and fell the trees, as he would the murderers of Christ, with such violence that the wound in his skull burst open and he died.

Physicians figured conspicuously in the tales of the Red Branch Knights. There was an organised army medical service attached to the Ulster forces during the war of the Tain. Their commanding officer was Fingin Faithliaig (the prophetic leech). King Conchubhar's personal physician, Faithliaig, had an official residence on Sliabh Fuaid, near Armagh.

Each member of the medical service carried a bag full of medicines and dressings. At the end of a day's fighting, whether between armies or individuals, wounds were dressed and the warriors refreshed.

In a story of Fionn Mac Cumhail it is stated that a piece of the skin of a ewe was fixed to a skinless part of one of the warriors. This took so well that a fleece of wool, which had to be periodically shorn, grew from the graft.

The motto contained in the badge of the Army Medical Corps recalls a description of part of the Cattle Raid of Cooley as related in the *Book of Leinster*. This deals with a period of civil war shortly before the Christian era. The two chief heroes of the saga were Cuchualainn and Ferdiad. They engaged in single combat on successive days at a ford somewhere along the line of the present Border. At the end of each day's fighting they declared a truce and shared their provisions and healing herbs. This chivalrous action was described by the compiler of the manuscript in the words *comraind legis* or 'equal division of healing.' Freely translated, this may be rendered as 'impartial treatment of the wounded,' a worthy motto for a medical service.

King Cormac, who reigned about A.D. 227, made an order 'that all future monarchs of Ireland should be at all times accompanied by ten persons consisting of a chief, a judge, a druid, a physician, a poet, an historian, a musician and three servants. The chief was to sit at the king's shoulders; the judge to explain the laws and customs of the country in the king's presence; the druid for sacrifice and prophecy of good or evil to the country, by his pagan knowledge. The physician for attending to the health of the king, queen and household.' This order continued in force from Cormac's time to the death of the great monarch Brian Boru in the year 1014.

The Battle of Crionna (A.D. 266) was the occasion of an early example of medical sharp practice. At the battle Cormac defeated the three Ferguses of Ulster. Two Munster chieftains were severely wounded and remained at Tara. Cormac induced his physicians to insert poison, insects and foreign bodies into their wounds in order to delay their recovery. They were placed in separate rooms so that neither might witness what was done to the other. One of the princes, Lughaidh Lagha, became angry with the king during a bedside conference. His wounds burst open when he leaped up. The foreign bodies were ejected and he fled to safety. He sent Fineen, one of the leading Munster physicians, with three of his pupils to attend the other chieftain Teige, who was still isolated and unaware of what had happened.

When they arrived near the house where Teige lay his groans were audible from a distance. The pupils were expected to be able to diagnose the disease from the character of the groans.

There are few references to midwifery in early chronicles, probably because childbirth was regarded as a normal occurrence, seldom requiring unusual attention. Caesarean section was known and practised in pre-Christian times. The first reference to it concerns a sister of Maeve, Queen of Connacht in the first part of the fifth century A.D. When Maeve abandoned Conchubhar mac Nessa (mentioned above) he went to her father and requested the hand of this younger daughter, Eithne. When she was nearly nine months pregnant Eithne fell into the river anciently known as Claise Bearramain, in Co. Longford. She was rescued in a dying condition. Her side was cut open and a living infant boy delivered. He received the name of Furbaidhe, from *urbadh*, the ancient Gaelic name for Caesarean section. The name of the river was changed to Eithne; now anglicised as the Inny. The story of the incident is recounted in the *Book of Lecan*, now in the Royal Irish Academy.

Much of the midwifery was of a primitive and superstitious character. In the seventh century King Dermot had two wives. One of these was bald; the other barren. The sterile wife was given three doses of a specially medicated (blessed) water. After the first dose she brought forth a lamb. This was sacrificed as the first fruits of the womb. After the second she bore a salmon. Finally, a son, Aedh, was born.

Diancecht is said to have recognised fourteen disorders of the stomach. The prescription for 'Diancecht's porridge' has been handed down to recent times. It consisted of a brew of hazel buds, dandelions, chick-weed, wood-sorrel and oatmeal. It was used to relieve colds, phlegm, sore throat and worms, amongst other illnesses. Saffron he held to be a first-class pick-me-up.

Cupping was practised by the early Irish leeches, with a special instrument known as a *gipne*. This operation in which a vacuum is created over a painful skin area is seldom employed nowadays, although at times it may give great relief without the use of drugs. Tubes to drain off pus were in common use in early times.

Physiotherapy was practised extensively. On Inishmurray, and elsewhere, there are the remains of 'sweating houses' or *tighe nalluis*. These are stone houses about five feet by seven in area and some three or four feet high, having a narrow entrance. When they were to be used a great fire was lit inside, until the house became like an oven. The embers were then swept out and the patient, wrapped in a blanket, crept in. He remained inside until he sweated profusely. On emerging he plunged into a pool of cold water. He was then thoroughly rubbed until he glowed all over. Similar practices obtain from remote times in other countries, notably Russia and Finland.

The hot-air bath was probably introduced from the East to England during the Roman invasion. Whether the practice was then brought to this country by travellers returning from Britain or was a legacy from an older civilisation is uncertain. When the Romans left Britain about the fifth century A.D., the bath fell into disuse there. Despite this the sweating treatment was commonly practised in Ireland until within living memory. It was not employed solely medicinally, but also as a form of beauty treatment. In some areas the sweating houses were large enough to accommodate several persons at one time.

Healing stones or *cloca umra* were preserved in several places. They were supposed to be efficacious in many conditions, and their use is closely bound up with superstition. A special form of these were the *bullan* or brash stones. These had holes upon the surface in which water collected. Persons suffering from rheumatism would kneel in the water-filled holes. The water was also believed to be useful in eye diseases. Pregnant women were told to kneel at these stones and pray for their safe deliverance. From the *Annals of Tigernach* we learn that in A.D. 366 a princess died in consequence of swallowing a prepared poison, which indicates a knowledge of some form of pharmacy.

The Celts and kindred colonisers of Ireland originally came from the East. They brought their own customs and codes of laws, the Brehon laws, which were formed centuries before the birth of Christ, being the most ancient code in Europe. In the next chapter we will consider those sections of the laws which are of immediate medical interest.

CHAPTER TWO

THE BREHON LAWS

The *Senchus Mor* is one of the oldest and most important portions of the ancient laws of Ireland which have been preserved. It exhibits the remarkable modification of the Pagan laws by the coming of Christianity during the fifth century.

The Brehon Laws were first promulgated several hundred years before the birth of Christ. Their growth was gradual. There are many references in them to kings and judges, who added their own contributions piecemeal to existing laws. These contributions frequently contained acid comments on previous law-givers, such as 'the sudden judgements of Ailell.' Diancecht is mentioned as an authority on medical matters.

Physicians and their skill, or lack of it, were frequently mentioned. It is interesting to note that they were given a special standing in the community.

The person in charge of a sick man was responsible ' . . . for providing him with bed furniture i.e. plaids and bolsters. For providing him with a proper house–not dirty or snail-besmeared–not one of the three inferior houses, that is the cowhouse, sheephouse or pighouse–that there be four doors out of it that the sick man be seen from every side–and water must run across the middle of it–that the sick man be not injured by woman or dogs i.e. that fools or female scolds be not let into the house.'

A person engaged on such an errand of mercy as sending for a physician or compounding medicines was exempt from the law's attentions, until his task was done. Seeking a midwife for a woman in labour; struggling with an epileptic and securing a madman were further reasons for exemption from immediate payment of a fine or compensation.

Some form of medical registration must have been practised at the time, for it was laid down that an 'unlawful' physician should give notice of this fact before performing an operation. Failure to do this involved a fine for the unsuccessful removal of a joint or sinew or blood letting. Both the lawful and unlawful physician were expected, under penalty of a fine, to warn the patient who might not respond to treatment.

Provision is made in the *Book of Aicill* for a medical referee where a dispute arose between patient and physician as to treatment.

Compensation, including payment of a physician and male attendant, was payable by the aggressor in quarrels resulting in injury. The physician's share varied according to the social grade of the wounded person.

The fine for wounded of the highest rank was forty-two cows, of which eighteen went to the substitute of the disabled man, nine for diet, four and a heifer each to the doctor and nurse. The fine for maiming a houseless man was six cows. A houseboy or slave was valued at three cows.

The 'testing time' for cure of injuries to the head was three years. For the hand it was one year; for the leg fifteen months. If, within these periods, the wound gave trouble, the physician was fined, if it was shown to be his fault, if not the penalty fell on the aggressor. The negligent physician was bound to restore the cost of his food and keep during his period of treatment, as well as to pay the usual *eric** fine. In addition the case was turned over to another attendant.

Physicians and medical treatment are mentioned several times in those sections of the books which deal with the levy of distress. 'Distress' was the remedy for a great variety of wrongs. The plaintiff came to the defendant's residence and sat fasting at his door. This was a form of notice. If no food was offered and the fasting terminated at its due period, which varied with the gravity of the alleged wrong, the distress claimed became greater. If the defendant gave a security then the cause was in time tried by the judge.

The institution of fasting on a debtor has been practised in other countries with variations. In India, for example, a creditor would sit continously outside the debtor's house so as to force the latter to negotiate but fasting was not a part of the procedure.

In one of the many domestic laws of ancient Ireland of about the seventh century A.D., there is a reference to the care of aged persons. Three items of maintenance were allowed, maintenance in food, in attendance and in milk. For maintenance in food, half a wheaten loaf with salt and a vessel of sour milk daily; for attendance, his body to be washed every twentieth night and his head every Saturday; for milk, one milch cow every month throughout the year. Houses for poor aged men were to be at least seventeen feet long and made of basket work with weather boards.

Among the Celts, the relieving officer was entitled to levy a rate on landowners for the maintenance of 'the wretched and wandering

---

Eric was a fine levied in order to atone for bodily injury. It corresponded with the Teutonic *weregeld*.

poor.' His name in Irish signified 'Pillar of Endurance,' a cognomen with which many of their present day successors will be in whole-hearted agreement. Amongst the rules laid down was one that these officers should not consider themselves insulted by the abuse of beggars. The tribes were chargeable for the maintenance of beggars within their own districts.

According to the Brehon Laws the chief physicians sat in the Council of State, a prerogative which might with advantage be re-established to-day.

A king kept in his court an *ollamh*, or eminent member, of each profession: poet, historian, storyteller, physician, judge, builder, etc. Each of these gave his services to the king, for which a generous allowance was made, usually including a house and land. In addition, private practice was permitted with payment according to a fixed scale of charges.

The leech (*liagh*) ranked with the smith and workers in precious metals. His privileges included possession of twenty retainers, ten of whom paid him tribute without refection. His place, above the salt, at banquets was a distinguished one. From every cow slaughtered for the chief the kidneys were reserved for the physician.

Several sections of these laws are devoted to the care of the insane. Grades of mental defect were recognised. The lunatic who could do no work, or a madwoman, were entitled to a greater subsistence allowance than a weak-minded person who could do simple tasks or act as a minstrel.

Five cows is the fine for neglecting to provide for the maintenance of the fool who has land and the power of amusing and *his having these* is the cause of the smallness of the fine. Ten cows is the fine for neglecting the maintenance of every madwoman; and the reason that the fine is greater than that of the fool is, for the madwoman is not a minstrel and has not land. If the fool has not land or has not power of amusing, the fine for neglecting to provide for his maintenance is equal to that of the madwoman who can do no work.

Children were not presumed to be fools until they were seven years old, nor half-wits until they had reached their fourteenth year.

Persons of unsound mind were protected from the effects of their mental confusion. Contracts, loans, or borrowings made by sane people with lunatics were invalid unless they had been witnessed and permitted by the lunatic's guardian.

Lunatics were exempted from the punishments inflicted for many crimes. If incited by others to commit crime the punishment fell on the instigator of the crime instead of on the lunatic. If the lunatic was intoxicated during his crime, punishment was inflicted on those who bought him drinks.

The provisions for the care of the children of insane parents are of some interest inasmuch as they recognised that the children might be feeble-minded and that lunatic parents could not contribute to their upkeep. If a sane adult had any part in bringing about sexual connection between two lunatics, he was made responsible for children born of the union. He was even responsible for any crimes which they might commit. If no responsible individual could be found the responsibility fell equally on the tribes of both parties. A sane person who cohabited with an insane person was responsible for any children which resulted. Failing proof of this, the lunatic's tribe was held responsible. The effects of this law must have been far-reaching as it was to the advantage of every member of a tribe to prevent the birth of children with insane parents.

There is no record of institutional treatment of lunatics in these laws. Most probably they were allowed to wander freely within the tribal areas. Reference has already been made to the exemption from distress of a person employed to fetter a lunatic which would seem to show that some form of restraint was occasionally practised. It should not be forgotten that lunatics have always been regarded by primitive peoples as being under supernatural protection, both before and after the coming of Christianity. Even to-day the common expression in Irish for a lunatic is *Duine le Dia* (a person with God).

The Brehon Laws were codified in the years after St. Patrick. They were strengthened by being given a spiritual as well as a temporal authority. They were abolished in the reign of James I (1566–1625), but many of them were respected even by the Anglo-Irish up to the middle of the seventeenth century.

In the *Calendar of Judiciary Rolls*, Ireland, 1225–1303, there is an account of a court held at Drogheda in the year 1300. At this, a man who had committed an assault was fined six marks. The physician who healed the plaintiff was awarded half a mark compensation.

CHAPTER THREE

MEDICINE AND CHRISTIANITY

As we have seen, the physician carried on a limited health service amongst the early Irish. He occasionally treated the sick in his own house, but presumably those who availed of this facility were able to pay. Until the establishment of Christianity there was no centre to which the sick poor could go for constant attention.

The care of the sick was stressed as a primary duty from the earliest Christian times. In the Benedictine rule: 'The care of the sick is to be placed above and before every other duty, as if indeed Christ were being directly served in waiting upon them. The Infirmarian must be thoroughly reliable, known for his piety and diligence and solicitude for his charge—baths be provided for the sick as often as they need them.'

The first hospital staffed by nuns was opened when St. Patrick enrolled St. Brigid and her companions, bidding them collect together, nurse and minister to the ailing.

The traditional date for St. Patrick's arrival in Ireland is A.D. 432. One of the first references to him in Colgan's *Acta Sanctorum*, is of medical interest, for it reads: 'Patrick maintains a certain leper in his house and washes his sores with his own hands.' Although there are many references to leprosy in this country in the Middle Ages, it is not always certain that the disease was accurately diagnosed. Certain other skin conditions may be implicated. When we remember that the difference between measles and smallpox was not recognised until the tenth century by Rhazes, the Arabian physician, it seems very likely that the number of cases of genuine leprosy was much smaller than the chroniclers would have us believe. In the *Chronicum Scotorum*, words which may be translated 'mange,' 'scurvy' or 'leprosy' are used in entries of the year A.D. 550. Mange in dogs is caused by a mite similar to the itch mite of scabies. Norwegian scabies, a very severe irritation believed to come from infected wolves, is common amongst Norwegian lepers. Possibly a similar mixed, or wrongly diagnosed, infection gave rise to the apparently high incidence of leprosy in mediaeval Ireland.

One of the greatest monastic works was the establishment of leper

12

houses. Shortly after the first Danish invasion, A.D. 835, there is mention of a leper house in the *Annals of Innisfallen* under the date A.D. 869: 'Devastation of Armagh by Arlaf, so that the city was burned with its houses and hospitals (nosocomiis or leper houses).' Whether this was a monastic or secular institution is uncertain and doubt has been cast even on the existence of these hospitals.

In A.D. 1185, a leper house for the poor was opened in Waterford by the Benedictines. In 1192 a house dedicated to St. Brigid was erected at Kilbrixy, Co. Westmeath.

Prior to 1230, the leper hospital of St. Stephen was erected in Dublin on a site later occupied by Mercer's Hospital. There were probably others in the city, but the only records we possess are scanty ones of a building on Lazar's Hill (now Pearse Street). Tradition says that many miraculous cures of lepers were wrought here. It was probably founded in 1220 by Archbishop de Loundres as a sort of quarantine station for incoming pilgrims.

In 1408, Henry IV granted to the son of William Rochfort of Wexford the custody of a hospital for lepers.

In Hardiman's *History of Galway* there is a brief account of St. Bridget's Church and leper house. It reads: 'St. Bridget's Hospital in the town of Galway, was founded for the poor of the town and each burgess was obliged in his turn to send a servant to collect alms every Sabbath day for its support – a custom which was long after observed. This charitable institution was fortunately completed in the year 1543 when the sweating sickness broke out, and raged with great violence, destroying multitudes of the natives, and particularly the tradesmen of the town.' This building was destroyed at some time prior to 1648, when it was re-erected by Bishop Kirwan.

The first reference to a St. Lawrence's leper house occurs in 1275, when Catherine le Grant left legacies to the lepers of St. Stephen's and St. Lawrence's. This house was somewhere near Chapelizod on the main Lucan road. The institution was founded by the Knights Hospitallers in Kilmainham, but they gave no personal service, for they appointed a warden to take full charge. Apparently the hospital ceased to function about 1532. Lands in the vicinity known as 'St. Lawrence's' may mark the site of the old buildings.

In Waterford a leper hospital was erected by King John in the early thirteenth century. This was situated close to St. Stephen's Church on the site now occupied by Messrs. Keily's brewery. A lintel over one of the windows belonged to the old leper house. It bears the date 1632. The story runs that John founded the hospital as a thank-offering for recovery from an illness due to over-indulgence in salmon and cider when in Lismore. In 1661, an inquisition concerning the hospital was held. The tasks of the Revenue Commissioner must have been considerable in those days, for we read in a manuscript of the time:

'We find and present that Juan Murphy, sent unto the Widow Bennett, was enfected with the Leprosie, and in the time of the usurped power was presented to the then Commissioner of Revenue, who denyed to give her any releefe, whereupon she miscarried and died in a miserable condition.'

Lepers or alleged lepers were admitted to this hospital up to 1723 when Drs. Reynet and Donogan certified that Mary Tobin suffered from the disease. About 1740 the building was converted into a general infirmary with forty beds.

Although most of the monastic 'hospitals' were leper houses, some general hospitals for the sick were maintained by monks. The oldest of these in Dublin was founded towards the end of the twelfth century outside Newgate in Thomas Street. This was known as the priory of St. John the Baptist. It received large grants from popes, kings and well-to-do citizens. This institution continued its useful and charitable existence until January 1537, when Henry VIII suppressed it and granted its property to the Earl of Thomond for £14 18s. 8d. At the time there were fifty beds in the hospital portion. The present Church of St. Augustine is erected on part of the site of the old priory.

Probably any major surgery undertaken was performed in these monastic institutions. There is support for this view in the story of the trephining of Cennfaeladh, whose skull was fractured by a blow from a sword during the battle of Moyrath, Co. Down (A.D. 637). He was brought to Armagh, the seat of the Primate Senach. The Primate arranged for the patient to be sent to St. Bricin, the Abbot of Tuaim Drecain (Toomregan in County Cavan). St. Bricin seems to have been an accomplished surgeon as well as a scholar for he removed the injured portion of the skull and brain. The chronicle of this episode states that – 'his brain of forgetfulness was removed' – and on his recovery his intellect and memory were more powerful than ever. It is most probable that Cennfaeladh was submitted to some form of decompression operation which relieved the pressure causing his lethargy and dullness.

Few trephined skulls have been found in Ireland. There was an abbey at Nendrum on Mahee Island in Strangford Lough. The last reference to it in any chronicle was in A.D. 974, when it was destroyed by fire. Probably this was the result of a raid by Norsemen. In 1922 a number of skeletons was recovered from the stone-lined graves around the abbey. These are now in Queen's University, Belfast. One skull is remarkable in having an 8 mm. trephine opening in the left parietal bone.

In 1935 a mediaeval cemetery at Collierstown, Co. Meath, was excavated. This contained amongst other bones, the trephined skull of a child about thirteen years old. The edges of the opening had healed all around. Around the hole on the outside of the skull for a distance of 3 mm. the bone was bevelled as if it had been scraped away. There were no marks of injury or disease on the skull. The trephine opening was oval in shape and larger (29 mm. by 22 mm.) than that of the Nendrum skull and was situated in the right half of the frontal bone, close to the middle line. According to experts from the anatomy schools and the National Museum, the bone probably belongs to the early Iron Age, or early Christian period.

Chemistry and pharmacy have usually progressed in step with medicine and this occurred during the period under review in Ireland.

In the *Leabhar Breac*, a fourteenth-century manuscript, it is related that: 'St. Patrick being at Temar the Druid Lucat Mael put a drop of poison into Patrick's drink – Patrick blessed the drink and turned the vessel upside down – the poison dropped out but no part of the ale did. Patrick then drank the ale.' The *Leabhar Breac* is copied from an older book. Whatever the accuracy of the story it suggests that a knowledge of powerful poisons existed here prior to the fourteenth century.

The following extract, also from a fourteenth-century manuscript – the *Book of Ballymote* – proves that slow or cumulative poisons were familiar in Ireland at an early date:

A.D. 366 – Eoghy Moymedhon, monarch of Eirinn, died: He left four sons by his wife, Monghinne,the fair-haired, the sister of Crimthann More, King of Munster. This Crimthann on the death of Eoghy assumed the monarchy to the prejudice of the young princes. His sister raised a revolution – giving the supreme rule to Brian her eldest son. Crimthann marching into Connaught encamped on the bank of the River Moy. Monghinne invited her brother to a feast for the purpose of procuring his death by treachery. She then repaired to her brother's tent and made a pretended peace with him on the part of her sons. When they had inspected the feast she put a poisoned cup into her brother's hand requesting him to drink it.' Crimthann drank the cup but did not die, presumably from the effects of the poison, until he reached his own country in Clare. The place where he died and was buried was known as *Sliabh Oighidh an Righ*, or the 'Mountain of the King's death.

The first reference to an individual physician in Christian times occurs in the *Annals of the Four Masters* under the year 860: 'Maelodhar Ua Tindridh, the most learned physician of Ireland died.'

The first great epidemic recorded in Christian times is dated as commencing about A.D. 540. It was preceded by famine, and after lasting some thirty years was succeeded by leprosy. The disease was known as *Blefed Crom Chonnaill*, or *Buidhe Chonaill*, literally the corn-coloured yellowness. It was also referred to as *Buidhechair* or jaundice. Probably the disease was some form of yellow-fever or possibly a malignant malaria.

The histories of other countries furnish evidence of the widespread nature of this disease. The colloquial names elsewhere bear out that it was marked by jaundice. The *Book of Llandaff* states that St. Teile fled from Wales, first to Cornwall and then to Amorica (Brittany) on account of the pestilence which nearly destroyed the whole nation. Some of the Welsh who came to Ireland were possibly the carriers of the disease.

For thirty years this pestilence attacked both men and animals. Wilde's report on the census for 1851 contains an exhaustive list of references to the disease throughout Europe.

Towards the end of the epidemic, in 569, the *Annals of Innisfallen* refer to *Bolgach* or smallpox for the first time. This is one of the earliest references to the disease in Europe. It is possible, however, that this was really leprosy or some other sickness, as there is no supporting evidence for smallpox in other annals.

One hundred years later there was another outbreak of the yellow plague from about A.D. 656. The trouble began this time in County Wexford and continued for some twenty years.

During the year 675 there is a more definite reference in the *Annals of Clonmacnoise* to 'a kind of great leprosie in Ireland this year, called the Pox, in Irish, *Bolgach.*' In subsequent years there are several references to this disorder.

The *Codex of St. Gall* is a manuscript of the early ninth century. It was probably brought to Switzerland, where it is preserved, by wandering Irish scholars. There are a few references in it to incantations against illness and injury which have a joint Christian and pagan origin. Those against a thorn and against urinary disease are typical:

Nothing is higher than heaven, nothing is deeper than the sea. By the holy words that Christ spoke from his Cross remove from me the thorn, a thorn . . . very sharp is Goibnius' science, let Goibnius' goad go out before Goibnius' goad!

This charm is laid in butter which goes not into water and some of it is smeared all round the thorn and it goes not on the point nor on the wound and if the thorn be not there one of the two teeth in the front of his head will fall out.

Against disease of the urine. I save myself from this disease of the urine

. . . save us, cunning birds, birdflocks of witches, save us. This is always put in the place where thou makest thy urine.

Despite the influence of Christianity the idea that disease was due to evil spirits remained current for many centuries. Even the Four Masters refer to 'Druidical or magic sickness caused by demons in the East of Ireland.' According to Wilde the names given to diseases were often more appropriate than their English or Latin equivalents.

The general names of 'illness' were *galar* (still in use) or *teidhm*. More modern forms are *tinneas* and *breoiteacht*. Tuberculosis was known as *anfobhracht*, or a skeleton. In the Brehon Laws the consumptive patient was 'one who has no juice or strength.' Murtagh O'Brian, a King of Munster, is supposed to have died of this disease in the monastery of Lismore.

The Christian influence is seen in the phrase *galar Poil* or 'St Paul's sickness.' This was epilepsy, so named from the belief that the saint was a victim. Sufferers were described as being *talmaidheach* or 'earthbound.' It is recorded that St. Eamin of Inis Cealtra died in A.D. 653 from *teine-brurr*, literally fiery swelling, or erysipelas. Those who have seen the disease will agree that the Irish name was an apt one. The more modern terms are *teine Dia* (God's fire) or *ruaidhe* (redness).

Reference has already been made to the occurrence of plague and the derivation of the place name Tallaght. Several other words were in common use for 'plague' as well as *tamh*. *Teidm* was occasionally used to denote a severe illness in an individual. Later *pláig* was borrowed from the Latin *plaga*. A widespread epidemic was referred to as *scuab* or 'sweeping.'

Sir William Wilde was able to tabulate seventy-five diseases accurately named and described from very early times.

Reference has been made to the belief that lunatics were under a peculiar Divine protection. Apart from restraint, however, there were no methods of treatment, possibly because it was believed that lunacy was incurable except by supernatural methods.

About eight miles west of Tralee, in Kilgobbin, there is the beautiful valley of *Gleannagealt* (the valley of lunatics). It was believed that all lunatics in any part of the country would eventually find their way there to be cured at the well known as *Tobernagalt* (the lunatics' well). Here they were supposed to drink the healing waters and eat some of the cresses on the margin in order to be restored to sanity. A very ancient tale describes how Gall, a youth of fifteen, took part in the battle of Ventry. The slaughter was so great that he fled madly from the scene, never stopping till he arrived in the lonely glen.

It is certain that practices similar to mesmerism were in vogue with the pagan Irish and were condemned by St Patrick. Notwithstanding this condemnation they were still observed long after Christianity was established. One of these, called *tiamh-las* or enlightenment, was definitely mesmeric in character. A full account is given in a manuscript purporting to deal with affairs of State about A.D. 20.

The evils arising from the delay attending the election of a king after the death of Edirsgeal led to a great assembly of the princes and chiefs at Tara and there, it was determined to practise the *tiamh-las* to ascertain the will of Heaven respecting the succession. A young man was selected by the Druids — a great number of solemn rites were performed; one of these consisted of breathing on him; and these operations continued till he was put in a deep trance and while thus entranced he was questioned as to the person who was to succeed Edirsgeal. He then returned intelligible answers, describing the person spoken of. The young man was kept entranced till the Druids sent to a place some six or seven miles distant which had been named by the young man and there they found the person described and sought for and they forthwith proclaimed him monarch.

A remnant of the Church's connection with medicine was the power granted to bishops to grant licences to practise physic, surgery and midwifery.

Several forms of licence, dated about the period of Charles II and James I, exist. The following originated in the diocese of Down and Connor. It was included in *Book of Precedents for the Ecclesiastical Court*:

To all Xrian people to whom these prts shall come: R by ye Grace of God: B. of L: Sendeth Greeting in ye Lord God Everlasting: Whereas for avoiding of any accident dayly happening to many of his Matie's, loveing Subjects by the unskilfull practizers of Surgerie. It was providently provided by speciall Acte of Parliament made for the reformation thereof. In the third yeare of the Raigne of our Late Sovereign Lord of famous memory King Henry the Eighth that it should not be lawful for any persons within this Realme of England to use or exercise the science or facultie of Surgerie except he were first examined approved, admitted, according to the Tenor of the said Statute. Know yee therefore wee the said Reverend ffather having received sufficient testimonie from R.W.C.L. ye Masters or govnors of the misterie and comonality of Barbers and Surgeons within the City of London incorporated by ye
Due examinacion of A: B: of the parish of St Sepulcher's wtout New gate London a free Brother of the said misterie heretofore approved and admitted to use and exercise ye said Facultie And examined the said A: B: concerning his sufficiencie therein, Doe now by these presents approve the said A: B: to be an able and sufficient Surgeon and he being first solemnly sworne before Sr E. S. Kt Doctor of Lawes our Chancellor to ye Supremacie of the

Kings most excellent Matie. Wee doe by these presents admitt him the said A: B: to use and exercise the said Misterie of Surgerie Soe farr forth as by the Lawes and statutes of this Realme of England, wee may lawfully admitt him thereto. In witness whereof we have caused the hand seale of our office to be sett unto these date ye–

It is probable that the bishops' power to confer medical degrees originated in the granting by their ecclesiastical superiors of licences to priests to practise. The degree granted by the Archbishop of Canterbury was a registrable qualification at the time of the passing of the Medical Act of 1858.

By the Council of Tours (1163) priests were forbidden to leave their cloisters to practise surgery. On the Continent the priests' servants began to practise and use the surgical skill they had acquired from the clergy.

A formal surgical profession did not develop in Ireland until 1446, when the Dublin Barbers' Guild received a charter from Henry VI. From 1765 licences to practise surgery were granted by the Surgeon-General. There are no records to show if any form of proof of knowledge was required from candidates for certificates.

CHAPTER FOUR

THE RENAISSANCE PERIOD

The renaissance of culture and learning which began in Italy about the middle of the fourteenth century had no effect on Irish medicine for many years.

From about the tenth century until the foundation of a formal medical profession, medicine in Ireland was practised by hereditary physicians whose families were attached to specified nobles and chieftains. Younger members learned from their elders and were expected to carry on the family tradition. Usually they continued in the same district but, at least one family, the O'Callenans, migrated from Cork to Galway. Their fame there became such that up to the eighteenth century it was said of a fatal disease *'Ni leighiseadh Callenan é sin'* — 'Even O'Callenan could not cure that.'

It has been stated that Edmund Haley, the celebrated astronomer, was descended from the O'Halghaiths, a family of hereditary physicians.

In his *Confessio Authoris*, published in 1648, van Helmont wrote: 'The Irish Nobility had in every family a domestic physician, whose recommendation was not that he came loaded from the college with learning, but that he was able to cure disorders; which knowledge they have from their ancestors by means of a book belonging to particular families that contains the marks of the several diseases, with the remedies attached; which remedies were vernacula, the production of their own country—for this reason, the Irish are better managed in sickness than the Italians who have a physician in every Village.'

The Ulster family of *MacDuinntsleibhe* (Dunleavy) was amongst the most notable. They were hereditary leeches to the O'Donnells. Their influence was such that, at one time, throughout the country the word *Ultach* was used as a synonym for 'physician.' Cormac Dunleavy (*circa* 1459) translated several Latin medical texts into Irish. One of these, in the British Library, contains a note: 'Ocus Cormac MacDuinntsleibhe basillar a fisigeact do cur a ngaigdeilg ocus do scrib do Deinis O Eachoidhe annsa caintsi he.' (Cormac Mac Duinntsleibhe, bachelor of physic it is, that has put it into Irish and written it for Denis O'hEachoidhe in this document.) He also translated Gualternus's treatise, *Doses of Decoctions*. On this occasion the book was done at the instance of Dermot MacDonall O'Line.

The MacDuinntsleibhes came originally from County Down, whence they were driven by the Norman, John de Courcy. The family were dispossessed in Donegal during the Ulster plantation of James I (1566–1625). In 1745, a member of the family residing in Paris wrote on non-medical subjects.

Nial O'Glacan, a physician who became Professor of Medicine in Toulouse, was born in Donegal. In *Tractatus de Peste*, published in 1629, he implies that he was educated by one of the hereditary physicians, possibly one of the Dunleavys. O'Glacan was appointed physician to the King of France. In 1655, at Bologna, he published several books on physiology and pathology.

In the south, the O'Callenans were hereditary physicians to the McCarthys. In 1403, in conjunction with Nicholas O'Hickey, Angus O'Callenan wrote a commentary on Hippocrates' *Aphorisms*. Some years later an Irish translation of a Latin text, *Regimen Sanitatis*, appeared under the title of *Regimen na Slainte*. This was very probably a product of the same partnership. The Irish text is contained in two manuscripts preserved in the Royal Irish Academy (*P*) and Trinity College Libraries (*H*). There is also a nineteenth-century transcript of the latter. The two original manuscripts seem to have been copied independently from one exemplar. There is considerable internal evidence by which we can fix the dates of the manuscripts. The manuscript *P* has a colophon 'Donncadh og O hIceadha do sgriobh an leabhar so. Anno Domini 1469.' (Young Donal O'Hickey wrote this book A.D. 1469.) *H* has a note: 'anno domini 1486, agus tabradh gach aon lefeas an leabur so beannacht ar anmain an ti sgriobh i.' (A.D. 1486–and let every reader give a blessing on the soul of the writer.)

Some of the O'Hickeys were physicians to the clans occupying what is now County Clare. Nicholas, a member of the family, translated *Lilium Medicinae*, a manual of medicine celebrated in its time. It was originally written in the fourteenth century by the Scotsman, Bernard de Gordon, who belonged to the school of Montpelier. His works had already been translated into several European languages.

The original manuscript of O'Hickey's translation is preserved in the British Library. By design or good fortune there are several dated references by which we can trace its career. They read: (1) 'The year of the Lord when this book was written 1482, and that was the year when Philip son of Thomas Barry slew Philip son of Richard Barry.' (2) 'I grieve for this news that I hear now: that my mother and sister are dead in Spain A.D. 1489.' (3) 'A prayer for Gerald the Earl, Justice of Ireland, that bought this book for twenty cattle. Two and twenty folded skins are in this book–this year in which I am, is the year of grace one thousand and five hundred years.' Gerald, Earl of Kildare, was Lord Justice of Ireland from 1478 to 1513.

In the *Calendar of Ancient Records of Dublin* (vol. II, p. 147) there is a note of the appointment of a Nicholas Hickey, presumably of the original family, to be physician to the city of Dublin in 1580:

That Nicholas Hykie, doctor of physick, in consideracion that he shall henceforward dwell and make his abode in Dublin, shall have and be payed by the hands of the thresorer of this cittie out of the thresorie and revenewe of the said cittie yearlie ten pounds, lawfull mony of Irland, begynning from Maie next, during his good behaviour and usadge, and shall observe the orders and dyrections following, that is to saie, taking for the vewe and loking of eche passientes uryn without visitacion, sixe pence sterling; for every visitacion of such passient and vewe of his water, twelve pence sterling; item for eche visitacion without viewe of his water, twelve pence sterling, over and besyds consideracion that if he undertake to cure any man for a certayne som of mony, then he to be at libertie to agre with the saide partie; also, that uppon lysence of Mr Mayor of this cittie for the tyme being, he may goo threskore myles out of this cittie, so as he return agayne within XII daies after, and that without lysence he may goo no further then that he may return within XXIIII howres after; and if the Mayor for the tyme being shall send for hym at any tyme he shall com to the said Mr Mayor presently, uppon payne of losing halfe a yeares stipend.

In late mediaeval times a crude form of urine analysis was practised. In the sixteenth century, Thomas Recorde in his *Urinall of Physick* made some effort to systematise the methods in vogue. He laid down that, 'the Urinall should be of clear glass, not thick nor green, without spots nor blots, not flat in the bottom nor wide in the neck, but widest in the middle and narrow towards the ends.' He exhorted the nurse to collect the urine and present it to the doctor as soon as possible, advice which was as sound then as it is to-day. Recorde kept a table of densities. Urine of the same density as rain water was judged to have come from a virgin suffering from a passion of the heart.

In the *Irish Journal of Medical Science* (February 1942) Winifred Wulff gave an account of some of the words used in connection with urinalysis in Irish medical manuscripts. The references are nearly all to the colours of various urines. These colours were compared to those of familiar, everyday objects as the following extracts show: '*mar uisge ngeal* – like clear water, *mar ubhall mbanbuidhe* – like a pale yellow apple, *mar bhan or* – like pale gold, *mar dearg chroch* – like red saffron.' Light colours indicated excessive cold in the nutritive members, especially the liver. A yellowish urine showed some measure of heat in these members and the beginning of digestion. Colours ranging from red to black showed the beginning of heat, the dominance of salt phlegm and choler in the veins, going on to 'burning of the liver and kidneys, corrupt blood in the veins, ulcers in the bladder.' Urine coloured like cabbage sap, black horn or shiny black horn was an indication of approaching death.

The Ui Caside were the hereditary physicians of Mac Uidhir (Maguire of Fermanagh). Their principal representatives were Finghin (d. 1322); Gilla na nAingel (d. 1335); Tadhg (d. 1450); Feoris (d. 1504) and Feidhlimidh (d. 1520). These are all mentioned in the *Annals of Ireland* as *ollamh leighis* or professors of medicine for a period extending over two centuries.

The death of Feoris is recorded somewhat fully in the *Annals of Ulster*: 'O'Cassidy of Ceul died this year–that is Maguire's Ollave physician and a well tried doctor in learning and physic in theory and in practise and a man who kept a house of general hospitality for every one and he died of *Cruith an Righ*.' This latter was a sickness of unknown identity which is mentioned several times in the *Annals* as occurring in epidemics. The name (King's Game in English) may arise from the belief that, like the King's Evil, it was curable by a royal touch. Tadhg wrote at least one treatise on medicine.

The O'Mearas, physicians to the Butlers of Ormond, were the first to publish medical works in Latin. Dermot O'Meara has left a book entitled *Pathologia Hereditaria Generalis* which was printed in Dublin in 1619. This book must have been of some importance as it was reprinted in London in 1665 and in Amsterdam in 1666. Dermot's son, Edmund, graduated at Oxford and became an Honorary Fellow of the London College of Physicians. A tract entitled *Hippocraticum Febrium Etiologium et Prognosim* has also been attributed to him. Three generations of this family practised in Ireland and London. In a letter, written in 1619 to the Lord Deputy, Sir Oliver St John, Dermot O'Meara gives an interesting account of his opinion of medical practice in Dublin. This differs markedly from the opinion of van Helmont already mentioned.

There are certainly more persons in Dublin at the present day practising the Art of Medicine than any other art, yet there are very few of them who have the six qualifications which Hippocrates requires in a Medical Doctor. Here, not only cursed Mountebanks, ignorant barbers, and shameless quack compounders, but also persons of every other craft whatsoever, loose women, and those of the dregs of humanity who are either tired of their own proper art and craft or inflamed with an unbridled passion for making money, all have free leave to profane the holy temple of Asculapius. Here might not one justly exclaim in the words of the poet,

> Here are those
> Who, groping in the dark, are licensed still
> To rack the sick, and murder men at will.

Malpractice, indeed, takes place in every country in the world but not everywhere with impunity. In every well-governed city and state legal precaution is taken that no one should essay medical practice unless one who is duly qualified by the public certificate and authorisation of some University. In these cities and states no barber dares to open a vein, no compounder dares to sell medicines, much less to attend patients, without a medical doctor's prescription. Thrice happy were this royal city of ours — thrice happy our whole state — had they the benefit of such wise legal precautions.

The O'Lees, who flourished under the patronage of the O'Flaherty of West Connaught in the fifteenth century, were looked on by many as magicians. Murrough O'Lee in particular was supposed to have received his knowledge from the genii of the enchanted island of Hy Brasil. A volume known by their name is surmised to have been written by a member of the O'Lee family. Copies of this are kept in the Royal Irish Academy and in the Library of the King's Inns, Dublin.

This book, which is a translation of a Latin text, is dated 1434 according to marginal figures which may not be accurate. The name 'P. Lee' appears on one page. It is written in Latin and Irish. It mentions the 'cardinal point' of heat or the temperature which influences diseases, the seasons of the year in which particular diseases occur and the ages at which they are most prevalent. The book is a complete system of medicine, dealing with putrid fevers, abscesses and pustules, wounds, hydrophobia, poisons, affections of the brain and spinal marrow, and diseases of the eyes, stomach and womb.

According to the legend, Murrough O'Lee was carried to the enchanted isle, and while there received a book from one of the inhabitants with instructions not to open it for seven years. This injunction he obeyed strictly until after the allotted period when he opened the volume, and 'at once became endued with the gift of healing and began to practise surgery and physic with wonderful success.'

There are curious tables of disease in the book. Each is divided into some ninety compartments, across, slant and vertical, coloured

red and black, showing various points of the disease in question.

The *Book of the O'Sheils*, written some time before 1657, when it was transcribed, contains the Hippocratic aphorisms, as well as commentaries on Galen, Avicenna and Vesalius with a dissertation on native plants.

The O'Sheils were physicians to the McMahons of Oriel and they held the estate of Ballyshiel on the banks of the Brosna in Offaly.

Owen O'Sheil was the first Irish physician to leave the country in order to study. He went to Paris in 1604, but took his diploma in Louvain, since he regarded the Paris Faculty as being 'somewhat lax at and favourable in the conferring of graduation.' After graduation he spent a year in Padua, then the centre of the medical world. After six months in Rome he joined the army of Albert and Isabella in Flanders. He worked as chief of the medical faculty in the Royal Hospital of Malines. In 1620 he returned to Dublin, and further army life, as surgeon-in-chief of the Leinster forces under Preston. In 1646 he transferred his allegiance to Owen Roe O'Neill. His letter to his former patient on quitting his service deserves to be quoted in full:

My right Honourable Lord,
  Having known the condition of your body this long while, and calling to memory also how some years since I have given directions in the Low Countries whereby your honour should abstain from all sorts of wine, only 'Vin de Pays' and 'Rhenish Wine,' excess in which direction was altogether excluded then; and now also, my Lord, according to my obligations I do once again forbid the same.
  Assuring your honour that no other end can be expected than to shorten your own days, whereby you will be an executioner of yourself if you follow the contrary. This much to discharge myself and my duty towards you I thought fit to certify, and so do rest and will ever remain,
                                        Your true servant,
                                          Owen O'Sheil.

O'Sheil died near Letterkenny in the service of O'Neill.

During the latter half of the fifteenth century a most important figure in Irish Medicine was the Englishman, John of Gaddesden, already dead one hundred years. His treatise *Rosa Anglica*, written about 1314, was a summary of mediaeval medical practice. The period was one of intense respect for previous authorities. Medicine and science made few efforts at independent thought and research. His book contains the three factors, ancient folk elements, degraded classical material and Arabic contributions. It is much more than a mere textbook, being an account of many family and intimate social matters in the contemporary life of the time.

Little is known of John of Gaddesden (1280–1361). He obtained degrees in arts and theology at Oxford before finally studying medicine. He apparently practised in Oxford and was eventually appointed Court Physician to Edward II. A fairly full account of his life is found in Friend's *History of Physick* (1726). He is mentioned by name in the Prologue to the *Canterbury Tales* and may have met Chaucer.

The *Rosa Anglica* is in five books in the first three editions. The Irish translation of the *Rosa* by O'Hickey was made about the beginning of the fifteenth century. A copy in the possession of the Royal Irish Academy is divided as follows:

A   Regarding Sanguine Fever, etc.
B }
C } Non-material sicknesses, i.e. ephemera and hectica.
D   Cardiac palpitations.
E   Swellings.
F   Lethargy.
G   Hernia.
H   Paralysis, etc.
I   Dropsy.
J   Smallpox.
K   Arthritis.

None of the Irish MSS is a complete translation from any of the Latin editions. Furthermore, the Irish translators took many pieces wholesale from Bernard of Gordon's *Lilium Medicinae*, which work John of Gaddesden had already used freely in compiling his original manuscript. There are several Irish manuscript translations, in the Royal Irish Academy, Trinity College, Dublin, and the British Library. In addition the work is referred to in other manuscripts, notably one in the Library of the King's Inns in Dublin.

The language of the text is Early Modern Irish. Except for technical and philosophical terms it is easily readable by a present-day Irish speaker. Some of the manuscripts are in very poor condition. In one copy in the Royal Irish Academy the scribe has made many mistakes and used contractions, sometimes for whole sentences. He uses the figure 3 indiscriminately for both drachm and ounce the notation for which was rather similar. The results to patients must, on occasions, have been extremely unpleasant.

Space does not permit of more than a few excerpts from this manuscript, and interested readers are referred to Winifred Wulff's commentary and translation published by the Irish Texts Society in 1923.

The book opens with a quotation from Galen: 'As Galen says: do not frequent too much the courts and halls of the great, as I never did, until you have (a knowledge of) your books.' Throughout the book Galen is quoted as an authority; as in dealing of phlebotomy for certain fevers. 'Galen says, when we bleed a patient in acute fevers it is till weakness seizes him for that cools the whole body at once, quenches the fever and relaxes the bowels; the sweat breaks out, and many folk have I seen cured thereby. Therefore it is meet to bleed a sick man *usque ad syncopem.*'

Concerning haemorrhoids, John of Gaddesden advises opening them externally, subsequently applying a poultice of boiled onions. The enema advised for constipation was composed of boiled violets, mallows, mercury (the plant), bran, cassia and a little salt.

The author's comments on a good water supply would cause much uneasiness to modern analysts.

Note these are the conditions of good water. One condition is that it heats easily and cools suddenly. Another that there be no foreign bodies visible therein. Another that it be not turbid. Another that it be not ugly and evil-tasting. Another condition is: that if two waters be taken and a little lixivium (lye) mixed therein, then whichever does not become turbid is the better of them. Another condition: take two identical cloths and wet them entirely in two waters equally, and dry them equally; whichever cloth dries quickest, that water wherein it was is the best water. Another condition: take equal quantities of two waters and whichever is lightest is the best. He (Galen) says not to use water that goes through pipes, for according to all true doctors it is not good.

Some good advice about drinking and the morning after is given in *Rosa Anglica*:

It is a rule that it is not right to drink wine without eating something first. It is not proper for a man who has a weak head to drink wine, except a little with water; so anyone who is at a feast or drinking with friends if he cannot keep his head let him eat peas or the stalks of cabbage, or its seed after his meal. If ill hap cause him to get drunk, as he will notice first by his tongue stumbling, let him get up and vomit. If it be a man, wash his extremities and rub them and his testicles with salt; and if a woman, wash her extremities and her breasts; let water be dashed on the face and rub the head with rose-water, and let him be a day and a night without food or drink. On the following day, let him do work and bathe, and let him eat something late, avoiding things hard to digest.

The prescription which was 'good in every weakness of the heart, whatever time it occurs' contained twenty-two ingredients. These were—a drachm and a half of cinnamon and one drachm each of: spikenard, lignum aloes, sanders, anise, endive; half a drachm each of red roses, ganofil, cummin, and red sanders; a scruple each of cardamomum, burnt ivory; half a drachm each of storax, calamint, borage flowers, bone of stag's heart, unbored pearls; and one pound of sugar. This was to be made with two parts of honey and rose-water and the third part of water of borage.

A teaspoonful of gold filings was advised to prevent cardiac syncope and palpitation.

The 'cures' for warts were as numerous then as now. Droppings of goats, vinegar, urine, ashes of snails, stale unsalted lard, unripe figs in vinegar and finally the 'cure in which there is no deceit,' water in which a dead man has been washed, are all mentioned as treatment for the troublesome little swellings.

The diagnosis of rupture was an unpleasant ordeal for the patient. 'Let a fire be made him of elder wood and when he who suffers from this disease smells the smoke thereof the entrails fall down and there is a great hacking pain and roaring in the abdomen and intestines which is heard throughout the house.' The author had a fair knowledge of the prognosis in rupture: '– is easily cured at the beginning, especially in children, but it cannot be cured in old people.' His directions for non-surgical treatment which include the avoidance of violent exercise and straining, small meals and avoidance of constipation are sound by modern standards.

John of Gaddesden knew something of the uses of thermal treatment. In the section dealing with dropsy he recommends a bath containing various herbs for the sick man. Apparently the patient was to be totally enclosed in this bath while the herbal brew was boiled under him: 'The sick man sits on a cushion well filled with bran or cotton or unwashed wool, till he sweat, and let him be rubbed with a linen cloth. When the pulse shall be felt to weaken, put him in his own bed and when cold begins give him some of the aforementioned electuary.'

Although the writer considered that smallpox was due to corruption of the menstrual blood, his powers of observation and ideas on prognosis in this disease were not negligible. ' – the pustules are best when they are few and large – the fever accompanying them is low – should the pustules appear now and go in again and be purplish accompanied by weakness of the force it typifies death.' This can be read as a reference to haemorrhagic smallpox, a most malignant infection. The section on smallpox is quoted as proof that John of Gaddesden was sometime Court Physician – 'Then take a scarlet or other red cloth, and put it about the pox; as I did to the King of England's son when this disease seized him and I permitted only red things to be about his bed, by the which I cured him, without leaving a trace of the smallpox pustules on him.'

The writers quoted as authorities in this book are numerous. Throughout, great respect is shown for classical learning. Sympathetic cures and causes for disease abound, such as the cure for lethargy; the heart of a robin is hung around a patient's neck to keep him awake. The reason for the selection of the heart, the part that continues to move during sleep, is obvious. The use of urine in dropsy is interesting when it is considered that a hypertonic solution of urea has a diuretic effect.

A page from a copy in the Royal Irish Academy of most of Book I of the *Rosa Anglica* which has pieces from Bernard of Gordon and Gilbert the Englishman interposed is illustrated. This copy which is in fair condition may have been written at Corcumroe, Co. Clare, according to internal evidence. There are many large illuminated capitals similar to that on the page reproduced. These are finely interlaced. Most of them are coloured with yellow.

The King's Inns' Library in Dublin possesses several manuscripts of medical interest of about this period. MS No. 15 is a large book written on vellum. The greater part of it was written in 1512 by Malachy, one of the O'Lee family. A small portion of the first part of the book was written by some unknown author. Like the other manuscripts of the time it is based on the works of the schools of Salerno, Montpelier and Arabia. The authorities quoted range from Avicenna to John of Gaddesden. The subjects treated include boils, ulcers, fevers, greyness, baldness, epilepsy, coma, quinsy, phthisis, hiccup and diseases of the heart, stomach, intestines and liver.

In the MS there are many marginal notes in English, written much later than the text. These seem to be random jottings by subsequent owners. They have no relevance to the subject, being mainly notes, rhyming jingles, proverbs and calculations. One of these is a promise By X . . . Brady to pay Luke Reilly one pound on the 15th of June, 1759.

MS No. 17 in the same collection dates probably from the twelfth or thirteenth century. Small figures on the first and fifth pages represent the dress of the people of that time. In the course of the book the writer declares that it was written 'for the glory of God and out of love for the Irish people, for the benefit of my friends, fostersons and tribe.' The frontispiece of this manuscript has been damaged by time. Nevertheless it is quite clear that its design must have been a matter of many hours' work. Scrolls and intersected lines cover an area of some 80 square inches.

Very few surgical operations were practised in the sixteenth century. The first operation of lithotrity ever recorded was performed in Dublin in 1567. The distinguished patient was Sir Henry Sidney, then Lord Deputy. (*State Papers*, Book III., p. 259 February, 1567).

My Lord President, being of the age of XXXVI years went into Ireland a hole man, not touched with the stone and so remained one yeare and a half or thereabought, and then, after long grief, avoided two stones which were very big such as few men have been known to have avoided. After this he took his journey into the North parts of Irelande–he avoided one other stone broken by the surgeon his instruments into divers pieces, for that it was so great that otherwise it could not be taken out, for all the pieces laid together might make the quantity of a nutmegge.'

Old Dublin never lagged behind the spirit of the age, and as she had her maternity hospital years before London so she early possessed a leper hospital represented in Speed's map of Dublin (1610) as being on the site later occupied by Mercer's Hospital. The earliest reference is in 1230 in an ancient charter. In 1244 it was alluded to in Gilbert's *Municipal Documents*: 'Dublin Commynalty, A.D. 1244, Terram–quae jacet inter terram quam idem Ricardus tenet de domo Sancti Stephani.' There is also mention of it in the Memorandum Roll, 17 Richard II (1394) in the record office, which relates that 'one Blena Mocton lately founded the aforesaid chapel for the relief of such Dublin citizens as might be smitten with leprosy.' Archbishop Alan, in his *Repertorium Viride* recorded in his census of the Dublin Diocese, in 1533, that the lepers held the church of St. Stephen for their own use. The present district of Leopardstown receives its name from the fact that there was a sort of convalescent home for the sufferers there. Through the years Leperstown has become converted to the less gruesome modern form.

In the *Calendar of Ancient Records* for Dublin under the date '1491, Fourth Friday after 24th June':

It is ordined, by auctorite of the semble holdyn the fourth Friday next after the fest of the Natyvyte of Sent (John the) Baptiste that every fre man and woman of this cite enfected with lepyr be received and take into the house of Saint Stewnes within the fraunches of this cite frely, without anny fyne paying to anny person or persones. And whosoever attempt the contrary to pay xl.s., halfe thereof to the maire and Bailiffs for the tym beyng, and the other half to the tresory of the said cite.

In common with other great and consequently overcrowded cities, Dublin suffered in the sixteenth century from recurrent outbreaks of plague. The *Calendar of Ancient Records* contains many references to these and to the measures employed to combat the menace, particularly in 1575.

In June of that year so many inhabitants had fled the city that there were not enough able-bodied men to perform the duties of the watch and the Municipal Council were obliged to threaten severe penalties on those who neglected their civic duties.

An Assembly of the Council held in September decided:

That Denis Collier, phisician and surgien shalbe and is admitted to the fraunches, fryudomes and libertyes of the cittie of Dublin in consideration that he nowe adventured his life in this contagious tyme of plague into the cittye, attendyng upon the Maire and every other that shalbe in danger or neede of phisicke or surgrye; that he shall continue during his life in service of the cittie, as well in the tyme of plague as in all other tymes, doying his duety, taking for his (fee?) as the patient and he shall agree, or as the Maire for the tyme being shall resonnablye order or adward.'

At the commencement of 1576 it was recognised that much of the spread of plague in Dublin was due to visits paid to infected houses by those ignorant of the sickness within. In order to remedy this the Municipal Council ordered that the head of any household affected by plague should inform the Mayor or his deputy within twenty-four hours under penalty of eighty days house arrest followed by disenfranchisement.

It was further ordered

That the great gardinge in Allhallowes nowe in the occupacion of William Stuoks shoemaker, is appointed to buylde lodgings in for the reliefe of the infected; also, that Mr Edward Peppard his house ther, and the steapell, bee in lycke sorte taken for lycke use as aforesaide; and that Mr Maior for the tyme beinge shall see lodginges made for suche as shall happen to be infected upon the cittie revenue; and that honnest house holders be apointed to keape the seyke foulkes and the parties that send any person being seyke thether shall fynde them meate and dryncke and all outher necessaries.

The plague must have continued throughout 1576 for, in October, officers were appointed to attend and bury the plague victims. Their salaries were fixed at sixpence per day.

The plague died out in the following year, but in May 1579 Nicholas Uriell, Physician, was admitted to the franchise on condition of dwelling within the city during his lifetime. This antedated by a year the appointment of Nicholas Hykie as an official city doctor (q.v.).

For practical purposes the end of the sixteenth century marked the end of a definite period in Irish medicine. Printing and easier travel, together with internal unrest, induced many would-be physicians to emigrate, at least temporarily. It was recognised that training and qualification in a formal medical school produced a more efficient doctor than did the handing down of traditional cures.

CHAPTER FIVE

TRINITY COLLEGE, DUBLIN, AND THE ROYAL COLLEGE OF PHYSICIANS

The early histories of the Trinity College Medical School and of the Royal College of Physicians are so closely intermingled that their consideration together is inevitable.

The foundation stone of T.C.D. was laid in 1593 by Thomas Smith, an apothecary, then Mayor of Dublin.

There is a reference in the College Records of 1598 to a government grant of £40 per year to the University for a 'Physitian's pay.' This may have marked the establishment of a Professorship of Medicine. More probably it was in the nature of a retainer for the services of a doctor to the College. In support of this it must be remembered that the foundation charter of Queen Elizabeth made no special mention of a Medical Faculty. By various statutes it was enacted that one of the Fellows should devote himself to the subject, but the elected Fellow did not always possess a medical degree or experience in the first instance.

The first statutes of the University contain a reference to courses of study for medical degrees about 1627.

– the student of Medicine – shall be a Master of Arts – shall have diligently devoted seven years to the study of medicine – he must on six occasions prelect in the School of Physicians; that he must be present at three anatomical dissections; that he must on four occasions successfully carry to a conclusion the cure of different diseases; that after frequent attendance in the laboratories of the apothecaries he must know and keep clearly in his mind all the simples that are met with in the laboratories; and lastly that he must on three occasions respond and as many times oppose in his faculty.

In spite of these regulations only one degree in Physic was granted in the first twenty-three years of the University's existence.

In 1626, Charles I in a letter to Lord Deputy Falkland, expressed his desire that a college of physicians should be set up in Ireland. In 1628, Bedell, then Provost of Trinity, expressed a similar wish in letters to friends in English universities. Unfortunately, Bedell was appointed Bishop of Kilkenny in 1629 and his proposals came to naught. The Rebellion of 1641 and the eclipse of the monarchy in England put an end to plans for the establishment of a school of medicine.

In 1615, a building originally intended as a Bridewell was granted to the University under the name of Trinity Hall. This was situated somewhere between the present Exchequer Street and Trinity Street. It was used as a residence for students until the Rebellion of 1641. In the usual post-war period of confusion the title to the Hall was questioned by the city authorities. Fellows had been appointed under both Royal and Cromwellian regimes, in England, and the legality of each was open to question. One of the most notable figures of the day helped to solve the impasse.

John Stearne (1624–1669) entered the University in 1639, obtaining a scholarship two years later. In 1641, he went to England and studied medicine at Cambridge and Oxford. He returned to Ireland and received his M.D. in 1658, at which time he was lecturing in Hebrew. Following a dispute over salary he resigned his Fellowship in 1659. Despite this he featured as Senior Fellow and Registrar in 1660–1. At the same time he put forward a plan for the establishment of an association of physicians.

Stearne founded the 'President and Fraternity of Physicians' in Trinity Hall in 1654. The Hall was given to Stearne by the Provost and Fellows of Trinity, who appointed him President on the understanding that he would endeavour to secure a Royal Charter.

When the monarchy was restored in 1660, Stearne was reappointed President and the Fraternity was placed on a legal basis.

In 1667, Charles II granted the first charter of incorporation to 'The President and Fellows of the College of Physicians in Dublin.' This preserved the continuity between the University and the Fraternity. At the same time the Physicians were given the control of the practice of physic in Dublin and within seven miles thereof. The objects of the incorporation were to stamp out:

'the daily abuses of the most necessary and laudable art of physic in the kingdom of Ireland by the practice of mountebanks and empirics, and other ignorant and illiterate persons, to the impairing of the health and hazard of the lives of the good subjects there.'

Unfortunately the powers granted were not sufficiently wide, and at the request of the College a new Charter was given by William and Mary in 1692. This Charter, with a few alterations, still governs the College.

In the first Charter, Stearne was nominated President for life. After his death, presidents were to be elected by the Provost, Fellows, and Scholars of Trinity, subject to the approval of the Viceroy.

By the latter charter the Fellowships were limited to fourteen; no one might practise physic in Dublin or within seven miles thereof unless he were a Fellow or Licentiate of the College; nor could any but graduates in physic of Oxford, Cambridge, or Dublin practise in the rest of Ireland unless licensed by the College. The College was entrusted with the supervision of apothecaries, surgeons and midwives. The science, as distinct from the art of surgery, was declared a part of medicine.

The members of the College were exempted from various public duties, such as serving on juries or being chosen as constables or scavengers.

On Stearne's death, George Walker was elected 'Medical Fellow' in the University. He held the post for less than a year. William Palliser, later Archbishop of Cashel, was then appointed. He, too, left after a year and, on 9th September, 1671, George Mercer was chosen, *in medicum*. Neither Walker nor Palliser held medical degrees and Mercer did not secure one until 1681.

Thomas Margetson became Professor of Physick about this time, for an indefinite period. There is no direct mention of this in the University records, but it may be inferred from contemporary references. Margetson was succeeded in 1674 by Ralph Howard (1638–1710?) who was the first Fellow of the College of Physicians elected under the charter of Charles II.

Abraham Yarner (d. 1677) was elected President of the College of Physicians in 1672. Yarner appears to have been more interested in soldiering than in medicine. There are many references to him as Mustermaster-General of the forces in Ireland.

Although there is confusion as to the officers elected to the College of Physicians at this time there is no doubt that active work was being carried on.

An account book of the College of 1676 contains notes of payments made for a body for dissection. During the same period the Register of the University makes the first references to Bachelors' degrees in Medicine, the graduates being John Madden (1674), Henry Nicholson (1674), Allen Mullen (1679) and John Foley (1680). Of the four, Allen Mullen (1653–1690) is the best known. He was one of the most energetic members of the Dublin Philosophical Society. His published works included several papers on the comparative anatomy of the eye, and on the volume of blood in the body. Unfortunately, he based his findings in the latter case on wrong assumptions and lost his chance of sharing William Harvey's fame.

In 1680, the College of Physicians surrendered Trinity Hall to the University. In the next year Dr (later Sir) Patrick Dun (1642–1713) was chosen President of the College. Dun was a native of Aberdeen who had studied in France and seen service in the Williamite wars before settling in Dublin. He was elected a Fellow of the College of Physicians about 1676.

On 24th June, 1681, he was chosen President of the College and seems to have been re-elected annually until 1687 when Dr John Crosby succeeded him. He was again elected from 1690 to 1692 and was nominated first President under the new Charter of William and Mary. It is obvious that Dun was a leading spirit in College affairs, for he was usually amongst those who acted as representatives of the College at discussions with other bodies. Dun was appointed physician to King William's army in 1688 and was present at some historic events.

Although busy and successful in his practise Dun later decided to enter Parliament and in 1692 was elected to the Irish House of Commons as member for Mullingar, and for Killyleagh, Co. Down, but seemed to take little interest in his parliamentary duties.

By his marriage in 1694 to Mary, daughter of Colonel John Jephson of Mallow, Dun secured his position amongst some of the most influential families of the period. His only son, Boyle, born in 1697, died at an early age. In 1711, Dun drew up his will and celebrated deed for the establishment of a professorship of physic. In 1713 he died and was buried in St Michan's Church.

In 1687, the Provost and Senior Fellows of Trinity had decided that the kitchen garden should be made a physic garden at the charge of the College of Physicians. In the same year a dispute arose between the two bodies over the election of Dr Crosby as President of the College. Crosby had been elected a Fellow in 1674 and the earliest records of this body are in his handwriting. He does not appear to have been a graduate of Trinity College and was certainly not a member of the Established Church in Ireland. Whatever the cause of the University's refusal there is no doubt of its effect. For several years there was no co-operation between the two bodies.

When the government of William III was established in 1690, life became more stable. The physicians petitioned the Lord Deputy for a new charter giving them wider powers. In 1692, the King and Queen's College of Physicians was incorporated with Sir Patrick Dun as President.

The first meeting of the College of Physicians under the new charter took place in Dun's house on Inn's Quay. After his death his widow allowed the use of the house for some time. Before permanent premises were obtained in Sir Patrick Dun's Hospital (1808) the College met in the house of the President for the time being. On the completion of the hospital the central portion of the building was allocated to the College for a Common Hall, a Library, a Museum, a Lecture Room and private rooms for the professors.

The foundation-stone of the present College of Physicians building in Kildare Street, was laid in 1862 by the Lord Lieutenant, the Earl of Carlisle, during the presidency of Dominic Corrigan. The last

College meeting in the old premises at Sir Patrick Dun's Hospital was held on 1st July, 1864, and the first meeting in the new building took place four days later.

These premises remained almost unaltered for over a hundred years. But in the 1970's pressure on existing space became so serious as to warrant extensive structural work. Four new faculties of Pathology, Paediatrics, Occupational Medicine and Community Medicine had been established. There was a considerable committment to post graduate education. All of these played a part in straining accomodation to the utmost. The redevelopment cost some half million pounds. The first phase was financed from the College's resources, but a public appeal brought in generous support from individuals and organisations so that the new facilities could be opened in May 1983, during the presidency of Professor Dermot Holland.

By the charter of William and Mary the College was entitled to grant licences in Medicine and Midwifery, and to elect duly qualified persons to the Fellowship and Honorary Fellowship. In 1878, a Supplemental Charter was granted to the College. This created the order of membership open to licentiates of the College and to other qualified medical practitioners. Admission to the order is by examination or by thesis and Members alone are now eligible for election to the Fellowship.

Under the 1692 Charter the College of Physicians agreed not to admit anyone as a Fellow who had not a Dublin University degree in Medicine. In return the Provost and Senior Fellows of the University proposed that everyone to whom they granted leave to perform Acts for a medical degree should pass an examination by the College before the degree was conferred. Despite other elaborate regulations no provision was made by either body for the instruction of students. At the time there was no school of medicine in the entire country.

On 14th June, 1710, the Provost and Senior Fellows of Trinity College ordered that space at the south-east corner of the physic garden should be provided for a Laboratory and Anatomical Theatre. This building was opened in the next year as a Medical School with a staff consisting of Lecturers in Natural Philosophy, Anatomy, Botany, Chemistry and the Professor of Physic of the University.

The Anatomical Theatre occupied a position at the west end of the College Park. Old engravings show that it was a plain brick building, with little decoration. The internal accommodation was small. There was no water supply or drainage. The building was formally opened on 16th August, 1711. Two of the lecturers on this occasion were Richard Helsham (1683–1738) and Thomas Molyneux (1661–1733).

Helsham had a brilliant career. He entered Trinity College at the age of fifteen. After a few years he became a Fellow and Master of Arts. In 1706, he was elected medical Fellow and two years later proceeded to the degrees of Bachelor and Doctor of Medicine. In 1710, he was admitted a Fellow of the College of Physicians. He was first Professor of Natural and Experimental Philosophy, a chair founded under the will of Erasmus Smith. He was later Professor of Physic and President of the College of Physicians. Despite his medical activities he took a keen interest in municipal affairs.

Helsham asked that his body should be examined post mortem. In the *Gentleman's Magazine* for 1738 an account of the examination was published:

It was imagin'd that his disorder proceeded from a twisting of the guts, and he took quicksilver, which proved ineffectual – there was found in one of his guts an excrescence of three pieces of flesh, the smallest as large as a hen's egg, and resembling the flesh of the liver.

Thomas Molyneux also entered Trinity at fifteen years of age. When he returned, in 1687, after some years abroad he became M.D. and F.K. & Q.C.P. During the political unrest in 1689–1690 he remained in London. After the Battle of the Boyne he returned to Dublin and established a successful practice. Molyneux was elected President of the College of Physicians in 1701–1702, 1709–1713 and 1720. In 1711, he was chosen Professor of Physic in succession to Richard Steevens. In 1730, he became the first medical baronet in Ireland. Not only was he an eminent physician, but he more than held his own as a zoologist, botanist, antiquarian, classical scholar, political economist and statesman.

In 1712, following consultations between the College and the University it was decided that ' . . . every candidate Batchellor of Physick be examined in all ye parts of Anatomy relating to ye Oeconomia Animalis and in all ye parts of Botany, Chymistry and Pharmacy. Every candidate-doctor be examined as to ye aforesaid subjects and likewise in ye explication of Hippocrates's Aphorisms, and ye Theory and Cure of external and internal diseases, and ye President and Fellows of ye College of Physicians to examine.' The influence of Hippocrates still prevailed after two thousand years.

According to the University Statutes the period of study required of a student before presenting himself for the degree of Bachelor of Medicine varied with the period in his academic career at which he began the study of medicine. If he commenced immediately on matriculation he was obliged to complete eight academic years of three terms each. The Bachelor of Arts was required to study for three years before seeking a medical degree. For the Master of Arts the period of medical studies occupied only two years.

In his will Sir Patrick Dun bequeathed most of his property to the College of Physicians for the purpose of establishing a Professorship of Physick in Dublin. He also left his house and library for the use of the Professor and College. In 1715, at the request of Lady Dun, Letters Patent were obtained incorporating the Professorship in Perpetuity under the title of 'King's Professorship of Physick in the City of Dublin.' Amongst the functions of the Professor were public lectures on osteology, bandaging, surgical operations, botany and materia medica. He was required to perform public anatomical dissections on both human and animal bodies.

Dr Robert Griffith was the first holder of the chair, his examiners being Benjamin Pratt, the Provost; Thomas Molyneux, Professor of Physic; Richard Helsham, President of the College of Physicians, with William Smyth and James Grattan, the Senior Censors.

The value of the estates increased and in 1749 three professors were elected to the chairs of:

> Physic – Henry Quin, M.D. of Padua.
> Chirurgery and Midwifery – Nathaniel Barry, M.D. of Rheims.
> Pharmacy and Materia Medica – Constantine Barbour, M.B. of Dublin.

Their memories were perpetuated in Gilborne's *Medical Review:*

> Ingenious Quin with Erudition great,
> Averts the Blows of unrelenting fate,
> He teaches youth, the cures, the remedies
> And various causes of all maladies,
> The Speculative theoretic Rule,
> And the best Practice in the Physic School.
>
> The God-like Barry high in learning soars
> His prudent Skill the sick to Health restores
> He teaches Midwifes how to trace their clews
> Thro' mazy Labyrinths and how to use
> Their Instruments he shrews Chirurgeons bold
> All this in College by the sage is told.
>
> Wise Barbour can prolong the days of youth
> By maxims founded on undoubted truth;
> With pharmaceutic Art he plainly shews
> How to prepare, preserve, compound and chuse
> Drugs and Materials medical that will
> All indications curative fulfill.

Unfortunately, the co-operation between College and University came to an end. Both were at fault, in failing to carry out their agreement in the spirit, as well as in the letter. The University Board occasionally granted medical degrees to men who had not been examined by the College. The College refused to license these. On the other hand the Physicians, after 1753, refused to examine anyone who practised midwifery. In this way they reduced seriously the numbers who might seek degrees. The squabble came to a head in 1759. Fielding Ould (1710–1789) was a Licentiate in Midwifery of the College. Trinity granted him permission to sit for a Bachelor's degree in Medicine. The College refused to examine him. Despite this, Trinity granted him a degree in 1761. One year later the President and Fellows of the College of Physicians formally notified the Board of Trinity that the connection between the two bodies should be dissolved.

The Board at once decreed that examinations in medicine should be carried out by members of the University staff. Robert Robinson, the lecturer in Anatomy, was dismissed and George Cleghorn was appointed to his place. Cleghorn (1716–1826) was a graduate of Edinburgh. He was in practice as a surgeon in Dublin and was a first-class lecturer. His anatomy class in one year numbered ninety-five students. Unfortunately the other teachers were not of the same calibre. William Clements (1707–1782), the Professor of Physic, was not in active practice. James Thornton (1720 ?–1783) seems to have been most unsatisfactory. He was probably appointed through favouritism. On his supersession by Perceval he committed suicide by drinking an ounce of tincture of opium. Edward Hill (1741–1830) the Lecturer in Botany, controlled a botanical garden which, he said, possessed only one barren fig-tree.

It became obvious that the quarrel between University and College must end for their mutual benefit. Dun's estates had increased in value, so that each Professor received £300 per year for doing nothing. In 1783, the President and Fellows of the College again took the initiative and proposed discussion of plans which would be acceptable to both sides.

In 1785 an Act for the provision of a complete medical school was passed. This Act established Professorships of Anatomy and Chirurgery, Chemistry and Botany, Medicine, Pharmacy, Natural History and Midwifery. The importance of clinical studies was recognised. Directions were given that lectures should be delivered in the city hospitals. Unfortunately the hospitals refused the use of their wards for this purpose. In 1787, the College took a house in Clarendon Street, as a hospital with seventeen beds. This lasted only two years. No further constructive move was made until 1791, when an Act was passed empowering the College of Physicians to raise

£1,000 on Dun's estates in order to build a hospital. A house was taken on Blind (later Wellington) Quay and opened as a hospital with thirty-one beds, in November 1792. The visiting staff were the six University Medical Professors. The public gave little support and the hospital was closed four years later. There is no record of its ever having been used for its primary purpose of providing clinical material for students. In 1798, the professors came to an agreement with Mercer's Hospital to allow the use of certain beds for lecture purposes. The arrangement never appears to have worked well.

On 1st August, 1800, the second-last Act of the Irish Parliament was passed. It deflected the greater part of the funds of Sir Patrick Dun's estate to the purpose of building a hospital primarily for the instruction of students. Until this building was completed, in 1808, clinical lectures were given in the Meath Hospital by Whitley Stokes and in Steeven's by John Crampton. A fuller description of Sir Patrick Dun's is included in the chapter on the hospitals.

The moving spirit in the proposal and passage of this Act was Robert Perceval (1756–1839). He was a graduate of both Edinburgh and Trinity and had had some Continental experience. When he returned to Dublin, in 1782, he joined the staff of Trinity, first as lecturer, then, in 1785, as Professor of Chemistry. He was elected President of the College of Physicians in 1799, but had to resign this and his Fellowship owing to a clause in the School of Physic Act, forbidding Professors to hold office in the College. Although he was censured by the College for his part in the passage of the Act he received an Honorary Fellowship in 1800. In later years he devoted his energies to prison reform and theological disputation.

Perceval's aim was to establish a large clinical hospital, similar to the Royal Infirmary in Edinburgh. He was bitterly opposed by Edward Hill, who wished to devote all available funds to supplying a first-class botanical garden.

When the Act was passed it set forth that three King's Professors should be appointed, of the Institutes of Medicine, of the Practice of Medicine and of Materia Medica at a salary of one hundred Irish pounds, each, yearly. After certain expenses the remainder of Dun's estates were to be devoted to the establishment of a hospital named in his honour. This hospital was to be governed by delegates from both the College and University. The regulations for the general government of the School of Physic were laid down. Most of these are still operative.

The clause in the charter of William and Mary which admitted graduates in Physic of the University as members of the College of Physicians without examination was repealed. The King's Professorships were opened to persons of all nations who professed their faith in Christ, but the University Professorships were reserved to Protestants. Catholics were made eligible for election to the College of Physicians.

Shortly after the passage of the Act William Hartigan (1756 ?1812) succeeded Cleghorn as Professor of Anatomy. He had previously held the Chairs of Anatomy, Physiology and Surgery in the College of Surgeons as well as the Presidency (1797) of that body. He became assistant to Cleghorn in 1799, and succeeded to the Chair in 1803, holding the post adequately, if not brilliantly, until 1812.

As has been mentioned, the Botany Department was seriously handicapped by the lack of a suitable supply of fresh specimens. Successive professors had tried to remedy this without success. The story of their efforts is commemorated in the name 'Botany Bay' given to one of the College squares. This was originally the kitchen garden. For a time it was used to supply botanical specimens.

Edward Hill was the chief agitator for the provision of a suitable garden. He pestered the Dublin Society, the Legislature and the College of Physicians in an effort to have his dream realised. In 1800, he was compelled to resign and Robert Scott (d. 1808) was appointed his successor. Hill took an action against Trinity to recover money he had spent on the garden and, after a long fight, was awarded over £600 with certain lands he had held in trust for the University in anticipation of the establishment of a botanical garden.

During this dispute the Board went ahead with their own plans, and secured grounds at the junction of Landsdown and Pembroke roads in Ballsbridge. A small staff was appointed with James Townsend Mackay (1777–1862) as head gardener. He deserves great credit for the growth of these gardens. He was the author of a standard work on Irish plants in 1836 and was later given an LL.D *honoris causa* by the Board of T.C.D. The gardens finally closed about 1976 and the grounds are now occupied by hotel premises. Many of the trees have survived, amongst which is an unusual variety of arbutus estimated to be at least 120 years old.

In 1813, William Hartigan died and was succeeded by James Macartney (1770–1843) who brought the Trinity College medical School to its important position in the early nineteenth century. His history in the University was marked by many disputes beginning with his association, as a student, with the United Irishmen and ending with his resignation in 1837. He studied in Dublin and London and held the Chair of Comparative Anatomy at St Bartholomew's Hospital School for thirteen years before returning to Dublin to occupy the Chair of Anatomy. He published several important works on his subject, but his main claim to fame is his reorganisation of the Medical School.

Macartney's appointment to the Chair was made in the face of strong opposition from the friends of other candidates but his qualifications were such that the Board had no option but to select him. Even after his appointment he was subjected to obstruction and non-cooperation in his efforts to improve the School's accomodation. He probably made enemies and lost financially by refusing to sign attendance certificates for absentee students but this attitude was an integral part of his determination to raise standards all round.

Macartney's earliest attempt at reform was to press for a practical examination conducted in English as a part of the final medical examination. This met with strong opposition from the older professors who invariably conducted their lectures and examinations in Latin.

Largely as a result of Macartney's brilliant teaching the School of Physic became overcrowded. In 1815 an additional building was erected and other departments were moved so as to leave more room for anatomy. With the increased space available it was possible for extra lectures to be given; in ophthalmology by Arthur Jacob and in midwifery by John Pentland. As the Rotunda and the College of Surgeons both gave lectures in the latter subject it was a financial gain to Trinity to keep her students centralised. In 1820, there were so many students (303) that Macartney was obliged to lecture twice daily. As the old buildings were now very rickety, estimates were invited for the erection of a new medical school on the ground then occupied as a bowling green.

After many disputes and delays work started in 1823. When the building was nearly finished Macartney met the architect, Morrison, and expressed his adverse opinion of the work. Words led to blows and eventually the Professor broke his umbrella over the architect's head.

The events leading to Macartney's resignation concerned the clashing of hours at which lectures were given by different Professors. Macartney seems to have been at fault, and refused to alter his lecture times even at the order of the Board. Several letters passed and in July 1837 Macartney resigned. He was succeeded by Robert Harrison (1796–1858).

At this time the University Professors of Anatomy, Chemistry and Botany lectured in Trinity College. The lectures in Medicine, Materia Medica, Pharmacy and clinical subjects were still given in Dun's Hospital. The School of Physic was still under the joint control of Trinity and the College of Physicians. The students were of two classes, those who had an Arts degree and those, the larger number, who had merely matriculated.

The University was the authority for conferring degrees, but in theory no one could practise within seven miles of Dublin without the Licence of the College. In reality licentiates of both the College of Surgeons and the Apothecaries' Hall practised with impunity.

In 1820, a committee of the College of Physicians reported that the course of study should be lengthened, that clinical studies should be extended and that one year should be passed in a foreign centre, by each student. This last recommendation was dropped, when the implication that Trinity was unable to give complete teaching was seen. Consultations were held between the two bodies without concrete results. In 1823, the Irish College of Physicians were informed by the London College that they did not consider the School of Physic diploma a sufficient qualification on which to grant the right to be examined for a licence.

The situation now was that the University might qualify anyone by conferring a medical degree without consultation with the College of Physicians.

There was no medical man among the Senior Fellows and the Board was dependent on outside advice in medical affairs. To make matters worse the Professors failed to work well together. Macartney's zeal for action led him into constant squabbles with the King's Professors. He was in the habit of making post-mortem examinations on patients who died in the Hospital. As his findings were often at variance with the diagnosis during life, the clinicians objected, particularly as Macartney did not spare their feelings when demonstrating to a class. This, as much as the disputes over lecture hours, led to Macartney's resignation in 1837.

When Harrison was appointed to the Chair of Anatomy the Board insisted that he should sign a declaration of obedience to their orders. Harrison had already held the equivalent Chair in the College of Surgeons for ten years. His main contribution to the work of the Trinity College School was the establishment of an anatomical museum.

In 1839 a new and extended course of instruction for medical degrees was approved. The diploma given to those who had merely matriculated disappeared and a more liberal pre-medical education was demanded. Subsequently, 1846, it was made obligatory for all medical students to graduate in Arts.

In 1839, the College of Physicians elected Thomas Brady (1801–1864) Professor of Medical Jurisprudence and requested the Board of Trinity to make attendance on his lectures compulsory. This step was not taken until 1845, after repeated urgings. Even then the student was allowed to choose between attendance at Chemistry and Jurisprudence, although the course of study was lengthened to four years. This new curriculum also separated the Chairs of Surgery and Anatomy, as recommended by Harrison in 1842. Robert W. Smith (1807–1873) was the first appointee to the Chair of Surgery. Clinical teaching in hospitals other than Sir Patrick Dun's was now recognised and systemic lectures were all delivered in the School instead of partly in the Hospital as heretofore.

During this period two of the most distinguished men in Irish medicine joined the University staff. They were Robert James Graves and William Stokes. Graves became King's Professor of the Institutes of Medicine in 1827. He immediately introduced the system of clinical teaching which has been followed so widely elsewhere. In this the student observes the patient for himself under the eye of a teacher whose function is to help. Under the old system the student might pass through hospital without ever examining a patient. He 'learned' by trying to grasp a series of statements flung at him by an aloof, impersonal, unapproachable 'teacher.'

Graves' ability as a teacher was recognised far afield, particularly in America and France, where Trousseau entreated those of his pupils who understood English to consider Graves' Lectures on Clinical Medicine as their bible.

Stokes was elected King's Professor of Medicine in 1840. He held the post for thirty-eight years. An outline of his life is given in the chapter on nineteenth-century personalities. During Stokes' Professorship much medical legislation was passed. Even more was discussed.

In 1849, candidates for the M.B. were permitted to attend courses at the College of Surgeons, provided they spent one year at the University. A reciprocal move was made by the College. Unfortunately, before the proposals could be ratified a dispute arose over the right of the University to teach surgery and the scheme collapsed.

The students requested the foundation of a Professorship of Surgery in 1851. Despite strong opposition by the Surgeons both in Dublin and London the Board of Trinity decided to make the appointment on learning that the Army and Navy Boards would accept the University's licence.

James William Cusack (1788–1861) was elected Regius Professor of Surgery in 1852. In the same year the century-old squabble with the College of Physicians was healed. The President and Censors of the College resumed their places as examiners, and graduates were admitted to the licentiate without examination. The scheme did not last long; for, in 1856, a new examination system was evolved. The

College was not invited to participate. They did not formally sever their connection until 1858. In this year the regulations for the M.B. course were again modified. It was stipulated that the candidate should be a graduate in Arts and should have spent four years studying medicine. Two years later the examination was split; Anatomy, Physiology, Chemistry, Botany and Materia Medica were taken at the end of the second year's study.

In 1867, the School of Physic Act was altered. Religious disabilities were dropped. The election of King's Professors was placed in the hands of the College of Physicians whose Fellows became eligible for election. The Professor of Surgery and University Anatomist were required to lecture in Dun's Hospital in place of the Professors of Chemistry and Botany. A King's Professor of Midwifery was appointed. This altered legislation is commonly known as 'Haughton's Act' in tribute to the then Registrar of the School of Physic, Rev Samuel Haughton (1821–1897) whose energy was largely responsible for its promulgation.

In 1870, on the initiative of William Stokes, a diploma in State Medicine was established. This, which was the forerunner of the Diploma in Public Health was the first of its kind in the United Kingdom.

A Medical School Committee consisting of the Professors and Registrar was established in 1863. This resulted in a more balanced administration of the School. It became impossible for one man to upset the harmonious working of the whole.

Haughton, the first Registrar, had graduated in Arts. In 1851 he was elected to the Chair of Geology. He did not qualify in Medicine until 1861. He held the post of Registrar from 1863 to 1879. He then became Chairman of the Committee. Many societies and Universities honoured him. His awards included F.R.S. 1858, LL.D. Cambridge 1880, LL.D. Edinburgh 1884, Vice-President R.I.A. 1877.

Haughton took an active interest in Dun's Hospital. He established the modern system of nursing there and was responsible for the admission of surgical patients in 1864. His name is commemorated in the Haughton Medal for Clinical Medicine and Surgery which he founded in 1869. At the meeting of the British Medical Association in Dublin in 1887, Haughton read a paper on death rates. He attributed Dublin's high rate to the conditions in the slums.

In 1868 the Board adopted a resolution that no University Professor should hold a clinical appointment other than to Dun's Hospital. The College of Physicians passed a similar resolution shortly after.

A laboratory for Histology and Pathology was opened in 1881 under the direction of Professor John Mallett Purser. Purser was elected Regius Professor of Physic in 1917. His drive and initiative were largely responsible for the School's success towards the end of the nineteenth century.

The absent-minded professor is a familiar figure of fun. Benjamin George McDowel (1821–1885), who held the Chair of Anatomy from 1858 to 1879, might have been the original character. Although he was a brilliant and popular teacher he frequently forgot to turn up for lectures or to make arrangements for dissections. His assistant, Thomas Little, was not much better and the anatomy teaching suffered some reverses.

Alexander Macalister was appointed Professor in 1879 on condition that he devoted his full time to the duties of the Chair. He was even excused from giving clinical lectures. When Macalister went to Cambridge in 1883 Daniel John Cunningham was elected and the school commenced a new and prosperous era.

Cunningham's Anatomy is a familiar textbook to students of medicine. Daniel John Cunningham (1850–1909) was born in Scotland. After qualification he demonstrated anatomy in Edinburgh University for several years. He was elected to the Chair of Anatomy in the College of Surgeons' School in Dublin in 1882. He only held this post until the following year when he transferred to Trinity where he remained for twenty years. In 1903, he returned to Edinburgh, this time as Professor. The Cunningham Bronze Medal commemorates his name in T.C.D. It is awarded annually to the student receiving the highest marks in anatomy.

Cunningham was directly responsible for the erection of the present medical school buildings. Throughout his long period in Trinity College he received the constant and enthusiastic support of Samuel Haughton.

The comparatively new speciality of Pathology was interesting medical minds and in 1895 Haughton proposed that a Professorship should be established. The proposal was defeated, but Alexander O'Sullivan (d. 1924) was appointed Lecturer. He was given the Chair in 1922.

In 1898 the School of Pathology and Bacteriology was erected on a hillock close to the Lincoln Place Gate. Dental degrees were established in 1904 and six years later a School of Dental Science was opened.

In 1912 the Bicentenary of the Medical School was celebrated by an international gathering and in 1925 the centenary of the 'new' school was commemorated by a great banquet.

In 1948 for the first time the school received an annual governmental grant. This increased considerably the available facilities. At the same time the 'Moyne Bequest' through the generosity of the Hon. Grania Guinness made possible the establishment of a department of Social Medicine.

In the intervening quarter of a century one of the most important developments was the establishment of professorial units in the hospitals, traditionally associated with the T.C.D. Medical School. The facilities available in these were very variable at both teaching and research levels so that the clinical material could not always be used to the best advantage.

The Fitzgerald report of 1968 suggested that St Kevins (now St James) Hospital should be developed as a major teaching unit. Three years later a new statutory body was set up to run this hospital and in the following year a formal agreement was concluded which made St James a major teaching centre for T.C.D. This development was closely linked to that of the Federated Dublin Voluntary Hospitals to which reference is made elsewhere. With over 700 beds the pool of material available to T.C.D. students within one complex will be more than adequate for advanced teaching and research.

CHAPTER SIX

THE SEVENTEENTH CENTURY

About the beginning of the seventeenth century the power of the hereditary medical families began to decline. The establishment of formal schools of medicine on the Continent, the state of unrest of the country and the eclipse of their old Gaelic patrons all played a part in the disappearance of the hereditary leech.

The disturbed state of the country prevented the foundation of an organised profession and the period is marked by the efforts of active individuals, even after the establishment of the College of Physicians and the Corporation of Surgeons, both of whose work is recorded in separate chapters.

There was little encouragement for anyone to work outside of Dublin with its relatively large population. Despite this, some members of the old families continued to practise the hereditary calling both at home and abroad. Even up to the present day descendants of these families may be found in the old areas, sometimes living under very poor circumstances.

Prior to the seventeenth century medical books of Irish origin were few and insignificant except for the manuscripts already noticed. Possibly the first printed medical work by an Irishmen was Theobald Anguilbert's *Mensa Philosophica,* published in Paris in 1530. Its contents refer more to social than medical matters.

Dr Thadeus Dun practised at Locarno in Switzerland. He published *Epistolae Medicinales* in 1591. In 1619, he followed with a treatise on women's diseases entitled *De Morbis Mulieribus*. Amongst his original suggestions was the use of a warm bath in prolonged labour.

One of the most noted Irish physicians of this century was Neil O'Glacan, born in Donegal about 1595. He received his medical education abroad and occupied the Chairs of Physic at Toulouse and Bologna. These were both important schools of medicine at the time. Later he became physician and privy councillor to the King of France. His chief works are *Tractus de Peste*, 1629, and *Cursus Medici*, 1646. His worth was recognised in a eulogistic poem composed by Peter von Adrian Brocke, contemporary Professor of Eloquence at Lucca:

With healing art he arms us to repel
Dire troops of agues and of fevers fell,
Whatever ills the patient may endure,
Known, or unknown, unerring is his cure,
Nor more instructions from my muse inquire,
The sons of science him alone admire.
His works all Gallia with attention reads,
Sucks in his knowledge and reveres his deeds,
Hence Belgia smitten with his art divine.
Far distant Spain, and thou who drinkst the vine,
Hence Italy with ample presents sued
The sage when absent, and with honours wooed.
Bolognia, now with skill-imbibing ears,
Devours his lectures, and applauding hears,
While he unlocks the healthy mystic stores
Of princely Galen, and his path explores
His country, blessed in such a son, may boast,
'And this be thine Ultonia's ancient coast.'

From the other end of the country came Bernard O'Connor. Born in Kerry in 1666, he became physician to King John Sobieski of Poland, after receiving his medical education at Montpelier. After a period in Paris, O'Connor went to London, where he died at the early age of thirty-two. His written works include *De Humani Hypogastri sarcomatei, Dissertationes Medico-Physiæ*, and a peculiar rambling treatise entitled *Evangelium Medici*. In this he mooted the possibility of human generation being effected without direct contact between the sexes. O'Connor was one of the earliest writers to appreciate the connection between chemistry, physiology and pathology. In the *Philosophical Transactions* he published a description of a skeleton whose bones were firmly cemented together at the joints. Possibly this was a case of rheumatoid arthritis.

Two Dutch physicians, Gerard and Arnold de Boote, or Boate, published a book entitled *Philosophia Naturales* in Dublin in 1641. This was largely a criticism of Aristotle. They also published works of medical interest.

In Gerard de Boate's *Natural History of Ireland* (1652) he writes:

The rickets are of late very rife in Ireland, where few years agoe they were unknown; so on the contrary it hath been almost quite freed from another disease, one of the very worst and miserablest in the world, namely, the leprosie which in former times used to be very common there, especially in the province of Munster; the which therefore was filled with hospitals, expressly built for to receive and keep the leprous persons. But many years since Ireland hath been almost freed from this horrible and loathsome disease, and as few leprous persons are found there as in any other countrie in the world so that the hospitals erected for their use, having stood empty a long time, are quite decayed and come to nothing.

Boate puts forward the theory that 'the leprosie' was due to the excessive eating of salmon out of season and credits the strict game laws of the English with the disappearance of the disease.

In the Thorpe collection of pamphlets in the National Library, Dublin, there is preserved a printed extract of a letter written by Arnold in 1642. The title reads: *A remonstrance of divers remarkable passages and proceedings of our Army in the Kingdome of Ireland. Being An Extract of a Letter sent out of Dublin from Doctor Arnold Boat, Doctor to the State and Physician General to the Army, to his brother Doctor Gerard Boat, Doctor to the King's Majestie living in Aldermanburie.*

This is largely an account of the work of the occupying forces in various parts of Ireland. There is no reference to medical matters or to Boate's duties as Physician to the Army.

In 1659, William Bladen of Dublin printed for Dr John Stearne a work with the imposing title of *De Morte Dissertatio in qua Mortis Natura, Causae, Mobilitas Remorae et Remedia proponuntur; ac variae de Cadavere Anima separata controversiae enodantur.* A second edition was published in 1699. A copy of this is preserved in the Worth Library in Steevens' Hospital. It is a duodecimo volume of 308 pages and is an excellent production.

Stearne was born at Ardbraccan, Co. Meath, in 1622 (or 1624). He became a Senior Fellow of Trinity College. He was the first President of the Fraternity of Physicians of Trinity Hall in 1665–7, of the College of Physicians in 1667, and of the King's and Queen's College of Physicians in 1669 in which year he died. Stearne also wrote several books of a non-medical character.

In 1667 Cassin Conly of Offaly published a small volume vindicating the views on fever of Dr Willis, the celebrated professor of medicine at Oxford. The latter's opinions had been challenged by Dermot O'Meara.

Long Latin titles were fashionable in those times. In 1686 John O'Dwyer wrote a curious book giving an account of the medical profession and complaining of the intrusion of midwives and quacks. The title runs: *Querela Medica se Planctus Medicinae Modernae Status Athore. Joanne O'Dwyer, Cassiliensi Medicinae Liccintiato Urbisque Montensis Medico Pensionario. Montibus Ex Officina Aegidii V. Havort Sub Signo Paradisii* 1686.

James Wolveridge, a graduate of Trinity College, practised in Cork about 1671. He was probably the author of the oldest original book on midwifery published in English. The book contains two hundred and ten pages and thirty engravings. The title is *Speculum Matricis; or the Irish Midwives' Handmaid. Catechistically composed, by*

James Wolveridge, M.D., London; Printed by E. Okes; and are to be sold by Rowland Reynolds, at the King's Arms in the Poultry, 1671. This book may be considered as the forerunner of the popular 'catechism' series, well known to students cramming for examinations. The contents are in the form of a dialogue between doctor and midwife, Dr Philadelphos and Mrs Eutrapalia. Philadelphos is probably intended to be Wolveridge himself.

In the second edition the title is printed as the *Expert Midwives' Handmaid*.

In both editions the text and illustrations are typical of the knowledge of midwifery of the time. There is a passage in the preface especially directed to Irish readers. 'It hath an English dress under an Irish mantle; it being never intended for the Irish—whose fruitfulness is such that there is scarce one barren amongst them; and whose hardiness and facilitie is such as neither requires the nice Attendance of diligent, vigilant Nurse Keepers, or the Art of expert Anatomists, or the unwearied brains and skill of dexterous midwives.' He bases this opinion of the native Irish woman on the story of one of them who accompanied her husband to camp. When she went into labour she withdrew by herself and without assistance brought forth twins. She washed them and herself, after which she wrapped them up and marched twelve miles barelegged and barefooted to the next camp carrying the twins all the way.

There are three known copies of the English edition of this book, in the Royal College of Physicians in Edinburgh, in the Radford Library in Manchester, and in the Royal College of Surgeons, London. Two manuscript copies of this edition are in the keeping of the London Obstetrical Society.

There are only two copies of the Irish edition. One is in the Bodleian library at Oxford, the other in the University of Lund Library in Sweden.

In 1677 Sir John Temple published in Dublin a work on the cure of gout by Moxa. This substance, which was a species of night-wort, was in common use up to the end of the eighteenth century.

The lack of organisation in clinical work was only excelled by the complete lack of any medical relief or public health system.

Bills of Mortality were first kept in Dublin in 1661. Many of these have been destroyed but the few remaining give some idea of the numbers dying from various diseases in different years. An article in the *Assurance Magazine* for 1853 gives an account of those Bills still in existence. Even these are very incomplete as the births and deaths of Roman Catholics were not registered. The Bills contained information on Parliamentary orders as well as the vital statistics.

In 1690, Dr Charles Willoughby, mentioned elsewhere, compiled a paper entitled 'Observations on the Bills of Mortality and Increase of People in Dublin; the Distempers, Air and Climate of this Kingdom; also of Medicines, Physic, and Surgeons and Apothecarys.' Sir William Wilde published this paper in the *Proceedings of the Royal Irish Academy* in 1857. It throws considerable light on the subject of 'Political Arithmetic' or, as we should now call it, 'Vital Statistics,' which was then exciting much interest as a result of the writings of Captain John Graunt and Sir William Petty.

Petty had published the Bill for 1666 as well as 'Political Mortality' and 'Observations on the Dublin Bills of Anatomy.' Willoughby paid tribute to Petty's methods and employed them in compiling his own Observations. Willoughby's main findings were that the average yearly mortality was 2,236 out of a population of about 55,000. Of the deaths, 472 were due to smallpox and 661 to fever, the latter presumably including various febrile diseases.

Willoughby did not adopt a detached approach to his subject. He made several references to his personal opinions. As we have mentioned the Bills recorded christenings and not births. Willoughby mentioned 'fanaticks wch christen not their children at all and of papists which being more numerous in Dublin yn formerly made use of their own priests – and consequently their baptisms did not appear upon our church register. – The Irish are naturally lazy.'

The Irish climate seems to have changed little in 300 years. According to Willoughby

the air of our country is milder yn yt of England; warmer in ye winter and colder in ye summer; its only crime is too much moisture; 'tis very unconstant, and seldome continues 24 hours without some remarkable change as to heat and cold, wch makes it very difficult for us to cloath ourselves in ye morning soe as to serve for all day.

Quinine had been introduced to Europe from South America about 1663 under the name of Peruvian or Jesuits' bark. Willoughby mentioned it in highly laudatory terms 'it appears to me ye only specifick I know in nature. It attacks all intermittant feavors wth equal success, making noe difference whether ye patient be old or young or the disease in its beginning, hight or declination or of wht temper soever ye patient be–and I never knew it miscarry.'

Later, referring to Dr Thomas Sydenham's work in popularising quinine, Willoughby further states 'I can easily concur with him, in ye great admiracion he has for ye Jesuits bark, and doe believe opium to be one of the greatest remedys in nature.'

Outside of Dublin, there was little interest in social medicine or in any form of sick relief for the poor. In 1626, the Corporation of Cork had invited a Mr Meade, Doctor of Physick, to practise in the city for the sum of £10 per year. It was hoped, not ordered or agreed, that he would 'minister the poor physicke, out of charitable disposition gratis.' The neighbouring town of Youghal made a similar arrangement with Thomas Adams to open an Apothecary's shop about the same time.

From the earliest times, as mentioned, the armies engaged in Ireland were provided with medical services. In a *History of Ireland* written by Maurice Regan, servant and interpreter to Dermot MacMurrough, King of Leinster, there is a brief reference to the medical service of that king's army under the date 1169:

But the Kyng would not be perswaded to make anye stay untill they came to Lechlin where his hurte men moughte be better Relieved, than in the Field–and the next Daye (carrying their hurt men with theme) they marched to Fernes; where Dermond provided Physicians and Surgeons for the sick and hurt.

About the beginning of the seventeenth century we find the first references to Surgeons and Physicians General to the Army in Ireland. Sometimes they were termed Surgeons and Physicians to the State, but were invariably military officers.

In June 1600, Queen Elizabeth complained to the authorities in Dublin that the pay of army surgeons should be reduced to 20*s.* or 26*s.* 8*d.*, according to 'quality.' She referred to one William Kelly as a former Chirurgeon-General. Kelly died in 1597 in receipt of a pension of two shillings per day.

Dr Anderson was appointed Physician-General in 1594. When his successor Dr Turner died, the allowance made to him was transferred to the newly-founded Trinity College, Dublin, in 1598. This may have been the origin of the 'Physician's Pay' mentioned in the early records of the College. Only fragmentary accounts exist of early appointments to these posts and of the activities of the holders.

In a letter to Sir Robert Cecil, Secretary of State, dated 16th February 1598, Sir Ralph Lane refers to the fact that although they paid for the services of army surgeons these defaulted out of every company.

From 1610 until the middle of the eighteenth century, the terms Physician and Surgeon-General were practically synonymous with the titles Physician and Surgeon to the State. The payment was niggardly despite the high-sounding address. In July 1626, the Surgeon-General's services were valued at two shillings per day. The total of payment was reckoned according to the number of days actually served with the Army. About 1625, William Clowes and Michael Andrew, Surgeons to the King, petitioned His Majesty for grants of land in the forthcoming plantation of Connaught. We may wonder how they intended to keep up their estates on two shillings per day or less.

In Cromwell's army the Physician and Surgeon-General ranked as General Officers. The posts were held respectively by John Waterhouse and James Winter in Cromwell's staff. Thomas Trapham was Chirurgeon-General to 'the Horse.' An Apothecary-General was also appointed.

In the wars between James and William, Surgeons, Physicians and Chaplains were attached to both sides, but some regiments had neither medical nor spiritual advisers.

James Fountaine, who occupied the Surgeon-General's post in 1660, received an extra four shillings per day as Surgeon to the Military Hospital, Dublin. Later (1684) he was constituted joint Surgeon-General with Charles Thompson.

After the abdication of James II, Robert White was created Chirurgeon-General by a patent, dated 29th June 1689. He died ten years later and was succeeded by Thomas Proby, who accumulated a considerable fortune from his private practice. For the last year of his life (1728–29) Proby held the post jointly with John Nicholls, who occupied the position alone for a further thirty-six years.

Nicholl's successor was William Ruxton, who lived in Hoey's Court. This is now the 'Castle Steps' leading from Castle Street to Ship Street. Ruxton died in 1783.

In July 1774 Archibald Richardson occupied the office of State Chirurgeon as a civil post created by patent. In 1784 George Stewart succeeded Richardson, who became Chirurgeon-General. Stewart in turn occupied the higher post and was replaced by John Neill of Dominick Street.

In 1791 Gustavus Hume and Clement Archer were appointed joint State Surgeons. Archer died and Hume resigned. Gerard Macklin was appointed State Surgeon in 1806. The office died with him in 1844. Subsequently the salary attached to the post was transferred to the office of Surgeon to the Household of the Lord Lieutenant. In 1819, Philip Crampton was appointed Chirurgeon-General in George Stewart's place. He was the last occupant of the post.

The Physicians-General received better fees than the Surgeons. According to the letter of Queen Elizabeth, already mentioned, the physicians' pay was settled at four shillings per day. In the Army list for 1610 Dr Medcalf is mentioned as Physician-General. In 1660, when William Currer, an English physician was appointed Physician-General to the Army he was authorised to receive ten shillings per day. His successor's name, Daniel de Maziers des Fountaine, was similar to that of one of the Surgeons-General, but there was no relationship between them. Sir Patrick Dun, also received the fee of ten shillings daily. Dun's successor, John Friend, was the only holder of the post to be removed by the authorities for misdemeanour.

Amongst the better-known Physicians-General was Thomas Molyneux, appointed in May 1718. His house in Peter Street later became the Molyneux Asylum for the female blind.

This asylum is now situated in Leeson Park.

The last Physician-General was John Cheyne, M.D., Professor of Medicine to the Royal College of Surgeons. He held the office until its extinction in 1833.

Sir Thomas Molyneux, already mentioned, was the first holder of the post of State Physician under Letters Patent as a civil office. One of his successors, appointed in 1770, was Robert Emmet, father of the United Irishman of the same name who was executed in Thomas Street for his revolutionary activities. The elder Emmet's other son, Thomas, held the State Physicianship for a while. He too joined the United Irishmen. After a period in prison he emigrated to America, where he died in 1823.

The holders of the offices are listed below. It will be noted that the early records are fragmentary and that there were several instances in which an office was held jointly.

PHYSICIANS-GENERAL

John Waterhouse	*circa* 1642
Arnold de Boate	*circa* 1649
William Currer	1660–1668
Daniel de Maziers des Fountaine	1668–1688
Sir Patrick Dun	1688–1713
John Friend	1713–1714
John Campbell	1714–1718
Thomas Molyneux	1718–1725
Upton Peacock	1725–1745
Edward Barry	1745–1776
Nathaniel Barry	1749–1785
Charles Quin	1785–1819
William Harvey	1794–1819
Robert Percival	1819–1820
John Cheyne	1820–1833

SURGEONS-GENERAL

William Kelly	*circa* 1597
James Winter and	
Charles Thompson	*circa* 1642
James Fountaine	1660–1676
John Atkins	1676–1679

Charles Thompson.....................1679–1689
James Fountaine......................1684–1689
Robert White.........................1689–1699
Thomas Proby.........................1699–1729
John Nicholls........................1728–1767
William Ruxton.......................1767–1783
Archibald Richardson.................1784–1787
George Stewart.......................1787–1813
Philip Crampton......................1819–1854

STATE PHYSICIANS

Dr. Anderson.........................*circa* 1594
Dr. Turner and
Dr. Medcalf..........................*circa* 1610
Arnold de Boate......................*circa* 1649
Sir Patrick Dun......................1676–
Sir Thomas Molyneux..................1715–1730
Henry Cope...........................1730–1742
Robert Robinson......................1742–1770
Robert Emmet.........................1770–1803
Thomas Addis Emmet...................1783–1788
Stephen Dickson......................1788–1797
James Cleghorn.......................1797–1826
Alexander Jackson....................1803–1848

STATE SURGEONS

Edmund Cullen........................*circa* 1610
Archibald Richardson.................1774–1784
George Stewart.......................1784–1787
John Neill...........................1787–1791
Gustavus Hume and
Clement Archer.......................1791–1806
Gerard Macklin.......................1806–1844

At the end of 1604 Dublin was again threatened with a major epidemic of plague. In order to combat the danger the mayor and aldermen issued civic orders. A house was procured in St George's Lane for use as an isolation hospital. Four strong men were appointed to look after this house, to bury the dead and restrain infected persons from 'running abroad.' These officials were not allowed to enter the city without the mayor's permission and then only if they carried a white wand or stick. It was ordered that every inhabitant should burn a faggot at his door on Mondays, Wednesdays, and Saturdays, in order to purify the air.

Patients in the pest house were expected to contribute to their upkeep. At the same time a charge was levied on the city for the maintenance of the house.

In 1665, plague being once more rampant in London, the Dublin Municipal Council took measures to avoid any extension through the continual sea-borne traffic between the cities. Two houses were erected on the then Island of Clontarf for the reception of passengers and goods from abroad.

In Dublin's records of the seventeenth century there are many references to medical men both as individuals and as members of the city guilds. In 1650 Thomas Andrewes, physician, Richard Mitchell, barber-surgeon, and Henry Ballaerte, apothecary, were amongst those admitted to the franchise of the city.

There was a complaint some years later that certain guilds did not restrict themselves to their particular trades. Included amongst these were the surgeons who 'admit members of other trades such as apothecaries and vintners or indeed any other trade that will apply to be free of them and so the corporation that is injured is forced to implead the person so admitted, who by the others being wrongfully protected, animosities and troubles do arise.'

PROVINCIAL PRACTITIONERS

One of the most prominent provincial physicians of whom we have a record was Thomas Arthur of Limerick (1593–1674). He left behind several manuscripts now in the British Library. These give a good account of his own life and of medical practice of the time.

Arthur was a member of an eminent family whose members, for five hundred years had filled prominent positions in the diocese and corporation of Limerick. He was educated at Bordeaux and Paris, taking his medical degree at Rheims about 1618. His diary contains a list of his patients from 1619 to 1663, with their ailments and fees. A full transcript of the diary appeared in the *Kilkenny Archaeological Journal* for January 1867.

His closing entry in 1619 reads: 'The amount of my fees for this year past is £74 1s. 8d. for which and for other gifts conferred upon me, unworthy, I return boundless thanks to the Almighty God, Who has thus deigned to bless the beginning of my medical practice; and I beg of Him to vouchsafe to direct, govern and sanctify the rest of my actions, to the praise and glory of His Name, through Christ our Lord, Amen.'

Arthur travelled widely throughout the country. Amongst his first entries for 1620 are:

I went to Dublin to Mr George Sexton (gonorrhoea laborantem) who being thoroughly cured, gave me a horse of the value of £8 and £5 in gold.	£13 9 0
I then went to the lady of Arthur Chichester, the Quaestor or treasurer of this Kingdom, then living at Carrickfergus, in Ulster, whom, when labouring under dropsy, and forewarning her of the death within a few days after my prognosis, I attended upon; he gave me on the 25th of May.	£5 10 0
Being sent for on the 3rd of May, I went to Margaret Walsh, the daughter of Cormac O'Hara, who was pregnant, and became convalescent without injury to herself or the child.	£1 0 0
Sir Randal M'Saurley, then Viscount of Dunluce, sent for me to Dunluce, and gave me	£1 0 0

Arthur's practice improved slightly in this year and in his closing entry he records, with thanks to God, the receipt of £75 18s. 0d.

On 3rd November 1621, Thady O'Dereleo paid the sum of one pound for his relief with an emetic of an-antimony from a worm thirty feet long. On 24th July 1633, Sir Basil Brooke of Ulster paid a similar sum, following treatment for a urinary infection.

During the early part of 1626, Archbishop James Ussher, a distinguished scholar and churchman, was at Drogheda. He suffered from an obscure malady which English physicians had failed to cure. Although Arthur was a Catholic, Ussher, who was Protestant Primate of All Ireland, consulted him. Arthur took his episcopal patient to Lambay Island for several weeks. The successful result gained him many patients including Lord Falkland, the Lord Deputy.

In 1670 John Toland was born at Inishowen, Co. Donegal. He distinguished himself by his violent attacks on orthodox religion and medicine. His treatise *Christianity not Mysterious*, was burned by the common hangman. In his last illness he fancied there was some mismanagement on his physician's part. He thereupon started doctoring himself and after a temporary improvement wrote a pamphlet under the title, *A Dissertation to shew the Uncertainty of Physic and the Danger of Trusting our Lives to those who practise it*. Unfortunately for his case, he died two months after this booklet was published.

Sir Hans Sloane, President of the Royal College of Physicians in London from 1719 to 1735, was born at Killileagh in Ulster in 1660. He studied medicine at Paris and Montpelier. Sloane's most enduring monument is the British Museum, of which he was the founder. Extensive travel in his youth enabled him to build a large private collection of antiquities, herbs, gems, and curiosities of all kinds. His bequest, from which the Museum Library was started, contained over 40,000 volumes, printed or in manuscript. The collection contains vast materials for the study of the history of English and European medicine amongst many other subjects.

In his *History of Medicine in the British Isles*, Norman Moore refers to Thomas Molyneux (1661–1733) as the 'first great physician in Ireland.' While the claim may be challenged there is no doubt that Molyneux was a figure of great importance in the late seventeenth and early eighteenth centuries.

Molyneux graduated in T.C.D. in 1683. Immediately afterwards he toured through England and Holland. He was fortunate enough to meet some of the most prominent thinkers of the day. His enquiring mind made the most of his opportunities and when he returned to Dublin in 1687 he had received a broad professional and liberal education.

When the College of Physicians was reconstituted in 1692, Molyneux was named as one of the Fellows. He attained a considerable practice and was elected President in 1702. His medical writings are observations on conditions of his own times. He published an account of an epidemic of coughs and colds in the *Philosophical Transactions of* 1694. In the same *Transactions* he wrote on comparative anatomy, on natural phenomena, including the Giant's Causeway, and on insect plagues. He died in 1733 and is buried in Armagh.

Animal magnetism or mesmerism was practised in Ireland nearly three hundred years ago. About 1666, Valentine Greatrakes (1628–1681 (?)) of Affane, in Co. Waterford, obtained favourable results by passing his hands over the parts affected in various diseases. He was so famous as to be sent for by the English Court. The Royal Society, unable to define the effects he produced otherwise, spoke of 'a sanative contagion in his body, which hath an antipathy to some particular diseases and not to others.' Amongst those who bore testimony to his powers was Robert Boyle, the most celebrated member of an extraordinary family.

According to his own account, Greatrakes was inspired with the belief that he had healing power. His first patient, who suffered from scrofula, was cured within a month. Amongst the diseases cured he claimed rheumatism, epilepsy, deafness, and ulcers. For abscesses he advised poultices of boiled turnips as well as the laying on of his hands.

About 1657 another Irish mesmerist appeared. This was James

Finaghty, a secular priest of Tuam. He was credited with the power to relieve sickness and cast out devils. His popularity was such that thousands, both Catholic and Protestant, followed him. Finaghty seems to have been something of a confidence trickster. The only full accounts we have are those of the Franciscan, Peter Walsh, an admittedly hostile witness. Finaghty was accused of taking valuable presents from patients and of bullying people into saying that they were cured. Certainly he never lost his presence of mind when a treatment failed, as appears to have happened very often.

Finaghty demanded a public trial of his powers before the Viceroy. Amongst the physicians who examined the sick, prior to this, was Sir William Petty. Sir William submitted to the mesmerist's treatment for weak eyes without any success. He then wagered one hundred pounds that he could cure as many patients by orthodox means as Finaghty could by mesmerism. The wager was not accepted.

When the day of the public trial arrived, Finaghty pleaded a serious illness which necessitated his immediate return to Galway. He died some years later under episcopal displeasure.

According to an anonymous writer in the *Dublin Journal of Medical Science* (1918), Kilkenny was the site chosen for one of the few attempts to regularise medical practice outside Dublin in the seventeenth century. In 1687, James II granted a charter to Nicholas Shee, Walter Keyly, Richard Mading and others to found a 'Royall Colledge of Physitians in Kilkenny.' Nicholas Shee was named first president. The functions of the College were to be the

. . . supperviseing and correcon of ye sd Colledge or Community and all men exercising the faculty of Physick, Chirurgery, Selling of Druggs and Appothecaryes within our sd Cittyes of Kilkenny, Waterford, Queen's County, Tippary, Catherlough, Kildare and Wexford—noe pson or psons within ye sd Cittyes, Townes or Countyes shall exercise ye sd facultyes unlesse he or they be thereunto admitted by the sd President and Community.'

There are no records of any meetings or proceedings of this proposed College. The most outstanding point of the Charter is its recognition of the unity which should exist between Physicians, Surgeons and Apothecaries and the desirability of their inclusion under a single governing body.

Enquiries in Kilkenny failed to reveal any documents which would throw light on this College. In 1687 a priest named Donat O'Leary received a Royal Charter from James II creating the Royal College of St Canice in Kilkenny 'with authority to teach and confer degrees, in all arts and sciences, and moreover with all the privileges, immunities and faculties which are wont to be granted to such establishments.' There is some ground for believing that the building in which this College was to be housed was originally a hospital.

Kilkenny was also the birthplace, at the close of the seventeenth century of a man who, though not a physician, enjoyed widespread influence in medical circles. George Berkeley (1685–1753) was educated for the ministry at Trinity College, where he became a Fellow in 1707. After a period of travel in America he took the See of Cloyne about 1734.

During his American tour Berkeley had learnt the use of tar-water as a preventive of smallpox. He tried it with some success for an outbreak in his diocese. Carried away with enthusiasm, he then used it for every possible complaint. In 1744, he published a book describing his methods, including the preparation of what must have been a nauseating mixture. A quart of tar was boiled with a gallon of water. After forty-eight hours the tarry water was strained off and given in doses of a pint or more per day.

The success of this book was startling. It ran to five editions and was translated into most European languages. The medical profession remained hostile although the apothecaries reaped a rich profit from the sale of 'the Bishop's tar-water.'

After Berkeley's death the craze died down. Casual references are met in popular literature. Dickens, in *Great Expectations*, refers to a dose of a pint at a time. James Clarence Mangan, in the middle of the nineteenth century, took the medicine on occasion. He warned against the simultaneous consumption of alcohol. The warning was sound, for tar is more readily soluble in alcohol than in water. Up to the end of the century tar-water appeared quite commonly on the tables of Parisian restaurants.

Should we dismiss Berkeley as a quack and his tar-water as quackery? Tar contains guaiacol and creosote amongst other aromatic bodies. These have a marked action as expectorants and intestinal disinfectants. As a skin antiseptic tar derivatives are still in use. Many of the diseases treated by Berkeley had their seat in the lungs and alimentary canal, so that it is probable that he did give his patients symptomatic relief at least. Like others before and after he made over-enthusiastic claims which were further exaggerated by grateful patients. Despite this we cannot be so scathing as a modern American textbook of pharmacy which dismisses the subject in half a dozen lines. 'An aequeous extract of tar was claimed by George Berkeley, Bishop of Cloyne, in the early part of the eighteenth century, to be a panacea for all human ills, and he wrote a book upon tar-water, which is very interesting reading as an example of misbelief and credulity.'

During the seventeenth century, particularly in the remoter parts of the country, the housewife was physician, surgeon and apothecary to her family. Most households had their own pharmacopoeia of medicines compounded from easily available materials. In the *Journal of the Cork Historical and Archaeological Society* for 1913 a diary of this nature is described in full. It contains about 450 prescriptions for common ailments. It covers the period 1671 to 1714. A few of the entries follow:

For a chine cough (Whooping-cough).

Take some house Mice. Flaw them and dry them in an oven, then make them into fine powder and Lett the party take as much of the powder as will Lye on a broad Shillinge, in Beere or possett, first in The Morning and Last att Night.

In 1692, Robert Boyle had advised a syrup of Penny Royal (a species of Mint) and Sulphuric Acid as a treatment for Chine cough and stuffings of the lungs.

For the head Ache.

Take a sevell Orange and Cutt it in quarters and take of the yelow Rinde or peel of it and apply the Red side of itt nextt to the Tempels, Rubing them well first; soe bind it on and Iff you Can, sleep.

Earth worms are an Admirable Remidy for Cutt nerves being applyed to the place; Mazalldus saith thatt the powder off them, putt Into a hollow Tooth, makes itt drop outt.

The Head of a Young Kitte, being Burntt to Ashes and the quantity of A dragme taken every morning in a Little watter, is an admirable remedy against the Goute.

Crabbe eyes break the Stone and opens stopings of the Bowles.

The Lungs of A fox well dryed is an admirable strengthener of the Lungs.

We have not completely divorced ourselves from this form of medicine. A random dip into the files of the Folklore Commission produced the following 'cures' from contemporary sources.

Thrush may be cured by a posthumous child breathing three times into the sufferer's mouth.

Food left unconsumed by a man named Seán and a woman named Siobháin living together cures whooping cough.

Nose bleed may be cured by tying a string around the little finger.

Such folk medicine has more than a casual interest. The remedies quoted above all demand the use of readily obtainable ingredients. The plants and animals which go to make up the mixtures can all be found growing or living in the country. Occasionally more exotic ingredients such as precious metals, gems or foreign animals are named. The inference is that these are a remnant of invasion by an eastern race. Where such ingredients are mentioned within a small area only, it is possible that they may commemorate some individual casual traveller or settler who secured local fame both as a foreigner and as a healer.

Although Robert Boyle (1627–91), mentioned above, was not a medical man, his work on chemistry had a great influence on physick. He was the fourteenth child of the first Earl of Cork and had the advantage of a most liberal education in England and abroad. His interest in the spread of Christianity led him to procure a charter for the East India Company, to translate the Bible into Irish, Welsh, Hindu, Turkish and Malay and to found the Boyle Lectures for the defence of Christianity.

Boyle published several works of medical interest, including one (in 1691) on *Medicinal Experiments or a Collection of Choice Remedies*. The treatments advised show but little superiority over the folk-cures of the day as may be judged from the following examples:

For convulsions –

Take earthworms, wash them well in White wine to cleanse them but so that they may not die in the wine. Then, upon hollow Tiles or between them dry the worms with a moderate heat and no further than that they may conveniently be reduced to powder; to one Ounce of which add a pretty number of Grains of Ambergris both to perfume the powder (whose scent of itself is rank) and to make the medicine more efficacious. The dose is from one Dram to a Dram and a half.

Powdered earthworms, this time in hensgrease, were also recommended as a local application to piles.

Boyle was not free of a fair measure of superstition, for he recommended a bag of groundsel as an amulet against agues and powdered Mechoacam root as an amulet against cramp. This is a jalap tuber with very feeble purgative properties obtained from Mexico, apparently identical with the Ipomaea Jalapa found in the Southern United States. It is to be noted that Boyle did not administer it internally, though its purgative action might relieve abdominal cramps.

In common with contemporary opinion Boyle considered that the patient's own urine was a cheap and efficacious medicine. He advised a morning draught of the liquid whilst still warm as a sovereign remedy for intestinal obstruction. The advice 'to forbear Food for an hour or two after it' seems superfluous. A prescription in which ale is the principal ingredient must have proved much more popular.

The present-day patient who talks incessantly of 'my operation' had a counterpart in 1670, for a letter of Sir George Rawdon, written in October to Viscount Conway and Killulta, contains the following passage:

Your prescription so kindly sent, came when my distemper was in great measure gone, but Mr Brookes had practised a great part of the doctor's method upon me and observed his prescription for a purge. This I took on Saturday last and I hope it hath taken away the dregs of my disease, yet I am a little faint still and am grown lean with it. Moses Hill is so ill with flux from some other disease that he is not likely to recover. The Bishop of Dromore very weak and with gripes in the guts in a very sad condition – hear this is a sickly time in England – Tom Stanhope – says many are sick of agues and fevers there.

A later letter between Sir George and the noble Lord contains references to the 'siethica' (sciatica?) of the former's brother. This caused great pain in one thigh and leg. A postscript to this later letter has been damaged but is still readable:

When I was ready to close this I thought I should keep it till Monday morning in the hope that my wife might be delivered of her burden–the midwife is with her–and my Lord Bishop of Doune though he hath also had a very ill night.

The lady was delivered of a male child which died at birth.

The close of the seventeenth century marked a definite change in the character of Irish medicine. The new century was to be marked by the growth of voluntary hospitals, the organisation of the branches of the profession and the regularisation of medical education. Unity between the different branches was still more than a century distant.

CHAPTER SEVEN

THE ROYAL COLLEGE OF SURGEONS

During the Middle Ages, and for centuries afterwards, in Ireland as elsewhere, the division between surgeons and physicians was a wide one. Far from being regarded as co-equal specialists, in different branches of the same profession, they were looked upon as practitioners of totally different trades. The position was complicated by the individualism of the midwives, both male and female, and apothecaries, who regarded their own callings as quite distinct, and neither asked, nor were requested, to co-operate in any way.

Probably there were many barber-surgeons in Dublin in the early part of the fifteenth century. On 18th October 1446, Henry VI established by royal charter a Guild of Barbers under the patronage of St Mary Magdalen. He would hardly have taken this step if the number to be catered for was small. This charter enabled women as well as men, to be admitted to the freedom of the guild.

This was the first incorporation of medical practitioners in these islands. The use of the word 'Barbers' throughout the charter was in popular estimation the equivalent of 'Surgeons'. The original charter has been lost, but it is somewhat fully recited in the charter of Queen Elizabeth, granted in 1577 to the Guild of Barber Surgeons. This is preserved in the Library of Trinity College.

We learn from the text of the latter charter that a Company of Surgeons had come into being since the incorporation of the barbers, but there is no reference to their arts or practices being in any way different. The two communities were united for 'the promotion and exercise of the art of chirurgery.'

The arms of the Dublin Barber Surgeons Company were almost an exact copy of those granted to the London Company. In the grant by Dr William Roberts, the Ulster King-at-Arms, they are described as

Parted by a crosse of England charged with a lyon passant gardant argent crowned or these two coates armour quartered viz: the first Argent a cheveron gules betwixt three cinquefoyles azure. The second Coat Armour Azure a Harpe crowned or the third as the second the fowerth as the first the breast on a helme and wreath argent and gules St Mary Magdalene etc. Mantled gules doubled argent supported by a Leopard proper and an Irish greyhound argent each gorged with a Ducall Coronett and standing on a scrowle with their motto viz., CHRISTI SALUS NOSTRA.

There are many references in the grant to services rendered by the guild to the Crown. These consisted largely in the supply of surgeons to the Army and Navy. A member of the guild, James Crosbie, gave evidence at the trial of Charles I after being present at the battle of Newbury.

We have no records showing where the barber chirurgeons held their first meetings. In the record of the Christmas Assembly, in 1641, of the Dublin Corporation, the following entry occurs:

It is likewise ordered and agreed by the authoritie aforesaid (the Corporation), that the most worshipfull and fraternitie of the Corporation of Barber Chirurgeons in this Cittie shall have for the use of the said corporation a lease for the tenure of sixtie and one years to be given at Easter next of St Paul's Gate in the Cittie containing in length from south to north thirtie feete. At the yearlie rent of £ff. 5. (£5) and a couple of capons to Mr Maior for the time being, guarding the portcullis room in time of danger to the cittie.

Paul's (a corruption of Pole) Gate was situated in the old city wall close to Dean Swift's birthplace in Hoey's Court. The gate was taken down in 1700 owing to disrepair. The Barber Surgeons also had the use of a chapel in Christ Church Cathedral.

The third charter was granted to the Dublin surgeons on 10th February 1687, by James II. It is interesting to note that in this charter Barbers, Chirurgeons, Apothecaries and Perriwigimakers were mentioned together, so that 'their Arts and Misteryes may be the better exercised.'

During the period of existence of the companies of Barber Chirurgeons in both Dublin and London, there were surgeons who repudiated professional contact with the barbers. These were mainly men of liberal education, surgeons' apprentices of good standing and army surgeons. At the same time certain members of the uneducated classes who were not free of the brotherhood practised surgery and were occasionally prosecuted.

The regular mode of admission to a guild was by an apprenticeship of five, six or seven years. 'Foreigners' (those not regularly educated to the trade) were admitted on payment of 'quarterage,' at the quarterly meetings of the guild. In 1672, the Lord Lieutenant in Council framed a set of rules by which, on payment of a fine of twenty shillings, a 'foreigner' might join any guild including that of the Barber Chirurgeons. The large numbers of surgical practitioners in Dublin during the eighteenth century who were not attached to the guild proves that there was practically free trade in surgery at that time.

By the charter granted to the College of Physicians in 1667, no person could legally practise medicine within seven miles of Dublin without the licence of that College, a regulation which was not strictly enforced; except that in the early years attempts were made to prevent barber chirurgeons and apothecaries from administering internal remedies. The College petitioned Parliament in 1725 asking for powers to prevent illiterate persons from practising physic.

During the reign of Queen Anne (1702–1714) a tract was published by the free-lance surgeons, calling on Parliament to dissociate the surgeons from barbers, apothecaries and wig-makers. The pamphlet contains several vigorous passages, of which the following are fair samples:

The present Corporation in this city is composed of Barbers, Surgeons, Apothecaries and Peruke-Makers which (instead of encouraging the true Professors of Surgery) is a refuge for empiricks, impudent quacks, women and other idle persons who quit the trades to which they were bred and wherein they might be useful to the Commonwealth to undertake a Profession whereof they are entirely ignorant to the ruine of their fellow subjects.

It is requisite for a surgeon (to arrive to a tolerable perfection in his profession) to have a reasonable understanding of Latin and Greek whereas a peruke-maker or a barber may be masters of their trades although they are wholly illiterate.

Among the advantages claimed for the separation are '. . . the preservation of many subjects' lives which are lost by the gross errors and the barbarous and inhumane practices of impudent ignorant pretenders of which there are too many instances which daily offer to the great prejudice of the publick and discredit of the profession.'

In 1716, the corporation held a correspondence with Thomas Proby, who was practising without being free of the brotherhood. Proby wrote polite replies, but maintained his aloof attitude and expressed his doubts whether agreement could ever be reached among the city surgeons. In 1721, the Corporation proposed a meeting with the free-lance surgeons who had formed a society of their own. Nothing came of this meeting, if it ever took place, for there are no records of its having done so.

Like the other guilds, the surgeons were obliged to participate in various city ceremonies. One of the most important of these was the triennial perambulation of the city boundary symbolic of the corporation's jurisdiction. Many of the surgeons were averse to taking part in these Lord Mayor's shows. As late as 1767 *Faulkner's Journal* states that the corporation perambulated the city and its liberties and that the colours of the barber surgeons were purple, cherry and red and those of the apothecaries purple and orange.

From the end of the seventeenth century it became obvious that the union of barbers and surgeons would soon come to an end. Barbers were restrained from practising any surgery except bleeding and the extraction of teeth. At the same time the numbers of surgeons in the guild diminished and in 1742 no surgeon could be found to fill the Master's chair. About this time efforts at co-operation with the College of Physicians were made, without any great success.

At a meeting held on 12th October 1741, the surgeons resolved to present the freedom of the corporation to the President, Censors and Fellows of the College of Physicians. Shortly afterwards they passed a resolution requiring aspirants to the freedom of the corporation to undergo an examination by that College and to receive a certificate of competency. A similar regulation was to apply to apothecary candidates. It was also proposed that when twelve surgeons were available that they should conduct the examination in the presence of delegates from the College of Physicians. There does not seem to have been any response on the part of the physicians to these efforts at reform and unification.

That regularisation of the status and education of the profession was vital may be reckoned from the work of Edward Foster. Writing in 1768 he tells a story of a 'certain hospital where a patient ran away in the night, to prevent the surgeon next day from amputating his leg, a member, which he demonstrated knew its office much better than the surgeon did his and which was soon after perfectly cured.'

The Surgeons' Company were empowered to examine their apprentices as to their fitness for enrolment in the fraternity. There is no evidence that examinations were consistently carried out. When the freedom of the company was conferred on Chevalier Taylor in 1732, allegations were made that he bought the freedom with a subscription of £161. The corporation published a disclaimer in *Pue's Occurrences* on 4th April 1732 stating that the Chevalier had been submitted to a thorough examination.

Many of the faculty regarded Taylor as a charlatan and the anonymous denouncement may have been aimed more at him than at the guild.

At this time the Barber Surgeons were meeting in the Tailors' Hall in Back Lane. This hall, erected in 1706, was used by many guilds and societies who could not afford to build or buy premises of their own. Amongst those who used it were the Freemasons and the United Irishmen. It was converted into a school in 1841 after the abolition of the Dublin Guilds. Sometime later, an undenominational Christian body used it as a dispensary and medical mission. They conducted services and meetings there up to about the middle of the present century, when the building was scheduled for demolition under a town planning order. This was resisted and the complete structure has since been renovated. The site of the Tailors' Hall was previously occupied by a college of Dublin University and by a military hospital.

In 1745 the first signs of definite disintegration of the guild appeared. The apothecaries, who heavily outnumbered the surgeons, were granted, by George II, a separate charter incorporating them into the guild of St Luke. The governing body of this guild, consisting of a master, two wardens and thirteen assistants were to be elected annually. Previous to the incorporation of this guild the barber surgeons returned four representatives to the lower House of the Corporation of Dublin. This number was now reduced to two.

After this date the surgical importance of the original guild declined rapidly. Even amongst the barber members there were many who were interested only in the political benefits they could obtain.

The establishment of county surgical infirmaries in 1765 led the way for the establishment of an independent surgical body. According to law no surgeon could be appointed to an infirmary unless he had been examined and certified competent by a board consisting of the Surgeon-General and the Surgeons attached to Steevens' and Mercer's Hospitals.

This Board examined the first candidates on 1st September 1766. The candidates, who all received certificates, were: George Pope for Carlow Infirmary; Peter Concannon for Louth; William Cleapem for Meath; F. K. Gervais for Armagh; William West for Wicklow; Ebenezer Jacob for Wexford and Robert Travers for Roscommon Infirmary.

All subsequent meetings of the Board were held in Mercer's Hospital. The Board met for the last time on 3rd March 1796, when they passed Robert Young Armstrong for Cavan Infirmary. After this the Board's functions passed to the College of Surgeons.

The Board were apparently more concerned with the correctness of candidates' indentures than with the depth of their learning. Out of 109 candidates examined, three were rejected because of insufficient surgical knowledge, whilst thirteen failed because of defective indentures.

In 1784 the union between barbers and surgeons was for practical purposes dissolved by the creation of the Royal College of Surgeons in Ireland. The Barber Surgeons were not yet dissolved and they might still employ their original title until 1840 when the corporation, along with other similar bodies, was dissolved under the Municipal

Reform Act. The documents belonging to the guild were deposited in the Library of T.C.D.

In the provinces there were guilds of barber surgeons in existence. These had no royal charter and were constituted by the local corporations. The most important of these local guilds were those of Cork and Limerick. In 1732 the Cork surgeons made an effort to sever their connection with the barbers. This was resisted by the corporation of the city.

Very few surgeons belonged to the corporation in 1784. Of the founders of the College only one, Philip Woodroffe, was a barber surgeon. He does not appear to have been satisfied with the union of surgeons with barbers and wigmakers and, on 29th March 1780, was one of those who founded the Dublin Society of Surgeons.

Although this body met, as was customary at the time, in such taverns as the 'Elephant' and the 'King's Arms' in Essex Street, and the 'Eagle' in Eustace Street, they got down to work and drew up the following resolution on 18th June 1780:

That it is the opinion of this Committee that a Royal Charter, dissolving the preposterous and disgraceful union of the surgeons of Dublin with the barbers, and incorporating them separately and distinctly upon liberal and scientific principles would highly contribute, not only to their own emolument and the advancement of the profession in Ireland, but to the good of society in general by cultivating and diffusing surgical knowledge.

The society appointed John Butler to prepare a petition for presentation to the Attorney-General, and levied a subscription of a guinea from each of its members.

The petition was presented to the Attorney-General in the autumn of 1781. A draft of the proposed charter was also submitted. By order of the Lord Lieutenant these documents were forwarded to the Company of Barber Surgeons for their comments and recommendations. Their reply, under date of 3rd December 1781, spoke strongly against the proposed separation or dissolution of the original charter. It blamed those surgeons who absented themselves from corporate functions for the spirit of unrest and pointed out that some of those who signed the petition were freemen of the Company of Barber Surgeons and continued to benefit from that association.

The wrangle between the various parties continued over several years, but eventually the surgeons gained their point and, on 11th February, 1784, the Royal College of Surgeons in Ireland was incorporated under a charter of George III. The preamble to the charter reads:

. . . that the reputation of the profession of surgery is of the utmost importance to the publick and highly necessary to the welfare of mankind and that the publick sustain great injury from the defects in the present system of surgical education in our kingdom of Ireland; and the regularly educated surgeons of the City of Dublin (who are become a numerous and considerable body) find themselves incompetent (from want of a charter) to establish a liberal and extensive system of surgical education.

The first meeting of the College took place in the Board Room of the Rotunda Hospital on 2nd March 1784. On this occasion the following officers were appointed:–President: Samuel Croker-King; Censor: John Whiteway, Robert Bowes, Gustavus Hume; Assistants: Michael Keogh, Philip Woodroffe, Arthur Winter, Vernon Lloyd, William Dease (Treasurer), James Boyton, Ralph S. Obré and James Henthorn (Secretary). Archibald Richardson, the Surgeon-General, wrote refusing to take an oath or attend meetings of the College. His letter was regarded as a resignation. Fifty-one members of the College were elected. These members were granted Letters Testimonial entitling them to practise surgery before being elected members. At the present time Fellows of the College need not be Licentiates although they must be qualified and on the Medical Register.

During this first year much important work was done. Twenty meetings were held. At these, bye-laws were drawn up and advertisements issued that regularly educated surgeons might present themselves for the letters testimonial of the College. An interesting item in such 'leisurely' days was the bye-law which inflicted a fine of five shillings on those who were more than ten minutes late for College business. Absentees from meetings were fined one guinea; except where absence was due to sickness or absence from the city. Bye-law number fifteen enacted

That for the better advancement of the profession it shall be lawful for the College to elect or appoint a professor or professors, who shall annually give a regular course or courses of lectures on anatomy, physiology, the practice and operation of surgery and midwifery; and that all apprentices or pupils to the members of the College, whose names shall be duly registered as set forth, may attend the said courses gratis.

Members who wished to take pupils had to have them examined by a board of the College. A registration fee of five guineas was exacted.

The College revived the practice of the Society of Surgeons of dining together. A happy augury for the future was the acceptance, in November 1784, by the President of the College of Physicians of an invitation to dinner.

On the 8th January 1785, the College presented a petition to the Irish House of Commons requesting financial aid for the establishment of a school of surgery. This request was repeated a year later. At this period the College met in the Rotunda, in the William Street Assembly Rooms, and even in private houses. In October 1788, the College were obliged to forgo acceptance of a body for dissections as they had no place in which to store it.

The first premises obtained, in 1789, were in Mercer Street. They stood on portion of the ground which had belonged to St Stephen's Leper Hospital in the sixteenth century. Adjoining was Mercer's Hospital, which, in the nineteenth century, acquired the College buildings.

The first meeting here took place in 1790. It is notable as being the occasion on which a combined Society of Surgeons and Physicians was considered. The newly-founded Society shortly afterwards met in the Mercer Street premises. Their books formed the nucleus of the present College Library.

The College made many appeals to the Government for financial assistance. The generous response to these appeals requires some explanation. About this period Britain was waging war on several fronts, including Ireland, and the demand for army and navy surgeons greatly exceeded the supply. Almost illiterate medical orderlies were qualified as surgeons after a few months' training. It was regarded as a good insurance to have more competent men.

This necessity rather than a spirit of altruistic generosity to an occupied country explains the many donations made to the College. In 1805 alone, £6,000 was paid from State funds.

Of the College founders, William Dease (1752–1798), who was President in 1789, was one of the most energetic. An original member of the Society of Surgeons, he contributed liberally to the expenses incurred in procuring the College Charter.

Dease invented or improved upon several operations and instruments. His most important work was on instruments used for removing urinary stones and on injuries of the head. He originally practised midwifery, and was the author of a textbook on this subject. There are several versions given of his death. The only thing which is certain was that it was sudden and violent. One version states that he mistook an aneurysm for an abscess. When he opened it the patient died in a few minutes. Horrified, Dease opened his own femoral artery. Dr Madden in his *Lives of the United Irishmen*, asserts that a warrant was issued for Dease's arrest as a member of an illegal organisation. In order to avoid disgrace and possible execution, he committed suicide. A further account states that during a bout of vomiting he burst a blood-vessel and expired.

Several members of the College were attached or sympathetic to the United Irishmen. This does not seem to have been a common bar to advancement, but at the close of the century, William Lawless, then Professor of Anatomy, was expelled from his membership for having 'been notoriously engaged in the late rebellion.'

In July 1805 the College acquired a cemetery, belonging to the Society of Friends, at the junction of York Street and Stephen's Green. On St Patrick's Day 1806, the foundation stone of a new building was laid. After several further parliamentary grants this was completed by the end of 1809. The Mercer Street premises were occupied until 1812. Glover's Alley, on the north side of the present building became the entrance by which bodies were brought to the dissecting-room.

In 1813 Dr John Cheyne was appointed first Professor of the Theory and Practice of Medicine. In the same year a motion was put forward proposing the abolition of apprenticeship as the only portal of entry to the profession.

At this period the surgical education given at the Dublin College was superior to that obtainable elsewhere in the United Kingdom. The London candidate could scrape through after one year's dissections and one year in hospital. The Irish 'chronics' usually went to London or Edinburgh in order to pass their examinations. In 1817, Dublin took the initiative in proposing a uniform and improved system of surgical education in the United Kingdom.

In 1820 the Museum was reorganised. John Shekelton (1795–1824) a demonstrator of anatomy was appointed curator at £30 per year. Many of the most important exhibits are products of Shekelton's work. Unfortunately, he died in 1824, following a cut received whilst dissecting. At the time of his death the Museum contained over 1,300 exhibits, of which the majority were fresh preparations.

In 1824 the College resolved to apply for a new Charter, but later in the year the proposal was shelved indefinitely.

In 1825 the buildings were enlarged and improved. J. T. Kirby suggested the establishment of a hospital under the supervision of the College. This was refused, as was the invitation of the College of Physicians to co-operate in the publication of a new Pharmacopoeia.

In 1828 the new (or second) charter was granted by George IV. The most important charge in the constitution was the power conferred to admit candidates to examination who were not indentured apprentices. Bye-laws regulating the education of students were introduced. These were amongst the most progressive of any licensing body of the day. The Irish College was the only surgical one in Europe which required its students to have a classical education. That the regulations were enforced is evidenced by the large numbers of candidates who failed the examination. Men qualified elsewhere were rejected just as ruthlessly as students up for the first time.

In 1829 the College instituted a Diploma in Midwifery and the diseases of women and children. In 1832, the first meeting of 'The Surgical Society of Ireland' was held in the College. This body survived until 1883, when its amalgamation with the other Dublin medical societies resulted in the present Royal Academy of Medicine in Ireland.

When Sir Henry Marsh (1790–1860) resigned the Chair of Medicine in 1832 the College introduced a rule that only members or licentiates should be elected to the Professorship. This was in retaliation for the refusal of Trinity and the College of Physicians to recognise the certificates of the College of Surgeons. Later in the year the Surgeons refused to recognise lectures delivered in the Apothecaries' Hall on the grounds that it was not a medical corporation. Both these rulings were rescinded in 1844.

A few years later, in 1838, the College had another brush with the apothecaries, claiming that these latter were imperfectly educated usurpers of functions of both physicians and surgeons. Although the apothecaries generally resisted the College attacks, many of them wished to remain pure pharmacists, as in Continental countries. The men who held these views, led by Michael Donovan, formed the Committee of Apothecaries, which lasted only a few years.

In 1844 the College received a supplemental charter. Amongst the changes effected under this, were the institution of a Fellowship instead of a Membership, the formation of a Governing Council, and the creation of a paid body of examiners. Prior to this a surgeon was elected to the Membership because of his long practice or social position. After 1844, the Fellowship was a mark of superior surgical education proved by examination. Candidates for both grades were still obliged to have a broad general and professional education.

The first President and Vice-President elected under the supplemental charter were Sir Philip Crampton and Richard Carmichael.

All through this period medical reform was an ever-recurring topic at meetings of all professional bodies. Unfortunately it was most difficult to obtain agreement amongst them. The situation was complicated in Ireland by the establishment of the Queen's Colleges, which were competitors of both the College and Trinity. In 1857 the College, in conjunction with the other medical and surgical licensing bodies, promoted a private Parliamentary Bill, the provisions of which were:

(I) the establishment of a Medical Council.
(II) the publication of a Register of qualified practitioners.
(III) regular discussions on education by the licensing bodies.

This Bill did not become law, but the Medical Act of 1858 contained most of its important provisions.

Two further supplemental charters were granted to the College by Queen Victoria in 1883 and 1885. These dealt with matters of internal government. One clause in 1885 charter was a sign of the times: 'And we do hereby, for us, our heirs and successors grant, declare and appoint that all provisions of the Charter, Bye-laws, and Ordinances as to education, examination and granting diplomas to Fellows or Licentiates shall extend to include women.'

Abortive attempts were made on several occasions, in 1858, 1869, 1876 and 1883, to combine with either Trinity or the College of Physicians as a joint examining and licensing body. In 1887, the London Colleges of Physicians and Surgeons discussed the formation of a Medico-Surgical University. The proposal, which came to nothing, was watched with interest in Ireland.

A conjoint committee of the College of Physicians and Surgeons held, in 1885, several meetings and agreed upon a conjoint scheme for examinations. A clause of the draft scheme provided that five-eighths of the candidates' fees should go to the college of Surgeons. The College of Physicians objected and negotiations were broken off.

A provision of the Medical Act of 1886 rendered it necessary for the College of Surgeons to combine with a licensing body competent to grant medical degrees or diplomas. Negotiations for combination with the College of Physicians were brought to a successful conclusion. A conjoint committee, of whom three were appointed by each College, was formed and entrusted with the management of the examination for conjoint diplomas.

The College of Surgeons were unanimous in requesting that the apothecaries should be included in the combination, but a majority of the Fellows of the College of Physicians objected. So a second combination was formed with the Apothecaries' Hall. The first examination under this scheme was held in May 1888. The diploma granted enabled the holder to practise medicine, surgery, midwifery and pharmacy. The College of Physicians made unsuccessful efforts to prevent this combination. In 1894 following a complaint by the Physicians and an unfavourable report by the Inspector of the

General Medical Council the College withdrew from the combination
with the Apothecaries.

THE COLLEGE OF SURGEONS SCHOOL

One of the primary objectives of the founders of the College had
been the provision of a School of Surgery. In 1785, as we have seen,
it had been decided to appoint Professors of Anatomy and
Physiology, Surgery and Midwifery. Thomas Costello applied for
the Chair of Midwifery, but was rejected. In November 1785, John
Halahan commenced lectures on anatomy, physiology, and
bandaging. He lectured in his own premises but received a small
grant-in-aid from the College. Mr William Dease commenced
lecturing on surgery about the same time.

It was not until 1789 that steps were taken to provide teaching
accommodation in the College. Rules were laid down for the conduct
of the School, including the fees to be paid and the examinations
to be held, and the following appointments were made:

Anatomy and Physiology................William Hartigan
                                      John Halahan.

Surgery...............................William Dease
Midwifery.............................John Halahan
Surgical Pharmacy.....................Clement Archer

                                      Charles Bolger
Superintendents of Dissections.............Thomas Wright
                                      William Lawless

The Schools were open to registered pupils on payment of one
guinea per year. When the Government gave a grant of £1,000 in
1791 the College resolved to admit army surgeons and surgeons'
mates free to the lectures.

Those attending the lectures were divided into several grades,
'registered pupils' or apprentices, 'students' who intended to qualify
elsewhere, unregistered apprentices and army surgeons and mates.

In 1791, Walter Wade (d. 1825), Professor of Botany to the Royal
Dublin Society, commenced lectures in the College, although he was
not appointed to the Chair until 1804. In the latter year Abraham
Colles became Professor of Anatomy and Surgery. With Richard
Dease he brought these departments to an extremely high standard.

Until 1810 'the Schools' (of Anatomy and Surgery) functioned in Mercer's Street. In that year the anatomical department moved to Stephen's Green and was followed two years later by the botany and pharmacy departments. In 1813, John Cheyne (1777–1836) was appointed Professor of the Practice of Physic.

Whitley Stokes was appointed Professor of Medicine in 1826. Owing to arrangements of other schools with hospitals, he had no class to lecture to. He requested that his son William might be asociated with him so that his students could have the advantage of clinical practice in the Meath Hospital. Unfortunately the College refused and one of Ireland's greatest physicians went instead to the Park Street Private School.

James Apjohn (1796–1886) was elected to the Chair of Chemistry in 1828. He had already lectured in the Cork Institution and Park Street School. In 1841 he went to T.C.D., where he succeeded Dr F. Barker (d. 1850) as Professor of Chemistry. In 1832 he was one of the founders of the City of Dublin Hospital. For twenty years he represented the College of Surgeons on the G.M.C.

Apjohn was internationally famous as a scientist. He is best known abroad for his formula for the determination of the dew-point. His papers, published in the *Proceedings of the Royal Society* and the *Transactions of the Royal Irish Academy*, are numerous and still important. In the College of Surgeons his lectures became so popular that considerable extensions to the accommodation had to be made in 1832. Without detracting from his ability it should be noted that except at Park Street, and the temporarily moribund Trinity College School there were no other chemistry lectures available at the time. In 1840 he was requested to deliver annual lectures on Natural Philosophy to registered pupils.

In 1841 the School instituted the first Professorship of Hygiene in the United Kingdom. The first occupant of the Chair was Henry Maunsell (1806–1879). After his resignation in 1846 it remained vacant until 1864, when Edward Dillon Mapother (1835–1908) of St Vincent's Hospital took over. On his transfer to the Professorship of Anatomy and Physiology in 1868, Sir Charles A. Cameron was appointed and remained in office for the record period of fifty-three years. On his death in 1921 Dr Henry Bewley was appointed.

In 1851, the Government instituted a Regius Professorship of Military Surgery and attached it to the College, with a grant for its maintenance. Joliffe Tufnell (1819–1885) also of St Vincent's Hospital, lectured in this subject until 1860 when the Chair was abolished. He was well qualified to do so, having seen service in India, Ireland and the Crimea. In the latter war, his bullet extractor was extensively used.

In 1881 D. J. Cunningham of Edinburgh was appointed to the

Professorship of Anatomy. Throughout this period the School was undergoing constant development and enlargement.

In 1885, the School was opened to women. In the first session only one, Miss Agnes Shannon, entered. In 1877, Eliza Walker, of Bristol, had qualified M.D. Zurich, and also held a diploma of the College of Physicians in Ireland.

In 1888, the College passed a resolution in favour of amalgamation with certain of the private schools. Various recommendations were made to overcome the redundancy of Professors which would arise from the amalgamation, as well as the distribution of funds and fees.

Opposition to the amalgamation came from Mr Ledwich and Mr Broomfield of the Carmichael School. They were appointed College Anatomists, which effectually removed their objections. Mr T. Mason of the Ledwich School was similarly appeased by being offered a Lectureship in Physiology. The amalgamation, which was highly desirable, became operative by a deed signed on 19th September 1889. Later, legal argument was occasioned by the vague wording of portions of this document.

Although the amalgamation of the schools enabled more efficient teaching to be carried on at a less cost, the full benefits were not obtained for several years. This was due to the foundation of the Queen's Colleges, the revival of the Trinity College School and the opening of new English Schools.

The introduction of the Irish Universities' Bill in 1908 caused alarm in the College and renewed efforts to obtain State support. In 1911, a sum was guaranteed annually from the Technical Education Grant. The College were somewhat more successful in 1917 and 1919 when the Treasury voted sums of £2,000 and £500 respectively. When the Irish Free State was established an annual grant was continued though this was by no means generous.

During the Easter Uprising of 1916 the College was an insurgent position held by a small garrison under the command of James Mallin and Countess Markievicz. Mallin deserves the thanks of all medical historians for he gave orders that no wanton damage was to be done to the College. A measure of the discipline he exerted was the fact that in the following year an estimate of £764 was felt to be adequate for the repair of damage due to the rebellion. As the building had been under fire for several days the amount of damage incurred by and to the occupants must have been trivial.

Two years later a Roll of Honour of those ex-students who had served in the 'war to end all wars' was published. It contained some 1500 names.

Conflict was to touch the College again, for in 1922, during the Civil War, a special guard was mounted to protect the buildings, contents and personnel. As a result of the destruction of the Four Courts the Incorporated Law Society held lectures and examinations in the St Stephen's Green buildings.

During World War 2 many licentiates and fellows joined the National Army or decided to serve elsewhere in either a civilian or military capacity. In the College itself a public air raid shelter was constructed and facilities for lectures to Army and civilian medical corps personnel were provided.

In 1951 reciprocity in the primary fellowship examination was agreed among the several Royal Colleges of Surgeons. Further international recognition of the high standard of teaching was given by the approving authorities of the States of Massachusetts and Connecticut after inspection of the school.

About this time, the early 1950's, it became obvious that extensions to the College premises were urgently needed and after lengthy negotiations adjoining premises were secured so that the College now occupies a square bounded by St Stephen's Green, Glover's Alley, York St and Mercer's St. It was not until 1976 that the new building was formally opened by President Cearbhall O'Dalaigh. Later extensions provided linking facilities between the original and modern parts of the College.

The College student population from this time onwards became multi-national with some three quarters of its members coming from overseas. But, in some cases, the value of the diploma issued by the College was not recognised in countries where all physicians and surgeons possessed an M.D. In fact licentiates could not even sit for an M.D. without first gaining a university degree. Almost a hundred years previously the English Royal Colleges had tried to obtain a Royal Charter which would entitle them to confer Doctorates. Lengthy negotiations with the Government, the Royal College of Physicians and the National University of Ireland resulted in an agreement by which the College was declared a recognised College of the N.U.I., and on the 9th of June 1978 Senator Whitaker, Chancellor of the N.U.I., conferred for the first time Bachelor's degrees on those who were conferred with the licence of the Royal Colleges by their Presidents Mr Keith Shaw and Dr A. Grant. In the words of Dr T. Murphy, President of U.C.D., a debt of honour had been repaid, for in 1855 the Cecilia Street Medical School of the Catholic University, the predecessor of U.C.D., survived only because the R.C.S.I. recognised its teaching. The history of the College from this time is one of continuous expansion and consolidation.

An important part of any student's life is the recreational and extra curricular facilities enjoyed. In all universities debating and discussion societies play a big part in medical education. In the Royal College of Surgeons this is supplied by the Biological Society. Before the foundation of the present day 'Bi' in 1931, there had been student societies in the College but these had petered out. The first, formed in 1790, perished at some undetermined date. In 1862 the Junior Surgical Society of Ireland was established under the Presidency of Charles Benson, Professor of Medicine and a former President of the College. Despite objections by the Council of Professors, meetings were thrown open to all Dublin medical students. This Society flourished, largely thanks to the activity of Alexander Macalister who had entered the School at the age of fourteen and received his licentiate while only seventeen years of age. When he left to go to Trinity College the Junior Surgical Society collapsed.

When the R.C.S.I. Schools amalgamated with the Carmichael and Ledwich Schools the student's athletic and social life was considerably expanded, but it was not until June 7th 1910 that the College Council sanctioned the foundation of a Students' Athletic Union with grounds at Terenure, which was later moved to Bird Avenue, Clonskeagh.

CHAPTER EIGHT

THE APOTHECARIES

The first Dublin apothecary of whom there is a record was Thomas Smith, later Mayor of the city. He was not an Irishman, but a settler who had arrived from England prior to 1566. In that year he represented to Sir Henry Sidney, the Lord Deputy, that the native Irish found his wares too expensive. The majority of them consulted the hereditary physicians already mentioned.

The government in Dublin granted Smith a yearly contribution from the Lord Deputy, privy councillors and military officers. This was officially stated to be in order to enable him to provide apothecaries' wares for those of English birth, the nobility and others of 'the graver and civiller sort,' as well as to allow time for improvement in his profession. He also had the honour of laying the foundation-stone of Trinity College during his term of office as Mayor.

The powerful Barber Surgeons Guild of St Mary Magdalen received its first charter from Henry VI in 1446. This was renewed by Queen Elizabeth (1576) and by James II (1687). Under the third charter the brethren of the Guild were given power to punish every falsity, fraud, deceit, oppression, extortion and every other crime committed by barbers, chirurgeons, apothecaries, or periwig makers in Dublin, or within six miles of it, and the apothecaries were admitted to the freedom of the Guild. The apothecary is not mentioned specifically in Elizabeth's charter, so we may assume that the profession developed separately about the beginning of the seventeenth century. There is additional evidence for this in Keogh's *Botanologia Universalis Hibernica*, published in 1735. He states: 'in this very kingdom there were scarcely two (apothecaries) in a province one hundred years ago.'

Apparently the general public did not hold a high opinion of the apothecaries for, on the occasion of the 1676 session of the Dublin Guilds a ribald versifier wrote:

> See where the proud Apothecaries strive,
> Who most by frauds and impositions thrive,
> Whose monstrous bills immoderate wealth procure,

81

For drugs that kill as many as they cure,
Well are they placed the last of all the rout
For they're the men we most can do without.

During the seventeenth century small coinage was scarce throughout the country and many shopkeepers issued token coins exchangeable in their own shops. In the Aquilla Smith collection in the National Museum, Dublin, there are several tokens issued by apothecaries throughout the country, bearing various dates between 1654 and 1658. The names of those who issued tokens include Gerrard Colley at Red Cross in High Street, Dublin; Henry Bollardt; Henry Rugge of Castle Street, Dublin; Ro Nelson of Dungannon; and Richard Pearce of Limerick.

The charter of William and Mary granted to the College of Physicians in 1692 empowered the College to examine all who wished to become apothecaries' apprentices. Apothecaries who accepted apprentices without this preliminary examination were liable to a fine of twenty pounds. The College had also the power to enter apothecaries' shops, examine the drugs and destroy any unfit for use. In 1695 the College applied to Parliament for the confirmation of this charter. A few days later the Corporation of Barber-Surgeons and Apothecaries presented a counter-petition. In this they referred to their own charter and stated that the clauses in the College charter, which forbade the administration of internal medicines other than by physicians, militated unfairly against the surgeons whose cures might not be complete without drugs or potions. At the same time many surgeons prepared their own medicines as a matter of convenience. Finally, the restriction would weigh most heavily on the poor who could afford only the services of an apothecary or surgeon instead of the more expensive physician. When it was resolved that the Corporation's view should be laid before Parliament the proposed Bill was dropped by the physicians.

A committee was appointed in 1698 to prepare a Bill to regulate the practice of physic in Ireland. In 1703, another committee prepared a fresh Bill 'to regulate the practice of physic and surgery and of apothecaries in the city of Dublin.' In 1711, the Corporation prosecuted Thomas McAwee, who set up as an apothecary without being free of the guild.

In 1729 a formal indenture of apprenticeship was designed bearing the arms of the company. Six years later an Act was passed for controlling the production and sale of medicines. The College of Physicians were required to appoint four inspectors who would examines apothecaries' shops, with power to destroy unsound medicines therein. All apothecaries, chemists and druggists were required to register at the College. Regulations were laid down for the admission of persons to the Corporation and for the method of prescribing and dispensing medicines.

In 1741 the Society of Barber-Surgeons and Apothecaries decided that they were, at best, assistants of the Physicians. It was decided to grant the freedom of the Society to all members of the College of Physicians. A later resolution provided for the examination of candidates by surgeons, physicians and apothecaries combined. This was a distinct advance in medical education. It is difficult to discover how many surgeons or apothecaries applied to be examined under this rule. Later it became customary to confer the freedom of the guild on eminent men in unrelated occupations who had performed public services. Amongst those were Thomas Leland, S.F.T.C.D., a divine and scholar, and the Sheriffs W. Leghburne and Thomas Emerson, 'for taking up the robbers and vagabonds that infest this city.'

At the beginning of 1742 certain apothecaries in Dublin, headed by Alderman William Walker, petitioned for a charter which would give them authority to control the sale and manufacture of medicines. The petition was referred to the College of Physicians, who recommended the grant of the charter provided that they had a controlling voice in matters related to drugs generally.

This charter was granted in 1745. Henry O'Hara was appointed first Master. The Feast of St Luke, patron of the guild, was appointed for the annual elections to office. Meetings were held in the corporation hall in Back Lane until 1765. This hall was used by corporations which had no premises of their own. From then, until the Apothecaries' Hall was opened in 1791, meetings were held at the house of the Master for the time being, as well as in various taverns. At this time the guild was practically under the control of the College of Physicians, although the making of bye-laws was left in the hands of the apothecaries themselves. They exercised a general superintendence over matters relating to their profession. Until the establishment of the College of Surgeons, apothecaries were still eligible as members of the original Guild of Barber-Surgeons and Apothecaries.

In the proceedings of June 1761 there is notice of a suggestion by the Master, Samuel Burrowes, that a public hall and laboratory should be opened. The question was adjourned. In the same year Lucas' Act, which is still in force, was passed. This tightened the previous regulations relating to the inspection of apothecaries' shops and the supply of medicines.

In 1767 an Act was passed directing the use of £7,000 granted to the Dublin Society (later Royal Dublin Society) for the encouragement of various trades. Of this, £250 was devoted to the establishment of a poor persons' dispensary in Capel Street, under the control of John Wade, chemist. This plan was sanctioned by the College of Physicians. In the first two-and-a-half years over fifteen hundred poor persons were treated. Wade was most active and energetic in the performance of his duties. Indeed, he seems frequently to have exceeded them in his anxiety to relieve the sick poor.

In 1771 Wade published an account of the work of the laboratory, which he addressed to the Lord Lieutenant. In this he complained, amongst other things, of the uselessness of giving medicines to those whose most urgent need was food. In order to cover the cost of poor relief he suggested a tax of one shilling per annum to be levied on each house with a rent of more than ten pounds.

Wade's ideas about food being more important than medicine were echoed a hundred and fifty years later by Dr Michael Cox (1851–1926) of St Vincent's Hospital. He had examined a case in which malnutrition had done more harm than any infection; he prescribed a diet and medicine when he turned to the Sister-in-charge, handing her some money, and saying: 'No! She requires something more urgently than medicine. Take this, Sister, and get her champagne.'

Wade advertised regularly, though with strict regard to professional ethics, in the Dublin papers. In the *Public Gazetteer* for September 1766 (No. 834) he mentioned amongst other medicines aether for the treatment of headaches, whooping cough, tooth ache, hysteria, syncope, lethargy and rheumatism.

The social standing of the apothecaries was recognised by several Acts passed about this time which gave them equal status with surgeons, physicians and clergymen in the performance of public duties. In 1787 four members of the Corporation were selected to assist the College of Physicians in the preparation of a Dublin Pharmacopoeia.

The first London Pharmacopoeia had been published in 1618. In this James I, although he assumed the title of 'King of Great Britain and Ireland,' restricted himself to commanding: 'all and singular Apothecaries within this our realm of *England* or the dominions thereof that they and every of them . . . do not compound or make any Medicine except as set downe by the said booke.' This book was not official in Ireland, but was probably used as a guide in prescribing and compounding.

In 1791 a pharmacopoeia for the use of the sick poor was published in Cork by Anthony Mann, M.D.; Richard Walsh, M.D.; William S. O'Halloran, M.D.; John Lord, M.D.; William Lecky, M.D., and

Thomas Harris, Surgeon. They used the *Edinburgh Dispensatory* as a model.

In 1794 the King's and Queen's College of Physicians published their first pharmacopoeia. This was never officially sanctioned as a pharmacopoeia by the College but, through inadvertency or misinformation, it was printed as such by Dr Duncan in his *Edinburgh Dispensatory* of 1803 and subsequently. A College committee was appointed for the revision of the Pharmacopoeia in 1804. This committee, which was open to all members of the College, held weekly meetings from August 1804 until August of the following year. These meetings were usually held in a member's house, where a laboratory was available for practical experimentation.

A *specimen alterum* was prepared, printed and circulated amongst members of the College and in February 1806 the committee resumed weekly meetings in order to prepare from this an official Dublin Pharmacopoeia. In March 1806 the committee published a report, part of which deserves reproduction in full, showing, as it does, the high esteem in which the physicians held themselves and their correspondingly low opinion of other practitioners. '(the committee) have availed themselves of the observations of members of the College on the *specimen alterum* formerly printed, of the information and occasional assistance of the professor of Chemistry of the Royal College of Surgeons and of some intelligent gentlemen of the Pharmaceutical profession.'

The first official Dublin Pharmacopoeia appeared in 1807, the last edition being published in 1850.

When, under the Medical Act of 1858, the General Medical Council undertook the preparation of a Pharmacopoeia, the new publication was made official in Ireland, as it still is.

Charles Lucas (1713–1771) was a prominent member of the corporation in the latter part of the eighteenth century. Something of a stormy petrel, his interests were political as much as professional. He was M.P. for Dublin at one time and kept an apothecary's shop in Charles' Street. After quarrelling with the College of Physicians, he obtained a neat revenge. When the inspecting physicians next examined his shop he had altered the labels and disguised the contents of the bottles. He boasted that they passed a substance as rhubarb which was really a concoction of toast and turmeric. As early as 1745 he was honoured by the Guild, of which he was first Master, for his services. Lucas' great objective was the establishment of an Apothecaries' Hall, as a central depot for the supply of medical services throughout the country. The only institutions to which the sick poor might be admitted, with few exceptions, were lunatic asylums, fever hospitals and gaols. Skilled medical attendance was almost non-existent.

Lucas' plan was to qualify practitioners for a very small fee, then, by securing them a monopoly of the sale of drugs, to enable them to live in the small Irish towns which had a poor population. This plan developed favourably. Gradually there was added the qualification to act as medical officers to fever hospitals and asylums. That Lucas succeeded so largely is a tribute to his drive and tenacity. Unfortunately, he denounced usurious transactions in Dublin. Because of this and because of his advanced political opinions he was obliged to leave Dublin. He travelled to Leyden, where he graduated M.D. He then took up practice in London, where he was highly successful, particularly with the Irish population.

Lucas died before he could see the foundation of the Hall for which he had worked so hard. One of the lesser known of his activities was the foundation of the *Freeman's Journal* in 1763.

In 1768 Edward Foster, an M.D. of Edinburgh, published an *Essay on Hospitals, or Succinct Directions for the Situation, Construction and Administration of Country Hospitals*. This was primarily addressed to Lucas. It contained suggestions for the building of county hospitals and gave several plans and drawings of these which are of some interest, and in many essentials are of a similar plan to that of the most modern hospitals.

In 1777 the Guild rescinded an order by which none but practising apothecaries were admitted. The first person on whom honorary membership was conferred was Dr David McBride, chemist, physician and surgeon.

David McBride (1726–1779), one of the founders of the Meath Hospital, was of Scottish descent. His first medical training was as apprentice to a surgeon in Ballymoney, Co Antrim. He served for several years as a naval surgeon. After this he returned to medical and obstetrical studies at Edinburgh, although he took no degree. Later he received an honorary M.D. of Glasgow.

In 1749 he commenced practice in Dublin. He became a member of the Medico-Philosophical Society, to which he communicated several important papers, notably on scurvy, his interest in which had been developed at sea. His view was that the cure of scurvy depended on the fermentative powers of fresh vegetables. He suggested that malt, which could be kept indefinitely, should be used as an antiscorbutic. Malt is not rich in vitamin C, but as an aid to digestion it is valuable and has been used as an adjuvant to other antiscorbutic treatment.

McBride's work in the field of chemistry was wide. It included experiments on fermentation and putrefaction and the nature of

carbonic acid gas. The proceedings of the Dublin Society in 1768
contain a description of a new method of tanning leather discovered
by him and later in the same year record his decoration with a silver
medal.

For some years after he obtained his medical degree McBride
lectured to students in his own house. To help them he published
a *Methodical Introduction to the Study and Practice of Physic*. This
was later translated into Latin and published at Utrecht. He was
responsible for several other books and papers on medical subjects
as well.

Gilborne's Medical Review of 1775 contains a mild rebuke to over-
confident apothecaries.

> Apothecaries! Freedom you'll forgive
> A Clyster not your office is to give
> You know not what a mischief you may make
> If you the spine's direction should mistake,
> Make the decoction with due care and skill,
> Then cork the pipe, the bladder bind and fill
> But let the surgeon his injection make
> He must for that his patient not forsake.
>
> Keep clean your shops in eminent degree,
> From all annoyance, dust, and cobwebs free,
> Make up your medicines with the nicest care
> But to dispense them cautiously forbear.
> Mind your own bus'ness, study where and when,
> And ne'er forget that you are Gentlemen.

The history of the eighteenth-century government of Dublin is
marked by constant squabbles between the Aldermen and the City
Companies. The Surgeons and Apothecaries were to be found in the
thick of most of the disputes.

The original Guild of St Mary Magdalen elected four members
to the City Council. When the Surgeons broke away, they and the
Apothecaries elected two members each. They were amongst the
foremost opponents of the system by which parliaments were elected
for an indefinite number of years. A hint of current opinion on vote
purchase appears in the minutes of 1768: 'the guild will support Dr
Lucas and Lord Kildare for the Dublin election without any expense
to them on the guild's account.'

At the beginning of 1790 the Royal College of Surgeons were
specially convened to hear the following resolutions of the
Apothecaries:

That the establishment of an Apothecaries' Hall in this city would be a great National benefit.

That to make such an institution permanent and respectable, it is absolutely necessary to take in the aid of every branch of medicine.

That physicians, surgeons, apothecaries, druggists and chymists, following their respective professions in this kingdom be considered eligible to subscribe.

That a copy of these Resolutions be sent to the King's and Queen's College of Physicians and to the Royal College of Surgeons, to request their concurrence and aid in forming and digesting a plan for this purpose.

Signed,   John Clark, Chairman.

Following conferences with the two Royal Colleges the Apothecaries' Hall was founded.

The Apothecaries' Act of 1791 established the Hall, consisting of one Governor, a Deputy Governor, thirteen Directors and Subscribers. Henry Hunt was the first Governor. He held the post during six sessions. Membership of the Hall was opened to all apothecaries in Dublin on payment of one hundred pounds. Interest was paid on this annually, so that the Hall was legally a limited company. For many years the Apothecaries' Hall held a monopoly of the importation and distribution of drugs in Ireland.

Under the Act, apothecaries were forbidden to take as apprentices any person who had not passed an examination by the Hall in general education. Nobody might open an apothecary's shop without a certificate of proficiency issued by the Hall. Persons who considered themselves aggrieved by refusal to issue a certificate had the right of appeal to the Royal College of Physicians. Apprentices were bound to serve for seven years before admission to the final examination. The penalty for failure to comply with these rules was a fine of twenty pounds.

One of the early measures for the control of poisons is found in this Act. Apothecaries were forbidden to keep arsenic or painters' colours in the same premises as they used for compounding medicines. Further, the apothecary was forbidden to sell arsenic except to people whom he knew. Records of the sale of arsenic were to be kept and signed by the purchaser. At the same time members were not to be punished for dealing in oils and colours in separate apartments from their chemists' shops.

In February 1791, Alexander Cannon, an indentured apprentice, was examined as to his knowledge of Latin and was appointed assistant to Mr Patrick McLoughlin of Andrew Street. In March of that year another apprentice was 'advised to improve himself further and return after six months for a further examination.'

During this period the Court of Directors met at the houses of its members. This was inconvenient and several efforts were made to secure premises in Clarendon Street, Bolton Street and elsewhere. Permission was sought and granted in April 1791 to meet occasionally in the College of Surgeons' building in Mercer's Street. Eventually arrangements were made for the purchase of a house in Mary Street. The first meeting held here was on 1st May 1792. In September 1791 the Apothecaries made a further effort to control the sale of drugs. They circularised their country members to the effect that any grocer found selling medicines would be prosecuted. There are frequent references in the minute books of the Hall to action taken against unqualified chemists and those taking apprentices against the regulations.

A committee was appointed in July 1792 to consider the payment of the profession. In December of the same year they reported and recommended the following scale of charges amongst others:

	£	s.	d.
Bleeding by Masters from 5/5*d*. to		11	4
,, by Apprentices		2	0
For a Master being called out of bed to visit the sick	1	2	9
Attendance of Master on emetics		5	5
,, of Apprentices		2	0
Gargles from 2/- to		3	6
Sinapisms applied to the feet from 3/3*d*. to		5	5
Blistering plasters behind the ears		2	2
A strengthening plaster to the loins		2	0

The charges for children's medicines were approximately half those of adults. A footnote stated – 'Your committee are of opinion that surgeons supplying their patients with medicine often as they are informed at the expense of those institutions set apart for the relief of the indigent and druggists compounding medicines are as injurious to the publick as to the apothecary. But it is with great concern that they are not able at the time to offer a mode either of prevention or removal of these grievances.' This resulted in a conference between the College of Surgeons and the Apothecaries to discover a mutual agreement.

In a minute book of the Hall for May 1793 there is a record of fifty-two persons who offended against the rules of the Hall. They were fined sums ranging from five to sixty pounds. The offences noted were mainly the improper sale of arsenic and irregularities in taking apprentices. In November of the same year, several of these were named as having failed to pay their fines.

The Apothecaries came into conflict with the customs authorities in June 1794 when their request to be allowed to operate a still was refused to for fear that it might be used for spirits instead of water.

During all this period much active work was in hand, both in the examination of apprentices and in the fitting out of the Hall in Mary Street. Apparently the Hall was recognised as an analytical laboratory, for, in August 1794, there is an account of the analysis of the waters found at the new Spa near Leixlip. The Hall made no charge for the analysis. Such generosity seems unwise in view of the fact that a few weeks later they were asking Henry Grattan and others for advice on how to raise funds. The financial difficulties continued for several years and in 1798 an effort was made to raise £2,000 by the issue of debentures. Counsel's opinion was that this step would be illegal.

On the occasion of the 1798 rebellion the Court of Directors forwarded an address to the Lord Lieutenant in which they expressed their willingness to assist in crushing the insurgents.

In 1811 a brief note in the minute book records that the Hall voted twenty pounds to the Lord Mayor's fund for the relief of distress in Portugal.

From 1798 until 1828 the minute books of the corporation contain little beyond accounts and the results of examinations. One of the few references to policy occurs in resolutions passed in April 1813, when it was decided that 'samples of the most usual articles of medicine enclosed in glass jars be laid upon the examiners' table previous to each examination for Assistant or Master.' And 'Whensoever any person is examined to commence as Master particular attention be paid to his knowledge of Diseases and the mode of exhibiting medicine with the proper dose.'

In 1815 there were several attempts at personation during examinations and the Court of Directors resolved to prosecute in further cases. The attempts continued and the Provost of Trinity College was approached to dissuade his medical students from acting as impersonators. At the same time there was a lack of harmony amongst the apothecaries themselves.

In 1818 the Hall requested Sir Robert Peel, then Chief Secretary for Ireland, to help them to introduce legislation to improve their status and to enable them more satisfactorily to enforce measures against quacks. Peel was not very helpful and referred the matter elsewhere. His only concrete assistance was the promise of a conference with Mr Vansittart, a member of the Treasury, on the subject of stamp duty on medicines and certificates. Vansittart turned down the suggestion and the whole matter closed until a general meeting of apothecaries was held in October 1818. As a result of this meeting a committee of fourteen was appointed to consider how best to benefit the profession and the public.

Unfortunately this meeting, instead of leading to unity, caused dissension amongst those apothecaries who were members of the Hall and those who, though qualified, practised on their own. Edward Breen, on behalf of the general body of apothecaries, proposed a joint conference, but this was firmly refused by the Hall.

The free-lance apothecaries claimed that their rights had not been protected by the Hall and that any regulations made without their advice and consent might be similarly disregarded. They threatened to approach Parliament independently if necessary.

Towards the end of 1823 associations of qualified apothecaries who were not members of the Hall were formed in Dublin, Cork, Waterford and Limerick. These bodies generally favoured more vigorous and unorthodox methods of procedure against quacks than would be countenanced by the Hall. John Madden of Limerick was one of those who favoured swift action. He held many communications with the Hall on the subject. In 1824 the Limerick Association suggested a meeting of the Apothecaries of the whole country to consider new legislation, but the Hall were not enthusiastic.

In 1825 the Hall were asked to co-operate with the College of Physicians in the preparation of a new Pharmacopoeia. An *ad hoc* committee was appointed.

In 1826 a resolution was moved that the title of 'Master Apothecary' was degrading to the profession and that the term 'Licentiate' should be substituted.

The Hall appointed Inspectors of Apothecaries to the whole country. These kept a fairly strict supervision on shops, but quite frequently they and the governing body were defied by unqualified practitioners. They received a percentage of the fines levied which must have acted as a spur to their zeal.

On 28th January 1828 the Hall received a letter from J. R. Price, a licentiate apothecary, stating that he intended to open a school of pharmacy, materia medica, botany and chemistry. He requested that his lectures should be recognised by the Hall. A few months later it was resolved that only University and Hall lectures would be recognised.

In April 1838 the College of Surgeons charged the apothecaries as a whole with neglect of their business. Their main charges were that the apothecaries had become medical practitioners instead of compounders; that they left their shops in charge of unqualified persons 'and even women'; that their Medical School was an illegal one and that they had successfully prosecuted surgeons who had dispensed medicines.

The Apothecaries replied that they conducted their affairs properly; that they were for centuries the doctors of the poor and that their school was not alone legal, but essential.

The quarrel died down some two years later when the introduction, by Sir James Graham, of a Bill to make State examination the only portal of entry to the profession convinced all medical men that they must unite to avoid Parliamentary interference. As a result, Graham's Bill failed and the Medical Act of 1858 recognised the Universities, the Conjoint Board and the Apothecaries' Hall as licensing bodies.

In November 1838 the Apothecaries proposed that a Board representative of all branches of the profession should be formed with power to grant degrees for general practice. They also suggested that all public appointments should be filled by competitive examination.

One of the notable events of 1838 was the formation of a committee of nineteen representatives of both the Hall and the other Dublin apothecaries. Their principal task was the preparation of the proposed amended Act for the better regulation of the profession. This task was widely interpreted and the committee protected the apothecaries' interest in many matters.

In 1792 the Apothecaries celebrated the first anniversary of the establishment of the Hall by founding a limited medical school in Mary Street. William Higgins, a native of Sligo and graduate of Oxford, was appointed chemist. Three years later he left to take up a post in the Royal Dublin Society. His name is associated with research on the atomic constitution of matter.

On 20th October 1815 it was resolved by the Court of Directors that lectures in chemistry and pharmacy would be useful. Directors were invited to give such lectures and a committee was formed to make the necessary preparations. In July 1816 a piece of plate value £30 was presented to George Kiernan for his course of lectures in pharmaceutic chemistry. In the following year he received a piece of plate value fifty guineas for another course of lectures.

Michael Donovan, appointed in 1820 as Professor of Chemistry, Pharmacy and Materia Medica, was one of the most able men attached to the Hall. He was a licentiate apothecary, but consistently opposed the claim of his own profession to be medical practitioners. In 1829, he published a pamphlet on the state of pharmacy in Ireland and started a periodical entitled *Annals of Pharmacy and Materia Medica*, which only appeared a few times. Donovan's solution of arsenic and iodide of mercury is still familiar to chemists throughout the world.

In 1832, a theatre, capable of affording accommodation for 150 pupils, was constructed in the laboratory, and Dr J. C. Ferguson was appointed Professor of Medicine. After this the College of Surgeons refused to recognise any of the lectures delivered in the School of Pharmacy, on the grounds that the apothecaries were incompetent to found a medical professorship.

In 1836 a number of apothecaries formed a company for the purpose of establishing a complete school. They chose the site of the ruined Theatre Royal in Crow Street. The buildings were finished in 1837. They comprised two large theatres, a dissecting room, three laboratories and other smaller apartments. Recognition was still officially refused by the College of Surgeons which set up its own Diploma in Pharmacy in an effort to freeze out the apothecaries completely. Relations remained strained until November 1842, when a truce was declared.

In 1854 the proprietors sold the buildings to the newly-established Catholic University. The premises were repaired, improved and reopened as a medical school, in 1855. On the establishment of the National University in 1909, the Cecilia Street school became a department of University College, Dublin.

The division between those apothecaries who wished to act only as dispensers and those who claimed the rights and privileges of medical men became more marked towards the middle of the nineteenth century, when the former founded the Pharmaceutical Society. At first this body had no official status. It existed to further the interests of pharmacy and chemistry. Confusion followed, as many apothecaries now refused to keep open shop. The resultant complaints by the public led to the passage of the Pharmacy Act. This enabled 'persons who although they do not desire to practise the art and mystery of an apothecary, desire and are qualified to open shop for the retailing, dispensing and compounding poisons and medical prescriptions, to keep open shop for the purposes aforesaid.' This and the amending Act of 1890 largely govern the practice of pharmacy in this country to-day.

The oldest pharmacy firm in Dublin is that of Hamilton and Long, founded in 1826 by Samuel Bewley. This firm originally acted as State Apothecary.

As a result of the Acts a pharmacist is one who is entitled to keep open shop for the dispensing of medicines on a doctor's prescription. An apothecary in Ireland is a medical man who holds the Licence of the Apothecaries' Hall of Ireland, which entitles him to registration and rights of practice under the Medical Acts. This licence also permits him to dispense other doctors' prescriptions as well as his own and to keep open shop as a Medical Hall if he so desires. Some hospitals have found it desirable to have a member of their staff so qualified. In a few cases their charters have required such appointments.

Up to 1971 the Apothecaries' Hall was an examining and licensing body. As it was not a teaching institution candidates were obliged to present evidence of adequate attendance both at lectures and clinical instruction in recognised teaching centres. In December of that year, the Medical Registration Council in Ireland and the General Medical Council in England withdrew the Hall's authority to issue licences to practice medicine despite protests by the Directors.

A curious situation immediately developed. As the Hall is a body established by statute it can only be dissolved by Act of Parliament. Under the Hall's constitution shares are held by the Governor and Directors. These can only be disposed of to an Apothecary and may not even be bequeathed. Probably many such shares are still in existance in many parts of the world, and it is not hard to imagine the legal tangle which could develop from any effort to close the Hall after almost two hundred years of activity.

There is still one function carried out annually by the surviving Directors. This is the organisation of the Sheppard memorial lecture delivered in memory of Dr John Sheppard, a distinguished Dublin general practitioner who had served the Hall as examiner, representative on the M.R.E. and G.M.C. and Governor for almost forty years. The lecture is given before an invited audience by a general practitioner usually on a subject of general practice interest.

About 1979 discussions were held with Irish members of the Royal College of General Practitioners to explore the possibility of some form of co-operation between the two bodies, but these proved fruitless. Possibly at some later date a means will be found to save an honourable institution from oblivion.

CHAPTER NINE

THE EIGHTEENTH CENTURY

The eighteenth century is medically notable for the growth of the voluntary hospital as we know it to-day. Dublin's lead in this development was largely due to the slum conditions in the city at the beginning of the period.

By 1728 the population of Dublin was 146,075, with scarcely any increase in the area occupied by buildings and streets. Under these conditions the spread of disease was accomplished with the utmost facility, particularly in the poorer districts, where malnutrition, combined with close personal contact, rendered such spread devastatingly rapid.

At that time no medical provision was made for the poor of Dublin. In 1699 the Corporation had set apart a plot of ground at Little Green as a hospital site, but the project fell through. There was a city doctor appointed by the Corporation, but his rather nebulous duties did not include attendance on the sick poor.

In 1703 the Irish Parliament passed an Act enabling the erection of a workhouse in the City of Dublin for employing and maintaining the poor thereof. A board of Governors was nominated to administer 'the ground walled-in at the South West end of James's Street, and a parcel of land adjoining thereto called the Pipes, containing about fourteen acres, on which are built several small houses called George's Folly.'

One of the sources of income of this house was the collection of money for licences of sedan chairs and hackney coaches, as well as a rate of three pence in the pound on the yearly valuation of properties in the city or liberties. Although the house was primarily intended for healthy persons it eventually made provision for those physically and mentally sick. A further reason for erecting the workhouse was declared to be 'to preserve the lives of illegitimate children and the educating and instructing them in the Protestant religion.'

The situation of unwanted children was miserable. They were the responsibility of the authority of the parish in which they were found. No parish wished to undergo this expense and usually the churchwardens employed a 'parish nurse.' Her slang name of 'the lifter' describes her activities much more accurately for she made nightly rounds and 'lifted' any infants found lying in public places. She brought them to an adjoining parish and laid them in any convenient spot. Sometimes she placed a dose of 'diacodium,' a narcotic, in the infant's mouth in order to prevent it crying. Such removes must have happened to many children, perhaps several times in one winter's night. At least they were soon out of their misery.

Following the findings of a House of Lord's Commission in 1730, a part of the workhouse was reserved as a foundling hospital. At one of the gates there was a basket fixed to a revolving door. Those who wished to abandon a child placed it in a basket, rang a bell and left. With a few minutes the door was turned from inside, and the baby received by a porter who could not see the depositor.

The babies who stayed in the home were fed on 'panada.' This was bread soaked in water with a little milk added. When an inquiry was held in 1797 the matron admitted that this mess was unfit to sustain life. Sixty-seven years had passed since panada was first employed in the hospital.

Some of the babies were 'nursed out.' A few lucky ones received good treatment. But the fee for foster-mothers was only £2 a year. The margin of profit was in inverse ratio to the amount of food given to the orphan. Advertisements appeared from time to time in the newspapers requiring the foster-mothers to bring their charges to the hospital in order to receive payment. All farmed-out children were branded on the arm. On one occasion thirteen such branded babies were found buried in a pit.

At one time the supply of Protestant foster-mothers ran out, and children were sent to the Cork home from Dublin. As the journey was done in an open cart in all weathers the number who arrived alive in the south was very small. Even in the home the mortality figures were appalling. In 1752, 365 died out of 691 admitted. From 1796 to 1826, 41,524 died out of 52,152, or nearly 80 per cent.

The majority of infants admitted to the hospital were healthy. When ill they were at once removed to the Infirmary. As this was tantamount to a death sentence, healthy children were sometimes transferred when the ordinary accommodation was overcrowded.

The only treatment sick infants received was 'The Bottle.' This was a narcotic mixture of some sort, for 'the children were easy for an hour or two after taking it.' It may have been the 'diacodium' already mentioned. During the five years 1791 to 1796, 5,716 infants were admitted to the Infirmary. *One* was discharged alive.

In 1797 a Committee was at long last appointed by the Irish Parliament to enquire into the hospital's affairs. They took speedy action, dismissing the physician, surgeon and apothecary as well as the whole Board of Governors.

Amongst the sanitary measures instituted by the new Board was the destruction by fire of the bug-infested cradles. This task was so nauseating that many of the workmen employed were taken ill.

Conditions amongst the older children were almost as bad. The food was scanty and verminous. Clothing was insufficient for even a cool day. Four or more children slept in one cot. All forms of disease due to dirt were constantly present. Savage punishments, such as nine lashes with the cat-o'-nine-tails for being slow in going to bed were commonplace. Treatment of sick children was such as to be largely unprintable. Two old women were in charge of sixty sick children, all under eight years of age. Two doctors were supposed to attend. Even when they did, their instructions were ignored. The dead were left until there were sufficient to make the task of preparing a burial-place worth the grave-digger's while. He rarely had long to wait. This part of the hospital was also improved following the Committee's report, until finally, in 1829, the house was closed as a foundling hospital.

But public-spirited benefactors of the sick poor were not wholly wanting. On 14th December 1710, Dr Richard Steevens, a Fellow of the College of Physicians, made his will. In this he bequeathed all his property in trust to his twin sister, Grizel, for her life, and after her death 'to provide one proper place or building within the City of Dublin for an hospital for maintaining and curing from time to time such sick and wounded persons whose distempers and wounds are curable.' Next day Dr Steevens died.

Madame Steevens did not wish the relief of the sick poor to be delayed until her death. This eventually occurred in 1747, when she was ninety-three. Dr Steevens' will was not established until May 1713, but before that his sister had presented a petition to Queen Anne, through the Lord-Lieutenant, the Duke of Ormond. In this, she set out plans for the proposed hospital, and prayed for a site to be allotted in the Phoenix Park. The death of Queen Anne in 1714, and the attainder of the Duke, quashed any hopes of success the petition might have had.

Undaunted, Madame Steevens embarked on a new plan. On 11th July 1717, she executed a deed whereby she appointed trustees to build a hospital, vesting in them £2,000 of her own money. On 14th August of the same year, the trustees bought for £600 'the piece of ground belonging to Sir Samuel Cook lying between the end of James' St., and Bow Bridge containing about three and a half acres.'

The work of building the hospital proceeded slowly despite the efforts of Archbishop King, who was by far the most energetic trustee. Although Madame Steevens and others made generous gifts, the main obstacle to a rapid finish seems to have been lack of money. Up to 1730 nearly £7,000 had been spent on materials and salaries. At the same time death played havoc with the trustees and interrupted the continuity of their work. In order to preserve this continuity the remaining trustees were incorporated in 1730.

The hospital was unable to accept its first patient until 23rd July 1733, by which time Grizel Steevens had contributed some £14,000 of her own money. Before the house was opened to patients she took up residence on the ground floor and probably kept an eye on all activities of the hospital. She died in 1747 and was at first buried in St James' Church. Later her body was moved to the hospital chapel. Her portrait hangs in the Worth Library or Board-room of the hospital.

At one time an absurd story was current that Madame Steevens was born with a pig's face. The tale ran that her mother rebuffed a poor woman shortly before Grizel's birth, telling her to clear off with her litter of pigs, presumably her many children. In revenge the beggar cursed the unborn child, which entered the world with a pig-like face. The story is an ancient and widespread one. References to it have been found in London and Amsterdam as early as 1640 and 1641, over a century before Madame Steevens' death. The present author can remember, as a child in Edinburgh, hearing the tale in another guise. It is possible that the story came to be applied to Madame Steevens from her habit of going about her charitable work wearing a heavy veil, in a vain effort to preserve her anonymity. There is no reference to the story as applied to her in the eighteenth century in any published records.

The bills for much of the furniture and equipment, bought when the hospital was first opened, have been preserved. They make interesting reading. '2 blue paragon beds for the matron and surgeon,' cost £13, with sheets at 1s. 3d. per yard. The patients fared more cheaply with wooden bedsteads costing 25s. each and sheets at 8d. per yard.

The patients' diet was largely a liquid one. For breakfast, each received a pint of gruel or small beer, and for dinner, broth or 'a quart of small beer.' As was customary at the time, the beer was probably brewed on the premises.

The salaries of the various officials provide an interesting commentary on the relative values set on their services to the hospital: resident surgeon, £30 p.a.; chaplain, £10 p.a.; steward, £30 p.a.; matron, £15 p.a.; four nurses, £12 each; laundry maid, £10 p.a.; cook and porter, £12 each. The total cost of furnishing a ten-bed ward was £72 5s. 1¾d. The average daily cost was about 1s. 8d. per patient.

In 1817 fever wards were opened on the top floor of Steevens'. During 23 months 4,778 patients were treated. The death rate was 3.04 per cent, the lowest for fever in the city. John Crampton published a report on the work of the fever department in 1819.

Steevens' Hospital was prominent in investigation and experiment. Dr Berkeley's tar-water, mentioned in a previous chapter, was given a trial without conclusive results, and considerable work seems to have been done in the use of mercury for 'salivating' or 'fluxing' patients.

Mercury was used both internally and externally from the beginning of the seventeenth century. Huge doses were given and the efficacy of the treatment was estimated by the amount of saliva produced. Between one and two quarts per day was considered essential. As the treatment was preceded by vigorous purgation and blood-letting it must have required a strong constitution in the first instance.

The earliest account of teaching in the hospital is dated 1756. Assistant surgeons were appointed, and each surgeon was allowed to have two pupils or apprentices in the hospital.

Amongst the trustees nominated by Madame Steevens was Edward Worth (1678–1723). The hospital library is named after him. Worth studied at Oxford and Utrecht, where he took his M.D. before returning to Dublin. He became M.D. of Trinity College and a Fellow of the College of Physicians. The few records of his professional life available point to him as being successful and popular. Because of some obscure dispute he refused the Presidency of the College.

During his life Worth built up a widely representative library of some four thousand books. He left the majority of these to the hospital with provision for their storage and cataloguing. He appointed his cousin and namesake, Edward Worth, as sole executor of his will. Very little was done about arranging the library until the young Worth was appointed a governor in 1734. During the following years the hospital minutes and accounts contain frequent references to work done in the library. By 1742 this had been completed. The room has now practically the same appearance as then.

There are only fragmentary records of the early surgical work of the hospital. There was no special operating theatre and the equivalent of the modern accident room was used. In 1787 a special room was set apart for the purpose, with two small wards for post-operative cases on either side. The passage-way to the present theatre is on the site of the original room.

The names of both patient and surgeon, together with the details of the operation, were regularly published in the popular press of the time. It is to these records that we owe much of our knowledge of day-to-day surgical practice. For example in *Pue's Occurrences* of 1736 we read:

John Nicholls Esq, the Surgeon-General performed a most wonderful operation by cutting a child of Mr Stockman's in Capel Street, of five years old for the stone, which stone was as large as a pullet's egg and weighed three quarters of an ounce. The child is now in a very fair way of recovery, hath a good appetite and is likely to do very well.

For many years, at least in the popular mind, Steevens was associated with the treatment of venereal disease when this consisted of prolonged administration of mercurial and arsenical compounds, but it is sometimes forgotten that, under the direction of Mr W. Haughton, pioneer orthopaedic treatment and teaching of a high order was carried on. In 1957 a burns service was initiated which covers severe burning incidents from throughout the country. In 1981 a small self contained isolation type unit was opened with its own cubicles, bathrooms, dressing rooms and a full operating theatre. A far cry indeed from the days when a struggling, unanaesthetised patient was held in the operating chair while a surgeon who had never heard of asepsis amputated a limb at lightning speed. The chair illustrated which dates from the late eighteenth century can still be seen in the Hospital.

Simultaneously with the development of Steevens', other hospitals were growing up. In 1718, six Dublin surgeons, at their own expense, had opened a house in Cook Street, for the reception of poor surgical patients. Their names were commemorated by an inscription on the walls of the original hospital:

SOLI DEO GLORIA. The Charitable Infirmary was first founded and opened August 1718, at the sole expense of the following surgeons–George Duany, Patrick Kelly, Nathaniel Hudson, John Dowdall, Fr. Duany, Peter Brenan–who served the poor without fee or reward.

In 1728 it became necessary to move to a house on Inns' Quay. There was now accommodation for fifty patients. Soon over 200 intern and 7,000 extern patients were being treated annually.

The earliest reference to this hospital as 'The Charitable Infirmary' appears in the *Gentleman and Citizens' Almanack* for 1738:

The Charitable Infirmary on the Merchant's Key, first projected in 1723 and opened 12th August 1728, is supported by several charitable contributions and by the attendance of surgeons where numbers of maim'd and wounded poor, both interns, who lodge and are supported in the house; and out-patients who daily flock to the Infirmary are attended and supplied with medicine at the expense of the Charity.

This house stood about four doors above Chancery Place (formerly Mass Lane).

Volume 91 of *Pue's Occurrences*, published in November 1746, contained an advertisement which read:

Whereas pursuant to the will of Mrs Susannah Maria Stafford, deceas'd, the trustees of the Charitable Infirmary on the Inns' Quay, have built and furnish'd appartments for the reception of twelve sick poor servants out of place and properly recommended. This is therefore to give notice that the trustees of the said infirmary are now ready to receive such sick persons according to the intent and meaning of said will.

In April 1771 a fire broke out in a small cabin somewhere in the slums. An old lady was burnt to death. According to the *Freeman's Journal*, 'her daughter narrowly escaped but was burned in a terrible manner; she was carried to the Inns' Quay Infirmary.' A few days later 'A sailor had his thigh broke between two vessels in Poolbeg and a Boy was dangerously wounded by a Cart going over him. They were carried to the Inns' Quay Infirmary.' Similar notices appeared frequently.

In 1786 the site on Inns' Quay was required for the erection of the Four Courts of Justice. The Charitable Infirmary's trustees bought No. 14 Jervis Street, the town house of the Earl of Charlemont. The hospital is now commonly known as 'Jervis Street.'

The house was not in good repair and in 1803 a temporary hospital was occupied, whilst the old building and the adjoining houses were completely rebuilt. A subscription list opened for this purpose met with a generous response from the public.

In 1792 the Governors of the hospital secured a royal charter. This was revised in 1820, with a provision that a governing committee numbering fifteen persons should be elected annually. In 1854 the Sisters of Mercy took over the administration of the hospital for the committee of management.

There were no great changes until 1877, when extensive premises adjoining the hospital were bought, demolished and rebuilt from the foundations as a hospital. The whole scheme took ten years. When it was finished, the hospital was complete in its accommodation for intern patients, but a suitable extern department was not supplied until 1910.

Jervis Street's importance as an accident hospital increased enormously with the development of motor traffic and industrial expansion in Dublin. During the period of war from 1916 to 1922 the Infirmary dealt with cases from all sides. Politics, religion or national sentiment were ignored. The only criterion for treatment was need.

In 1919, further extension became imperative. New premises, including modern operating theatres, were built. The respite from overcrowding was only temporary so that in 1927 and again in 1942 new extensions were undertaken.

An important landmark in the history of Jervis Street was the establishment in 1966 of a National Poisons Information Centre with the joint function of giving advice and admitting poisoning cases. The urgent need for such a service was reflected in the report on the first six month's working. Over two hundred enquiries for urgent information came from all parts of the country. Nowadays over six thousand calls are received annually.

In 1969 a Drug Addiction Clinic was set up. For a time, due to lack of space, this operated from a caravan sited in the Hospital yard. The first report of this centre stated that 'The drug problem in Ireland differs from elsewhere in that there are not many physically dependent on drugs'. By 1980 the report referred to the alarming increase in the numbers abusing heroin and cocaine reflecting their sudden availability on the streets. The original staff of four had expanded to thirty six, coping annually with 1,500 patients of whom 621 were new victims of this modern epidemic.

A further specialised development in which Jervis Street played a major role was genito-urinary surgery. Pioneer work in renal dialysis and transplantation was undertaken with a high success rate. When additional facilities became available at St Mary's Hospital this work expanded. About fifty renal transplants are now carried out annually.

In the 1971–72 report of Jervis St. Professor G. Doyle referred to the possibility of some fusion with the other two north city hospitals, St Laurence's and the Mater 'in ten to twenty years'. But by 1976 active moves to implement the idea of union were afoot and on July 20, 1977 representatives of Jervis Street and St Laurence's met the then Minister of Health, Mr Charles Haughey, and supported his decision to build a modern 730 bed hospital at Beaumont on the outskirts of Dublin. The first sod of the new site was turned by the same Minister in February 1978 with a four year dead line for completion, a target which has not been achieved to date (1983) and it appears that the earliest possible opening date would be the Spring of 1985.

Staff members of both the original institutions feel that a very appropriate name for the new hospital would be 'Dominic Corrigan' after the distinguished mid-nineteenth century Dublin physician who had been on the staffs of both Jervis Street from 1830 to 1840 and the Richmond (now St Laurence's) from 1840 until his death in 1879.

Grizelle Steevens has already been mentioned as the virtual foundress of a hospital. She was not an isolated representative of her sex, for in 1724 Miss Mary Mercer of Ship Street proposed to build a refuge for twenty poor girls. She received at a nominal rent a grant of land in St Stephen's Churchyard from the Church authorities, whereon she built a house. There is no record that she ever received into it the twenty poor girls but, in 1734, she executed a deed conveying the house (known as Mary Mercer's Stone House) to trustees for conversion into a hospital for 'diseases of tedious and hazardous cure, such as falling sickness, lunacy, leprosy, and the like, or of such other diseased and infirm poor persons as the trustees think proper.' The hospital was opened on 17th August 1734 with ten beds.

The minute book of the hospital for 1736 records that the sum of £402 18*s.* 2½*d.* was received in aid of the charity from the 'musical performance in St Andrew's Church.' In 1738 the following article appeared in the Dublin papers: 'On Tuesday last, the Te Deum, Jubilate and two coronation anthems composed by Mr Handel, were performed at St Andrew's Church with the greatest decency and exactness possible, for the support of Mercer's Hospital at which their Excellencies the Lord Justices and 800 persons of the first quality and distinction attended.' The annual musical service in St Andrew's was a chief support to the hospital for many years, bringing in on one occasion the sum of £600.

In January 1741 Mercer's received £805, the proceeds of a lottery. Unfortunately the moneys obtained by these and other methods did not always enter the proper channels, for in the minutes of 1738 it is recorded that the clerk, Robert Donnelly, absconded with 'a considerable sum of money.'

The standing rules of the house make strange reading after the lapse of two hundred years. The nurses were directed to change the bed-sheets every month 'or oftener if occasion required.' The steward was to read 'every Sunday a chapter of *The Whole Duty of Man* to the patients.'

On 5th November 1757, a new Mercer's Hospital was opened. This building remained in use, almost unaltered, for over one hundred years.

Early in the nineteenth century the Hospital took over premises formerly occupied by the College of Surgeons. In 1910 a further wing was erected. During the preliminary excavations numerous human bones were found, a relic, no doubt, of the anatomy school which had been on the site. As this is being written in 1983 the present

Mercer's is being run down in preparation for its new life as one of the Federated Dublin Hospitals. The future of the building is still undecided.

Towards the close of the eighteenth century the prison reformer, John Howard, visited Ireland. His comments on the state of the Irish hospitals were no less forthright than those he had made on English prisons. The following extracts are fair samples:

Mercer's Hospital in the middle of the city, was a few years since very dirty, offensive and unhealthy; but, now it is one of the cleanest in Dublin.

In Stephen's Hospital the wards are close and offensive; the windows were shut when the days were fine. The indiscriminate admission of visitants is highly improper, especially of men into the womens' wards, and more particularly, where the beds, as here, are enclosed with wood and curtains.

Simpson's Hospital for the blind and gouty is an excellent institution. The patients are kindly supplied with papers for their amusement; but are, improperly, indulged in the idle habit of taking tobacco and snuff, each having an allowance of four pence a week for that purpose.

The Lying-In Hospital is a good institution; the rooms in 1787 were quiet and clean. The greatest attention was paid to the patients.

Hospital for Incurables. Both outside and inside dirty; the rooms offensive; no rules; no diet table, the housekeeper in the country. The mistresses of such houses should never be permitted to be absent.

Howard was not content with inspecting Dublin hospitals. During the year 1787–8 he travelled through Ireland inspecting, criticising, praising, and reporting on gaols and hospitals in the most remote parts of the country:

The County Infirmary at Wicklow is a house rented by the county. It is out of repair–the ceiling of the kitchen fallen in. There were nine beds–the bedding very old, and linen only on one bed. Diet, a sixpenny loaf every four days, and three pints of milk every day.

Kilkenny County Hospital. A spacious house–but there were only five patients at my visits in 1787 and 1788. The housekeeper complained of the poverty of the hospital. Two medical gentlemen attend, each of whom receives £40 a year.

At Carlow, the County Infirmary is properly situated out of the town. The patients lay in close boxes. The wards were quiet. The floors were sanded, which I always consider as an expedient to hide the dirt.

The Infirmary at Maryborough for Queen's County is an old house in which are four rooms for patients–in a room called the tower, two patients, and a little dirty hay on the floor on which they said the nurse lay. This room was very dirty, the ceiling covered with cobwebs and in several places open to the sky. Here I saw one naked pale object, who was under the necessity of tearing his shirt for bandages for his fractured thigh. The surgery was a closet about ten feet by six; the furniture consisted of ten vials, some of them without corks, of a little salve stuck on a board, some tow and pieces of torn paper scattered on the floor.

In the County Infirmary at Cashel there are four good wards. The governors duly attend and great care seems to be taken of the patients.

In the North Infirmary at Cork all the rooms were close and offensive–not a window open in the whole house.

The County Infirmary at Tralee is a ruinous house–the roof falling in. There were eight old bedsteads in four very dirty rooms–never white-washed. The patients lay on a little hay or straw and found their own bedding.

Limerick County Infirmary–thoroughly repaired, white-washed and furnished with new bedding–a cleanly and notable matron.

The County Infirmary at Castlebar is an old ruinous house, very dirty and the windows stopt with straw. Only one room (eighteen feet and a half by fifteen and a half) for kitchen, turf-house and wash-house and for the nurse's lodging which is under the staircase.

Cavan County Hospital. All the rooms very dirty, an upper room full of fowls, a dunghill in the small front court.

Lifford Hospital for the County of Donegal–The payment of £3 8s. 3d. qualified a person to vote as a governor. I am well informed that the Surgeon (Mr Spence) spent £500 in procuring votes to secure his election. The same scandalous abuse, by which the lives and health of the poor are put up for auction, prevails, as is well known in many of the London Hospitals.

Dundalk Hospital for the County of Louth. The rooms towards the street. The bread good. Proper bedding and sheets. A book is kept for noting down the provisions as they come in.

Armagh County Hospital. Built by the Lord Primate in 1768. No baths; nor do I recollect any in use in other county hospitals, though very conducive to the health of the patients.

We may consider Howard somewhat of a fanatic and even a crank. His diatribes against the evils of snuff and tobacco are excessive. But he had no political axe to grind in Ireland and his reports on conditions here were just as objective as those he made on English prisons and hospitals. His insistence on cleanliness of both patients and wards, with white-washing, ventilation and repair of the latter is quite as strong as that of any hygienist of the twentieth century. He recognised the necessity for humanity in dealing with the sick and insane. This English philanthropist could, with justice, claim for his own the motto of the Irish Sisters of Charity 'Caritas Christi urget nos.'

There was little opportunity for professional discussion between medical men until 1744, when a society known as the Physico-Historical Society was founded in Dublin to promote the study of the antiquities and history of the country. It expired after a few years. Two of its medical members, Charles Smith and John Rutty, formed a private Medico-Philosophical Society, to further 'medical, natural and philosophical inquiries' in 1756. The minute books of this society which still exist are of considerable medical interest. The society held its last meeting on 7th October 1784. In April 1785, two Trinity College societies, the Palaeosophers and the Neosophers united to form the Irish Academy, which was incorporated by royal charter a few months later. The foundation of this body may have been indirectly responsible for the disappearance of the medical society.

About this time there was considerable agitation for improved status among the surgeons. In 1780, to further this object, they founded a society called the Dublin Society of Surgeons to 'promote the honour and advancement of Surgery in Ireland.' This was the forerunner of the College of Surgeons, incorporated in 1784.

Limerick has been the birthplace of many excellent doctors. During the latter half of the eighteenth century Sylvester O'Halloran (1728–1807) of that city stood high in public esteem. His reputation rested on his knowledge of both science and Gaelic studies. On his mother's side he was a blood relation of Seán Clárach Mac Donnell, the Irish poet.

O'Halloran pursued his medical studies at Leyden and Paris, where he made a specialised study of diseases of the eye. He wrote a treatise on glaucoma in 1749 which caused a considerable sensation.

On his return to Limerick his reputation as an ophthalmologist spread rapidly and he restored the sight of many otherwise doomed to total blindness. He established himself as surgeon at the County Infirmary, and in 1793 printed *A New Treatise on the different disorders arising from external injuries of the head, illustrated by eighty-five (selected from above fifteen hundred) practical cases.*

The faction fights of the time gave him considerable practice in this surgical speciality. In his preface he states 'without doubt there is no part of the habitable globe has afforded such an ample field for observations on injuries of the head—for our people soon catch fire; a slight offence is frequently followed by serious consequences and sticks, stones, and every other species of offence next to hand, are dealt out with great liberality—many of our fairs, patrons and hurling matches terminate in bloody conflicts.'

In 1775, John Gilborne, M.D., published a poem of 1084 lines entitled *The Medical Review*. This is a panegyric on the physicians, surgeons and apothecaries of Ireland marching in procession to the Temple of Fame. It was dedicated to Lord Trimleston and opens with some highly complimentary verses addressed to the noble gentleman, who is considered as reviewing the procession of medical men.

The leaders of the parade are the great doctors of the past: Galen, Vesalius, Boerhaave, Boyle, Harvey and others. A description of the Temple of Fame follows. The physicians of the day are named with a brief reference to outstanding points in their characters or achievements. The surgeons are classified under the institutions to which they belonged. After the section dealing with apothecaries, the gathering is addressed by the President of the assembly.

Although most of the names mentioned in this review are those of Dublin men, Gilborne made reference to several country practitioners. In some cases these brief lines are the only biographical details we possess of doctors who must have been well known, at least locally, in their day. Of physicians he mentions:

> The morning Star of Ossory is Drought,
> His Sound Opinion ne'er admits of doubt
> Clear Demonstrations all his Thoughts direct
> Point out the Cause and consequent effect.

> Matt. Dowdall who resides at Mullingar
> Thro' many Counties drives Apollo's Car;
> To those who suffer Anguish, Pain or Grief
> He gives immediate Comfort and Relief.

> John Martin practises with great Applause
> In Limerick which spurned Besiegers' Laws
> And Jeffry Connell has a Fortune made
> In Cork, a city of extensive trade.
> These two Physicians are so precious grown
> They can't be spar'd one Journey out of Town.

In the lines devoted to surgeons, Gilborne includes the following as eminent country practitioners:

> Young William Despard has instructed been
> In Maryborough County of the Queen.

There is no indication whether this instruction was merely Despard's ordinary schooling or whether it referred to professional training or apprenticeship.

> John Sproull, Chirurgeon of fair Town Strabane
> Cautious, defends the Patient's Back with Lawn
> Before he lays his Epispastic on.

> In Limerick O'Halloran abides
> And o'er the County Hospital presides.

Among the country apothecaries worthy of notice Gilborne includes:

James Donegan with precious Drugs supplies
The Country opulent that round him lies.
In Charleville he has his fixt Abode
From Cork to Limerick the thorough Road.

Of Durrow, Bathorn (George) full well is known
To Surgeon Broguen, who lives in Athlone.
To Surgeon Butler, who engrosses all
The fees that can afford both great and small.

I say that from Kilkenny to Athlone
The Fame of Bathorn is extensive known.
His sounding Mortar gave him vast Renown
He is too good for any Country Town.

All through the eighteenth century the difference between surgeons and physicians was such that they were scarcely regarded as members of the same profession. A physician held either the medical degree of a University or the licence of a College of Physicians, while the surgeon obtained his knowledge and qualification as the result of an apprenticeship. Very few surgeons possessed medical degrees.

This difference in status and education was not confined to Dublin. During the period of the Roman Empire there had been no distinction between physicians and surgeons. As far back as Hippocrates surgery had been equal in standing to medicine. With the dawn of Arabic predominance in medicine, surgery lost much of its status and by the beginning of the tenth century was practised almost exclusively by illiterates who had no proper training. The Edict of Tours (1163), *Ecclesia abhorret a sanguine*, although aimed at the malpractice of surgery by monks, was interpreted by many as a condemnation of all surgery. As a result the surgeon fell into still more disrepute.

Wilson's Dublin Directory for 1775 contains a list of physicians and surgeons practising in Dublin. Their numbers were as follows:

Fellows of the College of Physicians	11
Licentiates ” ”	10
Practitioners in midwifery (physicians)	12
Other physicians	15
Surgeons	49
Practitioners in midwifery (surgeons)	16

The apothecaries were the poor man's doctors and the nearest approach to general practitioners capable of dealing with all situations not requiring highly specialised skill.

Towards the close of the eighteenth century the authorities of

Trinity College became alarmed at the possibility of Nationalist sympathisers residing in the College and particularly of members of the College Corps, the equivalent of the modern F.C.A., being 'disloyal' to the occupying power.

As a result an investigation was made by the visitors to the College, Lord Clare, the Chancellor of Ireland, who was mainly reponsible for the Act of Union and Dr 'Paddy' Duigenan acting for the Archbishop of Dublin. The proceedings were most formal. The roll was called. As each member answered his name an oath was administered to him. He was then examined as to his membership or knowledge of unlawful organisations in the College.

One of the Fellows, Dr Whitley Stokes, admitted that he had been one of the United Irishmen in 1791, but had resigned as a result of their increased violence. He had protested against this violence but subscribed to a fund to relieve two imprisoned members. At the time of the visitation he was a captain in the College Corps. On one occasion when issuing ammunition to his unit he expressed the hope that it would not be used against fellow Irishmen.

As a punishment for his patriotism Stokes was precluded from acting as a tutor and disqualified for three years from sitting on the Board. When a vacancy occurred among the Senior Fellows in 1800 his name was passed over. After the Union he regained favour and received a Senior Fellowship in 1805. So much did he come into favour that he was appointed Regius Professor of Physic in 1830, a post which he held until his son William succeeded him in 1843.

Stokes was a great and humane man of wide sympathy and understanding. During the typhus epidemic of 1826 patients were housed in sheds, tents and even in open spaces, Stokes worked so whole-heartedly for their relief that he became a victim himself. Fortunately he recovered and graced his city until his death in 1845 at the age of eighty-two years. Wolfe Tone, in his *Autobiography*, mentions Whitley Stokes in appreciative terms, stating that his only fault was that he was too humane to be a successful revolutionary.

Whitley Stokes wrote little on medical matters. His treatise for the M.D. dealt with respiration, and in 1817 he published a small book on the necessity for isolation and disinfection in contagious disease. Apart from these, he published an English-Irish Dictionary, a reply to Paine's *Age of Reason* and a pamphlet refuting Malthus on Population. A little-known book of his was a satirical poem inspired by the circumstances attending the death of the Prebendary of Swords. The title reads *The satanical remembrancer, or, an interview between an apparition and an archbishop. A poem, founded on recent fact. To which is prefixed, an introductory letter with reflections on the reality of ghosts; addressed to Thomas C–bbe Esq., By Abednego Squib Esq.*

Although the importance of the medical individual declined slightly during the eighteenth century, with the growth of a corporate feeling amongst all branches of the profession there were several outstanding figures in contemporary life. Some of these have left permanent marks on the medical foundations, particularly in Dublin.

In 1755 Surgeon George Doyle, aided by a generous committee of lay people, established in Rainsfort Street a hospital especially for the treatment of venereal disease. Two years later it was transferred to George's Lane. In 1768 it went to Clarendon Street, and ten years afterwards it was transferred to the Buckingham Smallpox Hospital at Donnybrook. In 1792 premises in Townsend Street were occupied and a new board took over the management. The hospital was renamed 'Westmoreland' in honour of the Lord Lieutenant. The new board consisted of the Presidents and Vice-Presidents of the Colleges of Physicians and Surgeons, the Physician and Surgeon-General, the State Physician and Surgeon, the Surgeon to the King's Military Infirmary, the Professor of Surgery in the College of Surgeons and the two senior surgeons to the hospital. In 1819 the hospital was closed to male patients, who were subsequently treated at Steevens' and Sir Patrick Dun's. In 1946 the hospital was renamed for St Margaret of Cortona. However both medical and social developments made this hospital superfluous and some ten years later it was finally closed. The building was demolished and no trace now remains.

A private V.D. hospital in King Street was founded in 1758 but closed sixteen years later for want of money. There were also Lock Hospitals in Cork and Limerick, the latter of which was closed in 1849.

Henry Quin (1718–1791) was by far the most prominent Dublin physician of the eighteenth century. His family were of old native stock. At the time of Henry's birth in Dublin, they were scattered throughout the country in various walks of life. Henry's father was an apothecary, which may have decided his son's future. In 1743 he was admitted a Bachelor of Medicine of Dublin University. From that time until his reappearance in Dublin in 1749 as M.D. Padua, we have no record of his career. That his ability must have been recognised is evidenced by his appointment as King's Professor of Physic in Trinity College in the same year. He did not seek admission to the College of Physicians until the following year. In accordance with the rules of the College, he was not elected a Fellow for a further four years.

In 1762 Quin purchased a house in Stephen's Green (No. 101), which later became St Patrick's Nurses' Home. Although his practice and social influence must have been enormous, his name is often forgotten. He left no written works with the exception of a manuscript notebook, doubtfully attributed to him. He attached his name to no new process, treatment or disease.

During his attachment to the College of Physicians, Quin held many offices, including that of President on six occasions (1766, 1771, 1774, 1779 (twice) and 1781). His marriage into the Monck family secured his position in the highest social circles. He patronised the arts generously.

Charles William, Quin's second son, continued the family connection with medicine. He studied at Trinity College and Edinburgh University, where he qualified M.D. in 1779. On his return to Ireland he became Physician-General to the Army in Ireland and Physician to the Royal Hospital at Kilmainham.

Both the Quins had examined cases of what we now suspect to be tuberculous meningitis. They observed the minute tubercles on the membranes of the brain and recognised the inflammatory nature of the disease. Unfortunately, they failed to see its connection with pulmonary tuberculosis and missed a chance of medical immortality.

Richard Kirwan (1733–1812) was variously described as 'The Great Chemist of Ireland,' 'The Philosopher of Dublin' and the 'Nestor of English Chemistry.' Although not a doctor, his influence on the medical life of the eighteenth century was considerable. He was a member of many learned societies both at home and abroad as well as being President of the Royal Irish Academy for thirteen years. He was the only person ever to be granted the peculiar privilege of keeping his hat on while examining for the Fellowships of Trinity College.

In his youth Kirwan had been smuggled to France in order to study for the priesthood. After some years he found that he had no vocation and returned home to study science. His main interest was mineralogy. On this subject he published the first systematic textbook in English. His researches on minerals were of great importance both medically and industrially.

During the latter half of the eighteenth century patent medicines were advertised in all newspapers. Maredant's Antiscorbutic Drops which 'cured Leprosy, Scurvy, Ulcers, the King's Evil, Fistula, Piles, sore Eyes, and foul Blood' strove for supremacy over Fisher's Imperial Royal Golden Snuff, which 'infallibly cures all curable Disorders of the Head and Eyes especially Deafness and Noise in the ears; takes away all pains and headaches; instantly removes Drowsiness, Sleepiness, Giddiness, Vapours and Apoplexy.' Bennett's Stomachic Lozenges were sold, not by an apothecary, but by a cutler living in Essex Street. They were a 'speedy and certain remedy in Indigestion, Coldness, Weakness and relaxation of the stomach–as well as for the–Ill-effects of bad wine, sour Punch and stale Beer.'

Doctor Ryan, surgeon and man-midwife of Cope Street, advertised, complete with testimonials, his Pectoral Essence of Coltsfoot for coughs, colds, asthma, phthisis, wheezing and dyspnoea. His most notable cure was that of Captain Peter McLoughlin who, after only one bottle of the essence, was cured of galloping consumption with profuse bloodstained sputum. Dr Solomon, 'Operator for the Scurvy,' promised to publish lists of his cures three times a week in the *Dublin Evening Packet*.

In the cosmetic field Sieur du Bois' Pearl Water led from its rivals by streets. The advertisement deserves reproduction at some length:

(1) This Water (without being of the nature of paint) takes off those Freckles which fine skins are liable to and which are caused by Nitre in the air.
(2) It cleans the complexion, whitens a brown skin, opens its pores and gives it a new Polish.
(3) It dries up and heals pimples in a few days.
(4) It braces the skin and preserves it from wrinkles until old age.

John Fisher, bookseller, of Little Ship Street, also found patent medicines a good side-line, for he advertised Turlington's Balsam of Life, Genuine Jesuit's Drops, Anthony Daffy's Elixir of Health, Stoughton's Stomachic Drops and Genuine British Oil.

In general the eighteenth century was a strange mixture of empiricism, blind experiment, new discoveries and the beginnings of scientific method which were to lead to the great advances of the nineteenth. As usual, Ireland was handicapped by civil commotion. Although her population was increasing rapidly the great majority of these belonged to a proscribed faith, so that they could make little contribution to the general welfare.

Towards the close of the eighteenth century (1794) the Sick Poor Institution was established at Meath Street, Dublin, for the relief of the populous south-western quarter of the city. Some 60,000 persons were living, mostly in extreme poverty, in the Earl of Meath's Liberty and the adjoining streets. During the subsequent fifty years this area rapidly became a slum and breeding-ground for all forms of infectious disease. Without the services of the Institution even more serious epidemics than those of 1832 and 1847 might have arisen.

Reports of this Institution were published in the *Edinburgh Medical Journal* in 1830 and 1831 by Dominic Corrigan. All types of cases were admitted, and when Gordon Jackson, then senior physician, published his report in 1837, a total of 368,611 cases had been attended. Of these, 16,093 were seen in the preceding year. In 1830, a vaccination service was inaugurated and in 1851 poor-law dispensaries were established.

Portion of the premises was rented to the Poor Law Commissioners and the funds of the Institution were devoted to relieving the non-medical needs of the sick poor. The change of status was marked by the addition of the words 'Dorset Nourishment Dispensary' to the title. In 1893 a créche was opened, and since 1900 this has been the principal activity of the charity.

CHAPTER TEN

THE DUBLIN SCHOOL OF MIDWIFERY

In the eighteenth century the physician was the only medical practitioner with even a smattering of scientific training. The surgeons and apothecaries received their professional education as apprentices. Regulations as regards qualification and the right to practice were rarely enforced. Outside Dublin any quack could start practise and reap a rich reward. There was no hospital practice available, even for the physicians, except in Steevens', Mercer's, or the small Charitable Infirmary. Together these provided about 100 beds.

The positions of the obstetricians and midwives were even poorer. Midwifery was looked on by the physicians as wholly beneath their high calling. In case of difficulty they were sometimes called in consultation but, as they had never studied the subject, their advice was of little use. As for the midwives, their situation was worst of all. By their charter of 1692 the College of Physicians were given power to examine and license midwives. Prior to 1740 only four such licences were issued and of these only one was issued, in 1696 or 1697, to a woman, Mrs Cormack. Indeed the first definite statement on the subject was not made by the College until 1753, when it refused to licence in medicine any person practising midwifery. The general opinion on nurses and midwives may be gleaned from *Gilborne's Medical Review*:

> Of nurse-tenders a vile detested crowd
> And midwives screaming exclamations lowd,
> Their foul designs when disappointments cross
> With beggars' money they play pitch and toss,
> Their wretched fees stake down at dice and cards,
> At Wheel of Fortune risk their base rewards,
> They ramp and roar foreswearing blood and wounds
> And rage like hungry disappointed hounds.

This situation obtained elsewhere quite as much as in Ireland. Midwifery was learned the hard way, hard for the patient as much or more so as for the pupil midwife. A very few practitioners went

114

abroad to study along progressive lines. Dublin led the way to better things in 1745 with the foundation by Bartholomew Mosse of the first lying-in hospital in these islands.

Mosse (1712–1759) was born in Maryborough (now Portlaoise), where his father was rector. For his medical education he was apprenticed to a surgeon, John Stone. After a preliminary period in Minorca, as an army surgeon, he travelled extensively and studied midwifery in England, Holland and France. He returned to Dublin in 1742. Almost immediately, he was admitted a Licentiate in Midwifery of the King's and Queen's College of Physicians in Ireland. From that time, he specialised entirely in that subject.

When Mosse returned from the Continent he was horrified with the condition of the poor, lying-in woman; without skilled assistance in her home, she had no institution open to receive her. Mosse started agitating amongst his friends and, by 15th March 1745, had collected sufficient money to buy a house in George's Lane (now South Great George's Street) and install a few beds and meagre appliances. The building faced Fade Street, which would give its position as being approximately on the site occupied by Messrs. Cassidys or St George's Hall of the Dublin Central Mission, which is some yards withdrawn from the street. This house was originally the theatre in which Peg Woffington made her stage debut before her fifteenth year.

The first patient was Judith Rochford of St Andrew's Parish, who was delivered of a son on the 20th March 1745.

To quote again from the *Medical Review*:

> The founder was Bartholomew Mosse,
> Tho' dead! The Grateful still regret his loss;
> From small beginnings rose th' amazing plan.
> Few thought it would succeed when it began,
> He had no sooner crown'd his vast design
> Than cruel fate compelled him to resign.

A common method of obtaining money for charity was the presentation of concerts or drama. The first effort of this kind made by Mosse was the performance of 'The Distressed Mother.' Such a show attracted attention to the hospital as well as raising money directly. The proceeds of this and other plays enabled Mosse to enlarge the accommodation and lay on a piped water supply.

At the end of the first sixteen months the Governors of the hospital issued a report. During this period 209 women were admitted and 208 children were born. One woman died of puerperal fever and seven children of convulsions.

Subscriptions now began to arrive, in kind as well as in cash. James Taylor agreed to give six barrels of beer annually. The widow of the Archbishop of Cashel sent two beds with blankets and bolsters. Various other small gifts were received. Still the income was barely sufficient; expansion was impossible and Mosse decided to run a lottery. This met with some success, particularly as most of the winners subscribed to the hospital funds.

Mosse now determined to build a bigger hospital. He secured a site of four acres in Great Britain (now Parnell) Street, then a suburban area. On this he planned to build a hospital with 150 beds instead of the 28 available at George's Lane. At the same time he planned to lay out pleasure gardens which would pay for the upkeep of the new hospital. He was taking on a full-time task, for he was in sole charge of the existing hospital; he was deeply involved in the lotteries, and he depended for a livelihood on private practice. He succeeded in his plans and in 1757 the patients were transferred from George's Lane to the new Rotunda. The interest in the lease of the old building was transferred to the Governors of the Lock Hospital.

During the twelve and a half years of the original hospital's existence it had the following record:

Women Admitted	Children born		Twin Births	Maternal Mortality	Still Births	Infant Mortality
	Boys	Girls				
3,975	2,101	1,948	74	1.1%	119	10%

The new hospital received a timely grant of £6,000 from Parliament. Mosse received a further personal gift of £2,000.

The hospital was formally declared open on December 8th, 1757, by the Lord Lieutenant. On the same day Mary Rea and Elizabeth Knight were safely delivered of a son and daughter respectively.

There is very little information available about the early work and administration of the hospital. The infant mortality was at first very high, at one time over 12 per cent of all live births. The maternal mortality of less than 2 per cent was good for the period. The high infant mortality was mainly due to inexperience on the part of the attendants, inadequate equipment and lack of any aseptic precautions.

Despite his good figures Mosse still had to overcome the active opposition of his medical brethren. He was accused of self-advertisement, of fraud, and of all forms of malpractice. At one period he was imprisoned for debt. This has been disputed and he may have escaped imprisonment by leaving the country for some time. Despite these disappointments, he continued to plan for the expansion of his new hospital. At the end of 1758 he was taken ill and unable to attend to business. On the advice of friends he retired to Cullenswood, then a country district and now part of Ranelagh. He died there on 16th February 1759 at the age of forty-seven. He is buried in Donnybrook cemetery, but no stone marks his grave. Even in 1846 Sir William Wilde was unable to find any guide to its situation.

One of the features of the new hospital was the entertainment gardens. Concerts and amusements were provided here as a source of income. The yearly profit on them averaged £300. It was intended that the gardens should be decorated with statues standing on pedestals. On Mosse's death this plan was abandoned and the unoccupied pedestals still remain.

In November 1759, Dr (later Sir) Fielding Ould was appointed Master. His path was smoothed by a generous parliamentary grant both to the hospital and to Mosse's family.

Ould (1710–1789) had been assistant to Mosse for some years. During this period he published his Treatise on Midwifery, containing original accounts on the mechanism of labour, haemorrhage, destructive operations on the child, and other subjects.

Ould learned his obstetrics in Paris. When he commenced practice in Dublin in 1738 he was licensed in midwifery by the College of Physicians. According to the licence his practice was limited to that of midwifery. Despite this he undertook the treatment of non-maternity patients. In retaliation, members of the College refused to meet him in consultation.

Ould applied to Dublin University for permission to sit for an Arts examination preparatory to an examination for a medical degree. Special permission was given despite existing agreements between the University and the College. The College thereupon refused to admit obstetricians to medical degrees. When Ould eventually obtained a *liceat ad examinandum* from Trinity, it was refused by the College. In 1761, the Board of Trinity granted him their M.D. degree. As a result the College of Physicians broke off relations with the University. Towards the end of his life Ould was admitted a Licentiate in Medicine of the College, but never received a Fellowship.

Before the dispute Ould had been knighted. At the time he was the leading obstetrician in Dublin. Amongst the notable births at which he attended was that of the Duke of Wellington. Probably much of Ould's reputation depends on the period in which he lived, and that he was self-opinionated seems undoubted. At the same time he did much solid work, both administrative and clinical, and may be regarded almost as a co-founder of the Rotunda.

Until 1767, the hospital was known as the Dublin Hospital for

Poor Lying-in Women. In this year a new circular entertainment room was finished. This Round-Room, or Rotunda gave the now well-known name to the original foundation. Its primary purpose was to assist in raising funds. In 1947, negotiations were opened for the erection of a State Concert Hall on the Round-Room site, but this plan was later abandoned in favour of the present premises at Earlsfort Terrace.

One of Mosse's objects in founding a maternity hospital was the establishment of a teaching centre. Neither he nor Ould, however, was very successful in this, although students attended the practice of the hospital and received informal lectures. The subject became an urgent one about the middle of the eighteenth century with the development of schools in London and Edinburgh.

Under Sir Patrick Dun's will Nathaniel Barry was appointed Professor of Chirurgery and Midwifery to Trinity in 1749. It is doubtful if he ever lectured in midwifery. About 1763 John Charles Fleury was appointed Lecturer in Midwifery. In his memoirs he records that he gave practical instruction in patients' houses as well as theoretical lectures. He abandoned this instruction in 1769. The out-patient department was founded in 1771. It was temporarily closed in 1777 for lack of funds.

In 1770 during the mastership of William Collum (*circa* 1710–1782) it was suggested that instruction should be given in the hospital. In November of that year the Committee ordered that a room should be fitted-up as a theatre for lectures on diseases of women and children to both students and female midwives. David McBride was recommended as lecturer. A rather cumbersome method of selecting pupil-midwives from the counties was adopted with the dual object of spreading knowledge and advertising the hospital. The first midwives recorded as qualifying under these rules were: Mrs Shaw of Wexford (1772) and Mary Grogan of Limerick (1773). In 1773 it was decided to employ full-time nurses in the hospital as well as using the services of the student midwives. This is substantially the method adopted in most hospitals to-day.

The proposal to establish a school of midwifery met with considerable opposition. Several pamphlets and articles were published by both sides, including one which claimed that patients of the hospital would be subjected to all sorts of indignities by 'a parcel of Brats of Boys, the Apprentices of Surgeons and Apothecaries.' Curiously enough, Collum, although Master, was opposed to the foundation of a school. He was succeeded by Frederick Jebb in 1773.

Under Jebb, David McBride commenced a course of lectures which he repeated over a period of several years. From the time of Jebb, the Master and his family were obliged to reside in the hospital. Jebb held his mastership during most difficult times, as a result of which he was unable to make any great advances. He became involved in political affairs and was generally believed to have accepted a substantial bribe from the Government to stop publishing pamphlets attacking their corruption and ineptitude.

In 1785, an Act of Parliament was passed, imposing an annual tax of thirty-five shillings on all private sedan chairs in the city, the proceeds to be devoted to the hospital funds. This scheme brought in over £2,200 in the first six years. A similar scheme had been in operation since 1727 for the benefit of the Foundling Hospital.

The career of Henry Rock, who was elected Master in 1780 and died in office six years later, was marked by few outstanding events. He published the first annual report and was active in obtaining parliamentary support for the construction of new entertainment rooms. The records of the hospital during this period contain many references to financial difficulties, lack of space and suggestions for raising funds.

Joseph Clark (1758–1834) was appointed Master in 1786. His great contribution was a reduction of the infant mortality rate from 1 in 6 to 1 in 19. He stopped the practice of two women sharing a bed and introduced a students' register. Clark demonstrated anatomy in T.C.D. whilst in active maternity practice. This contributed to a high maternal death-rate during his mastership. At no time, however, did the rate touch that reached during one month of Labatt's mastership in 1820. Of 171 patients admitted, 61 contracted puerperal sepsis and 25 died.

The mastership of Thomas Kelly, from 1800 to 1807, was marked by constant bickerings and squabbles. He was accused by the matron and by the governors of discharging dangerously ill patients so that their deaths would not appear in the hospital returns. Kelly tendered his resignation in 1807 and sued the governors for defamation of character. He died in 1841 with his law case still unsettled.

After several serious outbreaks of puerperal sepsis, matters reached a climax in Robert Collins' (d. 1868) mastership in 1829. Things were so bad that patients were advised to stay at home and the Lord Lieutenant threatened to close the hospital. Collins adopted vigorous measures, mainly fumigation of the wards with chlorine, roasting of mattresses and linen, whiter washing the walls with chloride of lime and the use of wards in rotation. Treatment still consisted of frequent bleedings, leeching, violent purgation and hot stupes to the abdomen.

Evory Kennedy, who held office from 1833 to 1840, had the melancholy distinction of publishing the highest maternal mortality rate in the annals of the hospital. Typhus, cholera, dysentery, and other diseases reached pandemic proportions throughout Europe in 1833. In Ireland nearly 25 per cent of the doctors died of some infectious disease and in Dublin alone there were 5,600 deaths from cholera in one year.

Although Kennedy's figures for deaths from puerperal sepsis and other diseases were bad, he cannot be blamed as overcrowding and poor sanitation combined to make outbreaks of this disease truly deadly.

In 1869, nearly thirty years after his mastership ended, Kennedy read a paper to the Obstetrical Society which showed evidence of close study of the teachings of Holmes and Semmelweiss. This work was entitled 'Hospitalism and Zymotic Diseases as more especially illustrated by Puerperal fever or Metria.' This paper occupied in all eleven meetings of the society, two for its reading and nine for discussion. One of Kennedy's most important points, that infection could be carried by doctor and nurse from case to case, was ridiculed by many of his hearers.

Kennedy's most lasting monument was the gynaecological department which opened in 1835 as a single ward 'for the humane and beneficial purpose of alleviating the suffering of patients labouring under the diseases peculiar to women.'

The mastership of Charles Johnson (1840–1847), who had previously been Professor of Midwifery in the College of Surgeons, coincided with the famine period in Ireland. Elsewhere several great events came to the public eye for the first time. Oliver Wendell Holmes read a paper on 'The Contagiousness of Puerperal Fever' in Boston. Horace Wells used nitrous oxide anaesthesia. Semmelweiss recognised some of the causes of puerperal sepsis. Simpson was using chloroform in labour. Theodore Hermann of Berne described the axis traction forceps. In Ireland the potato famine with the resultant fever and emigration reduced the population by some two million people.

During the 1840's the main problem interesting obstetricians was the employment of chloroform in midwifery both in labour and in the control of convulsions. The Dublin school took a prominent part in the discussions of this as well as the problem of puerperal fever. Unfortunately their record in the latter is a poor one. There were several outbreaks of sepsis in the Rotunda. Better ventilation was introduced and unnecessary draperies around the beds removed. Washing and sanitary facilities for the inmates were improved, but the first water-closets were not erected until 1855 in McClintock's (1822–1881) mastership.

Sir William Wilde, the noted Dublin ophthalmologist, had studied with Semmelweiss at Vienna. The terrible results of puerperal sepsis were well known to him. His comments while still a young man show that he recognised how the unhealthy surroundings of the patients had much to do with the spread of the disease:

The doctors did not consider it infectious and therefore no precaution is ever taken to prevent its spread by cleansing, fumigating, white-washing or shutting up certain wards where it has particularly prevailed for any length of time. I myself have seen a newly-delivered woman placed in a bed scarcely yet cold, in which a death from puerperal fever had taken place not two hours before! From my own observations I am inclined to attribute the frequency and fatality of this terrible scourge to the want of proper ventilation in addition to the necessarily crowded state of the wards and to the most unjustifiable practice that I have just detailed.

The Rotunda was closed in 1866 during the mastership of John Denham (1806–1887) owing to a severe outbreak of puerperal sepsis. Despite the work of Semmelweiss the use of isolation wards in childbirth fever was not suggested in Dublin until 1870 by Evory Kennedy. Arthur Macan (1843–1908), Master from 1882 to 1889, was the first in Ireland to insist that students of an anatomy school should not enter the Rotunda.

In 1889 Macan recorded the first successful Caesarean section in the Rotunda. The undertaking was doubly notable, as Macan later confessed that he had relied solely on written accounts of the operation and had never seen it performed. In 1816, Charles Hawkes Todd had performed Caesarean section on a woman named Elizabeth M'Lorey at Loughbrickland, Co. Down. The mother died four days later, but the child survived.

During Macan's mastership his assistant, William Neville, read a paper on his traction handle for Barnes' forceps. This is now a standard modification of Barnes' original design. By reason of its multiple joints Neville's axis tractor allows the child's head and the forceps' blades to move as one during delivery. An arrow on the tractor indicates the correct direction for the traction to be applied.

Lombe Atthill (1827–1910) was one of the most progressive Masters of the Rotunda. He developed the use of blood transfusions in post-partum haemorrhage; reorganised the extern maternity service and insisted on the use of carbolic washing of the hands before examination and delivery. His book, *Clinical Lectures on the Diseases Peculiar to Women*, was translated into French and Spanish. Atthill abandoned the use of the clinical thermometer lest it should worry the patients.

One of the things of which the Rotunda Hospital has the most reason to be proud is its record in the fight against eclampsia, a condition in which pregnant women become poisoned by an unknown toxin with the occurrence of violent convulsions. During the first half of the nineteenth century a death-rate of 20 per cent. was constantly recorded. It was recognised by Sinclair and Johnston, writing in 1858, that antenatal care could do a great deal to prevent the disease from developing. They recommended purgation, rest and a light diet as a preventive, with opium and bleeding for an established case. They recognised an association between albuminuria and eclampsia.

In 1896, E. H. Tweedy (1862–1945) read a paper before the Royal Academy of Medicine in Ireland in which he disputed many of the current views on eclampsia. He recommended: control of the convulsions by morphine; starvation, except for copious fluids; efficient purgation; and stimulants and bleeding if necessary. As a result of this treatment the maternal mortality rate from eclampsia was halved.

Tweedy has ample claim to be considered one of the great Rotunda Masters. Aseptic precautions were improved and enforced during his term of office. New beds were opened and individual cases could be kept for a minimum of eight days. In 1907 a new nurses' home was opened. In 1910, an intern mortality rate of 0.35 per cent was recorded, the lowest to that date for a complete mastership.

Henry Jellett's (1872–1948) name is familiar to every English-speaking student of midwifery, for his textbook on the subject ran to many editions. He was appointed Master in 1910, but left to join the British Army in 1914. During his absence the hospital was under the joint mastership of William J. Smyly, Richard Dancer Purefoy and Tweedy, all previous Masters. During this period Dr Mabel Crawford, the first woman Assistant Master in the history of the hospital, acted. Jellett returned in 1917, with a *Croix de Guerre* and other decorations. He was permitted to resume his mastership until 1919, when he retired to live in New Zealand until his death.

Gibbon Fitzgibbon held office during the stormy period of the Anglo-Irish and Civil Wars. Despite this, much sterling work was done in the Rotunda and many advances were made. During his term of office (1919–1926) there were 13,234 deliveries 'on the district.'

At the beginning of Bethel Solomons' mastership in 1926 the hospital was still dependent on subscriptions, legacies, gifts, rents and paying patients for its upkeep. In 1932 the Governors decided to participate in the Irish Hospitals' Sweepstake scheme.

The most outstanding event during Andrew Davidson's term of office (1933–1940) was the introduction, in 1936 by Domagk, of Red Prontosil for the treatment of puerperal sepsis. In the first full year for which a Rotunda report was issued after this discovery only one death from childbirth fever occurred in the hospital.

During Ninian McI. Falkiner's mastership, in 1945, the hospital entered on its third century of service to the poor lying-in women of Dublin. Owing to emergency conditions no celebrations were possible until July 1947, when an International Gynaecological Congress was held in Dublin. On the occasion of this congress Dr O'Donel Browne, later Master, compiled and published a comprehensive history of the hospital from its foundation until 1945.

The welfare of the newly born baby has always been a prime concern of the obstetrician but from the 1950's onwards sophisticated equipment made pre-natal assessment ever more accurate with greatly improved chances of fragile babies being delivered at the optimum time. In the Rotunda since 1971 these developments received major help from the independent fund-raising Friends of the Rotunda one of whose primary aims is to finance research into the causes and prevention of congenital mental and physical handicaps. In 1976 the Rotunda research facilities were further improved when the Chester Beatty Research Laboratory was set up in the Department of Obstetrics and Gynaecology of Trinity College. One can visualize an approving if slightly puzzled Bartholemew Mosse watching the developments of his great idea after nearly two and a half centuries.

THE COOMBE HOSPITAL

In October 1823, John Kirby, in association with two members of the staff of his private medical school, Michael Daniell and Richard Gregory, opened a general hospital with fifty beds in the house in the Coombe which formerly had been the Meath Hospital. His main reason for doing so was that his students might have the advantage of clinical instruction, which was necessary for Army and Navy Surgeoncies at the time.

Of all Dublin hospitals, the Meath seems to have been the most peripatetic. Founded in 1753 in the Coombe, the hospital moved in 1757 to Skinner's Alley, in 1760 to Meath Street, in 1766 to Earl Street. On returning to the Coombe in 1771 there was no further move until the present site in Long Lane and Heytesbury Street was occupied, in 1822.

In 1826, there was a combination of fever and severe weather which rendered the lot of the Dublin poor more miserable then ever. In October of that year it was stated that there were 1,381 fever patients in the Dublin hospitals and 3,433 ill in their own homes. The Rotunda was still the only lying-in hospital and it was turning away patients daily.

A committee was formed to collect subscriptions and a large ward was opened in Kirby's hospital for the reception of maternity patients. At the same time arrangements were made for attendance in their own homes of those who did not wish to come into hospital. On 5th February 1829, the hospital was devoted entirely to maternity work, Richard Reed Gregory being appointed first Master. He died within a year, of typhus.

The hospital, when opened as a lying-in institution, contained thirty-six beds, divided amongst four wards. One of these was a pay ward. Shortly afterwards a fifth ward, containing six more beds, and an out-patient department, were opened.

In the first report of the hospital, issued in 1830, Gregory recorded '691 patients have been delivered in the hospital and 196 attended in their own homes.' Of 703 children born in the house, 55 were still-born. There was no account of maternal mortality or morbidity.

In order to raise money a Grand Dress Ball, attended by the Lord Lieutenant and his family, was held in Morrison's Great Rooms in February 1831.

After Gregory's death, the hospital remained closed for eight months. Thomas McKeever then took over the mastership until 1835, when he resigned. In this year, Hugh Carmichael and Robert Power were appointed joint Masters, with a resident medical officer.

In 1836, for some unexplained reason, the Governors of the Coombe included an Ophthalmic Dispensary in the scope of their work. For nine years a dispensary was held daily and although there are no records of an intern department, presumably cases were admitted when necessary. Robert Graves and John Kirby, the physician and surgeon, were both attached to the National Eye Hospital. Hugh Carmichael was also interested in ophthalmology. These circumstances may have been responsible for the addition. It seems rather an unwise move in view of the efforts of the Rotunda to discredit the Coombe as a maternity hospital.

A glance at the hospital records at this time is interesting. During the ten years ending 1841, there had been admitted 4,349 women, who gave birth to 4,010 live children; 38 of the mothers died and 388 children. There were 376 still-births.

The hospital continued to maintain the connection with Kirby's school and its successor, Ellis's. It developed a teaching tradition and Coombe certificates were recognised by the Colleges of Surgeons in Dublin, Edinburgh and London, as well as by the Army, Navy and Indian Medical Services. The authorities of the Rotunda saw that their pre-eminence was being challenged and made several attempts to discredit the work of the Coombe.

Carmichael, Power and, later, William Jameson were all attached to the Peter Street Medical School. Their students had the benefit of lectures and practice under the same teachers. In the hospital there was accommodation for six resident pupils as well as an extern class.

The fees charged were lower than those in the Rotunda and, for a while, a price-cutting war was waged between the two hospitals. Both issued certificates of proficiency to their students. Evory Kennedy petitioned the Council of the College of Surgeons to refuse recognition of Coombe Certificates on the ground that the Rotunda was the only chartered lying-in hospital. He failed in this, as well as in attempts to introduce clauses unfavourable to the Coombe in the Medical Charities Bill. In accordance with the custom of the day, both sides published and distributed pamphlets.The Rotunda claimed that the whole design and site of the Coombe was unsuitable for its purpose. The Coombe pointed out that despite this it had had only two cases of puerperal fever in six years, while at the Rotunda the disease was almost always present.

The Coombe emerged victorious from the battle; so much so that the Select Committee, which investigated the Dublin hospitals in 1854, recommended that a Parliamentary grant of £200 per annum should be paid to the hospital. In addition private persons were so impressed by the clinical and educational work of the Coombe that several large sums came as gifts and legacies.

In 1851, Benjamin Lee Guinness, Lord Mayor of Dublin, presided at the first annual public meeting. Thus began the happy connection between the Guinness family and the Coombe; a connection which redounds so much to the credit of the former and the benefit of the latter.

When Carmichael and Power resigned in 1841, their places were taken by Michael O'Keeffe, John Ringland (1816–1876) and Henry Cole. In 1845, O'Keeffe John Ringland (1816–1876) and Sawyer (1812–1875). In 1847, Cole resigned. His place was not filled.

The Coombe system of mastership differed considerably from that of the Rotunda. The joint Masters and the assistant were non-resident and appointed for an indefinite period. The routine work was done by a junior Resident Apothecary and Accoucheur, who held office for a brief period. As the senior officers held important and lucrative posts outside the Coombe, it was possible for the hospital to have able men on the staff despite the difficult financial position.

In 1864, it was decided that Ringland and Sawyer should hold office for life, but that from the time a vacancy occurred it would be filled by a single Master only. Future Masters were to hold office for seven years. One or two assistants were to be appointed for three-year terms. The general charge of the house was entrusted to a Resident Apothecary. In cases of abnormal labour he was bound to call the Master or an assistant. A pupil midwifery assistant was appointed to take charge of the extern midwifery under the direction of the apothecary. The dispensary was controlled by a special medical officer.

In 1858, the Rotunda made further efforts to discredit the Coombe on the occasion of the passage of the Medical Bill in Parliament. The Rotunda Governors claimed that as their hospital was chartered, it was entitled to have its Licentiate in Midwifery recognised as a registrable qualification. The Poor Law Commissioners thereupon became doubtful of the validity of the Coombe Licentiate for Poor Law Medical Officers, although in practice it had been accepted for several years. After some difficulty and delay the Coombe obtained a charter in 1867.

Unfortunately, the buildings were now in a ruinous condition; so much so, that for eight months, all patients were sent to the Maternity in Peter Street, where the Governors paid for their maintenance at the rate of one shilling per day. Benjamin Guinness came to the rescue with a sum of £2,500 for a new wing, Out-Patient Department and isolation ward. This work was not completed until 1872 owing to legal and architectural difficulties. At one period the ground under the new buildings subsided and the work of years was ruined. Mr Guinness gave a further £2,500 to cover the increased cost of the work.

In 1873, Mr Quinn, the contractor died suddenly. The architect declared that his estimate was hopelessly inadequate and that any new tender would be much higher. The Residency now showed signs of collapsing and the medical officers were obliged to move to Cork Street. As if this were not enough, the popular press commented unfavourably on the high daily cost of maintenance of patients in the Coombe. This effectually quashed any hopes of obtaining money by public subscription.

Sir Arthur Guinness now proposed to the Governors that the hospital should be handed over to him, with any available moneys, that he would complete the building and hand it back when the work was finished. His offer was accepted and in 1877 the new hospital was opened. Outside of his original proposal, Guinness refurnished the buildings and handed them over as a going concern. Unfortunately, neither Ringland nor Sawyer lived to see the new Coombe.

In 1876, George Hugh Kidd (1824–1895) was appointed Master for seven years, the first under the new charter to be elected for this period. He had had wide experience in midwifery and gynaecology. As well as his work in the Coombe he was interested in the welfare of feeble-minded children and the foundation of the Palmerston Institution for such cases is largely due to his efforts.

Kidd's appointment was marked by the introduction of aseptic and antiseptic methods to the practice of the hospital. His first report contained recommendations for the disinfection of clothing which had been in contact with septic patients. Despite improved techniques, however, the average maternal mortality rate in Kidd's mastership was still about 1.5 per cent. Like Semmelweiss, he recognised the relationship between students' attendance at post-mortems and the incidence of puerperal sepsis. In the year 1879–1880 only one woman died out of five hundred delivered.

In 1884, the hospital admitted the then record number of 782 patients as well as giving attention to a total of 8,201 in the dispensary and 1,818 women in their own homes. In 1893, the Guardians and Directors of the hospital sought for a sworn enquiry into alleged irregularities in the conduct of hospital affairs. The Board of Superintendence of the Dublin Hospitals duly held the enquiry and issued recommendations for the improved staffing and management of the hospital. These included the election of a matron, increased numbers of nurses and strict control of drugs and antiseptic precautions.

The recommendations and improvements did much to restore the reputation of the hospital and in the following year the Visiting Committee of the Dublin Hospital Sunday Fund reported a marked improvement in the condition of the buildings.

In 1897, 418 deliveries were conducted in the hospital without a single death, a striking tribute to the antiseptic technique of the staff.

Since that time the work of the hospital was marked by steady progress on the educational and clinical side. The centenary was celebrated in 1926 by the holding of a gynaecological congress in Dublin.

In 1939 plans had been prepared for the rebuilding of the Coombe on the site to be vacated when the Cork Street Fever Hospital moved elsewhere but, as with so much else, these were disrupted by building shortages due to the war and it was not until 1967 that the Coombe Lying-in Hospital was transferred to the present site at Dolphin's Barn, Cork Street, the first patients being admitted on the 27th of July that year.

These much more extensive premises have a total bed complement of 310, divided betwen maternity, gynaecological and paediatric services, the last being largely responsible for the remarkably low death rate of 1 per 1000 normal live births. In 1981 the only maternal death recorded was due to a non-obstetric cause.

Recent developments included the establishment of a teaching unit and a Research Committee. In 1981 Dr Bernard Stuart was awarded a Florence and William Blair Bell Lectureship by the Royal College of Obstetricians and Gynaecologists, the first time this prestigious honour was granted for work done in Ireland, though three previous Irish graduates had received it for research carried out elsewhere.

The later Masters of the Coombe were:

S. R. Mason		1883–1890
J. C. Hoey	1890–1893	(resigned)
F. W. Kidd		1893–1900
T. G. Stevens		1900–1907
M. J. Gibson		1907–1914
R. A. McLaverty		1914–1921
L. L. Cassidy	1921–1928	(died in office)
T. M. Healy		1928–1935
R. M. Corbet		1935–1942
E. A. Keelan		1942–1949
J. K. Feeney		1949–1956
J. J. Stewart		1957–1963
W. Gavin		1963–1970
J. Clinch		1971–1977
N. Duignan		1978–

THE NATIONAL MATERNITY HOSPITAL

The 'National,' in Holles Street, is the youngest of Dublin's maternity hospitals. Towards the end of the nineteenth century the Rotunda and Coombe provided adequately for the North City and the congested district about St Patrick's Cathedral. A few small private maternity hospitals whose primary purpose was the provision of midwifery certificates to medical students had closed after the reorganisation of professional education. As a result the Ringsend, South Quays, and Westland Row districts were left with no convenient maternity service.

In 1884, a hospital was opened in Holles Street under the supervision of Dr William Roe. This lasted until 1893, always in a very poor financial state.

In the following year, under the joint mastership of Sir Andrew Horne (d. 1925) and Dr P. J. Barry (d. 1919) the hospital was re-opened. Two adjoining houses had been bought and an influential committee of management appointed.

Although the medical and lay staff of the hospital was an efficient and energetic one the buildings in which they worked were quite unsuitable. Large sums of money were required to keep them in repair and expansion was impossible. Two houses were purchased in 1901, but lack of funds prevented their proper development.

In 1902, the hospital received a royal charter which assured its future management. In 1906 a new wing was built. This made it possible to provide an operating theatre and to double the number of patients admitted. These improvements involved the hospital in an overdraft of £4,000. In addition to the work done in the hospital, 10,000 visits per year were paid to patients in their own homes.

During 1907, the tenure of office of the first Masters came to an end. Sir Andrew Horne elected to remain, with Dr R. J. White (d. 1942) as joint Master.

In 1913, the architect to the hospital reported that structural alterations were impossible and that a new site should be sought without delay. The first World War both doubled maintenance costs and made new building schemes impracticable. By great efforts sufficient funds were raised to clear outstanding debts. Until 1930, in the last years of Dr P. McArdle's (d. 1946) mastership no improvements could be carried out. In that year the Irish Hospitals' Sweepstakes were inaugurated, with the active participation of members of the National Maternity Hospital's Board. The Hospital's urgent need was made a first charge on Sweepstakes' funds and in 1934 a new wing was opened.

Dr (later Professor) John Cunningham was appointed to the mastership in 1931. In recognition of his ability and resource in pushing forward the great improvements in the building, his term of office was considered as beginning with the opening of the new wing, so that he held his post for ten years. The hospital's charter was amended in 1936 and in the following year the second portion of the hospital was opened.

Dr Alex W. Spain was Master from 1941 until 1948, a period during which enormous advances were made in clinical midwifery, but during which building and reconstruction were almost impossible. During Spain's mastership a record low maternal mortality figure of 1.2 per thousand was achieved in 1946.

The most recent Masters of the National Maternity Hospital have been

Arthur P. Barry	1949–1955
Charles F. Coyle	1956–1962
Kieran O'Driscoll	1963–1969
Declan J. Meagher	1970–1976
Dermot W. Mac Donald	1977–

By 1968 the hospital was bursting at the seams and there was a very real risk that crowding and pressure of work would reduce the high standards now regarded as normal. A 45 bed extension with additional delivery and laboratory facilities eased the situation but even though Holles Street is now one of the largest maternity hospitals in Europe some 9,000 births per year pose huge problems of accommodation and clinical services.

A great deal of pioneer work has been undertaken, ranging from the use of highly sophisticated techniques such as electronic monitoring of the foetal heart to the more personal but equally important relaxation of visiting rules and the involvement of husbands and other family members in what is still basically a natural human function.

THE TEACHING OF MIDWIFERY

Although the final place to learn midwifery thoroughly must be the labour ward, theoretical training is of importance. For this reason the teaching bodies and the hospitals must always find themselves in ever closer alliance.

The association between the Rotunda Hospital and the College of Surgeons has always been a particularly cordial one. It was fitting that the College's Chair of Midwifery, founded in 1785, should be the first in Ireland.

The first applicant was not accepted and the Chair was not filled until 1789, when John Halahan (1753–1813), the Professor of Anatomy and Physiology, was appointed until 1793. He was succeeded by Sir Henry Jebb (d. 1811), whose brother Frederick was Master of the Rotunda from 1773 to 1780.

The first occupant of the College of Physicians Chair of Midwifery was William Montgomery (d. 1859), who was largely responsible for its foundation in 1827. In 1837 he published *An Exposition of the Signs and Symptoms of Pregnancy, the Period of Human Gestation, and the Signs of Delivery*. When he died, Arneth of Vienna in an obituary notice said: 'He leaves a name which is known and honoured wherever Midwifery is practised.' His museum of obstetrical subjects was sold to Queen's (now University) College, Galway, where it is still in use for teaching.

Fleetwood Churchill succeeded Montgomery in 1856. He published numerous books and papers on obstetrics, paediatrics and gynaecology. He resigned the Chair in 1867 and retired to Tyrone where he died in 1879.

In 1865, the Chair was raised to the dignity of a King's Professorship. Shortly after this Edward Sinclair (d. 1882) took over from Churchill. Sinclair opened a scheme for training soldiers' wives as midwifery nurses, in 1869, in Dun's Hospital. In recognition of this he received a knighthood in 1880. The Mastership of Obstetrics

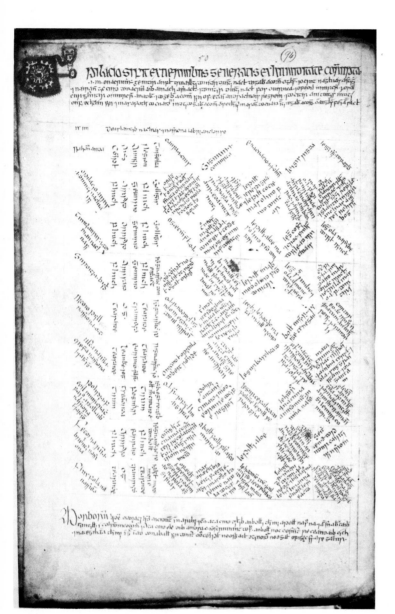

1. A page from the *Rosa Anglica*.

2. Sir Patrick Dun (1642 – 1713).

Orders and Resolutions with respect to S.
Patrick Dun's Will. Feb. 2ᵈ 171⁴/₅.

Ordered that it be entered as the Resolution
of the College that a Sum not exceeding one
hundred Pounds Sterling be expended by the
Committee, Dr. Cummyng, Dr. Molyneux
and Dr. Worth towards defraying the charges of making Sr. Patrick Dun's will effectu-
al for the use of the Publick.

Ordered at the same time that a Letter of
Attorney be drawn empowering the Committee
aforesaid to act in behalf of the College in
expending the said Sum for the said Use. —
and that the Seal of the College be thereunto
affixed with the Hands of the President and the
rest of the Fellows. —

Ordered that the Professor Dr. Molyneux and
Dr. Helsham do wait on the Provost to acquaint
him with the design of setling a Professor in
the College of Physicians of Dublin by the Kings
Letters Patents.

Rickd: Helsham   Ja: Grattan Prov.
Bry: Robinson   Bryan Cummyng   Tho: Molyneux
                 Richd: Hoyle   Wm: Smyth

3. Instructions relating to the will of Sir Patrick Dun.

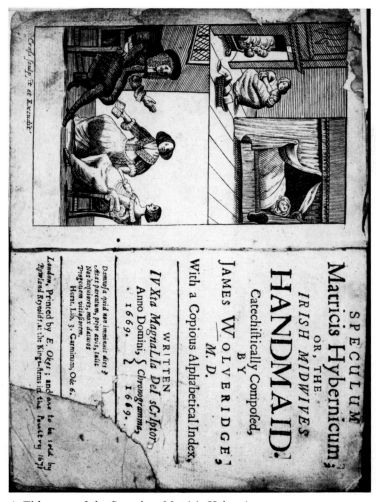

4. Title page of the *Speculum Matricis Hybernicum*.

The 15 *th. preternatural birth cured,
with the feet, what is to be done in this
case?*

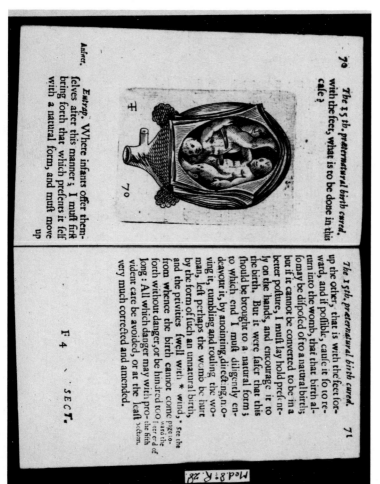

70

Answer.

Entrap. Where infants offer themselves after this manner; I must first bring forth that which presents it self with a natural form, and must move up

---

up the other, that is with the feet forward, and if possible, cause it so to return into the womb, that that birth also may be disposed of to a natural birth; but if it cannot be converted to be in a better posture, I must lay hold presently on the hands, and encourage it to the birth. But it were safer that this should be brought to a natural form; to which end I must diligently endeavour it, by anointing, directing, moving it, tumbling and rouling the woman, lest perhaps the womb be hurt by the form of such an unnatural birth, and the privities swell with * wind; * from whence the birth cannot come forth without danger, or be hindred too long: All which danger may with provident care be avoided, or at the least very much corrected and amended.

See the page toward the ter end of the fifth section.

F 4 SECT.

5. Twin births from the *Speculum Matricis Hybernicum.*

6. Charles Lucas (1713 — 1771).

A Yearly Bill of Mortality for the City and Suburbs of Dublin Ending the
26th of December, 1762

| Males buried this Year | 1273 | Males baptized this Year | 1043 |
| Females buried this Year | 1217 | Females baptized this Year | 1447 |

Increafed in Burials this Year   198
Increafed in Chriftnings this Year 281

Of the Difeafes and Cafualties this Year

Aged	225	Fits	200	Suddenly	46
Afthma	43	Flux	4	Small pox	370
Ague	2	Gout	18	Suffocated in Lime-kiln	5
Bloody-flux	6	Gravel	2	Sore Throat	01
Child-bed	2	Jaundice	11	Spotted Fever	03
Confumption	79	Inflammat. Lungs	2	Teeth	65
Convulfions	3	Lunatick	2	Murdered	04
Decay	184	Meazles	86	Worm-Fever	03
Drowned	14	Palfey	7	Executed	04
Dropfy	8	Quinfey	23		
Fever	960	Rickets	5		

7. Bill of Mortality for the City and Suburbs of Dublin, 1762.

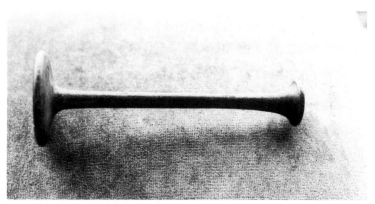

8. An early stethescope.

COLLECTANEA
HIBERNICA MEDICA.

BEING

A COLLECTION of, and REPOSITORY for,
PAPERS of ADVICE, DISCUSSION, and RE-
SEARCH, in all Departments of MEDICINE.

INTENDED

Not only to hand to Pofterity, in abftract Pieces
of Difquifition, the Refult of our Improvements
in that Line, but alfo to excite a Spirit of
Medical and Phyfico-Medical Enquiry
through this Kingdom.

NUMBER I.

Written ENTIRELY——as an Experiment of Public Tafte,
as well as to make a Beginning.

As thofe PAPERS will in future be collected, and pub-
lifhed in fubfequent Numbers,

By RICHARD HARRIS, M.D.
PHYSICIAN at CLONMELL.

———— *Quid tentare nocebit ?*
OVID.

———— *Fungor vice cotis, acutum*
Reddere quæ ferrum valet, exors ipfa fecundi.
HOR.

DUBLIN:

Printed by J. EXSHAW, No. 98, Grafton ftreet
M DCC LXXXIII.

9. Title page of the first issue of the *Collectanea Hibernica Medica*.

(M.A.O.) was established in Trinity in 1876. The B.A.O. degree was not established until 1887.

Under present regulations the medical student is obliged to attend lectures in midwifery and gynaecology both in his school and in a recognised hospital. The requirements vary slightly between the various examining bodies. Those of the College of Surgeons summarised below are typical. A candidate must produce evidence of having attended a recognised course of lectures in obstetrics and gynaecology and, in addition, of having spent a month in residence in a maternity hospital during which he or she has personally conducted a number of labour cases. Gynaecological and Obstetrical practical instruction as well as experience in the care of the newly born is also required.

When the first edition of this book appeard a very major part of the medical students obstetrical experience was still obtained 'on the district'. Students would attend maternity patients in their own homes and conduct normal deliveries. If complications arose they were expected to send for assistance from the hospital. The system had the educational advantage of introducing students to the very area in which much of their work would later be carried out, the patient's own home. They were likely to be asked questions from far outside the field of midwifery. Unfortunately there was the possibility of complications due to student inexperience and in retrospect one feels that the system must have involved many mothers in undue distress and delay.

While there are other maternity units both public and private in Dublin the three maternity hospitals continue to carry the heaviest load. Between them they cover some 25,000 deliveries annually with a remarkably low maternal morbidity and death rate, something of the order of 0.02%. Hopefully some day even this tiny number of personal tragedies will only be a sad memory.

CHAPTER ELEVEN

A CENTURY OF PROGRESS

Historically the middle of the nineteenth century was the Golden Age of Irish Medicine. Hospitals were built. Medical education and practice was regularised. Inventions from other countries were applied successfully to Irish patients. The clinical observations of the Dublin teachers, Graves, Stokes, Corrigan and Colles secured them an eponymous immortality. A Public Health Act seemed about to usher in a new era of peaceful progress. The country, despite famine and political unrest, was alive and a factor in medical affairs.

At the beginning of the century four corporations conferred medical, surgical or pharmaceutical qualifications, as we have seen. The University of Dublin conferred degrees in medicine only. The King's and Queen's College of Physicians (now the Royal College of Physicians) had two orders of qualification, the Licence and the Fellowship. The Royal College of Surgeons had likewise two orders, Licence and Membership. The Apothecaries' Hall conferred a licence as an Apothecary. There was no co-ordination between these bodies and few relations, even social, between their members. The licensing bodies had little control over their own members and co-operation between doctors was almost unknown.

The first effort at organisation, apart from the learned societies noted elsewhere, was the foundation of the Irish Medical Association, in the College of Surgeons, on 29th May 1839. The main instigators of the agitation leading to this association were Richard Carmichael and Arthur Jacob. As a first step, Jacob had, in January of the same year, founded *The Dublin Medical Press*, where he carried on vigorous propaganda for a united medical front.

Carmichael took the chair at the first meeting of the Association. He set forth in detail the profession's grievances and his own recommendations. He pleaded for a betterment of the conditions of dispensary medical officers, who were dependent on the good-will of their local authorities and had no central control. As at so many meetings, medical and otherwise, there was unanimity on the bad conditions and a desire that 'someone should do something about it.' Unfortunately there was not the same unanimity on the steps to be taken and few concrete reforms were obtained.

Failure to gain the support of the licensing bodies and of the Government nullified many of the founders' early efforts. The only notable results of this first meeting were the establishment, some years later, of the Royal Medical Benevolent Fund, and the grant, in 1844, of a supplemental charter to the Royal College of Surgeons which put its constitution on a democratic basis. The College thenceforth became more active in public affairs and in protecting the interests of its members.

The avowed aim of the Association and of *The Dublin Medical Press* was the union of all medical men under one governing body. The College of Physicians opposed this plan to the extent of allying itself even more closely with Trinity College. The Surgeons in turn refused to recognise the Apothecaries.

Such unification as was then attempted has never come about, but the movement did good by bringing various branches of the profession together socially and by giving them a common ground for discussion.

The violence of medical controversy at this time may be judged from a letter in the *Lancet* (2nd May 1840) on the subject of the Irish reformers (Maunsell, Williams, Jacob and Porter). ' . . . all the tag-rag and bobtail of the college school–hatched in corruption, though they still linger about their dunghill that gave them birth–robber pirates who, under false colours, ply their buccaneer trade from the same motives that animate robbers and pirates.' The letter purported to come from 'An Indignant Licentiate of the Dublin College.'

The Irishmen at home possessed an equally vigorous literary style, for in *The Dublin Medical Press* of 1839 (p. 235), they refer to 'the chronic medico-literary diarrhoea under which the learned professor has so long laboured.' The learned professor was Robert Graves.

One of the points about which argument raged was whether or not doctors should advertise. Graduates of the University and Colleges regarded themselves as specialists whilst the apothecaries were the G.P.s or poor man's doctors.

As the number of surgeons and physicians became larger they were forced to take on work formerly considered beneath them. Several of them advertised in a more flamboyant manner than the present discreet notices permitted by the M.R.C. would allow. The following examples appeared in the *Freeman's Journal* in January 1855:

Dr Hayden's Advertisements Defended And Explained.

1. This Christmas completes the tenth year of the General Practitioner system as adopted by me aided by the advice and sanction of that great and good man, Richard Carmichael.

2. The atrocious attempts–*per fas aut nefas*–of the Council of the College of Surgeons to crush my system and trample upon me, were as unavailing as they were wicked because this system was good, true, required to meet a public want; and I was upheld not by man but by God.

3. I have spent upwards of £4,000 in the publication of pamphlets, letters, circulars, cards and advertisements, for the followed reasons marked A, B, C:

A) To defend my character, moral and professional, from the disgraceful assaults of vindictive, fiendish and powerful enemies. The late Mr Carmichael truly observed that 'The conduct of the medical profession, particularly towards each other, is too often maintained in the spirit of mean jealousy and low underhand intrigue.'

B) To develop and defend a new system in the teeth of lying and influential opponents, novel machinery and powerful arms were required for both offensive and defensive warfare.

C) It is my decided opinion that a professional man (hear it, O Aristocracy!) is but a trader, for his services are simply a thing in the market, and hence he may legitimately use ADVERTISEMENTS, or the lawful means which my friend Sir Harry Gallop adopts–namely advertisements by LOCOMOTION! (not locomotive advertisements which are unlawful).

Scale of Fees for 1855

G. T. Hayden, Physician and Surgeon, respectfully informs the public that the following scale of terms will be adopted by him for Surgical and Medical Advice from 1st January 1855:

	£	s.	d.
(1) At home, 82 Harcourt St.		5	0
(2) Immediate City		7	6
(3) Immediate Suburbs		10	6
(4) Remote suburbs	1	0	0
(5) Three to four miles from General Post Office, Dublin	3	0	0
(6) Any distance greater than that mentioned in No. 5 charged at the rate of £1 for every mile.			

N.B. The medicines prescribed in each case are compounded at 82 Harcourt Street, by a licentiate Apothecary and are furnished to the patient gratuitously. Dr Hayden prescribes for patients at his residence (Sundays excepted) from eight to nine a.m., from eleven to five p.m. and on the evenings of Mondays, Wednesdays and Fridays from eight to ten o'clock.

Immediately below this the following appeared:

PUBLIC NOTICE FOR 1855

THOMAS SPOONER PALMER, M.D.

Finding the Apothecaries have now adopted the title of General Medical Practitioner, under which name I have practised for the past seven years, and as my system has been and will be in direct opposition to their encroachment on the profession, I must now publicly relinquish that appellation.

To remove professional jealousy I discontinued advertising for three years, and am now only giving publicity to this alteration, feeling I can do so with perfect safety to myself, the Public having had an opportunity of testing my practical experience in the various branches of my profession which has established my present practice.

This may be gratifying to those who might have considered I compromised myself and on which some (of the would-be-aristocrats) might have presumed; but knowing my respectability did not rest on the profession I felt I had a right to excuse my discretion and adopt any system or accept any fees I thought proper.

To those families whose confidence I have obtained, I return my grateful thanks and beg to say I shall continue to attend them on the same terms as I have done and for the benefit of others. I make no alteration in my Fees (my minimum fee being 5s.) which may be paid at the first visit, every fourth visit, at the end of attendance or half yearly as preferred. Families as usual attended by the year. Medicine given gratuitously or prescriptions as required. Hours of attendance and Scale of Fees, see Prospectus to be had at my residence.

32 Merrion Square North.

Another member of the profession was the forerunner of the patent-medicine-by-post system which aims to cure all ills.

Dr Robert Wall, Surgeon and Accoucheur, 29 Lower Abbey Street (corner of Marlborough St), gives advice and medicine as usual for 5's. either at his own residence or the patient's in any part of the city within the Circular Rd., and when consulted by letter, sends a prescription for 5's. This system—essentially the 5's system—Surgeon Wall adopted on commencing practice some years since, and expended a great deal of money in establishing. He should deem it most unwise to make any alteration therein now that it is so highly appreciated by a great portion of the Public. At home daily from Twelve to Five p.m. and from Seven to Nine in the evening and on Sunday from Ten to Twelve morning, and from Five to Seven evening.

In 1820, the sufferings of the people during the epidemic fevers of 1817, 1818 and 1819 induced the Lord Lieutenant to institute a General Board of Health in the City of Dublin for preventing a repetition of such a calamity or of mitigating its effects. The members of the Board were:

John David la Touche, Peter la Touche, William Disney, Robert Perceval, M.D.; George Renny, M.D.; Philip Crampton, Rev. James Horner, John Cheyne, M.D.; Samuel Bewley, William Harding, Thomas Crosthwaite, John Leland Maquay, Francis Lea and Francis Barker, M.D., Secretary.

An important part of the Board's work was the collection of statistics about local health conditions. As a means to this end they sent a questionnaire to prominent and well-educated members of rural communities. This requested information under the headings of (1) Dwellings, (2) Clothing, (3) Diet, (4) Fuel, (5) Employment, (6) Contagion, (7) Epidemic and General Diseases.

In 1822, the Board published a digest of replies received from correspondents in the Province of Munster.

In general the condition of the people was extremely miserable. Their houses were badly adapted to the purposes of ventilation, cleanliness or the preservation of health. Their diet was monotonous though healthy when in sufficient quantity. Despite the warnings of several correspondents that a potato crop failure would spell disaster, no provision was made for an alternative diet or crop. The average wage of a labourer was eightpence per day, or fourpence per day with food. The principal causes of the spread of disease were the crowding of apartments; attendance at wakes and funerals; collections of manure about houses; wandering beggars. The situation seems to have been similar for working classes throughout the country.

The middle and rich classes fared tolerably well in sickness. Though the sanitation in their homes was primitive or non-existent there was less crowding, and the sick person could be attended in a separate room. In the 'Liberties' and poorer parts of the cities the living conditions of both sick and healthy were horrible.

In the *Dublin Journal of Medical Science* for May 1845, Thomas Willis published a review of the social conditions in the North Dublin Union. He paid particular attention to the infant population, nearly 50 per cent of whom died before the age of two years. When we read Willis' description of conditions in St Michan's parish we are inclined rather to wonder how the other 50 per cent survived.

A large proportion of the houses have not necessaries and those that have are in very few instances connected with a sewer, but must be emptied by carrying out through the house. Water closets are scarcely known unless in public buildings; there may not be above a dozen in the entire district. . . . Of those houses let to weekly tenants not one in ten has the water conveyed into it by branch from the street main. The tenants in such cases are dependent for their supply on the public fountain. . . . The water is not constantly on in these fountains. The wretched people have no vessels to contain a supply; the kettle and the broken jar are the only ones to be seen in these abodes of misery. Nothing marks their poverty more than when congregating round the public fountain, struggling to have their little supply. There are many lanes and courts in which a tumbler of water could not be had fit for drinking.

Willis went on to note that the same water was used for several different purposes. The only cleansing stairs or floors ever got was with 'this noisome semi-fluid poison,' as he describes the much-used water. Of course this finally ended in the streets for want of branch sewers.

In some rooms in these situations it is not an unfrequent occurrence to see above a dozen human beings crowded into a space not fifteen feet square. Within this space the food of these beings, such as it is, must be prepared; within this space they must eat and drink; men, women and children must strip, dress and sleep. In case of illness the calls of nature must be relieved; and when death releases one of the inmates, the corpse must of necessity remain for days within the room.

Many of Willis' recommendations were later incorporated in Public Health Laws. They included periodic lime-washing of walls, the appointment of health officers, the prohibition of underground sleeping rooms, and increased water supply.

Under these circumstances it is no wonder that infectious diseases were rife in Ireland in the first half of the nineteenth century. There were frequent serious epidemics of typhus, cholera, relapsing fever, typhoid, measles, scarlatina and smallpox. Yet, in 1801, Steevens' was the only public hospital in Dublin which would accept these cases. In that year, a house in Brown Street was opened as a fever hospital. Two years later it became the Hardwicke Hospital with some 60 beds.

Added to inaccurate diagnosis, insufficient accommodation and a low standard of nursing was the barbarous treatment meted out to 'fever' patients. Repeated bleedings, violent purgatives, drastic emetics (masquerading as 'sedatives') and 'such a low course of diet as shall co-operate with the other remedies,' all played their part in reducing the already stricken patient to a dying state.

The teaching of the Quaker, John Rutty, who a century beforehand had related: 'I am assured of seventy of the poorer sort at the same time in this fever, abandoned to the use of whey and God's good providence, who all recovered,' had been completely forgotten and was not to be practised again until the time of Robert Graves, the descendant of a Cromwellian planter, who more than atoned for his ancestor's misdeeds in his adopted country.

An example of the treatment employed appeared in an obituary notice published in *Saunders' News Letter* on 22nd October 1822:

After an illness of ten years duration, during which she was bled upwards of 500 times, Mary, only daughter of William Moore, Esq., of Grimeshill, near Kirkby, Lonsdale.

We are given no information about Mary's illness, but a diagnosis of anaemia would probably be correct as a contributory, or even primary, cause of death.

One of the great killing and disfiguring diseases of the eighteenth century had been smallpox. In 1796 Edward Jenner of Gloucestershire had discovered vaccination and this method of protection soon gained great popularity. The first vaccination centre in Dublin was opened at the Dispensary for Infant Poor at 26 Exchequer Street, in 1800. In the first years of its operation over 9,000 children were vaccinated.

John Creighton (1768–1827), the Surgeon to this Dispensary, was one of Jenner's earliest and most ardent disciples. In 1801, he vaccinated nineteen children. The Surgeon-General, George Stewart, attempted unsuccessfully to inoculate these children with the smallpox virus. Seven years later, another attempt also failed. Creighton's belief in the method was amply testified by the fact that one of the human guinea-pigs was his eldest son.

In 1804, the number of requests for vaccination was so large that a special Cow-Pock Institution was established at 1 North Cope Street. An announcement in the *Dublin Evening Post* of 21st January 1804, read:

COW POCK INSTITUTION,

NO. 1 NORTH COPE STREET

Under the patronage of His Excellency Earl Hardwicke.

We the undersigned physicians and surgeons in this city convinced of the advantages likely to arise from a more general diffusion of Cow-Pox have associated for the purposes of inoculating the children of the poor and of supplying the different parts of this kingdom with infection. And we do hereby pledge ourselves that no infection shall be issued by us which we do not believe to be of the most genuine kind.

Joseph Clark,	George Stewart,
James Cleghorn,	Ralph Obré,
Thomas Evory,	Solomon Richards.

P.S. On Tuesdays and Saturdays between two and three o'clock all children coming to the Institution will be inoculated. Wet nurses of character will find it their interest to bring their infants as a regular registry of their places of residence will be kept. Packets of infection with printed directions which may be easily transmitted by post, at half-a-crown each. Surgeons of the Army and Navy to be supplied gratis.

All letters to Dr Labatt, Secretary, at the Institution. To be transmitted free of expense to the Charity.

In the first year 578 patients were inoculated and 1,012 packets of material for inoculation were issued to doctors. Of these 236 were sent to Army Surgeons.

Some years later the Institution was transferred to premises at 55 Sackville Street. Unfortunately there are no accurate records of the incidence of smallpox in those inoculated and in patients not so protected, but in the 1823 report of the Institution, Dr Joseph Clarke, a Director and Physician of the Institute, stated:

Since the beginning of this century when vaccination was introduced generally among the upper ranks in Dublin no family has lost a child, in previous good health, by smallpox after vaccination; nor has even one eye been extinguished by this pestilential disease, so far as I am informed.

In the same report it was stated that it was the practice of the Institution to buy in material in quantity and to use it for vaccination after a lapse of several months. This material was sent as far afield as the Mediterranean, Constantinople and elsewhere and was used successfully. This is completely at variance with modern practice in which emphasis is laid on the necessity for using fresh calf-lymph.

In July 1863 an Act was passed making vaccination compulsary and requiring parents and guardians to have their children vaccinated under pain of a fine of ten shillings. Dispensary Medical Officers received one shilling per vaccination. The registrar, usually the Dispensary M.O. received the munificent sum of three pence for recording the vaccination unless he performed it himself, when he got nothing for the extra clerical work. Failure to register a vaccination could cost him a fine of one pound.

The National Vaccine Institute was founded in 1889, when the Cow-Pock Institute moved to Upper O'Connell St and became the Vaccine Department of the Local Government Board. This building was destroyed in the fighting in 1916 and the Institute moved to premises in Sandymount, which had been purchased in 1896. All operations were carried out there until the early 1960's when, mainly because of greatly relaxed regulations both at home and for travellers abroad there was little demand for vaccination, they closed during the Directorship of Dr Peter Denham, great grandson of John Denham who had been Master of the Rotunda a century earlier.

Although Cork Street Fever Hospital is by no means the oldest Dublin hospital, its building between the years 1801 and 1804 is worthy of special note, for the energy and expedition with which a group of Dublin laymen went to work in days which we consider leisurely.

These charitable gentlemen decided that, as 'no adequate hospital accommodation has hitherto been provided for the relief of the sick poor of Dublin afflicted with fever,' they would provide it themselves.

On 28th October 1801, having collected some thirteen hundred pounds, they summoned a meeting of subscribers, at the Royal Exchange and set to work on their self-appointed task of building a new hospital for their city. Amongst the subscriptions was one of sixty guineas from the Apothecaries' Hall. As the general practitioners of the day, the Apothecaries would have a special interest in the foundation of a fever hospital.

The names of those who sat at this first meeting were: Samuel Bewley, Edward Allen, John Barrington, Randell McDonnell, William Disney, Joshua Edmundson, Arthur Guinness, Lewis Hodgson, George MacQuay, William Harding, John Orr, George Renny, Nicholas Roe and Luke White. John David la Touche took the chair.

Within a month, this energetic group had split into several sub-committees; had secured a subscription of 300 guineas from the Lord Lieutenant; had appointed officers and had advertised for an architect. Samuel Johnston was appointed architect, but his plan was found unsuitable and the building committee produced one of their own for 'a House of Recovery, to occupy the Widow Donnelly's premises in the orchard lying south of Cork Street.'

On 26th April 1802, six months after the preliminary meeting, the foundation stone was laid. On 14th May 1804, the hospital received its first patient.

Built by direct labour in two years, for the reception of eighty patients, at a cost of £11,318, Cork Street was eventually enlarged to hold 280 beds, pending the long-awaited building of a modern fever hospital of adequate size for the capital and surrounding country.

The stethoscope was introduced to the Meath Hospital in 1822 by William Stokes. At first there was great prejudice against its use. But the usefulness of the little instrument soon became obvious, and even patients became familiar with it. The crude wooden tube soon gave way to a more elaborate instrument which was the centre of a story going the rounds in Dublin for a while. Dr (later Sir) Henry Marsh was riding towards Dublin from the mountains when he was surprised to hear a voice shouting: 'Postman! Postman! You will lose your horn if you don't take care. It is joggling out of your pocket!'

The last objections to the stethoscope disappeared when post-mortem after post-mortem revealed the accuracy of diagnosis made with its aid. But, as late as 1872, proficiency in the stethoscope was mentioned in students' certificates as something worthy of note.

Another aid to diagnosis, the microscope, was in common use elsewhere. The first Dublin doctor to employ this instrument was John Houston (1802–1845), a surgeon at the Royal City of Dublin Hospital and Curator of the College of Surgeons' Museum from 1824 to 1841. His first written contribution on the subject appeared in *The Dublin Medical Press* in 1844 under the title 'On the Microscopic Pathology of Cancer.'

The miscroscope was still at a crude stage of its development. The preparation of objects for examination was tedious and unsatisfactory so that for several years clinicians were chary of putting much faith in reports from microscopists. In the words of Richard Butcher (1819–1891):

Some sneer at it because they do not wish the trouble of studying it; and others lay it aside because it sets at naught some previously conceived views in relation to pathology.

In 1852 the Surgical Society were still debating as to whether the microscope was of any value or not.

In 1854, a select committee reported on the state of the Dublin Hospitals. Edward Hutton of the Richmond informed the committee that this hospital possessed a cheap microscope purchased by the surgeons themselves. He agreed that better instruments were an essential part of a hospital's equipment.

The first course in Dublin on microscopic anatomy was given by

Robert Dyer Lyons in 1851 at the 'Original' School of Medicine, Peter Street. In Cork the first course was given by Thomas Holland (1828–1857) at the Royal Cork Institution.

Holland saw what others neglected, that the day of purely clinical teaching was finished. He realised that for the future the clinician and the pathologist must work as a team and that intimate knowledge of the underlying pathology was of immeasurable benefit in investigating and treating disease. He predicted that in the year 2000

Physicians would write what may be called chemico-physiological and pathological prescriptions the composition of which will be suggested by an accurate knowledge of the pathological states under treatment and the physiological and chemical actions of the remedies used for their removal.

The Dublin Microscopical Club met during 1864–65. Several doctors were members, but the specimens exhibited were all of a botanical nature.

Despite these faint beginnings of medical microscopy and laboratory investigation the healer's main fields of action for long remained the wards and the operating theatre.

Surgery had still to wait some years for the safety conferred by antisepsis. Anaesthesia was just around the corner.

Prior to 1846, the most important assistants to the surgeon were those who restrained the patient. To take three minutes over the amputation of a leg was regarded as dawdling. Opium and whiskey were the only soporifics known and speed was a surgeon's most valuable aid. In America a dentist, Horace Wells (1815–1848) and his student (later partner) William Morton (1819–1868), experimented with nitrous oxide and ether to put patients asleep during operations. After several setbacks Morton was successful in demonstrating the usefulness of ether as an anaesthetic. A new era in surgery had dawned.

On 1st January 1847 the first operation under general anaesthesia was performed in Ireland. The surgeon was John MacDonnell (1796–1892) of the Richmond Hospital. The operation was the amputation of the arm of a young country girl, Mary Kane of Drogheda.

MacDonnell tested the effects of ether on himself before using it on his patient. In his paper in *The Dublin Medical Press* he wrote:

I rendered myself insensible for some seconds, five or six times, and the following observations were made. The pupils dilated—my pulse rose at the beginning of each inhalation. My complexion was rather raised each time and, on one occasion only, my lips became blue.'

Amongst those who were present at the operation were Mr Carmichael, Dr Hutton, Dr Adams and Mr Hamilton.

MacDonnell recognised that his crude apparatus was not suitable for long operations and that permanent injury to the brain could ensue from anoxaemia. He proposed animal experimentation to develop a system by which known ratios of air and ether could be given to the patient.

The case was discussed at a meeting of the Surgical Society a few days later. Mr Hargrave mentioned that several years previously he had used ether to control epileptiform convulsions in a young girl. Henry Kennedy remarked that anaesthetics were unsuitable for cardiac and pulmonary cases.

Ether quickly became popular and a committee consisting of Drs McDonnell, Tufnell and Bellingham, appointed by the Surgical Society, decided that it should be used with care in all cases and was unsuited for patients with diseases of the heart and lungs.

For some time chloroform supplanted ether as a safe anaesthetic. The longest administration ever of the former was recorded in St Vincent's Hospital, Dublin. In a case of ilio-femoral aneurism under the care of Dr Mapother, anaesthesia was maintained for twelve hours. Six days later the same patient was anaesthetised for four and a half hours, also with chloroform. This lengthy administration of an anaesthetic was necessitated by the 'Dublin method' of treatment of an aneurism. Aneurisms, large swellings on main arteries, were common and of great interest to surgeons in those days. Indeed the Surgical Society was known facetiously as the 'Aneurysmal Society,' so many of these cases were presented. The only known method of cure was to tie the artery and cut off the blood supply. Anaesthesia had rendered surgery painless, but the septic complications were still appalling.

O'Bryen Bellingham (1805–1857) suggested in a treatise published in 1847, *Cure of Aneurysm by Compression*, that the supply of blood to the diseased artery could be diminished by continuous pressure from the outside and that a cure would result. The method was a resounding success. Usually relays of medical students were employed to apply the pressure over periods of several hours.

MEDICAL REGISTRATION

The first Medical Act was passed in 1858. The G.M.C. formed by this was empowered to keep a register of qualified medical men. In Ireland the registrable qualifications were, the Fellowship and Licence of the Colleges of Physicians and Surgeons, the Licence of the Apothecaries' Hall, the degrees and licences of Universities in the United Kingdom. The Council was empowered to supervise professional study and examinations and to report defects to the Privy Council. The Act empowered the Council to erase the names of those adjudged guilty of infamous conduct in a professional respect. Some eleven amending Acts were later passed. Of these, one of the most important was that of 1886, which required all doctors to be qualified in medicine, surgery and midwifery.

The Act of 1886 resulted in some paradoxical situations. It recognised no distinction between teaching and non-teaching universities. It partly disenfranchised the Colleges of Physicians and Surgeons, yet conferred full powers of examination and registration on the Apothecaries' Societies. But one good effect was that the Colleges of Physicians and Surgeons were drawn more closely together in order to confer the necessary 'conjoint' Diploma. A higher standard of professional conduct was obtained with a disappearance of many of the undesirable aspects of unethical advertising and quackery in general.

The evolution of the Diploma in Public Health dates from 5th June 1867. At a meeting of the G.M.C. it was proposed that in order to encourage the study of Hygiene, an additional registrable qualification should be instituted. The proposal was negatived. In 1869 a memorandum asking for their views was forwarded to the various licensing bodies. It is gratifying to record that Trinity College, Dublin, was able to reply that plans were already prepared for a Diplomate in State Medicine.

The first examination in State Medicine took place on 12th June 1871. Four candidates entered and were successful. They were: Arthur Wynne Foot, John William Moore, John Todhunter and Gerald Yeo.

In 1869 also, a meeting of the Medical Officers of Sligo and Leitrim presented a memorial on the subject of Public Health Administration to the Lord Lieutenant.

Unfortunately, the administration of the Health Acts and the payment of medical officers were so haphazard and variable that their full potentialities were not used. In general the district medical officers were so wretchedly paid that their lives were one long struggle against penury. Notwithstanding the efforts of the various Medical Associations, there was so much bickering between individual groups of practitioners that unified action was almost impossible.

Many shopkeepers who were Guardians issued 'red tickets' for the doctor's attendance in order to attract business. Well-to-do farmers applied for free medical attention and, while the doctor could in theory bring such abuses to the ears of the Guardians, in practice he dare not do so for fear of losing his meagre salary and all chances of private practice. Many doctors, as a result, were not so well off as the skilled labourers they were called on to attend as a Poor-Law patients.

In 1878, a Public Health (Ireland) Act was passed. Dispensary doctors became Medical Officers of Health for their own districts. Their duties were not clearly defined and their salaries ranged from £5 to £25 per year. The Irish Medical Associaton urged that the posts should be more adequately paid and the duties defined. The Local Government Board refused to give any help. For this reason, as well as for the fact that most of its clauses were permissive rather than mandatory, the administration of the Act was uneven and unsatisfactory. It was patched and altered by several amending Acts so that by 1925, when the Free State Government turned its attention to Public Health, the sanitary system of the country was in a chaotic state. The Public Health Act of 1947 was an attempt to codify and modernise the patchwork of legislation made up over the fifty Acts and innumerable Ministerial Orders. While the original object of the Act may have been achieved, it was soon overtaken by the changing medical scene and in the intervening thirty six years several more Health Acts were passed as described in other chapters.

FURTHER SURGICAL ADVANCES

John H. Maconchy, of the County Down Infirmary, was the first Irish surgeon to report a case in which Lister's methods had been employed. His report appeared in the *Dublin Journal of Medical Science* in May 1868. At the time he and his assistant, Dr Nelson, had practised antisepsis for over nine months.

The case reported was the excision of a knee-joint under chloroform anaesthesia. No antiseptic preparations were made, but dressings soaked in 1/30 carbolic acid were applied after the operation. Pus appeared in the wound on the fifth day. According to Maconchy, the only advantage of the cabolic acid in this was was to keep the pus free from odour. Sinuses formed in the wound and a chronic bone infection developed; however, the patient eventually recovered. In a footnote to his paper Maconchy recorded:

Every bubo treated here since last August (1867) has been opened under a rag steeped in carbolic acid and oil, squeezed out under the rag. The the carbolic acid putty applied: in twenty-four hours the putty has been replaced by a rag similar to the first–this process was repeated daily until no further matter came–in one case the dressings were left off too soon, the orifice had not healed, air got in and chronic suppuration was established.

Other cases reported by Maconchy included compound fractures, gunshot wounds, and similar serious injuries. Like other operators of the time, Maconchy considered that the air which entered a wound was of itself harmful and devoted his energies to keeping the wound airtight.

The first paper from a Dublin surgeon reporting the use of carbolic acid came from Henry Gray Croly, surgeon to the Royal City of Dublin Hospital, about August 1868. Croly also administered Peile's Antitetanic Pills, composed of aloes, antimony and opium, to his case, which was a serious compound fracture of the thumb and index finger. Prior to this, compound fractures nearly always resulted in the loss of a limb and not infrequently in death from sepsis or tetanus.

The antiseptic lesson had not reached the obstetricians in February 1866, for Fleetwood Churchill, addressing the Dublin Obstetrical Society, said

Modern researches have thrown some light on puerperal fever. Not that we are in possession of the means of prevention or cure.

On 26th June 1879 Lister came to Dublin for the purpose of receiving the Honorary M.D. of Dublin University. He visited the Richmond Hospital and gave an explanation of his method of dressing wounds before a large audience of surgeons and students. In the course of his address he derided as absolutely unnecessary the custom of 'our earnest German friends who before they operate on a part carefully cleanse the skin with ether and soap and water.'

Despite the advances made in anaesthesia and antisepsis most of the body was still forbidden territory to the surgeon. Amputations, lithotomies, opening of abscesses, excision of joints, repair of hare-lip and occasional removal of easily available organs, such as the breast and penis, comprised his entire operative experience. Abdominal conditions were treated by purges, emetics, hot stupes, enemas, opium and leeches, and except for the tapping of empyemata, the surgical treatment of chest conditions just did not exist. Some operators aspirated ovarian cysts with a high mortality rate.

Blood transfusion in a case of tetanus was reported in the *Dublin Quarterly Journal* in November 1870. The donor and operator was Robert McDonnell (1828–1889) of Steevens' Hospital. The operation had been performed in 1865. No effort was made to type the blood, which was stirred vigorously and strained through muslin into a bowl 'previously rinsed with hot water.' McDonnell mentioned that his very simple apparatus was equally useful for the injection of salines in cholera and that this treatment was worthy of an extended trial.

In August 1878, the *Dublin Journal of Medical Science* reported cases in England in which the abdomen had been opened and a case in which a brain abscess was drained.

On 6th June 1878, Thornley Stoker, Professor of Anatomy in the College of Surgeons, removed the uterus and one ovary from a patient suffering from a large uterine tumour. This was the first successful abdominal hysterectomy in Ireland. Stoker was acute enough to recognise the advantage of leaving the healthy ovary in place.

In 1881, Thomas Little, surgeon to Sir Patrick Dun's Hospital, reported two cases of strangulated hernia successfully treated by abdominal operation. Other surgeons, notably Henry Gray Croly, soon reported similar cases.

In November 1882, William Stokes reported a number of cases of removal of ovarian tumours, a panhysterectomy, hernia operations and an abdominal section for the relief of a strangulated hernia. This last operation was performed in the Richmond Hospital on 19th July 1877. Unfortunately, although the obstruction was relieved, operation had been delayed too long and the patient died.

Eventually it was recognised that sepsis was due to a living organism entering a wound and not to air of itself. In 1882, Kendal Franks, of the Adelaide Hospital, read an address on 'The Germ Theory.' In 1884, Franks operated on two cases of obstruction of the small intestine and from then on abdominal operations became common.

The first reported cases of brain surgery in Ireland, with the exception of trephining, came from the Richmond Hospital. The pioneer was again Thornley Stoker. The first case was a tumour on the right side of the brain. The second was an abscess. Operation gave temporary relief in the former and complete cure in the latter.

In March 1896, Bolton McCausland, a surgeon to Steeven's Hospital, used X-rays for the purpose of finding a needle embedded in the palm of a girl's hand. The needle had been embedded for twelve months and had resisted all attempts at removal. Professor Barrett and Mr Jefcote of the Royal College of Science took the photograph.

With the improvement of anaesthesia and asepsis, hospitals lost many of their dangers and terrors for the patient. Erysipelas, hospital gangrene, pyaemia, and laudable pus became rare rather than commonplace. But the hospital remained the poor man's refuge and the paying patient who had to undergo an operation stayed at home. His bedroom was converted into an operating theatre.

Gradually the idea that operations should be done in a special house gained ground and the Private Hospital or Nursing Home was born about the end of the nineteenth century.

The facilities available in these homes varied greatly. Several of them in Dublin were run by persons with no medical or nursing qualifications. The majority were converted private houses, totally unsuitable for the purpose to which they were diverted. Surgical patients were put into beds lately occupied by infectious cases with disastrous results. Lavatories and bathrooms were quite inadequate whilst the noises of trams, milkcarts, street musicians and hawkers did nothing to help the patient rest.

In 1895, Sir John Moore, writing in the *Dublin Journal of Medical Science*, appealed for regular inspection and licensing by the Public Health authorities, with a high standard of staffing and sanitary facilities.

A specialised Nursing Home was that devoted to the care of maternity patients. These ranged from small homes with half a dozen beds, to large units capable of dealing with most emergencies including caesarean section. All of these were subject to health authority inspection and licensing. The very necessity to maintain high standards was a major factor in their virtual disappearance, for sophisticated modern techniques are expensive and often require specially trained staff.

The title 'Nursing Home' nowadays usually means a 'long stay home' for aged people and for these the controls are inadequate. The only real sanction available to the Health Authority is to refuse to pay for Health Act patients if the home is sub-standard.

Towards the close of the century the tempo of medical life in Dublin slowed down. The flamboyant jack-of-all-trades gave way to the specialist. Mr (later Sir) Robert Woods was the first Dublin surgeon to confine himself absolutely to a specialised field, that of otorhinolaryngology. The brilliant operator whose speed was his great asset in pre-anaesthetic days was replaced by the man who could take more time and even modify his original plans during an operation. The surgical team had not yet appeared.

The most important change was the standardisation of medical education. Instead of an uneven standard varying from school to school and in a given school from year to year, there was now a consistently good standard of unified teaching. The mediocre lecturer stood less chance of securing employment whilst the talents of the brilliant teacher were not dissipated on a few students. Unfortunately, most of the new teaching was of discoveries made elsewhere. For many years the Irish school was eclipsed as a centre of independent thought and research.

CHAPTER TWELVE

THESE NAMES WERE NEWS

As did other periods, the nineteenth century produced its medical giants. Amongst the galaxy of medical men in the Dublin School at the beginning of the century, no star shone more brightly than that of Richard Carmichael (1778–1849). As a reformer, philanthropist and teacher he was outstanding.

Carmichael's medical education was obtained entirely in the College of Surgeon's School as Peile's apprentice. He qualified towards the end of the eighteenth century. Following the custom of the time, he spent some years as an army surgeon, before setting up on his own in Dublin. In 1816 he was appointed to the House of Industry (later the Richmond, now St Laurence's). In the winter of 1826, a 'School of Anatomy' attached to the House of Industry was opened in Channel Row; here Carmichael gave courses of lectures in surgery, anatomy and physiology. Despite recurrent and crippling attacks of sciatica and gallstones he taught for many years.

Carmichael's devotion to his hospital was a deep one. On the death of his colleague, Ephraim McDowel (1798–1835), two candidates, Robert Adams (1793–1875) and John McDonnell (1796–1892), sought the vacant surgeoncy. Both were able and distinguished. Both would serve their patients well. The rejection of either was a step that the governing body was reluctant to take. To solve the impasse, Carmichael resigned his own position, leaving two vacancies, to which both candidates were duly elected.

Carmichael was President of the College of Surgeons in 1813, 1826, 1848. On relinquishing office for the third time his reply to an address from the Fellows and Licentiates contained the following generous statement:

Since the termination of my year of Presidentship, I have relinquished all practice, except in my own house, or out-of-doors, in consultation. This determination has, in great measure, arisen from a wish to show a good example to my contemporaries, which, I trust, will in due time be followed for the benefit of their juniors.'

Carmichael's greatest reform was the union of the surgical and medical branches of the profession with the establishment of the Apothecaries as members of a separate profession. His principles were embodied in the Medical Act of 1858, which established the G.M.C. and the Medical Register. A little-known episode concerns his efforts in 1808 to establish a hospital entirely devoted to the treatment of cancer.

The circumstances of his death were sad. In his seventy-first year he set out to ride across the strand between Dollymount and Sutton. He was drowned within sight of the residents of his house. In his will was a provision for a bequest of £10,000 to the College, to revert on the death of his widow. With self-denial such as that of Griselda Steevens one hundred and thirty-nine years before, Mrs Carmichael advanced the sum during her life. The interest on this money now provides funds for the triennial prize awarded for the best essay on 'The State of the Medical Profession in Ireland.' A Carmichael Scholarship of £15 is also available for third-year students of the College of Surgeons.

In 1843, an obscure country practitioner in Mountmellick, one Henry Croly (1807–1893), brought out the first complete directory of medical men ever published in Ireland. Croly was an M.D. of Edinburgh and a Fellow of the College of Surgeons in Ireland. In his own words, in a later edition (1846),

the want of such a publication as this has long been felt by the profession, and how its usefulness has been appreciated may be learnt from the free use which has been made of the volume for '43, in *Thom's Official Directory* where many whole pages have been unceremoniously transcribed without even the grace of an acknowledgement.

Croly later settled in Rathfarnham, Co Dublin, where he built up an extensive practice. His son, Henry Gray Croly (1836–1903), was twice President of the College of Surgeons, and a pioneer of surgery in the last quarter of the century.

The inventor of the commonest medical instrument next to the stethoscope was an Irishman. Francis Rynd (1801–1861) was born in Dublin. He received his medical education from Sir Philip Crampton at the Meath Hospital and at Trinity College. He took a full part in the social and sporting life of the city even as a student. Despite this, or more probably because of it, he developed a most successful practice. As a teacher and friend to his students he was in the first rank. He was on the surgical staff of the Meath from 1836 to his death. Rynd's great contribution to medicine was an early form of hypodermic 'syringe.' His original communication on the subject appears in the *Dublin Medical Press* of 12th March 1845.

Rynd's instrument had no plunger such as we know to-day. The fluid entered the body by force of gravity only. Further, he does not seem to have conceived that the subcutaneous administration of drugs could affect distant parts of the body. He used it principally for introducing large doses (upwards of two grains) of morphia in the vicinity of nerves to relieve the pain of neuritis. Rynd's death was due to a heart attack brought on by an altercation following a street accident.

Seven noted Irish figures in the medical world of the nineteenth century had a common initial: Carmichael, Croly, Colles, Crampton, Corrigan, Cusack and Cheyne.

Abraham Colles (1773–1843) first appeared in the *Dublin Almanack* of 1796 as L.R.C.S. He then practised in Chatham Street. His fees for his first year of practice amounted to £8 10s. 7½d. In later years he averaged £5,000, a sum of much greater value then than now. While studying in Edinburgh, whence he walked to London in eight days, he records that he lived for three days on a tenpenny codfish. Six years later he was elected President of the College of Surgeons, and in 1804 entered on a thirty-years tenure of the Chair of anatomy and surgery. He was an excellent lecturer, although no orator. His teaching was clear, practical and attractive to the students.

Colles wrote on three subjects which have immortalised his name. Colles' Law, that a syphilitic infant cannot infect its own mother; Colles' fracture of the lower end of the radius and Colles' fascia about the perineum. Colles' lectures to the College of Surgeons were published after his death, which occurred following a long and obscure illness. At his own request a post-mortem examination was performed. A dilation of the great vein leading to the heart was found.

Colles operated in the days before anaesthesia was discovered. In an effort to render the patients insensible in order to allow of manipulations in strangulated hernia he used to inject an enema of tobacco smoke into their lower bowel by means of a silver tube connected with a long bellows. It is curious to note that the same instrument was used to resuscitate the apparently drowned and in the treatment of tetanus by O'Beirne.

In those pre-anaesthetic, pre-antiseptic days Colles tied the great artery which runs underneath the collar-bone. His own description of the first operation is arresting. In the small operating room a crowd of students and assistants jostle about the surgeon and his patient, the latter awake or possibly drunk. Colles cuts along the collar-bone and dissects among the vital and complicated structures lying about his objective. The patient struggles, but is restrained by the onlookers. The operation takes over an hour.

Colles performed the operation three times. Unfortunately the patients all died within a few days from septic complications, for the use of antiseptics was not discovered until 1867.

Colles' work in anatomy has been greatly neglected by his successors. Yet he was the first to describe several structures about the area of the groin, notably Colles' fascia, and assisted in the dissections from which the drawings, illustrative of Astley Cooper's work *On Hernia* were taken.

Sir Philip Crampton (1777–1858) was appointed Surgeon to the Meath Hospital within one year of qualification. That the choice was a good one may be judged from the fact that he held the post until his death, sixty years later. During this period he aided in establishing the system of bedside teaching with its intimate association of teacher and learner for which Dublin became famous. As a teacher, Crampton excelled both in hospital and in his private medical school at the rear of 49 Dawson Street. Throughout his career he never lost his interest in comparative anatomy and published papers on the 'Anatomy of the Eyelid in Birds' as well as on other zoological subjects.

In 1810, Crampton acquired considerable fame by opening the windpipe of a waiter who was choking in a tavern and thus saving his life. With the usual perversity of the public this exploit was talked about and advertised when more difficult and skilful work of Crampton's was forgotten.

Up until 1959, when it was removed after it had partially collapsed, there was a fountain nicknamed 'the Cauliflower' at the junction of D'Olier St and College St. This had been erected to the memory of Crampton and bore an inscription which read:

This fountain has been placed here, a type of health and usefulness, by the friends and admirers of Sir Philip Crampton, Bart, Surgeon-General to Her Majesty's Forces. It but feebly represents the sparkle of his genial fancy, the depth of his calm sagacity, the clearness of his spotless honour, the flow of his boundless benevolence.

There are various versions of the circumstances which gave rise to a *bon mot* concerning Crampton. He appeared at Dublin Castle in the splendid uniform of the Surgeon-General. An enquiry as to his identity elicited the reply variously attributed to Judge Norbury, Crampton himself or others: 'A General in the Lancers, Sir'

The name of James William Cusack (1788–1861) is not so familiar as that of his great contemporaries, probably because he wrote little and gave his name to no instrument or operation. Cusack studied at the College of Surgeons, Steevens' Hospital and T.C.D., where he won a scholarship and the Berkeley Gold Medal. When he qualified he went back to Steevens' as Resident Surgeon for several years until 1825, when he commenced practice at No 3 Kildare Street. In all he had seventy-eight apprentices. The last survivor of these, Dr Tweedy of Parnell (then Rutland) Square, died in 1907, aged ninety-two. Like Crampton, Cusack became a public figure overnight by his speedy first-aid treatment of a patient who was bleeding to death from a severed artery. Cusack held many appointments. He was surgeon at various times to Steevens', Swift's, City of Dublin, Rotunda, and St Mark's Hospitals, as well as Regius Professor of Surgery in T.C.D. (1852). His reputation was deservedly high. He would often tell how he lay awake for hours planning the best means of tackling a difficult case. His portrait and bust at present adorn the Board Room and Hall of the College of Surgeons.

John Cheyne's (1777–1836) name is commemorated in the type of breathing known as 'Cheyne-Stokes respiration.' He was born at Leith, the seaport of Edinburgh, where he graduated M.D. in his eighteenth year. He entered the Army and was sent to Ireland, where he saw active service at the Battle of Vinegar Hill, in County Wexford. He returned to Scotland to spend nine years as his father's assistant. In 1809 he came to Dublin, where he complained that most of the physicians paid but little attention to pathology. He was admitted a Licentiate of the College of Physicians in 1811 and was elected a Fellow in 1824.

Cheyne's experiences should provide a grain of comfort for the medical man building a practice. For the first half year his fees amounted to three guineas. Later his income averaged £5,000 per annum.

From 1813 to 1819 Cheyne held the Professorship of Medicine in the College of Surgeons. His lectures dealt mainly with military affairs and were largely attended by army and navy surgeons and surgeon's mates. He was probably the first physician of good standing to meet apothecaries in consultation. His worth was recognised by his appointment as Physician-General in 1820.

Cheyne published works on diverse subjects, *Pathology of the Trachea and Bronchia* in 1809, *Cases of Apoplexy* in 1812 and *Dropsy of the Brain* in 1815. In 1821, with William Barker, he published an *Account of the Rise, Progress and Decline of Fever lately epidemical in Ireland*. This ran to 837 octavo pages in two volumes, and dealt with the statistics and official aspect of the typhus epidemic as well as clinical records. In 1831, he presented to the Lord Lieutenant a Report on the Prevention of Cholera. His last work, published posthumously, was *Essays on Partial Derangement of the Mind in Supposed Connection with Religion.*

The description of Cheyne-Stokes respiration appeared in Stokes' *chef d'œuvre, Diseases of the Heart and Aorta,* in 1854. Stokes recorded with another colleague a number of cases of very slow pulse accompanied by fainting attacks, the 'Stokes-Adams syndrome.'

Robert Adams (1793–1875) was Dublin-born. He passed in the College of Surgeons in 1816 and secured the M.D. of Dublin University in 1842. In 1861 he received the newly-instituted qualification of Master of Surgery.

Adams was a first-class surgeon and anatomist. He taught both subjects for many years in private schools and hospitals. He left many pathological specimens to the museum of the Richmond Hospital. In 1863, Adams was a member of the College of Surgeons delegation which presented an address to the Prince of Wales on the occasion of his marriage. He was President of the College in 1840, 1860, 1867. In 1861 he was appointed to the Regius Professorship of Surgery in T.C.D.

James O'Beirne (1787–1862) has a claim to honourable mention for his treatment of intestinal conditions when abdominal surgery was non-existent. He was a member of the College of Surgeons and an M.D. of Edinburgh.

He entered the British Army and served for eight years in the Artillery. He was the first person in Ireland to hold the office of Surgeon-Extraordinary to the King in Ireland. He was Surgeon to the Charitable Infirmary, Jervis Street, and later to the House of Industry hospitals.

O'Beirne's important papers include 'Description of the Anatomy of the Rectum,' 'Tobacco in Tetanus,' 'Mercury in Hip Disease,' 'Extirpation of the Lachrymal Gland' and 'Taxis considered as a Means of avoiding Operations and its application to the different Stages of Strangulation.' In this paper the importance of removing intestinal contents in obstruction is pointed out. In the *Lancet* for 1843, a paper appeared on 'Case of Strangulated Hernia successfully treated by the Exhausting Syringe attached to O'Beirne's Rectal tube.' O'Beirne, who was first Surgeon-in-Ordinary to Queen Victoria in Ireland, dedicated one of his books on rectal matters to the Lord Lieutenant.

O'Beirne was President of the College of Surgeons in 1843 and was named first President under the supplementary charter. He died at Bayswater, London, on 16th June 1862, and was so poor that the cost of his funeral was covered by the Catholic Bishop of the district.

The first Medical Officer of Health for Dublin was Edward Dillon

Mapother (1835–1908). Mapother was educated at the College of Surgeons and Carmichael Schools, and at Queen's College, Galway. Before he was nineteen years old he began to teach anatomy in the College of Surgeons and conducted large classes for many years with great success.

In 1864 he was elected to the Chair of Hygiene in the College of Surgeons, thus filling an eighteen-year-old vacancy. Mapother's lectures were open to, and largely attended by, the lay public. He held the Chair of Anatomy and Physiology in succession to Jacob from 1867 to the amalgamation of the College and private schools in 1889. He was a Surgeon to St Vincent's Hospital from 1859 for almost thirty years, when he went to reside in London. His published works include: *A Manual of Physiology, Lectures on Public Health,* and *Complete Pressure in Treating Aneurysm.* In the *Irish Monthly* for 1878 four essays from Mapother's pen on 'Great Irish Surgeons' appeared.

A book which has been of the greatest assistance to the present author is Sir Charles Cameron's *History of the Royal College of Surgeons in Ireland.* Cameron (1830–1921) was born in Dublin. He studied medicine in the Apothecaries' Hall, the Dublin School of Medicine, the Ledwich School and the Meath and Coombe hospitals. His first appointment, at the age of twenty-three, was that of Professor to the Dublin Chemical Society, an institution in which chemistry was taught for some years prior to the foundation of the College of Science. After holding various teaching posts, he succeeded Mapother in the Chair of Hygiene in 1867. His appointments and honours were numerous.

In his brief appearance on the Dublin medical scene Valentine Flood (1800–1847) left his name to a ligament in the shoulder, 'Flood's Ligament,' which helps to preserve the integrity of the joint. His career illustrates the loss which science may suffer when those trained in research and laboratory work must abandon their studies in order to earn a living. At the beginning of his career Flood was rich in fame but not in money and was forced to take up practice in the poorer districts of the city. Here he was a failure. As a result he was obliged, in 1846, to take an appointment to a village fever hospital at Tubrid, Co. Tipperary, where he died of typhus in the following year. Flood's published works were few but sound. They dealt with anatomy and its application to surgery. His paper on the ligament in the shoulder was published in the *Lancet* of 1829.

In the year 1832, a dark, ferrety-looking young man left Roscommon, for Dublin. Thirty years later the young man was to become the central figure of a *cause célèbre* and the father of Oscar Wilde.

It is unfortunate that these two incidents should be seized on as the most outstanding in Sir William Wilde's (1815–1876) life. In his book, *Victorian Doctor*, T. G. Wilson has given an exhaustive survey of the less exciting, but more fruitful episodes of Wilde's life.

His early days were spent in the West at a time when racial persecution and agrarian agitation were violent, a fact which must have influenced him considerably. Wilde attended the Park Street School and was apprenticed to Abraham Colles at Steevens' Hospital. Colles recognised his pupil's abilities early and praised him publicly in a lecture delivered to the College of Surgeons.

When the cholera epidemic of 1832 hit Dublin, Wilde was brought home by his parents. The disease spread, however, and no part of the country was safe. Some years later Wilde suffered from a fever which was probably typhus. After qualification he spent several months travelling in the Canary Islands and Egypt. On his return he settled at 199 Great Brunswick (now Pearse) Street, where in the intervals between seeing his few patients he studied and wrote on archaeological, botanical and meteorological topics. Unfortunately, his extra-medical life was not a blameless one. He spoke quite shamelessly of his brood of children born of various mothers. Nevertheless he became a social lion in Dublin society.

In 1839 Wilde decided to specialise in ophthalmology, prompted no doubt by his experiences with trachoma in Egypt. He went to London and studied at Moorfields for several months, later moving to Vienna, then the outstanding ophthalmological centre. When he returned to practise in Dublin, Wilde opened his own Eye Hospital which later became the celebrated St Mark's. He distinguished himself about the same time as a Census Commissioner, for which service he was awarded a knighthood.

Wilde's name has been given to two medical entities. One was 'Wilde's incision' for acute inflammation of the mastoid; the other 'Wilde's cord,' an area in the brain.

Apart from medicine, Wilde's most important work was the preparation of the reports on the Census of 1841 and 1851. His account, in the latter, of the Famine is a standard work of reference. Wilde died in Dublin in 1876, aged sixty-one. His wife, 'Speranza,' a minor poetess and fearless Nationalist, survived him for many years.

When Wilde started practice in 1841, diseases of the eyes and ears were treated in the most primitive fashion. Many surgeons and physicians had never seen an eardrum. Accurate diagnosis of eye and ear conditions was impossible and the patient left to the care of his relatives or the local wise-woman did as well as, or better, than the patient who attended a doctor. Strong corrosive liquids, even nitric acid, were commonly applied as 'cures' to the delicate structure of the inner ear. When Wilde died ophthalmology and otology were firmly established as 'respectable' branches of medicine.

Amongst the famous Dublin physicians of the nineteenth century none have a more secure position in history than Robert Graves (1796–1853) and William Stokes (1804–1878).

Robert Graves' life was an adventurous and full one. After qualifying in T.C.D. he travelled extensively in England, Germany, Austria, France and Italy. In Austria he spent ten days in prison, on the grounds that his German accent was so perfect he could not be a foreigner and therefore must be a German spy. In Switzerland, Graves made the acquaintance of J. M. W. Turner, the artist. Over a period of several months the pair became close friends. During a sea voyage from Genoa to Sicily the vessel on which Graves travelled got into severe difficulties. The crew threatened to abandon ship in the only lifeboat, leaving the passengers to their fate. Graves stove in the boat with an axe, mended the leaky pumps with leather from his own boots and rallied the faint-hearted crew to bring the ship safely ashore.

On his return to Dublin in 1821 he was appointed physician to the Meath Hospital and helped to found the Park Street School. He introduced the present system of bedside teaching in which students are obliged to examine the patients for themselves.

Graves' claim to immortality rests largely on his description of exophthalmic goitre, a condition of the thyroid gland in which the patient becomes highly-strung, with bulging prominent eyes. His description appeared in his collected *Clinical Lectures* (1843) which was translated into French by Trousseau, who asked his pupils to consider it as their breviary. One of Graves' great reforms was the elimination of starvation, purging and bleeding from the treatment of fevers. Indeed, so keen was he on his own methods that he suggested for his epitaph, 'He fed fevers.'

Graves' younger associate, William Stokes, son of Whitley, was, in the happy phrase of T. G. Wilson in *Victorian Doctor,* a member of a dynasty rather than of a family. The dynasty has been ably represented in Ireland from 1680 to the present day. Stokes was a tremendously hard worker, from his student days at the Meath Hospital, and later in Glasgow and Edinburgh, until his death in 1878, the year in which the Public Health (Ireland) Act was passed. In his lifetime Stokes advocated many of the provisions of this Act.

William took his degree at Edinburgh in 1825 at the age of twenty-one. In the same year he published a paper on the stethoscope, an instrument which had been discovered by Laennec six years previously, but was not yet in popular use. His reputation was greatly enhanced by two books on *Diseases of the Chest* (1837) and *Diseases of the Heart and Aorta* (1854).

In 1845 he was appointed Regius Professor of Medicine to Trinity College, in succession to his father, which position he held until his death. On the foundation of the G.M.C. he was the obvious choice as the T.C.D. delegate.

Stokes was the central figure in a coincidence as unusual as any fiction writer could conceive. During a fever epidemic he treated a refugee priest from France. The date of this is uncertain, but it was probably during 1848. The priest was penniless and departed without paying for his treatment. Many years later Stokes was travelling on the Rhine. When his steamer drew into a small port there was great confusion and obvious preparations for the reception of some important passenger. Stokes was watching when his arm was touched. He turned and confronted an unknown clergyman who addressed him by name. It was the priest whom he had treated many years before. He was now chaplain to the Empress Eugenie. As a token of thanks he presented Stokes with a ring which is still in the possession of his descendents.

Stokes was familiar with the ravages of typhus, cholera and smallpox. Long before the concept of preventive medicine as we know it to-day he urged that public health was a specialised branch of medicine in its own right. A Sanitary Commission sat in Dublin in 1863–64. At this, and as President of the B.M.A. meeting in Dublin in 1867, Stokes urged the State's responsibility for the collective health of its citizens. His labours in this field were crowned by the establishment by Trinity College of the first Diploma in State Medicine in 1870. Not for another five years did Cambridge and Edinburgh follow Dublin's lead.

Two clinical entities bear Stokes' name: the 'Stokes-Adams' syndrome,' a condition in which an abnormally slow pulse is accompanied by fainting attacks, and 'Cheyne-Stokes respiration,' a type of intermittent breathing already mentioned which usually heralds the approach of death.

The third great Irish physician to give his name to a disease was Dominic Corrigan (1802–1880). Like his predecessors, Corrigan qualified in Edinburgh. He settled in Dublin and became one of the most prominent physicians of the day.

Corrigan's mother was an O'Connor. She claimed descent from the royal O'Connor family, one of whose members was the last High King. Much of Corrigan's later fame–in his latter days he was earning £9,000 per year–was due to the fact that he was the best-known Catholic doctor in Dublin. The Catholic Emancipation Act of 1829 had withdrawn the shackles from his religion. Corrigan was educated at the lay college attached to the great seminary of Maynooth, some twenty miles outside Dublin and the contacts he made there stood to him in later years. He often mentioned that in his early days he was advised by a senior member of the profession to advertise himself ethically by appearing at balls and other respectable functions as well as by giving generously to well-known charities, who published subscribers' lists.

Corrigan's butler died a richer man than his master. In those days doctors did not keep appointment books and the time at which one was seen by a fashionable doctor depended entirely on the tip given to the great man's butler. Those who tipped well were admitted first. Those who tipped badly or not at all might wait for many hours. Corrigan's principal work was done on diseases of the aorta. In 1832 he wrote a paper for the *Edinburgh Medical and Surgical Journal* on disease of the valves separating the heart from this great artery. His description of the characteristic pulse found in this disease was so striking that it received the name of Corrigan's Pulse. Years later in France, he had the unusual experience of being asked whether he was any relation to the physician who had given his name to 'la maladie de Corrigan.'

His name is also attached to a small instrument known as 'Corrigan's Button'. The knob of this is heated and applied to painful areas such as those found in lumbago and sciatica. The term 'Corrigan's disease' has sometimes been applied to a chronic fibrosis of the lung which he described in 1838.

Born in the slums, the son of a small shopkeeper, Dominic Corrigan was knighted and became five times President of the Royal College of Physicians in Ireland. A beautiful stained-glass window facing the door of the great hall in the College perpetuates his memory.

In 1980 the Section of the History of Medicine of the Royal Academy of Medicine in Ireland held a joint meeting with medical officers of the Charitable Infirmary, Jervis St and St Laurence's Hospital to commemorate the centenary of Corrigan's death. An exhibition of memorabilia, with lists of his papers and contributions to medical journals, indicated how wide were his interests. These had been presented to the Royal College of Physicians of Ireland in 1944 by Mr F. C. Martin, a descendant of Sir Dominic.

One of the lesser-known medical dynasties was that of the Quain family. Jones Quain (1796–1865) was born at Mallow. He studied medicine at Dublin and in Paris. From 1831 to 1835, he was Professor of Anatomy in London University. His best-known work was the textbook *Elements of Anatomy*, first published in 1828. It reached its tenth edition in 1890.

His brother Richard (1800–1887), born at Fermoy, was Professor of Clinical Surgery in University College, London, from 1848 to 1866. He became Surgeon-Extraordinary to Queen Victoria and President of the College of Surgeons of England in 1863. On his death he left £75,000 to University College, London, for education in modern languages and natural science.

Sir Richard Quain (1816–1898), born at Mallow, was Lumleian lecturer at the College of Physicians in London in 1872 and Harveian orator in 1885. His honours were many, including Physician-Extraordinary to the Queen; Ll.D. Edinburgh, 1889; President of the G.M.C. 1891, in which year he was created a baronet. He edited the *Dictionary of Medicine* in 1882. Sir Richard was not in the direct line, but was a first cousin to Jones and Richard.

Through the courtesy of the late Revd Chancellor O. Madden and his sister I was enabled to examine letters written by Jones Quain to his first cousin, Owen Madden. Some of his advice on the feeding of children has a very modern touch:

I recollect to have observed the way in which his nurse fed him. It was irregular and improper in every way, never at fixed hours or stated intervals – no adjustment of the quantity and a bad selection of the sort of food -- as an instance, eggs with cream. Nothing is more injurious to children than the habit of eating in different places.

Owen Madden's child apparently suffered from a squint for he was told to

Make a small stiff green shade and tie it over the *straight* eye to compel him to use the other solely for some time, say a fortnight, and see whether he does not acquire more power over it and squint less.

It is remarkable that the Quains rose to such eminence in London having no influence and only small means from their father's property in Mallow. Their sound medical diagnosis and treatment was, no doubt, an important reason for their success in practice.

There could be no more fitting figure to close this chapter on the famous men of the nineteenth century than Sir John W. Moore (1845–1937). He was in many ways a link between the spacious Victorian days and the crowded, hurried life of the period between the wars. His services to medicine are amply testified by the honorary degrees and memberships of professional societies which were offered to him throughout his long life. In Dublin his services are best remembered for his representation of the Royal College of Physicians on the General Medical Council and his editorship of the *Dublin Journal of Medical Science*.

Moore was Stokes' last house physician and immediate successor at the Meath Hospital. In 1882, as a member of the Dublin Medical Society, he moved the resolution which led to the foundation of the Royal Academy of Medicine in Ireland. At one of the first meetings he was elected Secretary for Foreign Correspondence. He held this post until he was elected President in 1918. In 1935, the Honorary Fellowship of the Academy, its highest award, was conferred on him. Closely associated with his activities for the Academy was his editorship of the *Dublin Journal of Medical Science*, in succession to Sir William Wilde, for forty-seven years (1873–1920). The most difficult of the *Journal's* years fell during this period. Without Moore its survival might not have been possible. He prepared, in all, ninety-four volumes for publication. Even when a new editor took over he continued to make his experience freely available.

In this review of great names we have left out many. Throughout the country, doctors who added in some little way to the history of their profession and their country worked, away from the publicity of city practice. Their names and the stories of their lives would fill a volume more than twice the size of this.

CHAPTER THIRTEEN

MEDICAL ADMINISTRATION

The relief of the destitute, the treatment of the sick and insane poor, as well as the control of Public Health have been looked on as Government functions here for over two hundred years. The system has much to recommend it for ease of administration. Unfortunately, the 'Poor-House' stigma became attached to the district hospitals and many sick people preferred to die at home rather than enter an institution. The administration of the Public Health services was frequently centred in the County Home with a resultant dislike for the treatment afforded by the County Medical Officer and his subordinates.

Prior to the dissolution of the monasteries relief was afforded to the sick poor, by the monks, as a charitable function. The use of the word 'Hospital' in this connection refers more often to a place where hospitality was obtainable than to an institution for the sick. In the medieval boroughs meaures for the relief of destitution and sickness were sometimes undertaken by the guilds.

In 1765 the Irish Parliament passed a Bill enabling the grand juries to provide funds for the provision of hospitals in each county. Within the year several had been opened. The office of County Surgeon was restricted to those who had passed an examination by the County Infirmaries' Board established for the purpose by Act of Parliament. When the College of Surgeons was organised the office was limited to licentiates of that body. This situation lasted for seventy-five years.

It is not possible to determine the exact year in which a dispensary system was initiated. About the end of the eighteenth century certain landlords formed friendly societies for the relief of their sick tenants. In 1805 they received Government grants for this purpose. The system worked very unevenly and it was not always the most deserving cases who received free attention.

The first Boards of Health were set up in 1818. As with the dispensaries there was no co-ordination and the Board's success in coping with sanitary problems was very limited. A central Board of Health was established by the Fever Act of 1846 to cope with the emergency arising from the Famine. The Board had wide powers of control over the local authorities, but it was dissolved when normal conditions returned. During this period other central and local authorities developed, each concerned with some small section of the rudimentary health legislation.

The first comprehensive measure of public relief was the Poor Relief Act of 1838, which established the workhouse system in 130 Union Districts, administered by Boards of Guardians. This Act did not come into full operation until 1845, the year in which the Famine started. The coincidence of Famine destitution being relieved in the newly-established workhouses did nothing to popularise them.

The Famine had such an impact on the life of the country that its consideration is essential in any work dealing with nineteenth-century Ireland, from any aspect.

The population of Ireland at the beginning of the Famine period was 8,295,061, which represented an increase of over one-and-a-half million within a quarter of a century. About a third of the population, mainly in Connaught and Munster, was almost wholly dependent on potatoes for their daily existence. The wretchedness of their living conditions may be judged from the remarks of J. G. Kohl, a German traveller, in 1843:

From Edenvale to Kilrush, sixteen English miles – a main road for the county, I passed not a single village, nor a single hut fit for human habitation. Even in Hungary, Esthonia, Lithuania, I scarcely remember to have seen such miserable cabins as in this part of Ireland – the poorest among the Letts, the Esthonians and the Finlanders lead a life of comparative comfort.

The political and economic conditions leading to the terrible effects of the Famine do not concern us here except in so far as they produced overcrowding and lower vitality, with the effect that infectious diseases piled further misery on the suffering people.

Although the 1845–47 failure of the potato crop was a disaster of previously unparalleled magnitude there had been several lesser failures during the previous century. The first recorded failure followed a severe and early frost in 1739. This lasted for two years. It was complicated by peculiarly malignant and fatal forms of typhus and what may have been cholera. This latter disease was at the time known as 'the bloody flux.' So great was the mortality, that the ordinary burial-grounds were insufficient to receive the large numbers who died by the roadside, or in deserted cabins. Numerous deaths occurred amongst persons occupying high places in society. Amongst these latter were the Mayor and several members of the Limerick Corporation, as well as a judge.

Several minor crop failures occurred, in 1821, 1831, 1835, 1836,

1837, 1839 and 1842. On all of these occasions relief measures proved adequate to prevent severe distress.

In the autumn of 1845, it was found that the potato crop in many areas was affected with a mysterious disease which had appeared in North America during the previous year. The first indications were small brown spots on the leaf, which increased in size until the foliage withered and the stems became brittle. Underground, the tubers were arrested in growth at the size of a pigeon's egg. The whole process was complete in a week. Early crop potatoes and other crops generally were not affected and it was hoped that the visitation was purely transitory.

In 1846 the blight appeared about the beginning of August and caused almost total destruction of the crop. There was a general rush to use what remained to feed pigs and cattle for fear that it would shortly prove quite useless. The effects of the catastrophe were worsened by the fact that, unlike the previous season, other crops were very poor.

In 1847 the disease appeared again in a less virulent form. Largely owing to despair, apathy and the counter attraction of relief works only about a sixth of the normal acreage was planted, so that only partial relief was obtained. Fortunately other crops proved plentiful.

The labouring classes in this country had always subsisted on foods grown by themselves and money wages were little known. It was necessary to devise some new mode of enabling them to procure food. This was done by establishing a system of public works consisting for the most part of improvements to existing highways. The desirability of this practice and the impracticability of working it form no part of a medical history, but are of the greatest sociological importance.

Of more direct medical interest is the situation which obtained in the workhouses. Sheds and stores were opened as auxiliary workhouses to accommodate the huge numbers seeking relief. The insanitary conditions and the low vitality of the inmates caused the mortality rates to soar to unheard-of figures. Inmates infected the workhouse officers. Ninety-four of the latter died between April 1847 and May 1848, chiefly of typhus.

A severe purulent ophthalmia, probably a form of trachoma, developed in several of the workhouses, notably those in Tipperary and Athlone. The Local Government Board requested Dr Arthur Jacob and Sir William Wilde to report on conditions throughout the country. Referring to his inspection of the Athlone Workhouse and its auxiliaries, Jacob wrote:

Of the nature of this ophthalmia, I have to state that it is not in general a very formidable or destructive species of disease, it is what is called mild purulent or catarrhal ophthalmia; but when it attacks people of feeble constitution or labouring under derangement of the general health, it becomes most destructive. In such case, the eye is either more or less injured or rendered altogether useless by rapid ulceration in the first stage; or it is subsequently injured by protracted disease of the inside of the eyelids.

There is a difference of opinion respecting this (the contagiousness of the disease − I advise the adoption of precautions calculated to prevent the spread of the disease in this way − a defective state of the general health predisposes to it, and when it occurs renders it much more destructive.'

Sir William Wilde, who inspected the cases in the Tipperary Union took a more serious view of both the severity and contagiousness of the disease. He reported:

The disease of the eyes under the effect of which the cases submitted for my inspection here labour, is an epidemic inflammation of the conjunctiva or external coat of the eye, commencing and chiefly having its seat in the inside of the eyelids, but in many instances extending rapidly to the globe and destroying, either by sloughing in the first instance, or by subsequent ulceration, the cornea or transparent external coat, and so producing complete or partial blindness in one or both eyes. I believe it to be a modified form of the disease, denominated Egyptian ophthalmia, which I have seen upon a large scale in Cairo and other parts of the Levant and which committed such ravages in the British Army.

It is manifestly contagious, as much so as fever, cholera, dysentery or any other established contagious or infectious disease. An impaired state of the constitution, broken-down health, and spirits, crowding together − have, I think, materially conduced to spread the epidemic in the Tipperary Union.

By a return obtained from all the Unions for 1849 and 1850, it appears that out of 1,737,986 persons admitted during those years to the workhouses 41,012 were treated for inflammatory diseases of the eyes. Of these, 795 suffered permanent partial injury to the sight, 316 lost one eye, and 117 were blinded. Of the last many were still living in blind asylums and workhouses at the beginning of the present century.

Under the Medical Charities Act of 1851 official dispensary districts were formed. Their management was placed in the hands of committees composed of Guardians and ratepayers. Under the Local Government Act of 1898 the Boards of Guardians were charged with the entire management of the dispensaries. They also provided infirmaries and fever hospitals as adjuncts to the workhouses.

Some co-ordination of the preventive and curative services was effected centrally by the establishment in 1872 of the Local Government Board for Ireland. In 1878, a new Act provided the machinery for improved central control.

Prior to 1878, Public Health in Ireland was controlled by innumerable brief Acts produced piecemeal to deal with sanitary situations as they arose. The whole formed a complicated and, at times, contradictory rigmarole productive of much litigation and little health.

The Public Health (Ireland) Act became law in 1878. This was a comprehensive measure which, besides introducing much new and necessary legislation, repealed, amended and codified most of the previous Acts relating to the public health. The Act gave comprehensive powers to sanitary authorities to deal, forcibly if necessary, with all matters relating to hygiene in their districts.

Under the Local Government (Ireland) Act of 1898 county and county borough councils were established. The sanitary authorities became elective urban and rural district councils. Eventually the county councils became responsible for special preventive services, including those concerned with tuberculosis, venereal disease, child health and the sale of food and drugs.

Between 1920 and 1922, Dáil Éireann initiated many changes in the Poor Law system. Most of the County Councils followed the Central Government's lead which aimed at abolishing the workhouses, removing the Boards of Guardians and codifying the operation of Public Health schemes throughout the country. The control of dispensaries and infirmaries (now county and district hospitals) was transferred from Boards of Guardians and Joint Committees to Boards of Health.

In 1923 the Local Government system was chaotic. The Local Government (Temporary Provisions) Act 1923 did something to reduce overlapping and empowered local authorities to introduce health schemes. Then in 1924, the Department of Local Government and Public Health was formed. For the first time the functions of the Local Government Board, the Inspectors of Lunatic Asylums, the office of the Registrar General, and National Health Insurance were controlled by one central authority.

Under the 1878 Public Health Act each Board of Health had been given wide discretionary powers, particularly in the matter of payment to the Dispensary Medical Officers. These were created Medical Officers of Health for their areas. Their duties were not clearly defined and the salaries were sometimes purely nominal. Many Boards only paid five pounds per year. A very few paid a maximum of twenty-five. Some were so niggardly that doctors died as inmates of the very workhouses to which they had been attendants. Despite strong urgings by the Irish and British Medical Associations the Local Government Board persisted in its short-sighted policy with the result that the Act was slackly administered. When the Local Government Act of 1925 was eventually passed the Irish Free State was more than half a century behind the times in Public Health work.

Under the 1925 Act, a new enlarged rural health district was created occupying the area of a county or county borough. The County Council became the sanitary authority for the district, but its duties were performed through a Board of Health consisting of ten members of the council.

The appointment of a full time County Medical Officer of Health responsible for the organisation and direction of local health services was made mandatory for County Councils. His responsibilities included water and milk supplies, food, housing, epidemic control, supervision of maternity and child welfare services, T.B. and V.D. schemes, blind welfare and school health. In most counties Assistant County M.O.s charged with the supervision of a particular part of the Public Health were appointed.

Medical relief for those unable to pay could be provided in three ways,(1) in institutions;(2) in dispensaries; and (3) in their own homes. 'Unable to pay' did not necessarily mean 'destitute'.

Local authority hospitals included both district and county types. The former dealt with minor medical and social problems and in some instances with maternity cases. In the latter most surgical operations could be performed but even by the standards of the day they were often understaffed and inadequately equipped.

The dispensary system lasted for just over 120 years. As with the hospitals penny pinching led to a service which left much to be desired. Buildings were inadequate, ancillary help for the doctor often nil and the supply of medicines basic in the extreme.

The medical officers were in theory part-timers with private practices contributing a major part of their incomes. In reality in poorer areas, whether urban or rural, the dispensary doctor was, for practical purposes, almost entirely dependent on his salary. Patients were expected to attend the dispensaries at fixed times and those who were too ill to venture out were required to procure a 'red ticket' (so called from the colour of the print) from the local relieving officer. This was an order to the dispensary medical officer to visit and treat the patient at home. The tickets could also be issued by members of the Board of Assistance. Many of these were local traders, so that the opportunity and temptation to make personal gain must have been very high in some cases.

The workhouses, still a dreadful memory to many families, now became County Homes. In some the change of name was accompanied by a change of attitude but to many old people admission to the 'Poorhouse' was still a fate too horrible to contemplate. Their feelings were summed up in a poem by an anonymous author found when one of the County Homes was being refurbished about 1970.

> They carved the name above the gate, 1849
> When they built the Workhouse on the hill
> Of limestone tall and fine
>
> A plague wind blew across the land
> Fever was in the air
> Fields were black that once were green
> And death was everywhere
>
> People came to drink the soup
> Ladled from greasy bowls
> They died in whitewashed wards that
> Held a thousand Irish souls
>
> And still the Workhouse looks to
> Heaven — the hills high-windowed dome
> The same for all its name is changed
> Today to the County Home.

Most of the County Homes have been greatly improved but they must still cater for a wide variety of residents, many of whom could be better accomodated elsewhere and the trend now is either to try and supply adequate support to enable people to continue living at home even if handicapped or to admit them to custom built units with properly trained staff where necessary.

The County Medical Officer and his team had played a major part in Irish Medicine for almost a century, particularly in the field of public health but the original concept of this officer's duties had become outmoded in the mid 1970's. Infectious diseases were both less common and less lethal. New industrial processes posed fresh problems of pollution. Some social problems such as drug abuse were on the increase.

In order to enlarge and improve the scope of the M.O.H. the combined post of Director of Community Care and Medical Officer of Health was established with specific roles in preventive medicine, epidemiology, all aspects of environmental health, medical administration, research and the development of medical information systems.

At about the same time a specialised training programme based on the Diploma in Public Health was developed. After three years professional training and an academic year spent obtaining the D.P.H., trainees may proceed to the Fellowship of the Faculty of Community Medicine of the Royal College of Physicians in Ireland which involves an examination as well as undertaking further research and in-service training with a Director of Community Care or the Department of Health.

Unfortunately the number of openings in this country and the remuneration for this very important post are both inadequate at the time of publication (1983), though pressures are being applied to remedy both shortcomings.

MENTAL DISEASES

Mental diseases have had for many years a strong 'official' association. Many mental cases are still treated in county homes. The State is obliged to make very special provision for such cases and although lunacy is no longer considered a crime, restraint of the lunatic must sometimes be practised. The assistance of the courts and of the police is still occasionally necessary and while our outlook may be more enlightened then formerly the mental patient still finds himself in a special category of illness.

One of the earliest references to the insane poor is a petition to the Dublin Assembly in 1699, setting forth a proposal to build a hospital for aged lunatics and other diseased persons. Although grants were made and a site selected, no such building was ever erected.

At this time and until well into the nineteenth century, lunatics were confined in prisons and not in special institutions. Their 'treatment' was similar to that given elsewhere. Purgings, beatings, bleedings and cold baths were routine. One treatment of this nature recorded in Ireland does not seem to have been practised anywhere else. The patient was buried for three days and nights in a shallow grave, leaving the head uncovered for the purpose of feeding, drinking and breathing. It seems highly probable that such therapy would increase the madness rather than cure it.

In 1708 six strong cells were built in the Dublin Workhouse for the reception of violent lunatics. By 1727, this number had been increased to more than forty. In 1711, the occupying military authorities provided cells for lunatic soldiers in the Royal Hospital at Kilmainham. Except for extensions in 1803 these cells were used until 1849 in their original state. After 1729, the Workhouse became almost entirely devoted to the care of foundling children, and Dublin was left without a mental asylum.

About this time Jonathan Swift, Dean of St Patrick's, was considering whether in his will he should bequeath a sum to the city for the foundation of a home for lunatics. Unfortunately his proposals and those of the Corporation were changed and debated until after his death in 1745. It was not until 1747 that the legal difficulties were cleared and St Patrick's Hospital was founded. The first four female patients were admitted on 26th September 1757. The generous action of the Governors of Steevens' Hospital in making a free grant of land helped the new hospital to find its financial feet. For many years this fifty-bed hospital had to suffice as the only refuge of the insane in Ireland.

The first paid physician to St Patrick's was Dr Robert Emmet, father of the United Irishman of the same name. He was one of the original governors and also acted as treasurer. In 1783, when he was State Physician, he was presented with a large piece of silver plate in recognition of his services.

The hospital flourished throughout the nineteenth century and in 1898 the St Edmundsbury estate, near Lucan, was purchased. This house originally belonged to Mr Vesey, a great personal friend of Dean Swift's. Later it was occupied by Edmund Pery, Speaker of the Irish House of Commons. During his term of office the hospital received great parliamentary help. A memory of this exists in a number of benches belonging to the Irish Parliament which are still in use in the institution. Swift's interest in the insane arose before he settled in Ireland, for, in the late 1940's a letter of his was discovered mentioning the fact that he was a governor of Bedlam Royal Asylum in London whilst still a young man.

The House of Industry, North Brunswick Street, was opened in 1773 for the relief and maintenance of beggars. A year later, medical and surgical wards were opened and in 1776 ten cells were arranged for the housing of lunatics. This number was quite inadequate and within the subsequent quarter of a century sixty-six more cells were provided. The conditions in the House of Industry may be judged from the fact that 3,679 persons died therein between 1799 and 1802; an average of almost three per day.

At the beginning of the nineteenth century, St Patrick's was still the only hospital dealing exclusively with the insane. Throughout the country lunatics were confined in prisons, in verminous cells in County Infirmaries or in the Houses of Industry in Dublin, Cork, Limerick and Waterford. Small private asylums existed in Dublin,

Downpatrick, Carlow and Cork, each of which cared for a few patients.

The private asylum at Cittadella, near Cork, was run by Dr William Saunders Halloran. He, at least, made some effort at active treatment. His name appears in the 1818 list of corresponding members of the Association of the King's and Queen's College of Physicians.,

Halloran published a small book in 1818 in which he outlined his theories on mental disease. His work shows evidence of study and the beginnings of a scientific approach. He recognised that there were various forms of insanity of which only some admitted of a cure. He was particularly shrewd in recognising that certain forms are accompanied by obvious organic lesions while others follow on severe mental strain or physicial excess.

He drew up a table of 1,431 patients admitted to Cork Lunatic Asylum from 1798 to 1818. These were classified according to the supposed causes of their insanity. Some of the headings with the numbers admitted thereunder make interesting reading'.

Terror from the Rebellion	108
Jealousy	45
Fever	8
Epilepsy	57
Religious Zeal	20
Venereal Disease	13
Head injury	21
Heredity	79

Of the 1,431 patients, 751 were cured, 429 died, and 251 were still in the asylum when the table was drawn up. In fairness to Halloran it should be stated that many patients were admitted in a very decrepit state which accounts for the high mortality rate. Halloran believed in the hereditary nature of mental disease, and devoted a chapter of his book to this aspect of the problem. He advocated prohibition of marriage between persons with bad family histories.

The cures recommended by Halloran included bleeding, emetics, purgatives, opium, camphor, blistering, mercury, baths and the circulating swing. This last apparatus was intended to amplify the effects of the purges and emetics. It could be rotated at one hundred revolutions per minute. Halloran stated that its use was sometimes followed by a sharp fever for several days and suggested that this might be the immediate cause of a favourable result. In view of the later use of high temperature in the treatment of general paralysis of the insane this suggestion is of no small interest. A modification of this machine was the rocking hammock in which a patient could be rocked gently to sleep or violently shaken until the desired purgative and emetic effect was obtained. In the author's words: 'The discharges which succeeded have surprised me, as much by their extraordinary magnitude as by their density and foetor.'

Halloran recognised that convalescent patients needed as much care as the acutely insane and that they should be educated, if possible, to a useful trade. He further pointed out that re-education of the family and friends was as necessary as that of the patient.

Grangegorman Mental Hospital, now St Brendan's, the largest in the country, was opened in 1815 with the assistance of a parliamentary grant. The present mental service developed from the Lunacy (Ireland) Act of 1821. The Lord Lieutenant was empowered to erect mental hospitals, to appoint local Governors, and to set up a Board of Control to superintend asylums generally. Under the 1898 Local Government Act, it became the duty of the County Councils to cater for the insane poor.

Until 1947, there was no satisfactory system by which a patient could be admitted to a mental hospital voluntarily. He had to go through a complicated legal process which was largely responsible for the stimga attached to treatment in a mental hospital. In that year the Mental Treatment Act of 1945 came into operation. It provided a more flexible procedure for admission, treatment and discharge of mentally ill patients. The patient was now admitted at the request of a relative or friend, backed by medical certificates. It was expected that most patients would be admitted under temporary certificates valid for six months. An important section of the Act enabled temporary admission orders to be made for the treatment of persons addicted to drugs or alcohol. Provision was also made for the establishment of out-patient clinics for the treatment of patients whose mental disability was trivial. These clinics prevented many minor mental disorders from becoming serious.

We are inclined to look askance at days when the insane were beaten and imprisoned and when a trip to Bedlam was a recognised afternoon's diversion. Can we afford to smile now, when those who commit crimes because of mental instability or because of poverty are locked up with those who offend to enrich themselves? Can we even afford to ignore the plea that all crime is pathological and should be treated by doctors and nurses rather than punished by judges and juries?

In the more enlightened approach of the present day, forceful removal to hospital is uncommon. Only a few years ago general hospital governing bodies resolutely refused to grant admission to mentally disturbed patients no matter how quiet and cooperative they were. The old concept of the 'madman' creating havoc all around him died hard.

In the nineteen fifties psychiatric clinics were set up in a few general hospitals and there are now in-patient facilities in some of these. The private psychiatric hospitals now play a major role in providing both in-patient and out-patient care within the overall scheme for mental treatment. One major bone of contention which still (1983) exists between general practitioners and the psychiatric hospitals is that the latter are reluctant to admit patients from outside their own firmly defined catchment areas.

Amongst those who have worked for the welfare and humane treatment of the mentally ill and handicapped, special mention must be made of the Brothers of St John of God, who celebrated the centenary of their arrival in Ireland in 1979. From tiny beginnings, near Clonmel, as an offshoot of the French Province of the Order the Brothers, now with full provincial status, operate facilities in over twenty Irish centres as well as having spread to Australia, the United States and Korea.

When Ireland was partitioned in 1921 medical administration in the Northern counties remained largely unaltered. Urban District Councils which were sanitary authorities in their own area had been established in most towns. Rural District Councils carried out similar functions but were not entitled to levy rates.

Boards of Guardians continued to administer poor relief and medical relief.

In 1927 a Departmental Commission reported that the dispensary system was working well and should be retained but both patients and doctors were dissatisfied with its functioning and many of the latter were in real financial difficulty particularly in rural areas with the small farmer who had previously paid his way disappearing to be replaced by large farmers, whose employees were often entitled to free treatment from the dispensary doctor. As there was no legal definition of a poor person there must have been many people benefiting from this scheme who should have been private patients.

In 1930 Lloyd George's National Insurance Act was implemented in Northern Ireland. This provided most of the poorer workers with a choice of doctor in return for a modest insurance contribution, some of which was used to pay the doctor. Eventually on 5 July 1948 the National Health service was established. Under this, all citizens were entitled to free medical services from the G.P.'s of their own choice as well as to hospitalization. The Dispensary Officers were absorbed into the scheme and were relieved of their duties as Medical Officers of Health.

Some 740 general practitioners agreed to provide services under the scheme, membership of which is obligatory, even for those who wish to continue private arrangements for their medical treatment. Payment to the participating doctors is on a capitation basis. At the beginning of the scheme most doctors were practising from their own premises, often in their family homes. There is an increasing tendency now for practices to be based on Health Centres with several doctors and improved ancillary services. Though fears were expressed that this trend would depersonalise general practice it does not appear to have done so.

The original intention of the N.H.S. was that all medical needs would be totally covered, free of charge and if the system was not abused this might be possible. Unfortunately there are always those who grab anything 'free' with both hands. In addition costs of medicines, appliances and hospital accommodation steadily increased so that charges have had to be made for some services, sometimes only for certain categories of patient. For example, low income patients are entitled to free prescriptions and glasses. Despite dire predictions in the early days the National Health Service is working well and it would be a brave or foolhardy government which would try to dismantle it.

CHAPTER FOURTEEN

THE BELFAST SCHOOL

The earliest reference to medicine in Belfast occurs after the defeat of O'Neill and the occupation of the city by Sir Arthur Chichester, in 1651. The commissioners for the area at the time were admonished by the Government not to pay more than £100 yearly to a doctor, nor more than £50 yearly to an apothecary.

In 1689, Schomberg's army in Dundalk retired into winter quarters at Belfast, then little more than a village of thatched cabins. A hospital was provided at the demand of Thomas Pottinger, the Governor, with a Dr Lawrence in charge. During the period November 1689 to May 1690, 3,762 men died. The deaths amongst civilians are not recorded, but papers of the period speak of ten funerals passing through the main street in one hour.

Two of the sanitary laws at this time read:

No one to make dunghills to continue longer than three days in the open street before the door or throw carrion, dying stuff, or any loathsome thing into the river, under a penalty of five shillings.

All blood (from slaughter houses) and garbage to be carried twenty yards beyond high-water mark under a penalty of twenty shillings.

Unfortunately there are few records of medical interest prior to the foundation of the *Belfast News Letter* in 1737. From those that remain it appears that medical men held a prominent and respected place in the community. John Tooley, a chirurgeon, is mentioned as the bearer of the mantle, helm and crest at the funeral of the first Earl of Donegal. Prominent among those who 'dug with the other foot' were Dr Marriot, composer of some of the 'Hearts of Steel' ballads, and Dr William Drennan (1754–1820), tried and acquitted for seditious libel. Part of the latter's will is a curious document:

I leave my wife a legacy of £100 by way of atonement for the many unmerciful scolds I have thrown away upon her at the whist table —

Until the establishment of the Irish licensing bodies most of the practitioners in the north of Ireland held the diplomas of one or both of the Edinburgh Colleges or the Glasgow Faculty of Surgeons. A few held medical degrees from Edinburgh University.

The Belfast Medical School had its origin in the establishment in 1792 of a dispensary by Dr James McDonnell (1762–1845) of Antrim. In 1797, the work of this dispensary had become so great that a small (six beds) fever hospital was opened. By the middle of October 1798 sixty patients had been treated with only one death. Only £5 remained of the original capital of £58 and a public subscription was organised. Unfortunately, all the members of the staff, including MacDonnell, contracted typhus and the hospital was temporarily closed.

In September 1799, a meeting was held to revive the hospital. The Rev William Bristow preached a charity sermon which realised £113, and with this small capital the hospital was re-opened in West Street, near Smithfield, with 20 beds. Following an Act of Parliament which helped the financial position a site was selected, in 1810, on which to erect a building designed as a hospital. On 5th June 1815, the foundation-stone of the new hospital was laid on the site in Frederick Street. In the centre of the stone were placed various objects, including a piece of pottery, coins, an almanac, a map of Belfast, a manuscript in Irish, and a small Bible. When the building was demolished in 1936 the stone could not be found. The years 1816 and 1817 were marked by severe outbreaks of typhus. The wards were opened on 1st August 1817, and, although the paint was still wet and the staircases insecure, 100 patients were immediately admitted. In 1818, 1,530 patients were admitted and in the following year, 1,258. Until 1821 only fever patients were admitted and no cases were refused either from city or country.

During the first year the Board of Management reported that:

The physicians and surgeons of Belfast should be invited to place their pupils here to acquire experience by observing its practice and in the course of a few years it might become a School of Physic and Surgery of no trifling importance to the young Medical Students of this neighbourhood and the Province of Ulster.

In 1820, in its third year, the hospital received pupils for the first time, as assistants to the staff. The first student was Mr W. Bingham. Formal clinical lectures were not given until 1827. At this time there was no definite Faculty of Medicine in Belfast. It was not until 1835 that a Medical School was opened in connection with the Royal Belfast Academical Institution. Prior to this three hundred students left Belfast and the northern counties every year for schools elsewhere. Classes in the new school commenced in 1835. The appointments to the faculty were:

Dr James L. Drummond	President, Professor of Botany, Anatomy and Physiology.
Dr John McDonnell	Professor of Surgery.
Dr Thomas Andrews	Professor of Chemistry.
Dr J. Drummond Marshall	Professor of Materia Medica and Pharmacy.
Dr Robert Little	Professor of Midwifery and Diseases of Women and Children.
Dr Henry MacCormac	Professor of Medicine (in 1837).

McDonnell did not occupy his post and was replaced by Thomas Ferran.

When founded the Faculty had no direct connection with the Frederick Street Hospital. As a result clinical teaching was impossible and the examining bodies would not accept candidates who had not adequate hospital instruction. A building known as the Old Barrack came up for sale in 1836 and was purchased by the Institution for £1,750, a sum which exhausted its funds. An epidemic of typhus came to the rescue.

A fever hospital had been erected at the rear of the General Hospital in Frederick Street in 1830, when Asiatic cholera was epidemic in Europe. When typhus struck Belfast in 1837, this hospital's small bed space was so overcrowded that the offer of accommodation and staff in the Old Barrack was gladly accepted. At the same time a teaching hospital became available for Belfast medical students. The famous Purdysburn Fever Hospital was not opened until 1906. This is now Belvoir Park Hospital.

This arrangement did not last long, and without facilities for clinical teaching in Frederick Street, the Belfast school would have failed.

In 1845 Queen Victoria assented to the founding of a number of colleges for higher education in Ireland. As a result Queen's College was opened in the Malone Road. Unfortunately this was on the opposite side of the city to the General Hospital. An agreement was reached whereby some of the staff of the General Hospital were appointed College Professors though not, as one would expect nowadays, to Chairs relevent to their specialties. For example the first Professor of Materia Medica was Horatio Stewart a surgeon who held the Chair until his death in 1857. Alexander Gordon also a Surgeon was appointed to the Chair of that subject and John Creery Ferguson formerly of the Apothecaries' Hall and T.C.D. became first Professor of Medicine. William Burden who had been Professor of Medicine in the Academical Institution since 1840 took over the same post in Queens.

The first Professor of Natural History was George Dickie of Aberdeen. This gentleman lectured at seven in the morning; a habit which made him most unpopular with his class.

Thomas Andrews was the first holder of the Chair of Chemistry. His later work on the latent heat of vapours and chemical combination was of outstanding importance.

Hugh Carlile was originally appointed to Queen's College, Cork, as Professor of Anatomy and Physiology. By a private arrangement he changed places with Alexander Carte. Carlile was a nephew of Professor Macartney of T.C.D., and had taught in the Park Street School in Dublin for nineteen years. He brought with him a valuable collection of anatomical specimens which are still in Queen's University, Belfast.

A Royal Commission held in 1858 revealed that the great needs of the College were clinical instruction and an adjacent dissecting-room. The old dissecting-room of the Institution was still in use. This system, involving a loss of several hours a week to the student, due to travelling difficulties, was not improved until 1866. The buildings erected were not, even then, complete. No physiology laboratory was included until thirty-one years later.

At this time about seventy students were attending the senior classes. There were only 200 beds in the General Hospital. As a result the opportunities for clinical instruction were meagre. After great trouble permission was granted for students to attend clinics in the Workhouse Infirmary. Later they requested and were granted permission to attend the Lock and Fever Hospitals. Certificates of attendance at the Workhouse were not regularised until 1926. Unfortunately a disturbance occurred following celebrations shortly after and the Guardians withdrew the privilege.

From its foundation, students of Queen's College, Belfast, sat for their University examinations in Dublin. In 1909, the College became The Queen's University of Belfast, with the power to examine and grant degrees. Prior to this, many students took the qualifications of the licensing bodies only. These latter were essential for appointments to the Army, Navy or dispensary services.

In common with the other Irish teaching bodies Queen's suffered from overcrowding. Despite many appeals to the Government no improvements were made until the beginning of the new century. About this time, too, several new chairs were created: Physiology (1893), Pathology (1901), Gynaecology (1920), Public Health (1921), Bio-Chemistry (1925), Pharmacology (1928). An autonomous sub-division of Dentistry was opened in 1920 in conjunction with the Royal Victoria Hospital, the descendant of the old General Hospital in Frederick Street which had been opened in 1815, with 100 beds, as 'the Fever Hospital'. Five years later medical students were admitted to courses of instruction. At this stage all the medical staff were general practitioners and they were far-seeing enough to recognise the importance to students of a period of hospital residence. From the beginning their apprentices, as they then were, resided within the hospital walls for specified periods.

Though the population of Belfast had quadrupled by 1860 the General Hospital still had only 100 beds. A further 86 were added by 1865 but the population had expanded even faster and by 1896 a new hospital was planned to commemorate the Diamond Jubilee of Queen Victoria though it was not opened and re-named the Royal Victoria by King Edward VII, in the present Grosvenor Road Premises until 1903.

The Royal Victoria has been one of the principal hospitals dealing with the appalling results of sectarian savagery which are so common in Belfast to-day. Whatever the personal feelings of the staff they have, in common with the other hospitals, extended their healing service to all bombing victims who sought it, without any consideration of creed, political belief or any other factor. Their experience of dealing with trauma particularly in the field of brain surgery is probably unrivalled in the world to day.

Another general hospital recognised for clinical teaching, since 1908, is the Mater Infirmorum, opened in 1883 by the Sisters of Mercy on a site opposite the present one in what already was referred to by a writer of the time as a 'venerable old pile'. Within ten years the original 34 beds had became inadequate but despite public meetings and fund raising efforts it was not until 1900 that the present hospital on Crumlin Road was opened. A maternity unit was added forty-eight years later.

As a voluntary hospital the Mater had to be self supporting but in 1948 when the National Health Service came into operation the Governing Body decided to remain outside the scheme and thus free of Hospitals' Authority jurisdiction. There were a number of reasons for taking this option but the most important was the Government decision not to implement a clause in the original Act which would enable hospitals in the Health Service to preserve their religious affiliations. For over a quarter of a century the Mater continued its independent existence. Eventually after lengthy negotiations the Hospital came into the Health Service in January 1, 1972 with a safeguard for its traditional religious associations being provided by a clause in the Health Services Act of 1971. With the extra funds which now became available the Mater was able to secure badly needed new equipment but the most urgent need and one very difficult to satisfy is still room for expansion though a new block is planned for building in 1984.

Two childrens' hospitals opened in the same year (1873) in Belfast and there is still discussion as to which was the senior. These were the Ulster Hospital for children, at 12 Chichester Street and the Belfast Hospital for Sick Children, at 25 King Street. A report in the *Northern Whig* of 1 August 1873 records that 101 out-patients had already been seen in the former.

Tentative efforts at amalgamation were made at an early stage but apparently the King Street Hospital Board were opposed to the Chichester Street Board's suggestion that adult female patients should also be admitted. Other stumbling blocks were the Ulster Hospital proposal to hold evening out-patient clinics to facilitate working people and a scheme for co-operating with the dispensary doctors.

One of the prime movers in the foundation of the Ulster Hospital for Children was Dr John Martin (1839–1884) of Newtownards who was a dispensary doctor. He served as a medical officer until 1876 when ill health forced him to retire though he remained on the Committee for a further five years when he resigned because he could not agree to the proposed opening of a Maternity and Gynaecological unit. The hospital opened with fourteen cots for non-surgical cases and in the first year 6,700 children were treated both as intern and extern patients and an additional 367 were visited in their own homes. With this volume of work it is little wonder that in 1876 a move had to be made to more commodious premises in Fisherwick Place, some 350 metres from 'the rival firm'. Twenty two cots were now available. William Whitla, later to achieve international recognition, was appointed to the honorary staff and is recorded as visiting all the intern patients, at least once daily.

Further fruitless approaches to the Belfast Hospital for Sick Children were made and in 1881 adult women were admitted to a ten bed ward and a midwife was appointed to undertake domicilary midwifery. About this time too students were admitted for instruction in midwifery, gynaecology and paediatrics. Four dispensary doctors were involved in this and each took pairs of students under his personal tuition, a forerunner of the attachment scheme so widely practised now.

In 1891 a further move was made to Mountpottinger where additional Eye and E.N.T. Departments were opened.

Yet another move was made in 1912 to Templemore Ave, where what was to be known as 'The Wee Hospital' did sterling work until 1941 when incendiary and explosive bombs demolished the buildings. Fortunately the children had already been evacuated to Saintfield House and Haypark where work was to carry on until 1944 in the former and until 1962 in the latter when the new Ulster Hospital was opened at Dundonald with over five hundred beds available for the treatment of a much wider range of illness then was ever envisaged by the pioneers of 1873.

What then of the other Childrens' Hospital? The opening date of the Belfast Hospital is firmly established as June 23rd 1873, 'on the same principle as the hospital in Great Ormond St, London'. Up to 4th August, of the same year only out-patients were taken but then a nine bedded ward was opened. At the end of a year 317 intern and over 5,000 extern patients had been seen and in 1874 it was decided to offer instruction in the diseases of childhood to medical students.

When further expansion became necessary in 1878 to a site in Queen St further efforts were made at amalgamation with the Ulster Hospital but this time the stumbling block was the absence from the Belfast Hospital's code of a rule sanctioning the admission of clergymen to the hospital. The Board tried to overcome the difficulty by making a regulation allowing free access of pastors to children of their own denominations and stressing that no efforts at conversion or prosletysing should be made. This did not satisfy the Ulster Hospital Board who insisted that there should be no restriction on Gospel readings by the matron and visiting ladies. No agreement could be reached and the two institutions went their separate ways.

The Queen Street premises contained forty beds and an out patient department which provided inter alia ophthalmological and dental services. During this period the training of both medical students and nurses became a major part of the hospital work, a situation which, combined with the large numbers of patients attending, eventually rendered the acquisition of new premises once again a matter of urgency. In 1932 a new 73 bed hospital was opened at the present site on the Falls' road with the assistance of a £10,000 bequest from the estate of Henry Musgrave.

This building was built in accordance with the most modern design of the time and became a medical show place of which the local people could be justifiably proud. A very advanced step for the times was facilities for mothers to remain with and help to nurse the children. Further extensions followed up to the outbreak of war in 1939, when in common with every other hospital the Belfast had to cope with staff reductions, patient evacuations and the possibility of air raid damage. Fortunately despite heavy raids on Belfast there was little material destruction to the hospital.

Immediately after the war plans for further development were thrown into chaos by the impending State take-over under the 1948 Northern Ireland Health Services Act. Under this the Belfast

Children's Hospital would be administered by a Group Committee responsible also for a number of other hospitals. Two weeks later the hospital was granted the appellation 'Royal' though the Northern Ireland Governor decided not to ask for Royal patronage as it would be 'inappropriate for an individual hospital under present circumstances' i.e. the nationalisation of the Health services.

The importance of convalescence and follow up in a healthy atmosphere was recognised from a very early stage but despite many efforts to provide suitable premises it was 1889 before a 12-bedded convalescent home could be opened at Newtownbreda with the title The Queen Victoria Convalescent Home for Children. For some reason none of the medical staff was invited to the opening ceremony. The home was always struggling financially and in 1908 after an outbreak of diphtheria this pioneer effort came to an end though in later years the idea was improved and expanded at Joymount in Carrickfergus a house which closed after only eleven years. There was no replacement until Lissue House near Lisburn which had previously been used as an emergency hospital during the war became available as a free gift thanks to the generosity of the family of Col D. C. Lindsay. This house was equipped and staffed rather as an annex of the main hospital than as a convalescent home.

On 21st January 1871, Mr Edward Benn, a well-known Ulster philanthropist, opened a small private hospital for the free treatment of eye diseases, in Great Patrick Street. He invited Dr William McKeown to take charge. The latter had already acquired considerable experience in his own private dispensary. McKeown's original work in ophthalmology is often neglected, but he had an international reputation, gained in the first instance by his use of the magnet for the removal of metal from the interior of the eye, which operation he performed for the first time in 1873 on a worker from the Harland and Wolff shipyard. His reputation for the surgical treatment of cataract was equally widespread.

The Belfast School of Obstetrics grew side by side with the Medical School generally. The story of its growth is largely the history of the Royal Maternity Hospital.

The Belfast Lying-in Hospital was first conceived in 1793 at a meeting held in the Linen Hall. The initiator was the Rev John Clark, then curate of St Anne's Church. The original name of the charity was to be 'The Humane Female Society for the relief of Lying-In Women.' The original 180 members subscribed 10s. 6d. each per annum. Refused the use of a ward in the Charitable Institution, they rented, for twelve guineas a year, a house in Donegall Street in which they had six beds. This house was opened for the reception of patients on 20th February 1794.

The records of the early days are fragmentary. No permanent medical staff was appointed. There was a separate ward for unmarried women. These were only admitted if they were first offenders. Weekly visitors were appointed from among the ladies of the committee. In the report book one of them states: 'I have endeavoured to make the midwife sensible that it is her duty to prevent the patients from spitting on the walls at the head of their beds.' Rather incongruously, she notes a few lines later: 'The House is as usual perfectly clean and in good order.' The diet was mainly milk, gruel, bread, rice, soup, arrowroot, butter and tea. During 1803, sixty-three patients were treated. This number increased steadily.

The resident staff were a nurse-tender or midwife and a maid. These two conducted the normal deliveries. A Dr Stephenson was called for difficult cases. This state of affairs lasted until 1830.

In 1828, the Ladies' Committee obtained rent-free land from the Charitable Society on the present Clifton Street. The building erected thereon was opened for the accommodation of eighteen patients in 1830. Patients were treated in their own homes as well as in the hospital. Dr Stephenson served in this institution until 1837, when his place was taken by Dr William Burden, who fought vigorously for the interests of his staff, students and nurses.

Medical students attended the practice of the hospital from 1854. Their work included lectures, demonstrations and the conduct of cases in the patients' homes. The curriculum contained no reference to gynaecology, which was still in its infancy as a separate subject. The 'resident' students were housed in lodgings in Townsend Street, and in Regent Street, near the hospital. Various systems of calling them were adopted, including the placing of a white sheet in the window of the labour ward. The students employed an urchin to keep the window under observation and inform them when they were wanted. Failure to notify or false notification involved the urchin in various penalties, including blood-curdling threats of ante-mortem dissection.

In 1855, Burden was appointed Master, with a staff consisting of Drs Dill, Purrie and Malcolm. As a result of this and the fees paid by medical students the Charitable Society, who were the ground landlords, now demanded rent for the premises formerly held rent free. The dispute was settled by payment of an annual rental of £3　3s.　0d. In 1900 the Society took an action for eviction against the Hospital Governing Body.

At this period fully-trained midwives were non-existent. The Sarah Gamps and handy-women attended cases by virtue of their own large families. The London Obstetrical Society granted a diploma by examination from 1872 and some hospitals gave courses of training, but in general this was sketchy, even for the few who attended. About 1860, in the face of strong opposition, Burden admitted a Mrs Hamil to a course of lectures. It was not until 1879 that the training of nurses was regarded as a vital part of the hospital's work.

Burden retired from the Chair in 1867 and from the hospital two years later. His departure and services to the College and Hospital were not officially recognised. The President of the College did not even mention that he had relinquished his post.

Robert F. Dill was now appointed Professor of Midwifery. As he had resigned from the hospital following a difference of opinion with the committee, he was in the difficult position of having no clinical material for his students. To overcome this he sent his students to poor women who wished for attention without going to hospital or paying a private doctor's fees. Dill, who had a large private practice, was city coroner and a prominent public figure. In one of the sectarian riots of the time he lost an eye.

The first student to reside in the hospital did so in 1868. He had already taken out his cases. The first students to reside there in order to do the necessary practical work were two ladies in 1898. They were given board and lodging at one pound per week on the understanding that they would leave if their beds were required for patients.

Following the deaths of eight women from puerperal sepsis in 1883 the medical staff wished to erect an isolation wing at a cost of £150. The Committee refused to grant the money. Two years later the nursing of patients in their own homes was instituted.

There are several references to clinical teaching in the annual reports of the hospital, but they seem to err on the side of optimism. Several of those who attended the hospital about the end of the century stated that no lectures were given except by the matron. One student, later a distinguished Professor, stated that he had never heard a clinical lecture in midwifery until he gave one himself! Students were frequently called on to perform obstetrical operations and give anaesthetics without qualified supervision.

In 1893, the hospital centenary year, Professor Dill died and the Chair of Obstetrics was taken by Professor Byers. The hospital became the Belfast Maternity Hospital; 'Incorporated' being added to the title in 1900, for legal reasons.

Byers did not come on the hospital staff until 1902. Even then he was only a part-time junior assistant, despite his College Professorship. His only opportunity to give clinical instruction at the hospital was when he was summoned to deal with emergencies on the district.

In 1900, following a renewed dispute with the Charitable Society the hospital was transferred to a site in Townsend Street. The medical staff were opposed to this site, but their wishes were overruled, as they were in many other matters. Due largely to Professor (later Sir John) Byers' exclusion from the administrative work of the hospital, the number of students fell off. An unpaid resident house-surgeon was appointed in 1904, after repeated appeals by the medical staff.

On Byers' death in 1920 Professor Lowry was appointed to the Chair of Midwifery and a separate Chair of Gynaecology went to Professor (later Sir) Robert Johnstone. Lowry was invited to join the staff of the hospital, which, mindful of the treatment meted out to Byers, he did on conditions. Within five years of his appointment the hospital was almost unrecognisable. There were two medical representatives on the Board of Governors; an ante-natal clinic had been opened; the medical staff were of senior status; a residence for students was opened and a university tutor had been installed. C. H. G. Macafee was the first holder of this post.

Until 1925, the Residency was a makeshift place, as were most of the wards and other accommodations. As a result, many Belfast students did their midwifery cases in Dublin or elsewhere.

The first refuge provided for mental patients in Belfast was the Grosvenor Road District Asylum, erected in 1829. This was of the usual pattern of the day. Its main function was the protection of the public, and in appearance the building was more like a prison than a hospital. There were numerous small, single cells whose tiny windows were heavily barred. Walls, locked doors and barriers of all sorts completed the prison-like picture.

Originally this building catered for Counties Antrim and Down as well as Belfast. In 1868 a special asylum was built for County Down and in 1897 separate arrangements were made for patients from Antrim and Belfast. In 1895, the Board of Governors acquired property at Purdysburn, five miles south of Belfast. Later purchases brought the total area available to 500 acres with about 65 acres for Purdysburn Fever Hospital.

In 1900, the Committee of Management decided to erect a new asylum on the villa colony principle, which accommodates patients in separate houses and permits of their classification according to physical and mental condition.

The principal units in this plan were a central block of buildings for sick and infirm cases with a number of detached villa residences. In Purdysburn these were designed to accommodate about sixty patients each. There is accommodation for a total of about twelve hundred patients. The colony is largely self-contained, as there is a shop to supply the patients' everyday small needs. The farm and orchards provide ample produce, and repairs to machinery and equipment can be effected in the colony's workshops. Catholic and Protestant churches for the use of the staff and patients are situated in the grounds.

Belfast led the way for the treatment of tuberculosis in Ireland with the establishment, in 1880, of the Provident Institution for Chest Diseases in Donegall Street. Prior to this, such cases were accommodated in the Union Hospital. In 1896, through the efforts of a generous Quaker gentleman, Mr Forster Green, the Institution was incorporated as the Forster Green Hospital, Fortbreda.

In 1904, the Poor Law Guardians acquired 'The Abbey' at Whiteabbey, Co Antrim, as an 'auxiliary workhouse' for the treatment of tuberculous patients. Two years later they commenced the erection of buildings to accommodate 265 beds. In 1914, the City Council took over the Sanatorium, renaming it the Belfast Municipal Sanatorium. During the same period various arrangements were made between the Corporation, the Insurance Committee, the Forster Green Hospital and the Abbey to provide treatment and relief for poor consumptive patients. The Central Tuberculosis Institute was opened in 1918.

The Municipal Hospital for children suffering from non-pulmonary tuberculosis was moved from Graymount to Greenisland following the 1941 air-raids when the former buildings were seriously damaged. In 1947, the new hospital came under the control of the Northern Ireland Tuberculosis Authority and was renamed the Orthopaedic Hospital, Greenisland.

OPHTHALMOLOGY AND OTORHINOLARYNGOLOGY

Just as in Dublin, the study of eye diseases became a matter of importance in Belfast about the middle of the nineteenth century. An attempt had been made to form an eye dispensary in 1816, but it was not until 1827 that success prevailed. This dispensary lasted only twelve years.

In 1845 Dr Samuel Browne established the Belfast Ophthalmic Institute at 35 Mill Street. The site was changed in 1858 to Donegall Square Mews and in 1861 to Howard Street. There was an average annual attendance of one thousand, of whom some one hundred were ear cases and twenty cases of cataract.

The Belfast Ophthalmic Hospital was founded in 1867 by Lady Johnson. In the early days the intern staff consisted of a caretaker and his wife, who attended to the nursing. The first surgeon was Dr Samuel Browne. He was succeeded by his son, John Walton. Amongst other well-known members of the staff were Dr Wiclif McCready and Dr Cecil Shaw, whose textbook on ophthalmology was very popular about the beginning of the present century.

The Benn Ulster, Eye, Ear, Nose and Throat Hospital, founded in 1871, has already been noted, but the general hospitals also opened special departments at various periods. In 1882 the Royal Hospital decided to open special departments for diseases of women and of the eye and ear. This was done in order to meet the educational requirements of the Royal University. That the gesture was a nominal one may be judged from the fact that expenditure on the expanded service was not to exceed £20 per annum. A separate examination in ophthalmology and otology was not held until 1895, but from 1886 candidates for the final examination of the Royal University were required to have reasonable proficiency in the use of the ophthalmoscope and laryngoscope.

The Mater Infirmorum Hospital established a new eye, ear, nose and throat department on moving to new premises in 1900.

THE ULSTER MEDICAL SOCIETY

The Ulster Medical Society was founded in 1862 by the union of the Belfast Medical Society and the Belfast Clinical and Pathological Society. The Belfast Medical Society had been founded in 1806 by Dr S. S. Thompson with nineteen original members. Its objects were to hold medical discussions, form a library, and make a collection of anatomical preparations. The Society lapsed twice, but was successfully reconstituted in 1822. Its most important meeting was held in 1832, when proposals leading to the foundation of a medical school were discussed. This eventually became the present faculty of medicine of the Queen's University.

In 1853 certain members, led by Dr A. G. Malcolm, broke away to form the Belfast Clinico-Pathological Society. This society was extremely vigorous and published abstracts of its meetings for the benefit of country members. Unfortunately, none of these have been preserved. The services of the founder have been honoured by the foundation of the Malcolm Exhibition for students of the Belfast Medical School. Malcolm's *Inquiry into the Physical Influence of Mill Life* contains recommendations for the medical supervision of works, on the lines laid down in the present-day Factory and Workshop Acts.

In 1862 the two societies were reunited, this time as the 'Ulster Medical Society.' This society maintained a vigorous existence, both in the scientific and medico-political fields. On the formation of the North of Ireland branch of the B.M.A. in 1883, the society devoted itself exclusively to professional matters. The papers read and cases exhibited were of a consistently high standard. The principal social functions inaugurated were the Annual Dinner, first held in 1864, and an Annual Presidential Reception. The official organ of the society is the *Ulster Medical Journal*, which appears quarterly.

BELFAST AND ULSTER MEDICAL SOCIETIES' *TRANSACTIONS*

The first *Transactions of the Belfast Medical Society* were published in 1857–58. In 1859–60 they were continued as *Transactions of the Clinical and Pathological Society* and and from 1877 as the *Transactions of the Ulster Medical Society*. Until 1890 they were published by Falconer of Dublin, and subsequently in Belfast. These *Transactions* appeared at very irregular intervals and in 1932 it was decided to produce a quarterly journal particularly suited to the needs of the busy practitioner in Northern Ireland. The *Ulster Medical Journal*, which first appeared on 1st January 1932, is financed and controlled by the Ulster Medical Society. The first General Editor was Dr Richard H. Hunter.

Contrary to the expectations of many, the *Journal* was highly successful and attracted contributions from outside the immediate area. When war broke out in 1939 publication of the *Journal* was suspended until April 1940, when it reappeared every six months, in April and October, up to 1948, when quarterly publication was resumed.

No account of the Belfast School would be complete without reference to Sir William Whitla (1851–1933). His interest in medicine started when at an early age he was apprenticed to a chemist. Shortly afterwards he commenced a brilliant career in Queen's College, Belfast. His studies were rewarded by the M.D. in 1879. Within two years he had been appointed to the staff of the Royal Victoria Hospital. Before the end of his long life he received many honours from universities and learned societies, including a knighthood in 1902. In the same year he erected, equipped and presented to the Ulster Medical Society the Medical Institute, since renamed The Whitla Institute.

Whitla's *Textbook of Materia Medica and Therapeutics* ran to twelve editions before his death. When this book first appeared Whitla was carrying on a considerable surgical practice. The success of the book and his appointment to the Chair of Materia Medica in Queen's College decided his future speciality. Whitla's later writings included dictionaries of treatment and of medicine. A specially-bound copy of the latter, written in Chinese, was one of his proudest possessions.

When the Queen's University was founded, Whitla was appointed Pro-Chancellor and was elected first Parliamentary representative. Whitla's influence on and interest in the Belfast School lasted until his death.

This very brief account of the Belfast School will end with an outline of the life of one of the most progressive northern practitioners.

Henry MacCormac (1802?–1886) was born in County Armagh. He studied medicine in Dublin, Paris and Edinburgh, where he qualified. After a period of travel in Africa and America he returned to Belfast, and was appointed a Physician to the General Hospital in 1830. In 1832, he was given charge of the temporary cholera hospital at Frederick Street. He received a handsome testimonial in recognition of his work in this hospital. In 1835, MacCormac was elected to fill the Chair of Medicine in the new School of Medicine of the Royal Belfast Academical Institution.

MacCormac's fame rests most securely on his work in the field of tuberculosis. His familiarity with twenty languages was of the greatest assistance in the preparation of his book, *On the Nature of Consumption*, published in 1855. His main advocacy was for the fresh air treatment of tuberculosis. Unfortunately, the medical world was not ready to receive his message, although one of his critics admitted that his views were already five hundred years old. The *Lancet* and the London Medical and Chirurgical Society characterised a paper of MacCormac's on the subject of fresh air and consumption as being a waste of time. Fortunately other minds were more receptive and MacCormac had the pleasure of reading German and Dutch translations of his work. MacCormac's other publications dealt with stammering, hanging, humane killing, chemistry and dietetics. Up to the end of his life he worked from four in the morning until late at night on his self-imposed task of educating his fellows to breathe fresh air.

CHAPTER FIFTEEN

THE PRIVATE MEDICAL SCHOOLS

Prior to the foundation of the School of the Royal College of Surgeons there were no regular schools of surgery in Ireland. Their place was assumed by professional anatomists, who gave instructions to persons other than their apprentices. The following advertisement which appeared in the *Dublin Weekly Journal* for 19th October 1728, gives an idea of the services rendered by these men:

A course of Anatomy in all its branches viz., Osteology, Myology, Angiology, Neurology, Adenology and Enterology will be given by James Brenan, M.D., at his house on Arran Key the 18th November, 1728, at twelve of the clock and will be continued every Monday, Wednesday and Friday, until the whole is completed, the operative part by Peter Brenan, Surgeon.

N.B. The charge of this course is two pistoles (34*s.* 2*d.*). And if any students in Physic and Chirurgery be desirous to read Anatomy and Dissect they may be instructed and accommodated at the same place on reasonable terms.

Although the teaching of anatomy and medicine was centred in Dublin there were isolated pockets of instruction existing in provincial areas. An advertisement for one of these schools appeared in the *Dublin Journal* for 28th July 1767:

Mr Maxwell, Surgeon, of the Tyrone Hospital, being solicited by many of his friends to establish in this county an anatomical school for instruction of young gentlemen of the profession, intends on Monday 14th December, at 2 o'clock, to begin, at his house at Omagh, a course of lectures on anatomy and surgery with some practical observations in midwifery, on the following terms, viz:— for attending his lectures on anatomy, three guineas; dissecting pupils provided with subjects, six guineas; for attending his lectures in general and the practice of the hospital, and being taught to dissect and to perform all the different operations in surgery, twelve guineas per annum. Such pupils as choose to come under Mr Maxwell's more private tuition may be provided with diet and lodging in his own house at fifteen guineas per annum.

The greatest period of the private schools in Dublin was between the years 1804 and 1880. Some of these gave sound training, but, in many, due to economic and other circumstances, the teaching was inferior in quality.

The first unchartered school opened in the nineteenth century was that established, in 1804, in the stable at the rear of 42 Dawson Street by Sir Philip Crampton. In this building he gave lectures on anatomy, physiology and surgery. Most of his pupils came from the Meath Hospital, to which Crampton was surgeon at the time. When he became Surgeon-General, in 1813, Crampton closed the school. The last survivor of his class was Dr William Madden, several times Governor of the Apothecaries' Hall, who died in October 1866, aged 81 years.

Peter Harkan, who was a demonstrator in Crampton's School, was a prominent resurrectionist. On one occasion he led a party of pupils to Bully's Acre, where several newly-dug graves promised rich returns. Unfortunately, the party were surprised by night watchmen. With great courage, Harkan delayed his escape until all his pupils were clear. As he scaled the cemetery wall the watchmen caught his legs. His pupils caught him by the arms and for several minutes he was hauled backwards and forwards across the rough wall, before the students won. It is believed that his death in 1814, in his early thirties, was directly due to the injuries received during this tug-of-war.

Crampton was prominent in his efforts to regularise the supply of bodies for dissection. At one time he gave public lectures in order to stimulate lay interest and show that there was no disgrace attached to post-mortem examination.

About 1808, systematic courses on medicine and surgery were instituted in the Charitable Infirmary, Jervis Street. Dissections were carried on in a room at the rear of the hospital. In 1813, courses of lectures on anatomy, physiology and surgery were delivered by Samuel Wilmot, who was assisted in clinical surgery by Richard Dease. At the same time, Dr W. Brooke lectured on the theory and practice of medicine. There was very little teaching of anatomy in this school after 1818. In 1832 Drs D. G. Corrigan and Percival Hunt (1802–1848) advertised a course of lectures in the Jervis Street Hospital school. The fee of two guineas also entitled the pupil to attend the hospital practice. The school lasted twenty-five years. During much of this time it was imperfect, even by the not-very-severe requirements of the day.

In 1809, John Timothy Kirby and Alexander Read (1786–1870) opened a private medical school at the rear of a house in Stephen Street, near Mercer's Hospital. Part of the house was occupied by a laundress, whose signboard read 'Mangling done here.' The first lectures in this school were delivered between October 1809 and March 1810. The school was moved to 28 Peter Street (the site of the present Adelaide Hospital) in 1810 and renamed 'The Theatre of Anatomy and School of Surgery.' Kirby became sole proprietor of this school when Read retired about 1812.

When the Army required candidates for surgeoncies to produce evidence of hospital attendance, Kirby set up a hospital, which was dedicated to SS Peter and Bridget and opened on 2nd August 1811. The school and hospital enabled him to give the necessary certificates to prospective army and navy surgeons. As the 'hospital' only contained one bed the requirements of the army and navy cannot have been very strict.

In 1828, Andrew Ellis (1792–1867) was associated with Kirby as 'Professor,' the demonstrators being John Edward Brenan and Thomas Bunbury Young. The school closed in 1832 on Kirby's appointment as Professor of Medicine to the College of Surgeons. The museum was presented to the College, and the house stripped of its fittings. From 1836 till 1868 it enjoyed varying fortunes as 'The Original School of Medicine' under George T. Hayden. The Coombe Hospital was originally associated with this school. During the period 1868 to 1889 its name was changed to the 'Ledwich School.'

Hayden was obliged to resign his Fellowship of the College of Surgeons following charges that he advertised and practised pharmacy. In 1832, Hayden published an introductory lecture to his course on midwifery. Some of his observations refer to the doctor's social demeanour rather than to his obstetrical skill:

The accoucheur should studiously avoid all allusions to his profession in general society; he should not let the crotchet and forceps be seen on these occasions, like the surgeon, who had always a bougie sticking out of his pocket, as a barber erects a pole to invite passing customers.

It will be perhaps only right to cultivate an acquaintance with a newly married couple; but do not make a practice of thrusting yourself into their society, by visiting day after day, in order to secure the case.

In 1812 a school of medicine was set up in a building adjoining the lunatics' wards at the Hardwicke Fever Hospital; this was known at first as the 'School of Medicine Hardwicke Hospital.' In 1816, its title was changed to 'The Anatomical Theatre of the Richmond Hospital.' During the typhus epidemic in the 1820's, a large number of bodies of persons dead of that disease were dissected in this school. It was remarked at the time that none of the students who dissected the bodies contracted the disease, except those who were also attending in the fever wards. This was considered a strong proof that the contagion was not carried through the medium of dead bodies. Fracastorius had recognised typhus as a specific disease three hundred years before, but it was not until the early twentieth century, that

Howard Ricketts (1871–1910) who died of the disease demonstrated the minute causative organisms spread by the bites of lice, ticks and mites. Ralph Mahon of Ballinrobe had done work on lice as carriers of typhus about the same time. The Richmond Hospital School became extinct in 1826, but the Carmichael School could claim to be its direct descendant.

In 1820, William Wallace (1791–1837), a lecturer in anatomy in the Jervis Street School, set up on his own account in the rear of his Hospital for Skin Diseases at No. 20 Moore Street. He called his school the 'Theatre of Anatomy,' and later the 'Anatomico-Medical School.' The most notable occurrence in the life of this school was the admission of twelve pupils from the Royal Dublin Society School of Art. On Wallace's death in 1837, at which time it had been for several years merely a dissecting room for his own apprentices, the school passed into the possession of a butcher, and is now Messrs Hanlons' fish and poultry stores.

From 1821 to 1827 the School of Anatomy and Surgery at 36 Lower Ormond Quay, enjoyed a brief spell of popularity. It was added to the St Mary's Hospital and Dublin Eye Infirmary in 1821, when Andrew Ellis joined the founder, Francis White. In 1827, Ellis joined Kirby in the Peter Street School and the Ormond Quay School became defunct.

Ephraim MacDowell (1798–1835) taught anatomy to his pupils in a dissecting-room in the stable of his house at 64 (then 59) Eccles St. This later became St Georges Church Mens Club and is now with adjoining premises, Our Lady's Hostel for Boys. At the same time, Robert Adams instructed his apprentices in a back room in Mecklenburgh Street. Adams' house was wrecked by a mob in 1822 and he joined forces with McDowell. They continued in partnership at Surgeon O'Bryan Bellingham's house in Eccles Street, when they founded a second Richmond Hospital School.

The Park Street (now Lincoln Place) School was founded in 1824 under the title of the Medico-Chirurgical School. At the suggestion of James W. Cusack, it was built in the style of a Methodist chapel. His reason is stated to have been that the school might not last long and would prove an attractive ready-made bargain to the Methodist community. It was eventually bought by Sir William Wilde, and became famous as St Mark's Eye Hospital.

The names of the first teaching staff were notable:

Anatomy and Physiology: Arthur Jacob.
Surgery: James W. Cusack and S. Wilmot.
Practice of Medicine: Dr (afterwards Sir Henry) Marsh.
Institutes of Medicine and Toxicology: Robert Graves.

Chemistry: James Apjohn.
Midwifery: Samuel Cusack.
Demonstrators of Anatomy: Benjamin Alcock and George Greene.
Curator: Thomas Wilkins.

At the time of the school's foundation, Park Street possessed an unenviable reputation as a 'red-light' district. The teaching at the Park Street School was always of a high order. The majority of Professors at the Royal College of Surgeons between 1825 and 1847 had been pupils and teachers in the school. In 1849 the principal proprietor, Hugh Carlile (1796–1860), was appointed to Queen's College, Belfast, and the school was closed.

The School of Anatomy, Medicine and Surgery of the Richmond Hospital was established opposite the hospital in 1826. In the first session a course of dissections was given. On 8th January 1827, Richard Carmichael began lectures on surgery. Later in the same year he lectured on anatomy and physiology. He retired in 1829, but kept up his interest in the school. On his death (1849) Carmichael bequeathed the sum of £10,000 to the school. This money did not become available until 1864, when a new building was erected in North Brunswick Street. The school was renamed the 'Carmichael School' in 1849. The North Brunswick Street buildings were abandoned in 1879 for premises on the corner of Whitefriar and Aungier Streets. The number of pupils increased greatly on this removal. When the school amalgamated with the Ledwich School in 1889 to form the School of Surgery, R.C.S.I., over two hundred pupils were attending.

In 1879 night lectures were given at the Carmichael School and at the Ledwich School. This met with strong opposition from the Royal College of Surgeons, whose Council claimed that men who had worked in banks and offices during the day could not possibly apply themselves whole-heartedly to night study. The Carmichael School stopped the lectures immediately, but the Ledwich School continued the objectionable practice for a further three years.

In 1827, there had been a maternity hospital known as the Anglesey Lying-in Hospital at 50 Bishop Street, in connexion with which a medical school was established by Charles Davis and George Hayden. This was more of a 'grinder's' establishment than a regular school, but it was recognised by the surgical colleges in London and Edinburgh as well as in Dublin. The midwifery classes were particularly well attended as the result of the ready availability of practical experience. When Hayden set up in Kirby's house in Peter Street in 1836, the Anglesey school ceased to exist.

In 1831 Hans Irvine (1803–1882) and Malcolm Hillis opened a

school at 66 Marlborough Street. The maximum number of pupils ever to attend here was fifty, and the school was closed after only nine years.

The Dublin School of Anatomy, Medicine and Surgery at 15 Digges Street lasted for a quarter of a century (1832–57). Its foundation dates properly from 1825, when William Hargrave (1797–1874) commenced teaching anatomy and surgery at the rear of 123 St Stephen's Green. A notable addition to the teaching staff, in 1835, was Dominic Corrigan, whose lectures attracted pupils from all the other Dublin schools. Hargrave was appointed Professor of Anatomy in the College of Surgeons in 1837, and the popularity of the school declined. Philip Bevan (1808–1881) succeeded Hargrave as proprietor. The school amalgamated with the school at 27 Peter Street in 1841 under the name of the 'Dublin School of Medicine.' In 1846 Corrigan went to the Richmond Hospital School and Bevan left in 1853 for the College of Surgeons. Edward Hamilton carried on until 1857 when he was appointed Resident Surgeon and Lecturer in Anatomy to Steevens' Hospital and Medical College, whereupon the Dublin School came to an end.

The Theatre of Anatomy and School of Surgery at 27 Peter Street had a stormy history. Andrew Ellis and John Brenan assisted John Kirby in the original Peter Street School. In 1832 Kirby was elected Professor of Medicine at the College of Surgeons. Ellis wished to carry on the school, but could not come to an agreement with Kirby. He took the house next door (No 27) and fitted it out as a medical school under the title of the 'Theatre of Anatomy and School of Surgery,' which had been the name of the original school at 28 Peter Street. The anatomical and surgical lectures were successful, but Corrigan's influence drew the vast majority of students of medicine to the Digges Street School. In 1833–4 only twelve pupils attended at Peter Street to listen to George Kennedy's lectures on medicine.

In 1836, Mr Hayden reopened Kirby's old house at 28 Peter Street under the title of the 'Original School of Medicine,' dating its function from 1810. This procedure annoyed the proprietors of the school in No. 27, who claimed to be Kirby's successors. They published the following footnote to an advertisement of their fees and courses, in the *Dublin Evening Post* of 8th October 1836:

The proprietors beg to state that they have no connexion with a school announced as 'the original Peter Street School of Anatomy, Surgery etc, revived.'

It is true that Mr Ellis and Dr Brenan, in conjunction with Mr Kirby (the original founder of the institution), conducted the school in the house, now in Mr Hayden's possession, from 1827 to 1832; but on Mr Kirby's retiring from Peter Street, in 1832, Mr Ellis and Dr Brenan, assisted by other recognised lecturers, carried on *the* school since that period in the *present* building, whilst the old house has remained unoccupied as a school up to the present time. In giving this explanation, the proprietors are actuated solely by a desire to prevent confusion or mistake, as to whether their *long established* school or the one *about to be* established in its vicinity has the strongest claims to originality.

Their school fell on evil days about this time and despite additions to the teaching staff, including Hugh Carmichael (then joint Master of the Coombe), gradually became moribund until its amalgamation in 1841 with the Digges Street School.

In 1833 the building at the rear of E. Ephraim McDowell's house, 69 Eccles Street, was opened as a medical school. This second Eccles Street School lasted for only one session. It may be regarded as the direct successor of the Mark Street School, which also lasted for only one session. The latter was opened in 1834 and closed in the next year. Bryan Shanahan was lecturer in midwifery to both these schools. Refused recognition by the Royal College of Surgeons on the grounds that he was not sufficiently well versed in his subject, he set up two small maternity hospitals in Townsend Street and South Cumberland Street. The real reason for his non-recognition was his qualification of L.F.P. and S., Glasgow and L.A.H. He subsequently set up as a general practitioner in 147 Great Brunswick (now Pearse) Street, under the title of Bryan R. K. Shanahan, Count de Kavanagh.

When George Hayden reopened Kirby's house in Peter Street as the 'Original' Peter Street School of Medicine, he brought a small class with him from Bishop Street, and with this nucleus soon had a flourishing school. Up to 1856 the buildings were very inferior. A laboratory which could be used as a lecture theatre was built in that year. In 1863 this became a museum and the front of the house, which was formerly the Anglesey Lying-in Hospital, was taken over. The premises were enlarged and improved on several subsequent occasions. Amongst the distinguished pupils of the school were Arthur Hill Hassell, the English food analyst, who appeared on the rolls in 1836, and Charles Culverwell. Culverwell became famous on the stage in later years as Sir Charles Wyndham.

In 1868, the name of the school was, at the request of the pupils, changed to the 'Ledwich,' in memory of Thomas H. Ledwich, who had been largely responsible for the school's reputation in anatomy since 1849. In 1877 the Board of Trinity College refused to recognise any longer the certificates of the Ledwich School. One of the proprietors had improperly issued to a pupil a certificate of attendance at Mercer's Hospital. In May of the same year, the Council of the Royal College of Surgeons passed a resolution condemning the punishment of one institution for a fault committed in another. Trinity College recognised the Ledwich certificates in the next session. The school was amalgamated with the College of Surgeons and the Carmichael School in 1889.

A school of anatomy, medicine and surgery was started by S. M'Coy, Charles Davis, O'Bryan Bellingham, Bryan Shanahan and Richard Kelly, at Mark Street in 1834. Shanahan was still refused recognition by the College of Surgeons and Kelly did not deliver any lectures, having left the country before the first session opened. During the one session for which this school existed the attendances were: anatomy, 28; surgery, 26; materia medica, 13.

In 1857 a Commission on the grants to Dublin Hospitals recommended that a portion of the annual grant to Dr Steevens' Hospital be diverted to the maintenance of a school of medicine whose pupils would have the advantage of easily available clinical material. £2,000 was borrowed from the Board of Works and a well-equipped school constructed. This school, which had an average of eighty pupils attending, lasted until 1880 when it closed following a disagreement between the medical officers and the Board of Governors as to the appointment of Dr Warren to the vacant Chair of Anatomy.

Several incomplete medical schools were founded in Dublin during the early part of the nineteenth century. In 1794, a committee composed of both medical and lay men established the Sick Poor Institution at 25 Meath Street. This lasted as a dispensary until the introduction of the Poor Law. In 1832 there was opened at this address 'The School of Practical Medicine and Surgery', in which lectures on various subjects were given by medical men. There were no systematic dissections, but frequent post-mortem examinations were carried out. Many of the lecturers subsequently became attached to the regular medical schools.

A. Calonne, M.D., a graduate of Paris and Edinburgh, who taught classes at 82 South Great George's Street in 1815, was the prototype of the Dublin 'grinders.' His death occurred at 81 Middle Abbey Street, in 1833. In 1832, the surgeons of Mercer's Hospital advertised that they had arranged to give instruction in anatomy and surgical pathology. Leonard Trant took out a licence under the Anatomy Act to conduct dissections in an outhouse near Cork Street Fever Hospital, to which institution he was surgeon for many years. The Dublin General Dispensary was instituted in 1782, being located in Temple Court, Temple Bar. In 1826 Dr Patrick Clinton gave a series of lectures here on chemistry, materia medica and pharmacy, which were recognised by the College of Surgeons. At different times lectures in other medical subjects were delivered. About 1836

Edward Stratton's class-rooms in William Street were well attended by students of pharmacy, botany and materia medica. For several years C. Loughlin, the apothecary to the Lock Hospital, gave private lectures on materia medica and therapeutics.

With the large number of private schools, effective supervision by the licensing bodies was impossible and many of the certificates issued for 'diligent attendance' were fraudulent. Some of the teachers were only too glad to issue certificates of attendance to anyone willing to pay the necessary fee. The culmination of this system was that people already engrossed in full-time occupations every day of the week attended grinds or a night school for a few months before their examination, purchased the necessary certificates and with luck passed the examination by a narrow margin. Their weakness was not revealed until it was too late and an innocent patient had suffered.

THE PROVINCIAL SCHOOLS

Outside of Dublin there were few opportunities for medical education, but in Cork two schools supplied the needs of the students of that city during the first half of the nineteenth century.

In 1812 John Woodroffe (1785–1859) established a dissecting-room in Cove Street. In 1828 the examinations for the Letters Testimonial of the College of Surgeons being no longer limited to apprentices, certificates of attendance at lectures at once came into demand. The dissecting-room was transferred to Warren's Place and the course extended to embrace surgery, medicine, materia medica, botany and physiology as well as anatomy. At first Woodroffe's certificates were not recognised by the College. But in 1836 a Mr Wherland improved the accommodation. From then until its closure in 1844, the certificates were accepted. Woodroffe was charged in 1820 with malpraxis by a man named Reade, upon whom he had operated for stone three years previously. The College of Surgeons found the charge unfounded and brought for the purpose of extorting money.

Woodroffe gave lectures on anatomy at the Cork School of Art. Foley, the sculptor, whose statue of Father Mathew adorns Patrick Street in Cork, was among those who benefited by these lectures.

Another school was established on the South Mall in 1828 by Henry Caesar. Its certificates received recognition earlier than did those of Woodroffe's school, hence the name of 'Cork Recognised School.' The 'Recognised' was dropped on the extinction of the Warren's Place school. Caesar's school continued in existence until 1858, nine years after the establishment of an orthodox medical school in Queen's College, Cork.

Anatomy was taught for some years in the Royal Belfast

Academical Institution. In 1835, a regular school was formed. This had a fair measure of success until the establishment of the Queen's College Medical School in 1849, when it became extinct.

For many years the instruction given in the College of Surgeons and the private schools was not recognised by the University of Dublin, nor was the instruction in Trinity recognised by the College. Candidates who wished to hold both a diploma and a degree had to attend a complete course of lectures in both institutions. At this period the College recognised the teaching of the private schools. After prolonged wrangling, the University accepted, in January 1859, the certificates of the College Professors, provided that the candidates took out one *annus medicus* in T.C.D. In October of the same year similar conditions admitted the students of the private schools to University degrees.

The 'Resurrection' Men

The history of the Dublin medical schools is very largely the history of the constant fight by students and teachers to secure sufficient human bodies for dissection. Dublin was not the only medical teaching centre where work was carried on under difficulties. The story of Burke and Hare in Edinburgh is world famous.

So early as 1542, an Act of Henry VIII had given annually to the surgeons the bodies of four executed criminals for 'anathomyes.' The practice was confirmed by subsequent monarchs. This number was quite inadequate. In order to maintain a supply the law was constantly flouted. Inconsistently, the law required a thorough knowledge of the human body by all who practised medicine. As a further example of the strange workings of the legal mind, those who dug up and removed the bodies were solemnly charged with stealing, not the bodies, but the winding-sheet in which the bodies were wrapped. Although the theft of the body was a crime it was rarely mentioned in the charge. The penalty was transportation. From their nocturnal expeditions the students, and the gangs who made money by stealing bodies, gained the names of 'sack-em-ups,' 'resurrectionists' and 'body-snatchers.'

In 1896 James Bailey, then Librarian of the Royal College of Surgeons in London, published *The Diary of a Resurrectionist*. This is a fragmentary account of the activities of one gang of professional body-snatchers in London during the years 1811 and 1812. These gangs were composed of some of the most depraved ruffians in the cities. Unfortunately, they could command their own price for bodies. Should any teacher prove inclined to haggle, his school could be closed by the simple expedient of refusing to supply him; with no bodies for dissection his pupils would be forced to go elsewhere.

The character of the professional resurrection men may be calculated from the excerpts in the diary. During the one hundred and eighty-seven days recorded there are nineteen references to some or all of the gang getting drunk. These occasions were probably outstanding debauches. There are many allusions to disputes and rows in the gang between themselves as well as with others. The entries in the diary, some of which follow, refer to most of the cemeteries and medical schools in London and give details of the prices paid for bodies of various sizes:

Thursday 28th (November 1811). At night went out and got 3, Jack and me Hospital Crib, Benjn, Danl and Bill to Horps, Jack and me 1 big gates, sold 1 Taunton. Do St Thomass.

Saturday 30th. At night went and got 3 Bunhill Row sold to Mr Cline, St Thomass Hospital.

Tuesday 3rd (Dec. 1811). Went to look out and bought the shovels from Bartholomew. Met early in the evening at Mr Vickers. Butler and me came home intoxicated.

Saturday 14th. Went to Bartholomew, tookd two Brookes: Packd 4 and sent them to Edinburgh, came home to Benn. Settled £14 6. 2½d. each man, came home got up at 2, me Jack and Bill went to Bunhill Row and got 3. Ben and Daniel staid at home.

Wednesday 8th (January 1812). At 2 a.m. Got up, the party went to Horps, got 4 adults and 1 small. Took 4 to St Thomas's. Came home went to Mr Wilson and Brookes. Danl got paid £8 8. 0. from Mr Wilson. I recd. £9 9. 0. from Mr Brookes. Sold small for £1 10. 0. Recd. £4 4. 0. for adult.

Tuesday 21st. Lookd out, Jack and Butler drunk as before hindred us of going out. At home.

Friday 31st. Got 2 Guys and Thomass. Same night 3 Horps, 2 small: same night the cart broke down, took 2 to Guys.

Friday 7th (Feb. 1812). Met together me and Butler went to Newington, thing bad.

Sunday 8th (March 1812). Got 5 large. Bill and me went to the Big gates missd.

Many of the slang words in the diary were of an argot peculiar to the resurrection men. Some of these occur in the extracts given: 'Crib' — burial-ground; 'Adult' — adult corpse; 'Large-small' — body about three feet long; 'Small' — body under three feet long; 'Foetus' — infant corpse; 'Thing' — body; 'Lookd out' — watched to see what funerals took place; 'Thing bad' — body putrid; 'Missd' — failed to secure any bodies.

On 27 January 1830, a pitched battle between guards and body-snatchers took place in Glasnevin Churchyard, near Dublin. About sixty shots were fired over a period of half an hour. The police were summoned by the tolling of the churchyard bell at two o'clock in the morning. Several of the 'sack-'em-ups' were wounded, and broken gravestones showed the bitterness of the battle. *Saunder's News Letter* of 28th January 1830 contained the following news item:

A RESURRECTIONIST.

Arran Quay. – A fellow, named Fitzpatrick who is notorious for his prowess in this unenviable profession, was taken into custody on Tuesday night, in Watling Streeet on suspicion; he had a blunderbuss loaded with slugs in his possession. He was, it is thought, bending his steps to that celebrated acre where Kings and beggars sleep in kindred dust.

James Macartney was Professor of Anatomy in Trinity College from 1813 to 1838. Realising the grave shortage of bodies for dissection, he circularised his friends. Within a fortnight, he obtained ninety-nine signatures from clergymen, doctors, lawyers and titled persons to a declaration that each would leave his body for dissection. His own signature brought the list to one hundred. Another version states that his was the first of the hundred signatures. Macartney was one of those called to give evidence before the Anatomy Bill Parliamentary Committee. His evidence was revealing and contained many alarming statements.

A report propagated in Dublin that children were kidnapped for dissection became so currently believed that it was necessary to provide police protection for some of the anatomy schools.

The resurrection men sold the hair and teeth of their victims as a separate commodity for the making of dentures and wigs. In a letter to the papers Macartney stated:

I do not think that the upper and middle class have understood the effects of their own conduct in impeding the process of dissection, nor does it seem wise to discountenance the practice by which many of them are supplied with artificial teeth and hair. Very many of the upper ranks carry in their mouths teeth which have been buried in the Hospital Fields.

The Hospital Fields, or Bully's Acre, was the paupers' free burial-ground at the Royal Hospital of Kilmainham. As the poor could not afford to pay for safe graves or a watchman, this cemetery was a favourite haunt of the 'sack-'em-up men.' Those who could afford to do so interred their relatives' remains in 'mortsafes,' which consisted essentially of a heavy iron railing or grating around the grave. The best examples of these are to be seen in Greyfriars

Churchyard in Edinburgh. One bereaved parent went to the length of fixing a landmine to his child's grave.

Macartney testified that he had paid for the prosecution of people who had killed a resurrectionist. He admitted that students were frequently armed with clubs, or even firearms. A favourite trick was to carry a coffin filled with stones to the Cabbage Garden graveyard near Kevin Street. The body-snatchers, who were shabbily dressed, would pretend to guard the 'remains.' Meanwhile they fraternised with the genuine mourners and plied them liberally with whiskey well laced with laudanum. When the latter were helpless the students decamped with coffins holding bona fide remains. The market price of 'things' fluctuated considerably. Between 1820 and 1830 it varied from half a crown to fifteen guineas apiece.

St Andrew's Churchyard, Suffolk Street, situated in the midst of the medical schools, featured in many body-snatching incidents. In May 1732, the gravedigger in this churchyard received a prison sentence for having turned a blind eye to the activities of the resurrectionists. Ten years later his successor, Richard Fox, escaped from custody while awaiting trial on a similar charge. The church-wardens of the parish in an advertisement in *Faulkner's Dublin Journal* for December 1742, offered a reward of £5 8s. 6d. for information leading to his recapture. He was described as being: 'blind of one eye, a tall, thin, young man, wore a blue coat and pewter buttons.' In Swan Alley, a haunt of gamblers, there lived an eccentric character known as George Hendrick, alias 'Crazy Crow.' His legitimate occupation was that of porter to various bands of musicians. He was fined and imprisoned for body-snatching from St Andrew's about 1825.

The church officials of the time seem to have been an untrustworthy lot. In the issue of the *Dublin Journal* mentioned above an advertisement offers a reward of ten guineas for the apprehension of Thomas Owen, sexton of St James Church,

who most wickedly and feloniously removed the corpse of the late Mrs Murphy which it is supposed he sold. The said Owen is above the middle height, with red hair and wore black coat and breeches.

The Dublin resurrection men conducted a flourishing export trade to the great medical schools in Scotland. In January 1828, the discovery of a body about to be exported caused a riot, during which Luke Redmond, a porter in the College of Surgeons, was killed. The principal exporters were two men named Collins and Daly, who lived in Peter Street and D'Olier Street respectively. They were absolutely reckless and made no effort at concealment of their deeds. They even exposed naked dead bodies on the public road. Prior to 1828 they commonly used the College of Surgeons as a warehouse for their goods. They had such a stranglehold on their trade in Dublin that the price of bodies rose from one guinea to eight guineas within a few years. In December 1831, a London anatomist paid £38 for an Irish body.

The post of porter to the College of Surgeons was no sinecure. Christopher Dixon, who held the position in 1805, was an active resurrectionist. On one occasion he was captured in Bully's Acre. A rope was tied round his waist. He was then dragged to the Liffey and repeatedly immersed until he was nearly drowned.

At least one Irishman was famed as a resurrectionist in America. This was 'Old Cunny,' who supplied the Ohio Medical College with anatomical material. On one occasion some students played a trick on him. As a revenge he dug up the body of a smallpox victim and succeeded in infecting several students with the disease.

The passage of the Anatomy Act (3 and 4 Geo. IV., c. 75) on 1st August 1832, removed the disabilities under which the dissectors laboured and did away with the necessity for an illegal trade in bodies. The Act permits the provision under the supervision of regional inspectors of as many bodies as may be necessary for the proper teaching of anatomy. The Act respects the wishes of the deceased person and next of kin when an objection is raised to anatomical examination. The Act forbids the dissection of a body within forty-eight hours of death, or in cases where no death certificate has been furnished. Dissecting-rooms must be licensed and are subject to inspection. The remains must receive decent treatment, and at the end of the examination be interred in consecrated ground of the deceased person's religious persuasion. The first regional inspector in Ireland was Sir James Murray, of Dublin. Sir James was Physician-in-Ordinary to Lord Mulgrave (later Marquis of Normanby). He has a further claim to fame as the inventor of 'fluid Magnesia.'

Probably the most outstanding feat in the annals of body-snatching in Ireland was performed in 1760 by students of the Trinity College School when they captured the body of Cornelius Magrath, the 'Irish Giant,' whose height was said to have been seven feet eight inches. Robert Robinson was lecturer in anatomy at the time. When he heard of the giant's death he addressed his class:

Gentlemen, I have been told that some of you, in your zeal, have contemplated carrying off the body. I most earnestly beg of you not to think of such a thing; but if you should be so carried away with your desire for knowledge that despite my expressed wish, you persist in doing so, I would have you to remember that if you take only the body there is no law whereby you can be touched, but if you take so much as a rag or stocking with it it is a hanging matter.

The students took the hint, attended the wake, and made the deceased's friends hopelessly drunk. In the confusion they secured the body. Next day, when the relatives asked for the corpse they were told by Robinson that the students' zeal had been such that it was already dissected.

In the December issue of the *Dublin Journal of Medical Science* for 1913, Dr T. P. C. Kirkpatrick published the 'Diary of an Irish Medical Student,' written between the years 1831 and 1837. The writer, Dr Robert Thompson, started the study of medicine under Abraham Colles at sixteen years of age. In his first year he contracted smallpox, probably from a subject in the dissecting-room. He seems to have been unfortunate in this respect, as later he records attacks of 'flu and measles, as well as coughs, colds and vague fevers. The diary deals with the writer's social and family life as much as with his professional one. Many of the entries refer to financial difficulties and drinking bouts. There are no references to grave-robbing expeditions, although the writer was a student of anatomy for some months before the passage of the Act.

An echo of the old dispute between anatomists and the public appeared in the *Irish Independent* of 28th March 1907. A motion was proposed by Mrs Wyse Power at a meeting of the North Dublin Guardians, that the Master of the Workhouse should offer all the inmates a Christian burial. She stated that out of 221 deaths in a quarter, 40 bodies were sent to the medical schools and that the number was excessive. In his reply, the then Master stated that there was an order as old as the Board itself that all unclaimed bodies were to be sent to the schools. For each body so sent, 5s. was paid to him, 5s. to the doctor and 2s. 6d. to the porter. Every effort was made to find the relatives of dead inmates and when a person expressed a wish not to be dissected, this wish was respected. He added that Christian burial was given to the bodies after dissection and that if the supply of bodies from the Unions failed the medical schools would have to leave Dublin.

Nowadays there is much less aversion on the part of the general public to leaving bodies for dissection, but a new problem has arisen. With the advances in transplant surgery there is an increasing need for donors to give organs, either after death or sometimes before. Corneal grafts and renal transplants are almost commonplace. Heart transplantation is well established. Attempts to transplant other organs still come up against technical problems. But none of these techniques can succeed in the absence of donors who have given permission to have their organs removed after death and who have made the necessary arrangements, for sometimes a few minutes delay in securing an organ makes all the difference between success and failure.

A further faint echo of the old body snatching days was heard in 1983, when a leading Canadian criminologist, Duncan Chapell, speaking in Vancouver, forecast that in the 21st century criminals might well kill just to get bodies to sell for organ transplants.

CHAPTER SIXTEEN

SOME NOTED HOSPITALS

The Irish general hospital system has developed over the centuries along two paths, voluntary and state. The former which are or were owned and operated by lay boards or religious orders date from the early eighteenth century and some hospitals in Dublin and other areas have celebrated their bi-centenaries. By comparison the rate supported local authority hospitals are of more recent origin, few antedating the early 1800's.

A sketchy system of County Infirmaries had been established by an Act of 1765, later enlarged to provide for lunatic asylums and fever hospitals. In 1838 the Poor Relief Act established the workhouses, which are referred to elsewhere. Their main function was to provide the barest necessities of life under the most degrading conditions and only the simplest medical care was provided. In 1862 limited changes were made in their role, the medical facilities were somewhat improved and until the establishment of the Irish Free State in 1922 they remained the main hospital facility for most rural areas. Their subsequent changes are summarised in the chapter on medical administration.

During the development of Dublin as a medical centre many hospitals grew up which had no direct connection with the medical schools and for a long time Sir Patrick Dun's was the only one with an official attachment, in this case to Trinity College. Medical students of the other schools traditionally gravitated to certain hospitals, but there was considerable freedom of movement and students could attend the clinics of most of the teaching hospitals at will. This freedom of intercourse did much to overcome shortages of clinical material in the smaller teaching hospitals.

In the past twenty years the arrangements between the schools and the hospitals have been formalised with the result that teaching courses are more coherent but possibly some cross fertilization has been lost.

Most of the Dublin hospitals have been noted either in this chapter or elsewhere. Unfortunately, requests to some sources for historical detail met with little or no co-operation and the accounts of the institutions concerned are necessarily incomplete or lacking.

The number of voluntary hospitals outside the capital city was never very large. A few of these have been noticed rather because they are representative or their records were easy to trace, than because those unmentioned have done less valuable work.

Probably the first hospital established in Dublin was the leper hospital of Townsend Street, formerly Lazar's Hill. It was founded about 1220 as a temporary refuge for lepers intending to embark for the shrine of St James of Compostella, their patron saint. It was maintained by revenues obtained from lands near Delgany in County Wicklow.

Until the eighteenth century such hospitals as existed were either run by monasteries or were mere fever sheds inadequately maintained by the State.

The first voluntary hospital to be opened in the city was the Cook Street surgical hospital (1718) which has now become the Charitable Infirmary, Jervis Street. Dr Steevens' Hospital was not opened until 1733, although money for its construction had been available since 1717.

THE ROYAL HOSPITAL FOR INCURABLES

The first voluntary hospitals were intended for such cases as were curable. They received every variety of sickness. In them patients were kept a few days or some months before discharge as 'cured,' 'relieved,' or 'incurable.' These last, usually victims of cancer, tuberculosis, other wasting diseases or paralysis, were frequently carried by their friends to public places so that the sight of their suffering might arouse the charity of passers-by. In 1744, Dublin led the way to better things by establishing the first Hospital for Incurables.

During the middle of the eighteenth century, 'The Charitable Musical Society' was founded. Its members were talented, wealthy amateurs. They gave an annual concert, in aid of a selected charity, at the music-halls in Crow Street and Fishamble Street. In 1741, £400 was collected for the Charitable Infirmary, Jervis Street and Mercer's Hospital. When Handel's *Messiah* was first publicly performed, at the Fishamble Street Theatre in April 1742, the proceeds were given to Mercer's Hospital. In order that the accommodation might be utilised to the utmost, ladies were requested to come without hoops and gentlemen without swords.

In 1744 the Society rented a small house in Fleet Street and furnished a few rooms for the reception of incurable patients. Ten years later the hospital was moved to Lazar's Hill (now Townsend Street). Two grants of £50 each were obtained from the Government and the Grand Jury of the city. The oldest existing minute book is that of 1771. At this time there were about forty patients in the hospital. Inmates were provided with clothing as well as board and lodging and the treasurer was able to show a credit balance of nearly five thousand pounds. In 1780 matters were less satisfactory and numbers were limited to thirty until finances increased. In 1782 the hospital came within an ace of being amalgamated to, or rather annexed by, the House of Industry. The next year several vigorous new governors were appointed. Their arrival and some generous gifts infused fresh life into the hospital; so much so that one hundred patients could be accommodated in 1792. In that year the Lord Lieutenant proposed to exchange the house on Donnybrook (now Morehampton) Road, known as the Buckingham hospital for the house and premises in Townsend Street. The Buckingham was originally intended for smallpox, but was currently occupied by venereal cases. The exchange was agreed to and the patients transferred.

In 1800 the hospital was incorporated by royal charter. In 1815 a hurricane which did grave damage in the city caused the collapse of part of the roof. A helpless patient, Darby Kavanagh, was killed. Throughout the nineteenth century, the hospital was continuously expanded and improved. At one time it seemed probable that part of the Wicklow and Wexford Railway would run through the grounds, but the threat was averted by vigorous action on the part of the governors.

The Wicklow and Wexford Railway, later the C.I.E Harcourt Street line, disappeared in 1957 but the Royal Hospital ('for Incurables' was dropped in the nineteen sixties) still carries on the work for which it was established almost two and a half centuries ago.

Up to 1953 patients were admitted free of charge but rocketing prices made it necessary to seek state grants in order to maintain services previously provided by voluntary efforts. With an annual budget well into its second million pounds the impossibility of relying on charitable donations alone can be appreciated.

THE MEATH HOSPITAL

The first reference to the Meath Hospital appears in the *Gentleman's and Citizens' Almanack* in 1754. It was opened on 2nd March 1753. In the first seven months 4,095 out-patients were treated. In the same period only twelve intern patients were admitted. Like many similar institutions of the time, the Meath was conceived and established by medical men. The first of these were Surgeons Alexander Cunningham, Redmond Boat, David McBride and

Henry Harkshaw, who attended daily without remuneration. At this period the hospital was situated in the Coombe. When the lease of this house expired in 1756 the hospital removed to Skinner's Alley.

Of all Dublin hospitals the Meath was the most peripatetic. After only three years in Skinner's Alley it moved to Meath Street, where it remained for six years. In 1766 Earl Street was the site of the hospital. In 1770 it moved back to the Coombe. Finally, the present site at the junction of Long Lane and Heytesbury Street was occupied in 1822. At this transfer which took place on Christmas Eve, the patients were carried in long baskets made for the purpose. On the return journey a furious storm arose and the stretcher-bearers were glad to protect their own heads from flying slates, with the now empty baskets. In 1826 a fever epidemic arose. Sheds were erected in the hospital and a Government subsidy was applied to the relief of patients. Later special fever wards were built.

Most Dublin charities depended on bazaars, plays, charity sermons, lotteries and concerts for their support. The Meath was no exception. In 1767 Mr Sheridan appeared in *Douglas* in the Smock Alley Theatre at the request of the Board. In the same year £100 was given out of lottery funds. In 1773 a charity sermon by Mr Herries raised £73   10s.   0d. The first Government grant of £100 was received in 1774, when the hospital was constituted the County Dublin Infirmary.

In 1866 there was an outbreak of cholera in Dublin. The few beds set aside in the Meath proved quite inadequate in number. As was done previously, sheds were hastily erected and were soon packed to overflowing. It was noted that in the close, stuffy wards, the mortality rate was 54.5 per cent at one period. In the well-ventilated sheds it fell to 42.8 per cent.

Of the Dublin hospitals the Meath's staff roll is one of the most illustrious. The world-famous men who served her as surgeons or physicians included John Cheyne, physician, 1811–1817; Robert James Graves, physician, 1821–1843; David McBride, surgeon, 1753–1779; William Stokes, physician, 1826–1875; and Francis Rynd, surgeon, 1838–1861.

A list of those whose names are familiar in a narrower circle would fill several pages of this volume. Amongst those of relatively recent date, special reference must be made to Mr T. J. D. Lane whose hard work and dedication were directly responsible for the establishment of the internationally known urological unit in the Meath. After a period in general surgery Lane revisited the Mayo clinic prior to the second world war. Following this he decided to take the still unusual step of specialising in one branch of his field. He recognised that special facilities were essential for success, and, threw himself into the task of building up a custom built urological unit. The difficulties both internal and external were enormous. Dissention in the administration of the hospital eventually led to the passing of an act of the Oireachtas which brought about major changes. During the proceeding period of uncertainty little progress could be made in planning and even had all gone smoothly, implementation of building plans was impossible because of war time building material shortages.

Formal planning began in 1950, and eventually the foundation stone was laid on 27th January 1954, by the then Minister of Health Dr James Ryan. The architect, Mr Andrew Devane, spent several years studying the needs of the proposed unit before producing his plans, which came to fruition when the Department was opened in November 1955 by a different Minister of Health Mr (later Chief Justice) T. F. O'Higgins.

From an early stage teaching of nurses, under-graduates and post graduates was an important part of the department's work and ex-trainees, often holding key posts in their own countries, can be found in all five continents.

An important development was the inauguration in 1973, of the Irish Stone Foundation, originally intended for research into the causes and treatment of urinary calculi in Ireland, but now extended to deal with all types of urinary tract disease. The work of this foundation has resulted in an extension of the Meath hospital's reputation throughout the world. The Meath is part of the federated hospital group scheduled to move at some time to Tallaght in Co Dublin with every opportunity for increased work and service to the community.

THE SMALLER MATERNITY HOSPITALS

Besides the three present Maternity Hospitals several smaller ones were opened in Dublin during the last two centuries. In 1763 an obstetrical clinic was opened in the Meath Hospital. There are very few records of the work of this clinic, but, in 1833, William Stokes reported favourably on the use of the stethoscope for listening to the foetal heart. He illustrated his remarks by reference to cases in the Meath Hospital.

In 1832 a small lying-in hospital hospital was opened in Townsend Street for poor women who did not wish to go to the Rotunda. This never contained more than twenty beds and closed in 1836.

The South-Eastern Lying-In Hospital opened in 20 South Cumberland Street in 1834. There was accommodation for three pupils in this twenty-five-bed hospital. Being near to Park Street

School and the School of Physic, it made a special appeal to students of these bodies and was well supported, remaining open until 1852. Dr Thomas Beatty published several reports of this institution. Two hundred and ninety-nine women were delivered in the first year. The first recorded cases in which chloroform was used in midwifery in Dublin were in this hospital. They were reported at a meeting of the Surgical Society in December 1847.

For some time Sir Patrick Dun's Hospital accepted midwifery cases. In the School of Physic Act it was laid down that when one hundred beds were available, a King's Professor of Midwifery should be appointed and that one of his duties should be to deliver clinical lectures at the hospital. In 1827 William Fetherstonhaugh Montgomery was elected first Professor of Midwifery by the College of Physicians. He was appointed Physician Accoucheur to the hospital although only a few beds were available. The Governors permitted him to deliver a course of lectures on midwifery and the diseases of women and children. Montgomery resigned in 1856. In 1867 it was enacted that a King's Professor of Midwifery should be appointed, no matter how many beds there were in the hospital. Edward Burrows Sinclair was the first occupant of the Chair. He was very active in his duties, particularly in teaching. Two resident midwives were appointed.

A scheme was devised for the training of soldiers' wives as midwives in order to attend cases in the married quarters of the various barracks. In 1869 Sir Patrick Dun's was recognised as the Training School for Army Midwives stationed in Ireland. In the first ten years 323 such midwives were trained. The Maternity House was probably a building in front of the east wing, which became successively an Out-Patient Department, an Ear, Nose and Throat Unit and, after reconstruction in 1940, a residency for women students. In 1873 the Hospital Board ended the agreement by which Sinclair was the tenant of this house and took its management into their immediate care. In the following year efforts were made to organise training for civilian midwives. The plans did not mature until 1876, when a Midwives' Home was opened in Holles Street. Civilian midwives paid a fee of five guineas. When John Rutherford Kirkpatrick was appointed in 1882 he asked that Army midwives should pay the same fee. There were no funds available for this purpose and training of these ladies came to an end.

Dun's had no intern maternity department, but from 1868 to 1886, 57,741 poor women were delivered in their own homes. In 1891, at the suggestion of Professor Arthur Vernon Macan, medical students attending the midwifery course were allowed to wait at night in the dispensary. In 1900 thirty-three probationer nurses entered. Unfortunately, some who qualified as midwives represented themselves as fully-trained general nurses. The Hospital Board resolved that a distinction should be drawn between General and Maternity Nurses, and that Maternity Nurses should not style themselves 'Sir Patrick Dun's Nurses.' This was opposed by Macan and vigorous discussion followed between interested parties. Eventually the midwifery department was closed in 1903 owing to the controversy and lack of funds. To-day a flourishing gynaecological department exists.

The Western Lying-In Hospital was opened in 1836 by Drs Robert D. Speedy (1810–1864) and Fleetwood Churchill (who was also for a while attached to Dun's as Professor of Midwifery) at Agar House, 31 Arran Quay. About one hundred patients were admitted annually to this house, which closed in 1853.

The Wellesley Female Institution was opened in Mercer's Street towards the end of 1826. It was not intended as a hospital, but merely as a dispensary to which expectant and newly-delivered mothers might apply for medical attention in their own homes.

Samuel Cusack (1800–1853) an assistant surgeon to the Institution for the Diseases of Children published a report on the Wellesley Institution in the *Edinburgh Medical Journal* for 1831. In the first three years 701 patients were delivered. Of these, 679 were normal. In 1834, also in the *Edinburgh Journal*, Fleetwood Churchill, Physician to the Institution, published a report read at a meeting of the Surgical Society of Ireland. The Institution now catered for gynaecological as well as obstetrical cases for, of some 500 patients attending, about 200 were suffering from gynaecological disorders. The dispensary opened on three mornings a week during this period, and patients too ill to attend were visited in their own homes.

In 1833, in the same *Journal*, Henry Maunsell's report for 1832 was published. During this year 442 midwifery cases were attended. Of 431 children born, one in ten were still-born, mainly due to prematurity and syphilis. Only four maternal deaths were recorded.

Maunsell referred to the use of the stethoscope in assessing the foetal condition, but noted that the correct interpretation of sounds heard with its aid depended on the experience of the accoucheur. His *Dublin Practice of Midwifery*, published in 1834, was illustrated with cases from the Institution's practice.

The Anglesea Hospital in Peter Street was opened by George T. Hayden in an effort to give complete training in his medical school. It was closed on his death in 1857.

Dr Henry Coffin opened a maternity hospital with sixty beds in South Great George's Street in 1844, near the site of the original Lying-In Hospital. He gave classes for intern and extern pupils and applied for recognition as a teaching hospital by the College of

Physicians. This was refused, with the inevitable result that the hospital closed.

The effect of the smaller institutions was most keenly felt by the Rotunda and Coombe in the falling-off of students attending and paying fees. Evory Kennedy, during his mastership of the Rotunda, published a manifesto in the daily papers pointing out the advantages of studentship in his hospital. He stated that he intended to issue diplomas of proficiency and to publish lists of those holding such certificates. The private teachers asked the College of Surgeons for a ruling that Kennedy was not entitled to issue diplomas. The Governors of the Rotunda replied by reference to bye-laws made and approved under their charter. These laid down that a register of students was to be kept and certificates given to those who attended regularly. The matter does not seem to have gone any further, but, in 1836, the College of Physicians decreed that the Rotunda Governors were not entitled to issue a diploma permitting the holder to practise midwifery.

SIR PATRICK DUN'S HOSPITAL

This was the only Dublin hospital primarily intended as an educational institution and officially allied for many years to a teaching body, the Dublin University Medical School.

When Sir Patrick died in 1713 he provided in his will for a trust in perpetuity to the College of Physicians in order to endow a Chair of Physic. Nearly ninety years later the second-last Act of the Irish Parliament sequestrated most of these funds in order to found the hospital now known as Sir Patrick Dun's. The Trinity College professors had made several efforts to establish a hospital for teaching purposes during the closing years of the eighteenth century. In 1791, the legislature empowered the College of Physicians to raise £1,000 on Dun's estate to establish a hospital despite the opposition of certain professors of the Medical School. In 1792 a house on Blind (later Wellington) Quay was taken and styled Sir Patrick Dun's Hospital. Thirty-one beds were provided. The Medical Professors of the University attended daily. Two hundred and fifty-three patients were admitted during the first year. According to *Watson's Almanack*, the majority of these were suffering from contagious diseases. The hospital failed for lack of financial support and it never seems to have been used for teaching purposes. It was closed in 1796. A scheme to provide clinical material from the cases in Mercer's Hospital failed and in 1800 the School of Physic Act, establishing King's Professorships and enabling the erection of a new hospital, was passed. Pending the completion of this building clinical instruction was given in Steevens' and the Meath Hospitals.

In 1801 the Commissioners appointed under the Act selected a plot of ground in Artichoke Road (now Grand Canal Street). This very marshy ground required two years' drainage before building could be commenced. The foundation stone was laid by the Provost of Trinity College, Dr Kearney. The West Wing was completed in 1809 and was ready to receive thirty patients. The whole building was not finished until 1816.

The first clinical lecture was delivered on 7th November, 1809 by Dr George J. Allman, Professor of Botany in the University. The Medical Professors were required to lecture in the hospital. A Physician-in-Ordinary was appointed to attend those patients who were not suitable for teaching purposes. The appointment drew protests from the Professors, but on 3rd April 1877, James Leahy, later Professor of the Practice of Medicine, was appointed. As most of the professors regarded the hospital purely as a teaching unit rather than as a treatment centre, the appointment was fully justified. For instance, the name of Robert Graves is rarely associated with Sir Patrick Dun's although he lectured there from 1829 to 1841.

When the hospital was completed the central block was used mainly for administrative and teaching purposes. Male and female patients were admitted to separate wings. Originally the upper wards were employed for fever cases. During the epidemics of 1826–28 and 1846–48 over 10,000 cases of fever were treated. The first major architectural change was the replacement of the lecture theatre by an operating theatre in 1898. Thirty-two years later a modern operating unit was constructed.

In July 1850 the hospital was obliged to close for three months owing to lack of funds. After the re-opening in November, a ward was set aside for patients who could pay ten shillings per week.

The story of the hospital for the next fifty years is one of saving and stinting in order to keep as many beds as possible available. Some additional building was undertaken: in 1899, a small pathological laboratory; in 1903, an Out-Patient Department. The situation was not eased until the establishment of the Irish Hospitals' Sweepstakes in 1930. As with so many other Dublin hospitals financial problems were accompanied by increasing pressure on space as new specialities were developed all requiring room, personel and facilities. In Dun's there was little room for expansion and eventually, as has been described in relation to other hospitals, amalgamation into the Federation of Dublin Voluntary Hospitals became a matter of urgency.

DRUMCONDRA HOSPITAL

In common with many other Dublin hospitals the Drumcondra changed its name and site several times. Its early history is closely linked with that of the Parish of St George. In 1801 a parish dispensary was opened in Dorset Street to relieve the congestion in the existing dispensary in Cole's Lane. The following year a fever hospital was opened on the North Circular Road. St George's Place on the North Circular Road, and Dorset Place (formerly Dispensary Lane) mark the sites of the two buildings. The first medical attendants included Abraham Colles and Richard Carmichael.

The fever hospital was quite inadequate for the work it had to do. In 1816–18 a new building was put on a site originally intended for the parish church. This was named the Whitworth Fever Hospital. It could accommodate thirty-five patients. The early records are fragmentary, but since 1842, in which year general medical complaints were admitted for the first time, the minute books have been preserved.

For several years the hospital finance was very shaky, and, about 1848, amalgamation with the Adelaide Hospital was proposed for their mutual benefit. The negotiations came to nothing and the Whitworth was closed during 1849–50. At the end of the latter year, the house was re-opened for both intern and extern patients. In 1853, fever cases were excluded from the hospital. During this period patients had to supply their own food. A Ladies' Committee to provide meals for necessitous patients was formed, but they resigned *en masse* in 1856, because of religious differences.

The main sources of income for the hospital from 1863 until 1911 were bazaars, fêtes and concerts. As a result of the success of these, many improvements were made and new buildings erected. In 1884 water from the Vartry replaced the former supply from the Royal Canal. Despite the progress there was a period when the hospital threatened to become a refuge for chronic cases. At the same time there was a spirit of non-co-operation between the lay board and medical staff.

In 1893 matters were more satisfactory and the name of the hospital was changed to 'Drumcondra.' This was done in an effort to rouse parochial interest and support and to avoid the confusion of names with the other Whitworth. Letters and patients frequently arrived at the wrong institution. The hospital's finances improved about this time, so that necessary repairs and replacements could be carried out. In 1895, an ophthalmologist and gynaecologist were added to the staff.

James Weir left £1,500 to the hospital in 1897. This was expended on an operation theatre, a private ward and sanitary accommodation. A brass plate over the theatre recorded this generous bequest. In 1915 a pavilion for open-air treatment was erected by the Co-operative Congress in the grounds, in memory of Thomas Blandford.

Drumcondra Hospital continued to serve the area as a general hospital up to 1972 when increasing costs and the need for highly sophisticated equipment made continuation on a voluntary basis impractical. Arrangements were made for the Rotunda to take over after extensive renovations and improvements. Thirty one beds are now available for newly delivered patients and their babies who are transferred by ambulance from the main hospital.

THE ADELAIDE HOSPITAL

The Adelaide Hospital was established in 1834 at 43 Bride Street with fourteen beds. The hospital resulted from the idea of Albert Jasper Walsh (1815–1880) who, whilst still a medical student, conceived the plan of establishing a hospital for the exclusive use of Protestants.

Walsh was appointed first surgeon to the hospital, with John T. Kirby and Maurice Colles. Robert Graves was amongst the honorary physicians appointed. From the beginning, clinical instruction was given to students of the Ledwich School of Medicine.

In 1848 the full financial effects of the Famine were felt and the hospital was obliged to close. In 1850 a committee of clergymen investigated the possibilities of re-opening. They were unsuccessful until 1857, when they were able to purchase numbers 24 and 26 Peter Street. These houses were fitted as a hospital with 75 beds. In 1858 two adjacent houses were bought and their stables used as fever wards. There was now accommodation for 120 patients. The present buildings were erected in 1875. As a reminder of the past it may be noted that the boilerhouse and laundry occupy the site of the old Ledwich School of Medicine. Religious restrictions on the admission of patients have long been dropped and many non-Protestant patients are admitted, both as intern and extern cases. The Adelaide is now a member of the Federated Dublin Voluntary Hospital Group.

ROYAL CITY OF DUBLIN HOSPITAL

The Royal City of Dublin Hospital, popularly known as Baggot Street, was opened in 1832 with fifty-two beds. The founders were Professors of the College of Surgeons who were handicapped by having no beds for teaching purposes. They included Arthur Jacob, Robert Hannon, James Apjohn (1796–1886), Thomas Beatty

(1800–1872), Charles Benson (1797–1880) and John Houston (d. 1845), the last-named being curator and anatomical demonstrator in the College School. Abraham Colles, Sir Henry Marsh and Samuel Wilmot were appointed consultants. For many years the physicians and surgeons to the hospital were connected with the College of Surgeons School, as were the great majority of students.

The first legacy left to the hospital was the small sum of five pounds. It came from a poor woman who died of an incurable disease a few months after her discharge and was in token of gratitude for the kindness and temporary relief she had received as an inmate.

In 1838 one of the earliest wards exclusively for the use of children was opened. The money for this was raised entirely by the medical officers of the hospital. Four years later a special gynaecological ward was placed under the care of Professor Thomas Beatty, one of the founders.

Like the other Dublin hospitals, Baggot Street's history during the latter part of the nineteenth century is largely one of advances made in the face of great financial difficulties. On the foundation of the Nurses' Home in 1900, by Princess Christian of Schleswig-Holstein, 'Royal' was added to the hospital's title.

Sometime during the 1930's tentative proposals were made for an amalgamation of Baggot Street with Mercers and Duns Hospitals and plans were drawn up for a new hospital on the site of the last. As with so many other proposals war stopped this development which was superseded by the present Federation scheme.

Baggot Street's pioneer work in cardio-pulmonary medicine and surgery dates from 1954 with the appointment of Dr Terence Chapman, followed in 1958 by Mr Keith Shaw as pulmonary surgeon. Some 600 operations in this field are now performed annually. If the services of Baggot Street Hospital are all moved to a new Federated complex one wonders what cover will be available to the over 35,000 patients who annually pass through the out-patient and casualty departments of this 152 year old hospital.

EYE AND EAR HOSPITALS

The number of eye and ear hospitals founded in Dublin during the nineteenth century was large for such a city. Their development was very fully traced by Dr Somerville-Large in the *Irish Journal of Medical Science* in 1944.

In 1814 Commander Isaac Ryall R.N. (1781–1846), Oculist-in-Ordinary to the Viceroy, founded the National Eye Hospital at 10 Mary's Abbey. After ten changes of address and ten changes of name, this became the Royal Victoria Eye and Ear Hospital in Adelaide Road.

Ryall was an ophthalmologist of some note. His work on inflammation of the eyes in the new-born anticipated Credé in many respects. He mentioned the use of silver nitrate, for long an accepted treatment and preventive for the condition.

After Ryall's departure for England in 1827, the hospital was taken over by Richard Morrison, who appointed, amongst others, Richard Carmichael and John Kirby to the Board of Management. The Lord Lieutenant was invited to attend a charity sermon in aid of the hospital. He declined to do this, but dropped a hint that he would attend a ball. The hint was taken with the result that £600 came to the funds.

Morrison recognised that many diseases of the eye have an origin elsewhere. He made a real advance when he appointed specialists in other subjects, including Sir Philip Crampton, to the hospital. Later Stokes and Graves came on the staff for some ten years.

The hospital moved to Cuffe Street, in 1831. Matters were satisfactory until 1846, when it became the 'Dispensary for Diseases of the Eye.' This may account for the assertion by the Governors of St Mark's Ophthalmic Hospital that they were the only eye *hospital* in the city at the time.

By 1849 matters had improved so much that resident students were admitted to the wards. In 1853 the hospital lost its character as a specialised institution, becoming The National Infirmary and Dispensary. Sir Henry Marsh and William Colles now joined the staff. For ten years, until the appointment of J. D. Hildige in 1863 as ophthalmic and aural surgeon, little was done for diseases of the eye.

In 1871 Hildige retired. Henry Swanzy (later Sir Henry) (1843–1913) and Charles Fitzgerald (1843–1916) were appointed as ophthalmic and aural surgeons. From this period the hospital made continuous progress, particularly after the 1872 move to 97 St Stephen's Green. Daily dispensaries were conducted, operative work was increased and regular courses of instruction were given to students. Annual reports were published and some work in preventive ophthalmology was done. At this time a Dispensary for Diseases of Women and Children was opened in the hospital and functioned until 1882.

In 1880, the hospital moved to 13 Molesworth Street. The accommodation here was much better, and it was possible to provide private and isolation wards as well as a general ward of thirty beds. In 1889, it was suggested that the hospital should amalgamate with St Mark's Ophthalmic Hospital. This step was not taken until 1904.

The various moves and changes of name of the hospital are tabulated
below:

1814.	The National Eye Hospital	10 St Mary's Abbey
1817.	,, ,, ,, ,,	5 Nth Cumberland St
1822.	National Infirmary for Curing Diseases of the Eye	Upper Nth Gloucester St
1829.	,, ,, ,, ,,	44 Nth Cumberland St
1830.	,, ,, ,, ,,	47 Mid Gardiner St
1831.	,, ,, ,, ,,	10 Cuffe St
1843.	Dispensary for Diseases of the Eye	,, ,, ,,
1845.	National Infirmary for Curing Diseases of the Eye	,, ,, ,,
1846.	,, ,, ,, ,,	12 Cuffe St
1853.	National Eye Infirmary and Dispensary	,, ,, ,,
1863.	National Eye and Ear Hospital	,, ,, ,,
1865.	National Eye Hospital and General Dispensary	,, ,, ,,
1873.	National Eye & Ear Infirmary & Dispensary for Diseases of Women and Children	97 Stephen's Green
1880.	,, ,, ,, ,,	13 Molesworth St
1882.	National Eye & Ear Infirmary	,, ,, ,,
1904.	Royal Victoria Eye & Ear Hospital	Adelaide Road.

St Mark's Ophthalmic Hospital for Diseases of the Eye and Ear
was opened as a dispensary at the back of 11 Molesworth Street by
Sir William Wilde in 1841. For the first twelve months he bore all
the expenses of the institution. In 1844 he moved it to Mark Street,
where he had room for twelve in-patients.

In 1850 the building was found to be too small and was moved
to the Park Street Medical School premises. Wilde paid £1,100 for
this building and a further £200 on alterations. Twenty beds were
provided here, as well as a few for paying patients. Although the
clinical and operative work was of a high standard the administration
was poor. The nurses slept in the female wards and no matron was
appointed until 1877. Costs were extremely low, even for the times.
The average cost per patient until 1864 was less than one shilling
per day. All patients, except paupers, were asked to contribute a few
pence weekly to the hospital fund. The diet was a meagre one:

For an adult 24 ounces of the best wheaten bread and one quart of the best
milk is supplied on six days a week. On Sundays 16 ounces of bread, one
pint of milk and three half pints of broth with its meat.

At this time the operative work was of a high standard. Cataract and squint were treated surgically and in 1880 a reference was made to the transplantation of a rabbit's cornea. In 1880 a special ward, the Henry Wilson Ward, for trachoma cases was opened.

Wilde began clinical teaching in St Mark's in 1844. In 1853 attendance at an eye hospital was made compulsory for certain of the public medical services. In 1868 Trinity College made attendance at such a hospital part of its course of professional study. The standard of teaching in St Mark's was such that many English, Continental and American students attended.

On Wilde's death in 1876, Henry Wilson (1838–1879), his illegitimate son, succeeded him as surgeon. He died a short time later, leaving most of his property to the hospital.

The hospital was assigned by Wilde to trustees in 1862. The scandal of his trial in 1864 and the lack of an absolute authority led to a proposal, in 1879, for the amalgamation of the two Dublin eye hospitals. The first suggestion was made in the report of the Hospital Sunday Fund. In the following year the Committee of the National Eye and Ear Infirmary raised the question again. The Committee of St Mark's were now more agreeable and, by 1893, the details of the proposed amalgamation to form a 120-bed hospital had been settled, with the exception of the name. As a result of the wrangling, neither hospital secured immortality and the new institution was named for a foreign queen. The pioneers who gave the parent hospitals birth were forgotten and a name chosen that tells nothing of the hospital's early history. At first it was proposed to enlarge the Molesworth Street premises. Fortunately, a long-term policy was adopted and to-day the Royal Victoria Eye and Ear Hospital stands on its own grounds with room, if necessary, for further expansion. The first patients were admitted in 1904. In the first year 1,284 in-patients and 7,230 new out-patients were attended.

In 1819 Arthur Jacob established the Charitable Institute in Kildare Street as a Hospital for Eye Diseases. When he joined the Park Street School in 1823 he closed the hospital. In 1829 he opened the Ophthalmic Hospital at 8 and 9 Pitt (now Balfe) Street. The teaching of ophthalmology was probably one of his main reasons for founding this hospital. In 1834 his ophthalmic ward in the Royal City of Dublin Hospital became available as a teaching centre. As a result, the only hospital in Dublin exclusively devoted to eye cases was closed.

In 1872, Jacob's son, Archibald (1837–1901), established the Dublin Infirmary for Diseases of the Eye and Ear at 23 Ely Place. He had followed his father's lead, both as an ophthalmologist and as editor of the *Medical Press and Circular*. He had also followed him in his violent and abrupt manner. In his hospital he provided in-patient accommodation for eighteen poor patients as well as some pay beds. There was an operating theatre and out-patients' dispensary, so that accommodation must have been strained to the utmost. No mention was made of any clinical instruction being given. Evory Kennedy, Sir George Porter and John Cronyn were chosen as consultants to the hospital. When the hospital closed, after only three years, the era of the small eye institution in Dublin passed.

CHILDREN'S HOSPITALS

The problem of the sick child has always been one of peculiar difficulty. The differences of medicines and treatment between the child and adult are easily overcome, but the mental aspect, particularly of children *en masse*, is one requiring very special training, and accommodation. The sick child in an adult ward is either the spoiled darling of everyone, or a rather woebegone stranger in a very frightening place. The child in a children's ward or hospital is amongst people who have his own problems, fears, illness, likes, dislikes and mental outlook. The furniture is built to scale. Even that prosaic object, the bed-pan is not a yawning cavern into which childish buttocks may wedge themselves fast.

The National Children's Hospital in Harcourt Street is the direct descendant of the Institute for Sick Children founded at 9 Pitt (now Balfe) Street in 1821. The founders were Dr John Crampton, Sir Henry Marsh, Sir Philip Crampton, Dr Thomas Cuming and Dr Charles Johnston. Sir Charles Cameron, in his *History of the Royal College of Surgeons in Ireland*, refers to Thomas Cuming (1798–1887) as Assistant Physician and Lecturer to the Institution between the years 1821 and 1829. This seems to indicate that some teaching was carried on there at that time.

In 1835 Richard T. Evanson (1800–1871) and Henry Maunsell published a *Practical Treatise on the Management and Diseases of Children*. This was illustrated by cases admitted to the Institution. The authors referred to their experience there as students and medical attendants since the period of its establishment. Maunsell stressed the necessity for mental as well as physical hygiene in the education and care of the growing child.

In the *Dublin Hospital Gazette* for 1860 an advertisement for the Institution appeared. Its objects were stated to be:

1. The medical and surgical treatment of sick children.
2. To afford students the opportunity of acquiring a knowledge of the nature and treatment of children's diseases.
3. To impart instruction to mothers and nurses as regards

the proper management of children, both in health and disease.

The number of extern patients was stated to be more than five thousand annually.

Apart from the names of the physicians and surgeons to the hospital, there are very few records available prior to 1875 when Mr (later Sir) Lambert Ormsby (1849–1923) founded the National Orthopaedic Hospital at Upper Kevin Street. In 1879, this was transferred to Adelaide Road, under the name of The National Orthopaedic and Children's Hospital. In 1884 the Pitt Street and Adelaide Road Hospitals amalgamated as the National Children's Hospital. They continued in their original buildings with combined staff and administration until 1887, when premises in Harcourt Street were purchased. The last medical officer of the Pitt Street Institution was William Moore, M.D., who died in 1901. In the new premises work continued steadily, keeping pace with every modern advance but it became ever more obvious that development was being hampered by lack of space. Even had adjoining buildings become available their purchase and reconstruction would have run into enormous sums of money.

Eventually arrangements were made that Harcourt Street would become one of the Federated Dublin Hospitals to which reference is made elsewhere in the present volume.

The Children's Hospital, Temple Street

The Children's Hospital, Temple Street, began its career as St Joseph's Infirmary at Upper Buckingham Street in 1876, following the enterprise of a band of charitable young ladies. At their request, four sisters of the Irish Sisters of Charity were appointed to develop the struggling infirmary.

In 1879 the lease of the Buckingham Street premises expired. The bequest of Mr Richard Simpson made possible the purchase of a house in Temple Street. The Sisters for several months slept in the stables during renovations. Twenty-one beds were at first available. This has risen steadily until 139 children can now be accommodated at one time. A convalescent home, St Anthony's, was later opened at Herbert Avenue, Merrion, Co Dublin.

In 1908 the Sisters of Charity in charge of this hospital benefited by the legacy of Lady Martin (widow of Sir Richard Martin and daughter of Sir Dominic Corrigan). In her will she left Cappagh House, Finglas, to the Sisters for use as a convalescent home under the name of St Mary's. In 1921, it became obvious that 'surgical' tuberculosis of the joints in children could not be successfully treated either at home, in general hospitals, or in the few existing sanatoria. In this year, two new open-air wards for the treatment of bone and joint tuberculosis in children were opened at Cappagh. The site was regarded as peculiarly suitable as it was in open upland country, yet near enough to the city for parental visits to be easy.

Since its opening this hospital catered for the educational needs of the sick child as well as for its purely physical wants. Classes were held by qualified teachers. Many of the children received their first regular education in St Mary's. Emphasis was placed on positive health and on the maximum activity for every child. But with improvements in milk hygiene and public health generally bone and joint tuberculosis became uncommon and in Cappagh emphasis turned to the treatment of other musculo-skeletal defects. Advances in surgery and anaesthesia together with the development of new inert materials resulted, as in so many other centres, in the techniques which have rendered hip and other joint replacements everyday operations.

ST ULTAN'S INFANT HOSPITAL

Prior to 1919, there was no Dublin hospital in which infants, as distinct from children, could be nursed. St Ultan's Infant Hospital was opened in that year with two cots and a bank balance of £100. Until 1926, all work was carried on in a converted dwelling-house. In December of that year, the foundation-stone of a new wing was laid. This gave accommodation for an out-patients' department, kitchen and operating theatre. The in-patient accommodation was increased to 35 cots.

The advent of the Sweepstakes was a boon to St Ultan's and it became possible to expand in a more realistic way. By the 1940's there were 77 cots for up to two year olds and an annual out-patient attendance of some 9000 children up to five years of age.

In 1949 a special unit was built which served as headquarters of the National B.C.G. campaign as well as containing isolation wards for contact babies and a B.C.G. out-patient vaccination clinic. By 1952 this clinic had achieved an annual vaccination figure of 65,401 with an annual income of £23,384. Surely 30p per person was never better spent.

At the time of writing it appears that St Ultans is faced with closure as part of a rationalisation plan. Negotiations with St Vincent's Hospital were abortive and 83 beds will be lost to south Dublin children, unless some scheme can be devised.

NEWCASTLE SANATORIUM

The early history of Newcastle Sanatorium is marred by sectarian and personal prejudices of the narrowest and pettiest kind. A small sanatorium existed near Belfast for some years before Newcastle was built (1893), but otherwise tuberculosis cases were treated at home or in general hospitals. There were two previous abortive attempts, in 1878 and 1887, to found a large national sanatorium.

In September 1891 Miss Florence Wynne, in a letter to the press, suggested that a national sanatorium should be built for the exclusive treatment of pulmonary tuberculosis. She followed this by circular letters to public men and a provisional committee met on 20th November 1891 at 6 Merrion Square. At this meeting, which was attended by some of the foremost members of the profession, Miss Wynne acted as secretary. At subsequent meetings it was decided to build a 100-bed hospital, open to all, irrespective of religion, and providing as far as possible separate rooms for each patient.

In July 1892 the choice of a site lay between land at Ballycorus, near Shankill, and the present site at Newcastle, Co Wicklow. The medical committee decided in favour of Ballycorus. On receipt of this information Lady Zetland, wife of the Lord Lieutenant, threatened to withdraw her influence and subscriptions unless the Newcastle site was selected. Incredible as it seems, the committee allowed themselves to be bullied into reversing their decision, Miss Wynne strongly dissenting. In October Miss Wynne resigned following this and another dispute on the provision of places of worship in the hospital.

The hospital was incorporated on 6th July 1893 and opened on 19th March 1896 with 24 beds. In the publicity concerning the opening ceremony no mention was made of Florence Wynne, while great prominence was given to Lady Zetland. This drew strong letters of protest both from Miss Wynne and her sister Emily, pointing out that the former was the real founder of the hospital and that Lady Zetland had only joined the movement when it was well advanced.

By 1914 one hundred and twenty five beds had been provided. Additional buildings had been built, extra ground bought and an adequate water supply installed. The outbreak of the first World War and the local political upset prevented any great constructive work for many years. In 1931 an X-ray apparatus was installed. In 1935 mains electrical power was made available and in 1936 a modern operating block was built. This block proved of immense advantage, enabling operations to be performed as soon as necessary without the removal of the patient to Dublin.

For many years the relations between the board and the medical staff were unhappy. The board interfered unduly in the treatment of patients and apparently had little confidence in their staff at some periods. In 1912 Dr Crofton was appointed a visiting physician and the consulting and visiting staff resigned in a body. In March 1927, when Dr Crofton resigned, the staff agreed to return provided that two of their number were co-opted to the Board. Since that time the history of the hospital was one of steady progress.

In 1948, large additions were commenced. This building, upon completion was designed to provide two sections with 40 beds each, for men and women, complete with dining-rooms, recreation halls, visitors' rooms, etc. For practical purposes this was a self-contained unit with many of its own amenities separate from those of the main building. In 1949 further extensions were contemplated in order to bring the bed capacity to between 250 and 300 specifically for the treatment of all forms of tuberculosis. But shortly afterwards the patterns of disease changed in Ireland as elsewhere and in the 1960's the treatment of T.B. became shorter and more effective so that fewer beds were required.

On the other hand the treatment of and public approach to psychiatric illness was undergoing what can only be called a revolution. Custodial, almost prison-like, care was largely abandoned. New treatments both medical and surgical came into vogue. Most important of all patients, families and friends accepted that mental disturbance was no more 'shameful' than physical illness so that treatment was accepted on a voluntary basis at an earlier stage in the sickness. This meant that many more beds had to be provided and the obvious solution was to alter the function of many T.B. hospitals including Newcastle where the change over took place in 1966.

Newcastle is now administered by the Eastern Health Board and is recognised as a post-graduate training hospital. In addition to the main hospital there is a sheltered workshop in Bray and a residential hostel in Enniskerry. The hospital proper now has just over one hundred beds and serves the entire County of Wicklow with a catchment population of 89,000 people.

CORK HOSPITALS

THE NORTH AND SOUTH INFIRMARIES

The trustees of the South Charitable Infirmary were incorporated in 1722. The early history of the institution has been lost. By the Infirmaries Act of 1765 a County Infirmary was established at Mallow, and the Protestant clergy were created a perpetual corporation for the erection of such infirmaries.

In 1832 an Act to amalgamate the North and South Infirmaries was passed by Parliament and the Committees of both Institutions met as a joint Board of Management. When the original intention to build a single hospital was abandoned the two Boards again functioned separately.

In 1861, the County Infirmary was transferred from Mallow to the South Charitable Infirmary.

According to some authorities the North Infirmary was founded about 1719. F. H. Tuckey, in the *Cork Remembrancer*, gives the year as 1744 and states that the erection of the Infirmary was made possible by the charity of members of the Cork Charitable and Musical Society, who devoted their surplus funds to its support. Certainly the first map of the city in which the hospital appears was printed in 1750.

The honorary medical staff of the Infirmary in 1744 consisted of eleven physicians and five surgeons. There was accommodation at first for fourteen patients. An out-patient department was run and seems to have been the main part of the house, accounting for the relatively large medical staff. The administration was in the hands of the Board of Directors, chosen annually by the Musical Society from their own members and from subscribers. The medical staff were ex-officio directors. In the annual report for 1750 it is recorded that 1,267 patients were received with the following results:

Cured	721	Dead	75
Incurable discharged	69	Intern under treatment	14
Irregulars	230	Extern under treatment	158

An Act was passed in 1751 having for its object the establishment of an enlarged Infirmary. Eighteen trustees named in the Act, with nominees of the subscribers, constituted the Governors of the Infirmary.

In 1762 a number of charitable Cork citizens purchased, altered and equipped for patients a house in the suburbs of the city. Two years later this new institution was granted a charter and incorporated by an Act of the Irish Parliament. Under the title of South Charitable Infirmary the hospital proved a blessing to a population all too often smitten with cholera, typhus, enteric and infectious diseases of all kinds.

In 1858 the Commissioners for the control of Convict Prisons surrendered possession of premises which they held as tenants from the South Infirmary and adjoining premises came on the market. Considerable expansion was thus made possible.

By the Infirmaries Act of 1765 a County Infirmary was established in Mallow. In 1861 this was transferred to Cork City and merged with the South Infirmary as 'The South Charitable Infirmary and County Hospital.' The new hospital was opened in 1863. In 1899 the Sisters of Mercy took over administrative control of the hospital under the joint committee of management on which the Health Authority are strongly represented.

THE VICTORIA HOSPITAL, CORK

Following a public meeting, which was held at the Royal Cork Institution and which was presided over by Sir Thomas Tobin, 'The County and City of Cork Hospital for Women and Children' was opened in a house on Union Quay on 4th September 1874. There were 24 beds and an out-patient Department. The medical staff consisted of Dr W. J. Cummins (d. 1892), Dr Nicholas Grattan (d. 1896) and Dr H. MacNaughton Jones, Professor of Obstetrics in Queen's College, Cork. One hundred and twenty-eight intern patients were treated in the first year and in 1876 the hospital was moved to Pope's Quay, where there was more room for expansion.

After prolonged negotiations the old South Infirmary buildings were leased from the trustees and after rebuilding opened as a hospital in September 1885. These buildings were constructed in 1762 and used as a hospital until 1862. From then until 1876 they were used as a militia barracks.

In 1886, the lady superintendent, Miss M. H. Baxter, organised a thorough training system for nurses. In 1942, a scheme for State Registration in affiliation with the Adelaide Hospital was established for Victoria Hospital Nurses. This was abandoned in 1945 and the Royal City of Dublin Hospital was substituted for the Adelaide.

In 1901, the name of the hospital was changed to 'The Victoria Hospital for Women and Children.' Since then the history of the hospital has been similar to that of the other Irish hospitals, a constant struggle to keep abreast of medical advances under the heavy handicap of rising costs.

HOSPITALS OF THE SISTERS OF CHARITY AND OF MERCY

The Christian tradition of tending the sick has not diminished with the passage of time and we have now many medical institutions staffed and administered by religious orders. It is convenient here to note two great nursing orders founded in Ireland who now control numerous hospitals.

The Irish Sisters of Charity, founded by Mother Mary Aikenhead, began their work by visiting the sick poor in the meanest quarters of Dublin. The foundress sent three of her followers to study in Paris while, in the face of strong opposition, she collected funds for a hospital in Dublin. In 1834 she opened St Vincent's Hospital on Stephen's Green.

Amongst Dublin hospitals, St Vincent's will always hold an honoured place. Established when the destitution of the city poor was almost incredible, St Vincent's gave them new hope. It was the first hospital organised and staffed by women to be opened in these islands. The hospital was opened in the town house of the Earl of Meath in Stephen's Green. At first only 12 female patients could be accommodated. After a few months, 28 more beds were provided for women and children. It was not until 1836 that 20 male beds were made available in what became St Laurence's Ward. The adjoining mansion of the Earl of Westmeath was bought in 1841. Before it could be reconstructed it collapsed. From this time onwards the history of the hospital is one of acquisition, building and rebuilding; in 1858 a new wing, and living quarters; in 1860 a chapel; in 1861 a laundry; in 1869 a mortuary chapel; in 1873 a pathological laboratory – like the children's ward, the first of its kind in Dublin; in 1879 the student residency; in 1888, 58 and 59 Stephen's Green; in 1897 and 1899 the private homes 97, 96 and 94 Lower Leeson Street; in 1909 a new operating theatre; in 1919 a new out-patients' department, built with the legacy of Charles Lalor. This was opened in 1924. But it was already obvious that the premises at St Stephen's Green were becoming outdated and in the early 1930's plans were drawn up for the building of a new and much larger hospital at Elm Park on part of a golf course which still exists. Rising costs, building material shortages and the multiple arrangements necessary for such a large undertaking delayed construction into the late 1960's and it was not until May 1970 that the first patients were transferred to the new hospital which continues to expand in response to ever increasing demands on its service.

In 1864, a Mr Coppinger of Monkstown sold his mansion at Linden, Blackrock, Co Dublin, to the Irish Sisters of Charity. After a few alterations it was opened as Ireland's first convalescent home for poor patients. Originally 20 were accommodated; to-day, 160 are housed and there is a long waiting list. Talbot Lodge was added later for patients who can pay their way. These homes fulfil a vital need in catering for people who are too weak to work, but too fit to occupy a hospital bed.

The Irish Sisters of Mercy owe their foundation to Mother McAuley, who gathered a group of ladies to work for the sick poor. The greatest monuments to their work are the Mater Misericordiae Hospital of Dublin and the Mater Infirmorum Hospital of Belfast.

The Mater Misericordiae Hospital, Dublin, was founded in 1861 with 40 beds. From the beginning many members of the staff held appointments at the Catholic University Medical School. Of these the best known were Thomas Hayden and Francis Richard Cruise.

Thomas Hayden (1823–1881) held the Professorship of Anatomy from 1855 until 1865. On the foundation of the Mater Hospital he was appointed one of its physicians and remained so until his death. Hayden's qualifications were surgical and he had previously served on the surgical staff of the Anglesea Hospital in Peter Street.

Francis (later Sir Francis) Cruise (1834–1912) lectured on anatomy and the practice of medicine in the Carmichael College. In 1861, he was appointed to the Mater Hospital and retained the post until his death. Cruise was a pioneer of psychotherapy in Ireland. Apart from his medical activities he was well known for his translation of Thomas à Kempis' *Imitation of Christ*. He had the distinction of having a street in Kempen named after him.

The Mater Misericordiae Hospital always kept well abreast of medical advances. In particular we may note that their X-ray department, opened in 1907 under Dr Maurice Hayes, was for many years the only unit of its kind in Ireland under the control of a doctor practising this speciality exclusively.

The nursing in the Mater was originally done entirely by Sisters of Mercy, a number of whom were trained at the Hotel Dieu in Paris prior to their new venture. In 1891, a nursing school was opened with 16 probationers. To-day the Mater holds 365 public beds and has a nursing staff of about 180.

Though St Michael's Hospital, Dun Laoghaire, dates from 1876, the Sisters of Mercy had charge of a small hospital at Packenham Villas in nearby Monkstown from 1859 where the hospital of that name, which still plays a large part in the provision of medical services for the district, had already been established in 1835.

In the early nineteenth century Dun Laoghaire, then Kingstown, was a shabby down-at-heel village. In his *Irish Sketch Book*, Thackeray described the houses as having a battered rakish look and going to ruin before their time. There were some medical services, for the same writer refers to the 'Medical Hall – pompously described over very humble tenements'. Dr John B. Power, the first physician to St Michael's, wrote of the miserable courts and rows of wretched hovels where a healthy life was well nigh impossible. He ascribed, probably correctly, to these conditions the low birth rate, relatively high death rate and large number of admissions to the Workhouse.

St Michael's Hospital was built at a cost of £6,000 for forty beds and opened in June 1876. Michael A. Boyd was appointed first surgeon to the new hospital. He was a fervent believer in Kingstown's virtues as a health resort despite publishing a paper about the neighbourhood entitled 'Is drinking Sewage by Milch Cows a danger to Public Health?'. A long standing association with the Mater Misericordiae Hospital was foreshadowed by the appointments as Consulting Physician and Surgeon of Francis Cruise and Henry J. Tyrell, Professor of Surgery in the Catholic Medical School, both of whom were on the staff of the larger hospital.

For over sixty years all nursing in the hospital was carried out by the Sisters of Mercy. Sometime in the 1930's senior nurses were seconded from the Mater Hospital and in 1942 St Michael's was recognised as a teaching hospital by An Bord Altranais. In the late 1970's there were persistent rumours that St Michael's was to be in some way down-graded, a move which would arouse intense local opposition. From a forty bed unit caring for patients from a limited catchment zone it has grown to become a 175 bed hospital dealing with patients from a wide area and the author deeply appreciates both as colleague and patient the care still being provided after more than a century.

Reference has been made to Monkstown Hospital which was preceeded by the voluntary Rathdown Dispensary opened by charitable people of the area in 1812. The coming of age of this institution was marked in 1833 by the purchase of land on which a 16 bed hospital, originally intended for fever cases only, was to be opened in 1835. The staff consisted of Dr William Plant who was to serve for 43 years with a nurse and assistant employed at the weekly wages of seven shillings and three shillings respectively. From this date until 1878 the Hospital was known as the Rathdown Fever Hospital and did valiant work in the dreadful famines and epidemics which killed so many of our countrymen and women. Occasional accident cases were also admitted and at times there was such intense pressure on available space that two patients were forced to occupy one bed.

In 1876 the Committee of Management decided to admit general cases to a new wing opened in 1880. In the interim the name was changed to Monkstown Hospital because of the confusion with the Rathdown Union Hospital (now St Columbcille's) at Loughlinstown some 8 km away. Four years later the Hospital was selected as sick quarters for naval personnel taken ill while in Kingstown Harbour. After only eight years the new accomodation had become quite inadequate and further expansion and modernisation were required, as has happened at regular intervals since.

Many distinguished physicians and surgeons have served Monkstown Hospital in a consultant capacity throughout its one hundred and forty eight years of existence but there have only been four medical superintendents in all that period, they were:

Dr William Plant   1835–1878
Dr Joseph Beatty   1878–1919
Dr R. De Courcy Wheeler   1919–1955
Dr Desmond De Courcy Wheeler   1956–

OUR LADY'S HOSPICE

The concept of a special unit for terminally ill patients is sometimes thought to be of very recent origin. In fact religious orders and benevolent individuals had looked after such cases for centuries. In Dublin this care was put on an organised basis in 1879 by the establishment of the Hospice for the Dying at Harold's Cross.

The Irish Sisters of Charity had already been serving the Dublin poor for sixty four years but, with the limited therapies available, the failure rate was high and provision of a place where continuing care at a special level could be provided became a matter of urgency if active treatment beds were not to be blocked by patients for whom such treatment was no longer effective. Greenmount House at Harold's Cross had been in the possession of the Sisters since 1845 serving as a Novitiate, Mother House of the Congregation, a night school for the women and girls in the area and a centre for visitation of the sick poor in the district. No doubt this visiting of mortally ill patients in their own homes, often rat infested crumbling hovels, was a major stimulus to the provision of a Hospice.

In 1879 the Mother House was transferred to the present premises at Milltown leaving Greenmount House available for its new role. Even before the official opening deserving patients were admitted including Joseph Sharkey, a medical student, riddled with tuberculosis who came in on September 16th 1879 and died on November 5th of the same year. On December 9th 1879 the Hospice was officially opened with eight patients ranging from a young boy to a very old woman.

The original conditions for admission, which still appear on the application form, excluded those suffering from contagious diseases, mental maladies or epilepsy and specified that the applicants should have a very short expectation of life. These regulations always appear to have been interpreted in the most humane and generous way possible so much so that in the nineteen fifties some truly terminal cases could not be admitted because many elderly people with nowhere else to go had been accomodated. But, there was a further complicating factor, of itself a tribute to the care extended. Patients admitted in a truly desperate state apparently having only hours or days to live often rallied and remained alive for months or even years. According to the rules they should have been discharged. For many there was nowhere else to go and the Sisters practised the Charity of Christ which their Foundress had adopted as the Order's motto.

But it was obvious that some changes of policy would have to be made and the present day Hospice (no longer − 'for the Dying') has 130 beds for relatively long term admissions, 34 beds for cases of advanced cancer and in a seperate building but with some shared facilities St Joseph's wing with 70 beds for active rehabilitation of rheumatic and neurological patients.

Amongst the future developments planned is an out-patient pain control clinic with a visiting service working in close collaboration with family doctors and their patients. This would certainly allow many patients to remain at home for longer periods without anxiety to themselves or their relatives knowing that admission would be assured when matters had gone beyond home care.

GASCOIGNE HOUSE

On 18th August, 1904 the first patient was received into the Rest for the Dying in Camden Row, across the street from the Meath Hospital. This small building specifically intended for destitute Protestants was founded as a result of the generosity of Colonel French Gascoigne. In the intervening years over 3,000 patients have been cared for. Most of these are now in the later age groups, but in the early years many young people were admitted in the terminal stages of diseases which can now be relieved or cured.

In 1939 a Mary Martin who had served as a V.A.D. in the First World War saw one of her dreams fulfilled. Now Mother Mary Martin Foundress and Superioress of a new religious order, the Medical Missionaries of Mary, she took over in Drogheda a house intended as a 12 bedded maternity centre for the area. Despite the shortages and multiple problems of war-time construction this small building had been developed into a general hospital containing 75 beds by 1947.

By then the Hospital had been recognised as a training school for both general and maternity nursing.

A target of the Foundress had always been the establishment of a missionary training centre with emphasis on tropical diseases and plans had been agreed when fire almost totally destroyed the existing buildings in 1952.

Within a year active re-building was commenced and the International Missionary Training Hospital with over three hundred beds is the principle centre in the Republic for the investigation and treatment of tropical diseases, as well as being a vital link in the accident, emergency and general medical services of the area.

There is an extensive training programme for doctors and nurses from foreign countries as well as Ireland. In 1970 it was the venue for the first I.M.A/B.M.A (Northern Ireland) joint clinical meeting.

The Cork Fever Hospital Act of 1938 was the first in which the free status of an Irish hospital was challenged by the legislature. Under this the Cork Corporation was enabled to draw up a scheme for a new Fever Hospital. The old Committee of Management was to be replaced by a Cork Fever Hospital Board which was eventually to consist solely of Corporation and Board of Health members. As in other legislation of this nature the Minister was given wide powers of dismissal and arbitration. In practice he had almost complete control over the hospital.

The Dublin Fever Hospital Act of 1936 was a similar instrument, giving wide powers to the Minister for Local Government and Public Health. The history of this piece of legislation is of importance if we bear in mind its implications for the future of Irish hospitals.

The needs of the growing city engulfed the accommodation at Cork Street. In 1933 the Hospitals Commission recommended the immediate erection of a 400 bed hospital, with room for expansion. Such work was beyond the powers of the managing committee, and in 1936 the Parliamentary Secretary to the Minister for Local Government introduced a Bill in the Dáil for two specific purposes: the provision of increased accommodation, and the representation on the Board of Dublin city and county ratepayers. The managing committee, carrying on their tradition of self-sacrifice, gave up their buildings, their assets, their funds and their autonomy. In 1936, the Local Government Department assumed authority.

In 1944, three members of the Board, all nominees of the Minister, sent a list of complaints against their colleagues and demanded an enquiry, which was ordered by the Parliamentary Secretary. The enquiry was held in November 1944. Six months later the Board was dismissed and a Local Government Commissioner installed. The findings of the enquiry were not published and a storm of protest arose. When a change of Government came about in 1948, the Board was restored, with representation of all bodies concerned in the hospital's affairs.

The new Dublin Fever Hospital at Cherry Orchard, now controlled by the Eastern Health Board, was opened in 1953 with about 280 beds instead of the recommended 400. At the time the main infectious diseases were still diphtheria, typhoid, scarlet fever and poliomyelitis with outbreaks of small pox and typhus very real possibilities. In the intervening thirty years the pattern changed. Smallpox has disappeared and the unit originally intended for cases is now reserved for viral haemorrhagic diseases.

Some 75% of the beds are occupied by children many of whom suffer from gastro-enteritis and are admitted as much for socio-economic reasons as for their medical condition. There are still some patients suffering from respiratory paralysis as a result of poliomyelitis contracted many years ago.

Centralised control now reached out to affect general hospitals. The House of Industry Hospital (later the Richmond, now St Laurence's) owes its foundation to an Act of George III, passed in 1772. This Act (11 & 12 Geo. III) recited that:

strolling beggars are very numerous in Ireland and that it is become necessary to give countenance and assistance to those poor who shall be found disabled by old age and infirmities to earn their living as to restrain and punish those who may be able to support themselves by labour and industry and yet may choose to live in idleness by begging.

The Act empowered corporations to grant to such helpless poor badges and licences to beg in certain districts. The Act provided for the punishment of vagrants begging without a licence. It empowered Justices of the Peace to dispose of the children of vagrants by apprenticing them.

By virtue of this Act the corporation for the relief of the poor in the City of Dublin was instituted in 1773. For the first four years voluntary contributions sufficed to keep the House of Industry going, but in 1777 Parliament was obliged to make a grant of £4,000. For many years the Dublin House of Industry received vagrants from all parts of the country. The names Hardwicke, Richmond and Whitworth applied to various buildings of the hospital were derived from the Viceroys in office at the time of their construction.

Many Parliamentary Commissions and Acts dealt with the hospital, so that its history may be divided into four periods:

(1) From 1772 to Peel's Poor Law Act of 1838.
(2) From 1838 to 1856, when the annual subsidy was fixed by an Act passed for the better regulation of Dublin Hospitals.
(3) From 1856 to 1943, when the name was changed to St Laurence's.
(4) From 1943 to the present day.

Until Peel's Act the House was a mixture of workhouse, penitentiary and hospital. On the passage of this Act the workhouse was separated from the hospital and the penitentiary function disappeared.

In this first period conditions were horrible in the extreme. Young and old, sane and mad, male and female, healthy and diseased were crowded together without distinction. In 1774 two wards were set apart for medical and surgical patients and placed in charge of two physicians and two surgeons. In 1773 ten cells for lunatics were built. Two years later a separate house, later occupied by the Carmichael School, was built for 109 lunatics who were still treated as dangerous wild beasts. In 1857 the lunatics department was closed and most of the inmates were transferred to Lucan under the care of Dr Stewart, a former Governor.

In 1803 the Hardwicke fever building was opened with accommodation for 64 beds. In 1826 it was supplemented by a disused convent near St Paul's Church in King Street, which was hired under the name of the Wellesley Hospital. This held 133 patients.

Following an unfavourable report by La Touche's Commission in 1808, the Richmond Surgical Hospital was opened in 1811. This building was also originally a convent. The heights of the five stories from basement to fourth floor were respectively 8 ft. 8 in., 10 ft., 10 ft., 8 ft., and 7 ft. 8 in. The Museum and Library of this building attained great importance about the middle of the century.

In the year preceding La Touche's Commission the following details of conditions in four wards were given.

In No. 18, 48 female lunatics, in 24 single beds.
In No. 16, 42 males in 27 beds.
In No. 15, 50 males in 25 beds.
In No. 13, 50 females, each nursing a child in 25 beds.

The report stated that the House was not unduly over-crowded. The death rate was over 15 per cent of admissions.

The Whitworth Hospital was used as an auxiliary fever hospital for its first two years. Later it became a medical hospital. In 1829 another Commission revealed that there had been many improvements. The death rate was halved although many more patients had been admitted. During the late eighteenth and nineteenth centuries the hospital, familiarly known as the 'Richmond,' was remarkable for the number of distinguished surgeons who were members of the staff. No less than eleven Presidents of the College of Surgeons held office in the hospital during the period 1788 to 1900. They were:

	President R.C.S.I.	*Surgeon to Hospital*
Philip Woodroffe	1788	1780

Francis l'Estrange	1796	1786 (assistant)
Robert Moore Peile	1798 & 1816	1790
Richard Carmichael	1813, 1826, 1845	1816
Charles Hawkes Todd	1821	1809
Robert Adams	1840, 1860–1, 1867–8	1838
Edward Hutton	1852–3	1828
Christopher Fleming	1859–60	1851
Sir William T. Stoker	1893–95	1876
Sir William Thomson	1896–98	1873
Sir Thomas Myles	1900–02	1890

Robert William Smyth, Vice-President of the College in 1873, and John Hamilton, Vice-President in 1875, were appointed Surgeons to the House of Industry Hospitals in 1838 and 1844 respectively. The Vice-President succeeds to the Presidential office, if he so desires, as his election to the higher honour is never opposed. Smyth and Hamilton both died during their terms as Vice-President.

The most famous physician attached to the House of Industry was Dominic Corrigan, who worked there from 1840 until 1860. A more detailed account of his life appears in another chapter.

The hospital continued to teach, treat patients and make progress, often under difficulties, and in 1937 that portion known as the 'Old Richmond' was condemned as unsafe. As a result, alternative accommodation had to be provided for nurses so that thirty-six patients' beds were lost temporarily to the hospital. The meagre out-patient accommodation also required great improvement.

Shortly after this, in 1943, an Act which occasioned considerable uneasiness to hospital authorities was passed by the Oireachtas. This was the St Laurence's Hospital Act. It provided for the establishment near Dublin of a new general hospital to be called 'St Laurence's.' This was to take the place of the Richmond. The latter was to be closed. Fears were expressed that unduly wide powers in the internal control of the hospital were given to the Minister for Local Government and Public Health. In particular, he was given wide powers of appointment to the board of governors. When land for the new hospital was acquired, the board were required to submit plans for its erection. As these were subject to the Minister's modification he was in the position of being able to veto a whole scheme if he so wished.

The 1943 St Laurence's Hospital Act was followed in 1947 by the St Luke's General Hospital Bill. This provided for the establishment in or near Dublin of a new general hospital to be called St Luke's, in the place of Mercer's, Sir Patrick Dun's and Baggot Street, and for the closing of the three last. The Board of the new hospital were required to submit a scheme for its establishment. As in the previous Act, this was subject to the Minister's approval and modification.

Part VII of the original Bill contained a section which caused grave disquiet amongst hospitals not directly affected by the Bill. It read:

Whenever the Minister is of opinion that it is expedient that any non-participating hospital should be amalgamated with the new general hospital he may, for the purpose of effecting such amalgamation, make with the concurrence of the hospital (St Luke's) board, in relation to such hospital an amalgamation order.

The proposed hospital was to be governed by a board elected by the Dublin County Council, Dublin Corporation, and the amalgamating hospitals. The medical and other staff of the existing hospitals were to continue in equivalent positions in the hospital. The Minister for Health was empowered to make grants out of the Hospitals' Trust Fund for the erection and equipment of the new hospital. At the same time provision was made for the transfer of the property and certain assets of the amalgamating hospitals to the new Board. Liabilities, including pension rights of employees, would also be transferred.

Simultaneously with the publication of this Act an announcement appeared in the press to the effect that a small extra ward was being built in Dun's to relieve existing congestion. This original scheme never developed along the projected lines but was the foundation on which the present Federation of Dublin Voluntary Hospitals was built. This comprises the Adelaide, Meath, Mercer's National Childrens' (Harcourt St), Royal City of Dublin (Baggot St), Dun's and Steeven's together with St James (previously St Kevin's) the largest local authority hospital in the country. All of these occupy buildings more than a century old and have from 90 to 270 beds each. Services are frequently duplicated and while it is sad to see old establishments disappear one hopes that the amalgamation will result in even higher standards of care.

When the Federation was conceived it was envisaged that the hospitals would all move to a single site but the Department of Health now (1983) feel that they should form the nucleus of two major hospitals on the South side of Dublin, St James on its present site and the new Tallaght Hospital. It is intended that the cooperating hospitals should retain a large measure of autonomy apart from the monitoring of capital funds, the appointment of medical consultants, teaching arrangements with other bodies and the allocation of specialised departments. These functions will be carried out by a

Central Office of the Federation. At the time of writing the joint annual expenditure of the group for 1,200 beds is almost £32 million substantially met by direct allocation from the Department of Health. St James is to become the main teaching Hospital for the T.C.D. Medical School with Mercer's, Dun's and Baggot St, transferring their services there on a phased basis. The remaining hospitals will form the nucleus of the new Tallaght Hospital located some ten kilometres to the South West of Dublin.

BARRINGTON'S HOSPITAL, LIMERICK

Amongst the provincial voluntary hospitals, 'Barrington's' of Limerick has an old and honoured name. In 1821, Limerick was badly hit by outbreaks of fever, particularly in the Irishtown district. Although the poor were the worst sufferers, no class escaped completely. The Barrington family, from whom the hospital is named, carried on a pewter works at Charlotte Quay. Joseph, the father, was the moving spirit in founding the hospital. His sons, Matthew, Daniel, Croker, and Samuel assisted.

A site was obtained on George's Quay and construction commenced in 1829. Tradition says that during the work Sir Joseph Barrington had his favourite armchair, pipe and umbrella set down opposite the building and sat there all day long regulating the work and correcting the slightest slackness or inattention.

The building was entirely in cut stone. When finished, it had three storeys with stone stairs and a balcony leading to the main entrance. It had a pointed slate roof and at the top were three circular windows, the centre being occupied with a clock, surmounted by a tower. This clock was the first illuminated one in the south of Ireland. The roof was replaced by a flat one in 1933.

Lack of funds restricted the original plans, which were for a 200-bed hospital. As a result, the west wing is still missing. The east wing was presented by Matthew Barrington in 1837. On 28th July 1831, Barrington's was formally opened and handed over to the citizens. It was suggested that a monument should be erected to commemorate the founders, but the Barringtons refused to allow this.

The first medical staff elected were.—Physicians: James F. Carroll, William J. Geary and Michael Brodie. Surgeons: Richard Franklin, John Thwaites and Thomas Kane. John Allen was appointed first registrar and apothecary, a post he held for forty years. His wife, Catherine, was first matron; Anne Meagher and Ellen O'Dea were appointed nurse-tenders.

For the next five months the furnishing and equipment of the hospital occupied the minds of the staff. Accommodation for thirty patients was provided. Although no patients were yet admitted, the Hospital Board were mindful of their duties as guardians of the people's health. In November 1831, a sub-committee was appointed to examine the law relating to the cleansing of lanes and byeways. Subsequently a meeting of prominent citizens was held to devise means of appointing health officers in the city.

On 1st December 1831, the hospital was opened for the reception of poor patients and accident cases. The population of Limerick was 90,000 and in the first eight years 2,836 intern and 100,000 extern cases were treated. The Lord Lieutenant and the Grand Jury now made grants totalling £300. Several generous gifts and bequests followed.

In May 1832, the cholera epidemic which had reached Dublin in March assailed Limerick. In June, the Board of Health requested the Governors of Barrington's to lend the hospital for cholera patients. During the nine months for which the building was so used, 1,537 cases were treated, with a death rate of just over 35 per cent (551). In July 1833, it was returned 'in a clean state' to the Governors and non-fever patients were again admitted to its thirty-five beds.

In January 1837, a serious explosion occurred in Limerick as a result of which many citizens were injured. Nine of these were admitted to Barrington's and made full recoveries. During this period most of the accident cases admitted were the direct result of hard drinking.

Finances now became bad, following a severe winter, and Matthew Barrington founded, in connection with the hospital, a charitable pawnshop on the plan of the Monts de Pieté in France, Belgium and Italy. In 1847, this was leased as a police barracks. About 1883, it was finally demolished and the materials sold by auction. The fine stone pillars were said to have been bought for an American millionaire's home. The pawnshop issued its own token money.

In 1848–9, the Fever Board again took over the hospital in order to save the expense of erecting fever sheds for cholera victims.

Barrington's always held a firm place in the affections of Limerick citizens, who came to the rescue in many financial crises by personal subscriptions as well as by organising concerts, fêtes and collections. The Centenary Fund raised over £2,000 in 1929.

The advent of the Sweepstakes in 1932 relieved the hospital of some of its most pressing financial worries. Half the grants were expended on alterations, repairs and the provision of new equipment. These included a new nurses' home, service and patients' lifts, a new operating block, private wards, radiological plant and reconstruction of the laundry. The remainder was invested to give Barrington's a good start in its second century of service to the people of Limerick.

Many other Irish hospitals are worthy, not alone of mention, but even of separate chapters or separate volumes. Some day perhaps their history will be written.

CHAPTER SEVENTEEN

THE NATIONAL UNIVERSITY MEDICAL SCHOOLS AND THEIR PREDECESSORS

The visitor to Dublin is often confused by the apparent multiplicity of universities in that city. The National University, Dublin University, Trinity College, T.C.D., U.C.D., University College are commonly mentioned. When references are made to 'The Old Royal University,' 'The Catholic University' and 'The Queen's Colleges' confusion becomes worse confounded.

At present there are four universities in Ireland. They are the University of Dublin, which is for practical purposes, synonymous with Trinity College, Dublin (T.C.D.); the National University, of which there are four constituent Colleges, in Dublin, Cork, Galway (U.C.D., U.C.C., and U.C.G.), and St Patrick's, Maynooth, Queen's University, Belfast (Q.U.B.), and the new University of Ulster sited near Coleraine. The last two are completely independent of the others.

Although the National University was founded in 1908, it is commonly considered as the direct descendant of the Queen's Colleges, the Catholic University, the Queen's University and the Royal University. The Catholic University School of Medicine in Cecilia Street was the immediate forerunner of the Faculty of Medicine of University College, Dublin.

In 1845, Queen's Colleges had been established in Cork, Belfast and Galway. These were intended to place higher education on a secular basis. They were denounced by the Catholic hierarchy as 'dangerous to faith and morals,' and by the High Church party in the British House of Commons as 'a gigantic scheme of godless education.' The Belfast College succeeded, but the others failed.

Medical Schools were opened in each of these Colleges, although no provision had been made in the original plans for such establishments. Parliament provided grants for their maintenance and the professors' salaries. Every candidate for a medical degree in the Queen's University was obliged to spend at least one *annus medicus* in one of the Colleges. The total course of lectures extended over four years.

In 1850 the Colleges were incorporated into the Queen's

University. They now became Queen's University Colleges with wide local autonomy. Although they conducted their own courses and examinations, the University remained the conferring body. Most of the students came from the poorer classes of society. As in the Scottish universities, they were obliged to 'live out' under the ineffective supervision of Deans of Residence.

The Cork, Galway and Belfast Colleges maintained an unbroken existence until the foundation of the National University. In Dublin the situation as regards medical education and qualification underwent several important changes.

In 1857 a Royal Commission was appointed to consider the whole question of the Queen's Colleges, which were obviously achieving little success with the Catholic section of the population. A point on which most of the professors examined by the Commission agreed was that the University should have the right to grant a Diploma in Surgery. The Royal Colleges of Surgeons in London and Edinburgh received Queen's candidates for examination without any further attendance at lectures in these cities. But in order to obtain the diploma of the Irish College, candidates were required to reside in Dublin for two years. A surgical degree was necessary for most public appointments. As a result, many students emigrated who would otherwise have completed their course at home. On the other hand, the Queen's University required only one-third of its course to be attended in a Queen's College in order to obtain a medical degree. This was a great advantage to the newly-qualified licentiate of a surgical college who wished to obtain such an additional degree.

Some deficiencies in the staffing of the Colleges were revealed to the Commission. For example, no Professors of Medical Jurisprudence were appointed, and in the Belfast College this subject was taught by the Professor of Agriculture. While the London College of Surgeons did not require the subject, no M.D. degree or Diploma in Surgery could be granted in Ireland without it.

In 1854 the Catholic University of Ireland was established with John (later Cardinal) Newman as first Rector. Newman's *Idea of a University* set forth in beautiful prose his philosophy of education. Briefly, his hope was the development of a Catholic University for the 'upper' classes — not for the middle and poorer classes whose many small contributions had done so much to establish and support that University. Newman hoped that English rather than Irish Catholics would be attracted to the new University. Newman rejected utility as a note of liberal education. Despite this, he made provision for practical studies. In this, as in other points of administration, he was inconsistent with his avowed ideals. Newman resigned in 1857, deeply disappointed with his Irish experience. Although he was out of sympathy with, or did not understand, much of the Irish character, we owe Newman a debt of gratitude for the foundation of the Catholic University School of Medicine in Cecilia Street. His bust adorns a niche in the wall of University Church, Stephen's Green and the premises of U.C.D. at 86 St Stephen's Green have been renamed Newman House.

The earliest reference to a possible connection between a Medical School and the Catholic University appeared in the *Catholic University Gazette* of September 1854. It ran:

It is proposed to open at once in a respectable part of Dublin a lodging house for medical students, under the sanction of the Catholic University. The house will not be formally connected with the University, nor will the University be responsible for its inmates. They will in no sense be under its jurisdiction, or subject to its rules, or debarred from their free choice of lectures. The object contemplated is solely that of providing a dwelling, respectable and reasonable in terms, for gentlemen who are brought to the metropolis for the purpose of professional education.

The very reasonable terms of £7 per quarter were later lowered to £6 per quarter. In November of the same year the words, 'till the Medical Schools are set up,' inserted before, 'the house will not . . .,' seem to mark the formal decision to establish a Catholic School. During this time the offices of the University secretary were situated in the Medical School buildings in Cecilia Street, which had been acquired from the Apothecaries' Hall.

The Catholic University Medical School opened in the autumn of 1855; Practical Anatomy on 1st October, and Lectures on 1st November. Two classes of students were admitted to the teaching, viz: first, Matriculated students of the Catholic University, free of charge; second, Non-matriculated students at a fee of two guineas for each course.

The School set a high standard from the beginning. Catechetical examinations were held each Saturday on the work of the preceding week. The Demonstrators resided on the premises and were available for keen students at 7 a.m., or between the hours of 8 and 10 p.m. The lectures were immediately recognised by the Queen's University, by the Colleges of Physicians and Surgeons, and by the Army, Navy, and East India Medical Boards.

A public address, introductory to the lectures of the session, was read by Andrew Ellis on 2nd November 1855. The audience included the Archbishop of Dublin and a distinguished gathering of clergy, medical and lay men.

Thomas Hayden read his introductory lecture three days later. The school attracted favourable notice from at least one Protestant physician, Dr Robert Travers (1807–1888) of the 'Original' School of Medicine. In an address he defended vigorously the right of the Catholic University to establish a Medical School, and welcomed its students to friendly rivalry.

In July 1856, the first prize-giving of the school was held in the University Church, St Stephen's Green. An address was read by the Very Revd Rector, Dr Newman. The prizes were distributed by Dr Cullen, then Archbishop of Dublin; the first prize-winners of the school were: Francis B. Quinlan, Thomas Crean, William F. Hanley, Walter Morrin and Henry Devlin.

When the Cecilia Street buildings passed from the control of the Apothecaries' Company to that of the Episcopal Board of the Catholic University the favourable omens for the new school's success were few. The buildings acquired were old, cramped in accommodation, structurally unsound and already out of date for the work of a Medical School. The Chairs were only moderately endowed. Nevertheless, able men were attracted to the professorships and some first-class work was done. It is often forgotten that one of the intentions of the founders was that the establishment should be not alone a teaching centre, but a nucleus where research workers might have an opportunity of investigation denied them elsewhere. In the appointments to various Chairs, men were selected to fill those of Anatomy and Physiology who were practising physicians holding hospital posts. Specialisation in these subjects was still almost unknown, and they were joined as one Chair.

Amongst the well-known members of the school staff was Thomas Hayden (1823–1881), a cousin of G. T. Hayden of the Bishop Street and 'Original' Schools. Thomas started his career as an Anatomist in the 'Original' School. Later he became Professor of Anatomy in the Catholic School. He was appointed a physician to the Mater Misericordiae Hospital on its foundation, occupying the post until his death thirty years later.

William Kirby Sullivan (1826–1890) was first Lecturer on Chemistry to the new School. He held several other appointments, including professorships in the Albert Agricultural College and the Museum of Irish Industry (later the College of Science and now Government Buildings). He eventually succeeded Sir Robert Kane as President of Queen's College, Cork. Sullivan organised a well-equipped chemical laboratory and museum in the Catholic School.

The first Professor of Surgery was Andrew Ellis (1792–1867). After a period in the first Peter Street School and the Theatre of Anatomy and School of Surgery, he was appointed to the Apothecaries' Hall in 1837. When the Apothecaries' School became extinct he joined the Catholic School staff. Ellis was surgeon to Jervis Street Hospital. He produced some publications of surgical importance, notably 'Wounds of the Abdomen and their Effects' (*Lancet* 1832). In 1846 he published a volume of lectures and observations on Clinical Surgery while he was still on the staff of the Apothecaries' School.

Robert Dyer Lyons (1826–1886), first Professor of the Practice of Medicine, had a most adventurous career. In his twenties he was appointed Pathologist-in-Chief to the forces in the Crimea. He was present and rendered assistance to the French wounded at the battle of Tchernaya. In 1859, he reported to Pedro V of Portugal on the insanitary state of Lisbon. For these services he received the Cross and Insignia of the Portuguese Order of Christ. This report was published in *Atlantis*, the organ of the Catholic University in 1859, as were others of his works on other issues. Despite his wide foreign experience Lyons did not forget his own country, and in 1870 he served on the commission appointed to consider the treatment of Irish political prisoners in English gaols. Finally he served as a Member of Parliament for Dublin from 1880 to 1883. Lyons published one modest medical text book, *A Handbook of Hospital Practice or an Introduction to the practical Study of Medicine at the Bedside*, in 1859. Robert Cryan (1826–1881) of St Vincent's Hospital, a Licentiate of the Colleges of Surgeons and Physicians, formerly a lecturer in the Carmichael School, was appointed to the second Chair of Anatomy and Physiology. Henry Tyrell and John O'Reilly, both Licentiates of the College of Surgeons, were appointed Demonstrators of Anatomy. Henry Hennessy, a Member of the Royal Irish Academy, took over the Chair of Natural Philosophy.

In 1858 the School had the good fortune to come into possession of the 'Munich' Library. This was the product of the united collections made since an early period of the eighteenth century by a group of eminent medical philosophers of Germany. It was greatly enriched by the additions of Dr von Ringseis, Rector of Munich University, from whose hands it passed directly to the Catholic University. It comprised over 5,000 volumes, including many rare medical works. It represented the select medical literature of seven languages, Dutch, English, French, German, Greek, Italian and Latin.

A medical lodging-house, known as 'St Luke's,' was established at 41 York Street, Dublin, under the supervision of one of the Anatomical Demonstrators. The fees for board and lodging for an academic year were £30. This was distinct from the house already mentioned which catered for medical students of any school. Unlike the T.C.D. undergraduates, the students had no official residence and lived, like the Queen's students, with little supervision, in 'digs.'

Inevitably they developed a name for rowdiness and idleness which became all the more marked during the University's declining years. Frequently this provided a not unwelcome excuse for parents to send their sons to Trinity. Newman hoped that arrangements could be made whereby students would be examined for degrees by the Queen's University, but in this he was disappointed. A similar scheme put forward by the Liberal administration in 1886 was quashed when supporters of secular education appealed to the Courts.

In 1863 many of the staff of the Mater Misericordiae and Jervis Street hospitals lectured in the Medical School. This, in conjunction with the fact that the hospitals were administered by a Catholic religious order, resulted in their great popularity with the students of the Cecilia Street School and facilities were provided for lectures and practical work.

The battle of university education in Ireland at this time would provide material for many volumes. It was a direct cause of the collapse of Gladstone's ministry in 1873.

A Bill to establish a Royal University as an examining body only, was submitted to the Council of the College of Surgeons by the Lord Lieutenant. The Council remarked that no practising Licentiate or Fellow of the College appeared on the Roll of the proposed Senate, while the names of several physicians were prominent. His Grace expressed regret and promised to rectify the matter when a vacancy should arise. Six years later the Council were informed by the Royal University that their visitors found the teaching equipment of the College defective. The Council maintained that as the visitation was an unexpected one, there was no competent person to demonstrate the College's teaching resources.

Prior to the establishment of the Royal University, students of the Catholic University Medical School had practically no access to medical degrees. The majority had to content themselves with holding the conjoint qualifications of the Colleges of Physicians and Surgeons. They could not graduate at Trinity nor the Queen's University, and had not the benefit of a liberal as well as a technical education which a university can give. Although the Cecilia Street School was not housed in the same buildings as the Catholic University, the ties between the two were close. All the first year medical lectures were given at University College in St Stephen's Green, and the two bodies worked in close harmony. At the same time, many students took out Arts degrees concurrently with those in Medicine. The wish for harmony between the two was later generously expressed in *St Stephen's*, the paper conducted by the students of University College:

We hope that one of the effects of this publication may be to bring the students of the College and the Medical School into closer relations.

These closer relations became a reality in work, in debate, in social life, and on the sports field, and supplied many university benefits for the medical students. At one time they occupied a football ground beside the Star of the Sea Church in Sandymount. The University College men were allowed to use this freely as some return for the amenities they granted the medical students.

In 1878, Gladstone had proposed in his University Bill to set up a National University of which Trinity would form a part. This solution was unanimously condemned by Catholics and Protestants alike. Both sides agreed that it would be unfair for Trinity to lose her independent status and become subject to a governmental board. The Catholic Bishops had the further objection that under the Bill the Catholic University would be left penniless.

Ninety years later the question of some form of amalgamation of the two Universities again became a live issue when Mr Donacadh O'Malley was Minister of Education. His plans had reached a very advanced stage when he died suddenly, cutting short a brilliant career. His particular interest in medical students was given practical expression by his presentation of a fine cup awarded annually to the winners of an inter-medical school rugby competition promoted by the Irish Medical Students Association.

In 1879, the Royal University was set up in the place of the Queen's University. However, the Catholic University, now University College, Dublin, had not been endowed, and the Royal was merely an examining and conferring body. Under these conditions the Catholic community remained unsatisfied.

The regulations for medical education made by the Royal University were criticised in the *Dublin Journal of Medical Science*. The Arts curriculum was meagre by comparison with that of Trinity, and the total hospital attendance was twenty-four instead of twenty-seven months. However, certificates of attendance on fever and mental cases, as well as of instruction in vaccination and compounding, were required.

The University followed Trinity's lead in conferring a Diploma in Sanitary Science on its own graduates. The examination for the diploma was open to criticism as three out of the five papers were set by one examiner, and the Sanitary Law paper related entirely to Irish enactments. Then, as now, a huge majority of doctors qualified in Ireland were required to emigrate.

Full courses of instruction leading to the degrees of the Royal University were established in the Catholic University School in 1884.

The school still suffered under the grave disadvantage of having no public endowment. This situation was fully recognised by Mr Arthur Balfour, Chief Secretary for Ireland, when, in a speech delivered at Glasgow, he declared:

There was a time when all you required of a University was a water-tight roof, a certain number of teachers, a certain number of students, a few benches and some blackboards. But all that has been changed by the advance of medical and scientific training. In England and Scotland and in Ireland we are far behind some of our Continental brethren in our public recognition of the fact that in order to teach science and medicine properly, you require a most costly equipment. That costly equipment I do not believe will be provided or can be provided by the Roman Catholic population of Ireland, and my desire is to help them to provide it, and not to help them only, but to help for example, Queen's College, Belfast.

The public endowment for the professorships of the Faculty of Medicine in Belfast was £1,320 per annum; in Cork £1,380; and in Galway £1,450. In addition, the Queen's Colleges were well equipped in the matter of laboratories, museums and libraries. The sums mentioned were independent of outlay on repairs and maintenance, the whole cost of which was borne by the public through the Board of Works.

To many, including the Archbishop of Dublin, Most Revd Dr Walsh, the annual grant to Q.C.G. was a waste of public funds. In an address to the Catholic University School of Medicine in 1889, he pointed out that there had been only forty students in Galway in the preceding session. The largest class was that of Anatomy and Physiology, with thirty-four students. The salary of the Professor was £220, exclusive of class fees. In Midwifery, the class consisted of a solitary student, for lecturing to whom Professor Richard J. Kinkead received £150 of public money.

In evidence given before the Queen's Colleges' Commission in 1857, Richard Doherty, then Professor of Midwifery in Galway, revealed that he had no means of giving practical instruction to his class although attendance at a lying-in hospital was required for all students. Doherty used every means, including public lectures and appeals, to found such a hospital, but without success.

When the Royal University was founded, fresh fields of activity were opened to the Catholic School. The necessity of preparing students for examinations of a high standard and competitive nature led to the re-organisation of the school's teaching and staffing. In the first place, Anatomy was divorced completely from Physiology, and placed under the care of a special teacher. The professorship of Physiology remained in the hands of a practising surgeon,

Charles Coppinger (1846–1908) of the Mater Misericordiae Hospital. His assistant devoted his full time to Physiology.

The regulations of the Royal University required students to attend a three months' course of lectures on Pathology before presenting themselves for the degree examination. The Catholic University School was the first in Great Britain to appoint a Professor of Pathology with the obligation that he should confine himself exclusively to his special subject, including bacteriology. A Public Health Laboratory, the first of its kind in Ireland, was provided with what was then ample equipment for those working for the Diploma in Sanitary Science.

The students of the Catholic University School of Medicine had an extremely high record of success in the open examinations of the Royal University, in spite of their School's financial difficulties. In the seven years, 1885–1891, forty-one first-class honours were awarded by the Royal University. Queen's College Galway secured 1, Cork 7, Belfast 16, the Catholic University School 17.

In 1889 the great superiority of the Cecilia Street School was the subject of a question in the House of Commons. In 1889 and 1891 Studentships in Biological Science were offered by the Royal University. Both of these were secured by students of the Cecilia Street School–Alexander Blayney (1869–1925) and Denis Coffey, later the distinguished first President of University College, Dublin.

Following the passage of the Educational Endowments (Ireland) Act of 1885, the School became a body corporate. This gave it a legal position comparable to that of the other medical schools. It was managed by a Board of Governors created by an order of the Lord Lieutenant.

In 1891 the Bishops gave their consent that the School and its endowments should be dealt with by the Educational Endowments Commission. The endowments transferred to the new governing body were:

(1)   The buildings and equipment of the School;
(2)   A £1,000 bequest;
(3)   Stocks yielding about £55 per year.

In 1893, following urgent appeals, over £3,000 was raised by the Irish Bishops. This, with the £1,000 bequest, provided new anatomical, chemical, public health and physiological laboratories. Out of his private funds, Most Revd Dr Walsh, Archbishop of Dublin, provided the School with a bacteriological laboratory, the first of its kind in Ireland. As a result of the expansion, the interest of £55, with students' fees, was the total income of the School

Unfortunately, the capital fund of the Catholic University was exhausted and an important source of help at a critical time was not available. A very sound machinery for the expenditure of funds had been devised. Unfortunately again there were none to expend. The situation was so grave that for some twenty years the professors received no salaries.

Women were first admitted to the Medical Register in 1876, but it was not until twenty years later that the Catholic University Medical School received its first lady student. In October 1896 Miss Frances Sinclair requested permission to follow a course in Sanitary Science and Pathology. The Governing Body decided that her request might be granted, and gave a direction to the Faculty that if other women made application they might be permitted to follow senior courses. During the year six women, of whom four were Protestants, studied at the Catholic Medical School. One of these was Miss Jellett, the daughter of a former Provost of Trinity College, and Miss Ovenden, later Dr Ella Webb. In 1897 Dr Quinlan volunteered the use of some of his rooms for the exclusive use of lady students, and when these were fitted as waiting- and dissecting-rooms ladies were admitted to the full courses.

The battle for equal educational opportunities for all sections of the community proceeded throughout this period. James (later Viscount) Bryce proposed a reconstruction of Dublin University in which a new Catholic College would be founded. As this would be denominational the T.C.D. authorities vetoed the plan, and no satisfactory scheme was devised until 1907 when Mr Augustine Birrell brought in a Bill establishing two new universities – one, Queen's University, Belfast, the other the National University of Ireland. The latter was to be formed by a new University College in Dublin, together with University Colleges in Cork and Galway, previously Queen's University Colleges of these cities. Provision was made for the recognition of other institutions for teaching purposes. Under this, St Patrick's College, Maynooth, became a recognised College for instruction leading to degrees in Arts, Philosophy, Celtic Studies and Science.

The house at 86 St Stephen's Green became the Headquarters of University College, Dublin. Other buildings available to the infant university were those of the Royal University in Earlsfort Terrace which had been housed in the buildings of a former Dublin Exhibition. The present buildings (front portion) occupy roughly the same position as the front of the old exhibition buildings. There was a fine clock tower on the north-east corner of the original premises, which was taken down and re-erected as the main chimney for the block now occupied by Government Buildings. Cecilia Street remained the seat of the Medical School.

The University College premises in Earlsfort Terrace were erected during 1914–19, despite the difficulties occasioned by the World War and the Nationalist movements at home. All lectures were gradually transferred there, leaving '86' free for social functions. When plans for the new building were drawn up in 1914, the section designed for Departments of Anatomy, Physiology and Pathology was marked, 'erection deferred for the present.' When the National University came into being, a promise had been made that the Cecilia Street buildings would be closed within six months. Although various departments were transferred to the new buildings, the Cecilia Street premises were occupied by the Anatomy classes until 1932, when the final transfer took place and a ninety-six-year-old connection between the building and medical education was broken.

In the *National Student* of 1911, a contributor wrote a scathing article on the amenities of the Cecilia Street School:

. . . we arrive outside an ungainly, dilapidated block not unlike a jail or workhouse, painted a nauseating yellow, its windows almost opaque with the accumulated dirt of half a century. Students are requested not to wait in the hall, but there is nowhere else to wait unless they line up in the street outside. The students' waiting room is furnished in a style suggestive of a Police Station – a wooden table, three chairs (one with three legs) and two long deal seats running along the wall.

In Cecilia Street the two lecture theatres were singled out by Professors of Hygiene as awful examples of bad lighting and ventilation. An upstairs lavatory occasionally dripped on the heads of the class beneath.

When the Medical School was transferred to Earlsfort Terrace it was not possible to group all Departments together and lectures in Chemistry, Botany and Zoology were given in Science Buildings in Merrion St. In 1967 much of the College activities were transferred to the new campus at Belfield but Anatomy, Physiology, Pathology, Forensic Medicine and Community Medicine continued to be based in Earlsfort Terrace.

Amongst the distinguished alumni of the Royal University and the Cecilia Street Medical School, none has a greater claim to immortality than Ambrose Bermingham (1864–1905). He entered the Catholic University School in 1882 and almost immediately revealed his talent for Anatomy. During his course he took several prizes and exhibitions. Immediately after qualification in 1887 he was appointed to the Chair of Anatomy. Shortly afterwards he became Registrar of the Faculty, and the School took on a new lease of life. The dissecting-room became a workshop rather than a loungers' club.

The walls were covered with diagrams. Demonstrations were held regularly. Beautiful dissections were prepared and preserved for teaching. The increased attendance of students raised the teachers' keenness, so thåt idleness on both sides of the rostrum fell to a minimum.

Bermingham produced many papers on anatomical subjects. His most important work included the section on the abdominal tract in Cunningham's *Anatomy*, a textbook of international fame. He also produced a dissection manual, of which only one volume was published. His worth was recognised, at home by his appointment to the Presidency of the Section of Anatomy and Physiology of the Academy of Medicine, and abroad by his appointment as an Extern Examiner at Cambridge. Bermingham's hobby was photography. Even here he used his knowledge to further his anatomical work. Many of the lantern slides he prepared were, until recently, still used during Anatomy lectures at University College, Dublin.

One of Bermingham's plans for giving the students some social life was the foundation of 'The Cecilians' Dining Club,' which met in the Dolphin Hotel. At this, students and professors gathered on equal terms. Bermingham died, aged forty-one, from a progressive hardening of the arteries. His memory is commemorated in U.C.D. by the Ambrose Bermingham Gold Medal for Anatomy. The Bermingham Memorial Fund, formerly held by the Governors of the Catholic University School of Medicine, provides the income for the provision of this medal.

Bermingham's assistant in the anatomy department for many years was Patrick Joseph Fagan (1863–1910). Fagan started medicine at a later age than many of his fellow-students, and studied anatomy as a means to an end. With the determination to adopt surgery as a career he secured his F.R.C.S.I. in 1896. When he was appointed a surgeon to St Vincent's Hospital in 1897, he had an opportunity of combining surgical and anatomical teaching for the benefit of many students.

Fagan, who was an extremely modest man, made few communications to the Academy of Medicine in Ireland. All were on original observations in Anatomy, free from any contention. They included 'Irregular Distribution of Nerves in the Foot' (1892), 'Reports of Collective Investigations in the Anatomical Department of the Catholic University School' (1892–93) and 'Specimens of the Nasal Fossa' (1900). In the surgical field, Fagan presented a paper to the Academy on 'Tumour of the Testis' (1899).

The administration of University College, Dublin, in its early days was the primary responsibility of a medical graduate. A brilliant course in Medicine and Arts, followed by an appointment to the

Catholic Medical School Chair of Biology in his early thirties, was a fitting prelude to the career of Denis Coffey (1864–1945), first President of the College, who held office until 1940. During his Presidency, the Medical School developed from a small crowded department, hidden away in Cecilia Street, to a most important Faculty of the College. Although the College as a whole was Coffey's responsibility, the Medical School remained his special pride. Its academic and social functions could always be sure of his whole-hearted support.

At the last College meeting over which Coffey presided officially, he secured the adoption by the Governing Body of two schemes very near to his heart, one for the foundation of Catholic University Scholarships which formed an additional link between the Catholic University Medical School and the U.C.D. Medical School; the other for the establishment of the Archbishop Walsh Prize. This commemorated the great churchman who, more than any other individual, was instrumental in securing a University for Irish Catholics, and who had no more devoted supporter than Coffey himself.

Coffey represented the University on the G.M.C. for more than twenty years, and on the Irish Free State Registration Council, of which he was first chairman. Some years before he retired, the Irish Government appointed Coffey as its representative in the Health Section of the League of Nations and at the International Office of Public Health in Paris.

Since Coffey's retirement the Presidency of U.C.D has twice been occupied by medical graduates, in 1950 by James N. Meenan, Professor of Medicine, and from 1972 until the present by Thomas Murphy, then Professor of Social and Preventive Medicine.

UNIVERSITY COLLEGE, CORK

The Medical School of Queen's College, Cork, opened on 8th November 1849 with twenty students. Denis Bullan, a surgeon of the North Infirmary, was appointed Dean. The accommodation for the Medical School in the west wing of the quadrangle was soon found to be quite unsuitable. Appeals to the Government proved fruitless, but Lord Clarendon (1800–1870), then Lord Lieutenant, was more sympathetic, and the present medical school building is a monument to his generosity. The Queen's Colleges were not utilised fully by the Catholic population as a result of the ecclesiastical condemnation. This, of course, extended to the Medical Schools though not in so marked a degree. Relations between professors and students, too, were better in this faculty than in the others.

The first Medical Professors appointed were: Benjamin Alcock (Anatomy and Physiology), Denis Charles O'Connor (Medicine), Joshua Reuben Harvey (Midwifery), Denis Brenan Bullan (Surgery), Alexander Fleming (Materia Medica), Rev William Hinks (Natural History) and George Frederick Shaw (Natural Philosophy).

Benjamin Alcock was born in Kilkenny in 1801. He studied Anatomy at Trinity College under Macartney, later being indentured to Abraham Colles. From 1825 until his appointment in Cork, Alcock demonstrated Anatomy in various Dublin schools. Alcock's transfer to Cork followed the retirement due to ill-health of the original appointee, Dr Carte.

In 1853 a dispute arose between Alcock and the College authorities over the working of the Anatomy Act. As a result Alcock resigned and went to America. No further records of his life or death are known.

Joshua Reuben Harvey, the first Professor of Midwifery, had been a student in Cork, Dublin and Edinburgh. He was Physician to the Cork General Dispensary and Lying-in Hospital. In 1878 he prepared some of the Zoological exhibits in the Queen's College Museum. He published a few papers in the *Dublin Quarterly Journal of Medical Science*.

Harvey is sometimes confused with his son Reuben Joshua (1845–1881). The younger Harvey was educated in Trinity College, Dublin, where he later became a demonstrator and examiner. His name is commemorated by the Reuben Harvey Prize, which is awarded triennially to students or graduates of less than three years' standing from the Irish schools or licensing bodies. The prize is awarded to the author of the best essay upon a subject showing evidence of original research into animal physiology.

Denis Charles O'Connor, the first Professor of Medicine, qualified L.R.C.S.I. in 1833. He too, was attached to the Cork Dispensary and to the Mercy Hospital. His worth was recognised when he received the M.D. *Hons. causa* of Q.U.B. (1879) and Litt.D. (Cantab) 1880, as well as being elected a President of the British Medical Association.

Denis Brenan Bullan, the Professor of Surgery, was the first Dean of the Faculty. He held the responsible post of Inspector of Anatomy for Munster, and was a surgeon to the North Infirmary.

Alexander Fleming, the Professor of Materia Medica, had considerable foreign experience. He was President of the Royal Medical Society of Edinburgh, and Vice-President of the Parisian Medical Society. When he retired from Cork in 1857 he went to Birmingham. His paper on the use of aconite is commemorated in the synonym for strong tincture of that drug, Fleming's Tincture of Aconite.

Sir Robert Kane (1809–1890), first President of Q.C.C., was originally a chemist. In 1829 he became a Licentiate of the Apothecaries' Hall. He had already achieved fame as the discoverer of Kaneite, a natural arsenide of manganese, at the age of twenty. The Meath Hospital Medical Society awarded him the first of many honours, a gold medal for an essay on the effect of poisons introduced into the circulation. Kane's first teaching appointment was to the Chair of Chemistry in the Apothecaries' Hall. When the Apothecaries' Medical School was established in 1836 he assisted in the organisation of the new courses. Kane's years in Cork were anything but peaceful. He spent much of his time in Dublin, but refused to delegate his presidential authority. This led to constant friction with his staff.

In May 1862, the east wing of the college was destroyed by a deliberate fire. Many people suspected a Richard Burke, Clerk to the Waterford Union. When Burke's wife died, her viscera were sent to the Cork College to determine whether death was due to poisoning. Shortly after this the building took fire. Certainly Mrs Burke's remains were examined by Dr John Blyth, the Professor of Chemistry, but his report had been given to the Coroner nearly two weeks before the fire. Professor Bullan alleged that the fire had been started by College officials, and that Kane had suggested the publication of a report attributing the crime to the radical Catholic element who would not accept the Queen's Colleges. Bullan was probably hoping for Kane's post, but instead was dismissed following the Triennial Visitation of 1864. In 1873, after holding office for twenty-eight years, Kane resigned.

William Kirby Sullivan (1822–1890), the second President, issued his first report in 1874. He pointed out many defects in the buildings and equipment. His recommendations included the construction of a physiology laboratory and additions to most of the medical school departments.

Five years later, thanks to State grants and the generous gifts of W. H. Crawford, work was commenced on laboratories for Physiology, Biology and Pharmacy. The Medical School was Sullivan's constant care, although he was not a medical man. In 1881 he pointed out the need for lectureships in Sanitary Science and Physiological Medicine. In 1886, he recommended the establishment of Chairs of Human and Comparative Pathology, and of Public Health. Despite this, Yelverton Pearson, Professor of Surgery, in 1901, was able to complain justly that the arrangements for the teaching of Pathology were quite inadequate, and that there was no pathological service in the whole southern province. In 1886, Sullivan recommended that the Chair of Anatomy and Physiology should be divided. This was not done until 1907.

The third President, Sir Ronald Blennerhasset, appeared in the College once a year on a formal inspection. His successor, John Slattery, was another absentee President.

In the last decade of the nineteenth century the average number of students attending courses in all faculties was about two hundred, of whom three-fourths were medicals. Women students were unknown, and it was not until 1898 that Drs Lucy Smith and Dora Allman qualified M.B., B.S. of the Royal University.

The fifth President of the College, Dr (later Sir) Bertram Windle (1858–1929), who assumed office in 1905, was responsible for many improvements in the Medical School. These included a second dissecting-room, Physiological and Pathological laboratories, and an operative surgery department with a museum of instruments. A Department of Dentistry was added to the Faculty. Windle at various times held the Chairs of Anatomy and Archaeology as well as the Presidency. He was the first holder of a separate Chair of Anatomy, as suggested by Sullivan.

For the first few years after the establishment of the National University the medical students in Cork averaged about 200 in number. They comprised about half the whole student body. During the first World War their numbers increased. Afterwards their numbers fell steadily until in 1930 only 120 medicals appeared on a roll of some 500 students. From that time until 1941–42, a sharp increase in numbers brought the Medical students to a strength of over 360. Since the end of World War II the Cork Medical School has steadily expanded. The building of a large Regional Hospital with a wide range of specialised departments provided a welcome pool of varied clinical material. This has undoubtedly had the effect of attracting outstanding clinical teachers whose ability would otherwise have encouraged them to go to medical schools elsewhere.

UNIVERSITY COLLEGE, GALWAY

The Medical School of Queen's College, Galway, opened on 30th October 1849, with the paltry number of ten pupils. Two years later this had fallen to eight. Despite such a poor beginning the school developed, and in 1881 there were 122 names on the roll. The school gave complete training from its establishment in 1849 with the following staff:

Botany and Zoology   .   Alexander G. Melville

Experimental Physics	Morgan W. Crofton
Chemistry	Edward Ronalds
Anatomy and Physiology .	Charles Croker King
Surgery	James V. Browne
Medicine	Nicholas Colahan
Midwifery	Richard Doherty
Materia Medica . . .	Simon McCoy
Medical Jurisprudence .	Simon McCoy (Lecturer)

The Galway School must be one of the few in which professors and lecturers at one time outnumbered the students. Scholarships in the Faculty of Medicine were granted from the earliest days. The same names re-appear frequently in successive years as winners.

The most distinguished member of the Galway School was probably John Cleland, who was Professor of Anatomy and Physiology from 1863 until 1877, when he went to Glasgow as Professor of Anatomy. Whilst still in Galway he became a Fellow of the Royal Society. He lived to over ninety years of age. Among distinguished students were Peter Freyer, famous for his technique in prostate operations, and Edward Divers, the celebrated chemist, who afterwards became first Professor of Chemistry at the University of Tokyo.

James V. Browne, the first Professor of Surgery, was the subject of a curious story. Thomas Maguire, the Professor of Latin, became a Fellow of T.C.D. in 1880. When he went to Dublin he spoke of Browne to some of the people whom the latter had described as fellow-students. They, however, said that Browne had died shortly after qualification. Further enquiries revealed that the Professor of Surgery had posed as his deceased cousin.

William Brereton, the Professor of Surgery from 1887 to 1924, was a well-known authority on spiritualism. He refused to believe in microbes or the principles of asepsis. Despite this he was good on fractures and invented several very useful splints.

One of the best appointments to the school was that of Ralph Mahon to the Chair of Medicine from 1913 to 1932. Mahon had been in general practice in Ballinrobe, where he had done some work on lice as carriers of typhus.

When Cleland retired from the Chair of Anatomy and Physiology in 1877 he was succeeded by Joseph Pye, who remained in office until 1920. The chair was not divided until 1922.

The Galway College was subjected to the same changes of status and title as the other colleges. In 1929 an Act of the Oireachtas was passed in order to increase the annual grant and to ensure that

10. Dr. Halloran's Swing and Hammock for the Treatment of Lunacy.

11. The Lying-In Hospital, Great Britain St., Dublin.

Plate II   *To Face Page. 139.*

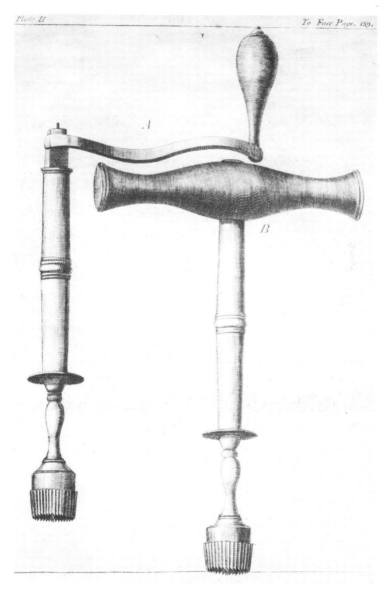

12. Croker King's Trephine, late eighteenth century.

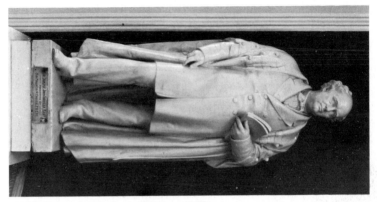

13. Sir Dominic Corrigan (1802 — 1880).

14. Richard Carmichael (1778 — 1849).

15. The Mater Infirmorum Hospital, Belfast.

16. Mortsafe, Drumcondra Churchyard, Dublin.

17. Watch Tower.

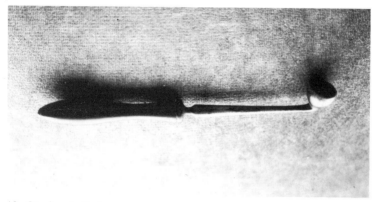

18. Corrigan's Button.

19. Mid-eighteenth century operating chair.

"*Your little Bill looks a healthy child to me, Mrs. Ryan, but maybe the doctors will discover a few spots on him.*"

20. Cartoon by JOD. Courtesy Mr. L. O'Sullivan, *Dublin Opinion*.

21. Elevation of the south front of St. Patrick's Hospital.

officers of the College would be competent to discharge their duties through the medium of Irish.

Up to the early 1950's Galway Medical students were handicapped by a scarcity of clinical material and a lack of specialised departments. Many of them came to Dublin to do their maternity residence. In 1953 the Galway Regional Hospital was formally recognised as a teaching hospital. Existing departments were expanded and new departments were established. As a result it became possible for the Galway Medical School to host both national and international meetings. In 1977 the researches of local workers in the field of coeliac disease were recognised when the third International Conference on this condition was held in Galway. Two years later a Digestive Disease Research Centre was opened.

One of the most outstanding Galway Professors was J. F. Donegan the width and depth of whose learning caused the Physiological Society to elect him to their Honorary Membership in 1976. The Galway medical school has always been aware of the importance of family medicine and had Professor E. O'Dwyer been given more support in 1973 there might now be a Chair of General Practice in U.C.G.

CHAPTER EIGHTEEN

THE ROYAL COLLEGE OF GENERAL PRACTITIONERS

Since the establishment of formal registration in 1858 the medical profession had tended to divide into two sub-divisions, 'specialist' and 'General Practitioners'. Though both had legally the same status and were each essential to the patient and to each other there was, in the minds of some people, both, within and without the profession a feeling that the specialist was, in some mysterious way, better than the G.P., whom many regarded as a failed consultant dealing only with trivial diseases.

As general practitioners played no part in the education of medical students, were sparsely represented on academic medical bodies and often had little or no access to post-graduate refresher courses, it is little wonder that the myth of general practice being inferior was perpetuated. Even some G.P.s subscribed to the idea and were content to accept a subservient role.

Attempts had been made to found a college, academy or association of general practitioners since the middle of the nineteenth century. Most of these were of English origin but particularly in the political climate of the day would have had a considerable impact on Irish general practice. Unfortunately all of them failed because of internal dissention, poor communications and sometimes, one suspects, from lack of mutual trust and goodwill.

For almost a hundred years nothing was done. Occasionally a letter to one of the medical journals, referred to the possibility or desirability of founding a college, but action was sadly lacking. In Britain the establishment of the National Health Service in 1949, with its implication for and dependence on the G.P.s of the country, brought matters to a head.

The many disappointments and frustrations of those who were keen to form a college, have been recorded in detail in the *History of the Royal College of General Practitioners* published in 1983 which is essential reading for anyone interested in that body's origin and birth pangs.

The College was founded on 19th November, 1952, under a

provisional constitution. The steering committee's report was published a few weeks later in the *British Medical Journal*. It was a report which suggested an Irish involvement. The present writer, who was then secretary of the Private Practitioners' group of the Irish Medical Association, wrote to the steering committee asking for further information. As a result a meeting of Irish General Practitioners, under the chairmanship of Dr Laurence Masterson, was held in U.C.D. on 15th March, 1953. After lengthy discussion and even some opposition, resolutions were passed approving the foundation of a college or faculty of general practice in Ireland and establishing a steering committee. These decisions were communicated to London and the writer was invited to join the College Foundation Council on 5th April, 1953. This Council met regularly until the first A.G.M. in the Great Hall of the B.M.A. when the members retired and were re-elected as the first College Council on 14th November, 1953.

At a very early stage decentralisation was a feature of the College's organisation and faculties were established in Great Britain and Ireland. There are four Irish faculties covering areas approximating to the traditional Provinces.

The Northern Ireland Faculty was founded on 30th April 1953 in the Whitla Institute, Belfast, under the Chairmanship of Dr J. Campbell Young. A Faculty Board with a wide geographical spread was elected from the 43 members who attended. For the first year, meetings were largely devoted to discussions about management of illness in general practice but members were concerned, not alone with increasing their own knowledge, but also with improving the standards and image of General Practice. Sub-committees dealing with criteria for admission to membership, undergraduate and post-graduate education, research and standards generally were set up. As the Faculty and the College gained strength their influence increased. A particularly notable result in Belfast was the establishment of a Department of General Practice in Belfast under the direction of Dr George Irwin. The Northern Ireland Faculty is widely recognised as the voice of general practice in its area, most importantly by the Ministry (now Department) of Health and Social Services. Members are regularly invited to give advice on health matters generally.

A note in the minutes of April 1954 records that the Chairman of the Northern Faculty was invited to attend the inaugural meeting of the Dublin (now East of Ireland) Faculty held on 1st May 1954. The early work of this Faculty ran parallel to that in the North. Organisation, education and research all attracted members who felt that at long last the G.P. stood a good chance of influencing local medical development. The sub-committees appointed were very active. The G.P. education group produced a detailed report which analysed all aspects of continuing education and, read with hindsight, was a document considerably in advance of contemporary thinking. Similarly, the Research Committee, chaired by Dr Nora McNally, suggested that general practitioners were in a particularly favourable position to study *inter alia* antibiotic effectiveness, dental care, stress, alcoholism and 'minor' illnesses which cause major personal and economic hardships. It also called for the adoption of normal anthropometric standards for Ireland as an essential pre-requisite for worthwhile research. The various reports of the undergraduate education committee foreshadowed the present attachment system, but for a long time continued to give prominence to the formal lecture method of teaching by both specialists and general practitioners. The first news letter of the Faculty announced the establishment of monthly clinical meetings and refresher courses for members and also noted that advice had been given about the foundation of two further Irish Faculties in Galway and Cork.

The first steps to found a West of Ireland Faculty were taken on 20th June 1954 when a preparatory meeting led to the establishment, with 23 foundation members, of the West of Ireland Faculty under the Chairmanship of Dr G. C. Maguire. Though this is one of the smaller Faculties the members' activity and involvement with College affairs has been remarkable. As early as December 1956 the U.C.G. medical school welcomed a proposed undergraduate education scheme of the Faculty though organised student attachments to general practitioners did not become a reality there until 1963. A proposal from the Western Faculty a year later, that part of the pre-registration year should be spent in General Practice, was approved in principle but has never been implemented for a variety of reasons. Despite this the Faculty has been continuously involved with the Galway medical school in both pre and post qualification education.

When the Royal College of General Practitioners held a joint meeting with the Canadian College of Family Physicians in Dublin in 1982, the largest of its kind held in the Republic or the United Kingdom, the elected Chairman of the Irish Council of the College was Dr James Kent from Galway. This occasion was marked by the presentation of an Honorary Fellowship of the Royal College of General Practitioners to President Patrick Hillery by Dr John Horder, President of the College.

The Cork Faculty was not alone the last to be founded in Ireland but also the last in these islands. The inaugural meeting was not held until 28th January 1956, over three years after the foundation of the College. Dr Joseph Walsh was elected first provost. Despite its tardy start the South of Ireland Faculty rapidly made up for lost time. Post-graduate refresher courses were immediately established and have continued without interruption in the intervening twenty seven years. In 1958 the first lectures to undergraduates were delivered and as a direct result student visits to various practices were introduced. A voluntary scheme for student attachment became so obviously valuable that it is now mandatory for Cork students to spend at least one week with a family doctor. In 1972 Cork pioneered a Vocational Training Scheme for young graduates intending to enter general practice. This was directly linked to the medical school and has proved very successful.

In 1961 it became apparent that the College faculties in Ireland had certain mutual problems, not always the same as those in the other Home Countries, and the College Council requested these faculties to appoint a steering Committee to consider the establishment of an Irish Council. After only three meetings it was able to draw up a constitution which was approved both by the College Council and the local faculties and the newly formed Irish Council met for the first time on 2nd December, 1962. The chairmanship of this fifteen member body rotates between the four faculties. This Council provides a forum for affairs relating to general practice on both sides of the Border and is commonly asked to comment on general practice matters at both governmental and other levels.

One of the most satisfying results of the College's work has been the upsurge of undergraduate interest in general practice as a possible career. For decades G.P.'s played no part in medical student education and the present writer is proud to record that at the invitation of Professor D. K. O'Donovan he delivered the first G.P. undergraduate lecture in U.C.D. on 8th May 1953.

For several years occasional didactic lectures by selected speakers were the only exposure students had to general practice and it was not until the mid-nineteen sixties that student attachment to general practices for periods ranging from single days to a continuous fortnight became common in this country. Even still, many students graduate with no real appreciation of what general practice entails. For those who decide to make a career in G.P. a structured programme of vocational training is now available combining teaching by established G.P's and consultants as well as practical experience as a trainee. Competition for places in trainee schemes is keen and the products judging both by results in the Membership examination and by working standards are of excellent quality.

As yet Belfast has the only Professor of General Practice (George Irwin) in Ireland though a distinguished member of the East of

Ireland Faculty (James McCormick) is Professor of Community Medicine in T.C.D. and other members in all four faculties either have specific teaching committments or take some part in training students. In 1982 University College Cork appointed a part-time Research Fellow in family medicine. The Fellow's function is not alone to initiate research projects but also to advise and assist members who have ideas for research as well as putting them in touch with colleagues working on similar lines. In West Cork, at the time of writing, an experiment in small group continuing education is attracting considerable attention from many people interested in Post Graduate training. It could well be that this pilot study will eventually be the model for a comprehensive scheme of post graduate education particularly among general practitioners.

A Consultative Council on General Medicine Practice was established in 1971 and in its first report published in 1973 stressed the importance of vocational training in general practice and emphasised that the hospital orientated pre-registration year did not fit the newly fledged doctor for the responsibilities of general practice. It was suggested in this report that education in general practice should be organised and co-ordinated by the Council for Post-Graduate Medical and Dental education or by some other broadly based body. This latter Council declined the task and suggested that training in G.P. should be under the guidance of an appropriate professional body. As a result of this The Irish Council of the R.C.G.P. convened a meeting with the Irish Medical Association, the Medical Union and other bodies leading to the establishment of the Irish Institute of General Practice, in March 1975, as the professional body competent to deal with Post-Graduate general practice education.

The stated objects of the Institute are broadly the promotion of education, vocational training schemes, and research into all aspects of general practice as well as the laying down of standards for training in G.P. A major break through in general practice education was the role of the Institute in approving hospital posts as being suitable for trainee general practitioners. Much of the routine work of the Institute is carried out by members of its three regional committees based on Dublin, Cork and Galway. Provision was made for the establishment as required of similar committees elsewhere.

From the first meeting in Dublin in 1953 the question of founding an independent Irish College was raised on countless occasions. There were many arguments for and against such a body. Would G.P's in Northern Ireland join, so that the new body would be truly Irish? Would there be sufficient interest anywhere to warrent such a step? There were some who felt that anything with a 'Royal' prefix was an anachronism. Others felt that loss of such a status symbol would be detrimental. Would membership of a new body be recognised either in Ireland or elsewhere as a registrable degree or as an asset when applying for a G.P. post? Most frequently the question raised was 'How is it to be funded?'. Matters came to a head in November 1982 when, following a decision of the Irish Council of the College, it was announced that with the full backing of the existing Royal College active steps should now be taken to form an autonomous Irish College of General Practitioners. After a number of meetings between representatives of the Institute of General Practice, the R.C.G.P., the I.M.A., and I.M.U., a Foundation Council was established to draft a constitution for a new Irish College. In May 1983 this Council held its inaugural meeting at which agreement was reached on many points including the name of the new body The Irish College of General Practice.

CHAPTER NINETEEN

THE TWENTIETH CENTURY

With the close of the nineteenth century Ireland's brief leadership in medicine passed elsewhere. Stokes had pointed the way to better things in the field of public health when, following his agitation, Dublin University instituted a Diploma in State Medicine – the first of its kind. Unfortunately, lack of money held back many advances and the death rate in Dublin was so high that unfavourable comments appeared in the *Medical Record* of New York and the *Pacific Journal* of San Francisco in 1900.

Ireland was abreast of modern advances in surgery, but Germany was undisputed leader. Lister's doctrines had been readily accepted and improved there. Karl Thiersch of Leipzig, Richard Volkmann of Halle, Theodore Billroth of Vienna and Friedrich Trendelenburg of Berlin were and are familiar names in surgical circles throughout the world.

The outstanding events of the first half of the twentieth century in Ireland were the foundation of a new university and the development of an independent State. However, the bad state of the public health did not pass entirely unnoticed and, in 1900, the Local Government Board appointed a Committee to enquire into the matter in Dublin. In their report, the Committee pointed out that the insanitary housing conditions of the poorer classes played a great part in the spread of disease, and that the low vitality of the people made them ill-fitted to fight infections which still ranked amongst the most important causes of death. The Committee also condemned the system by which dispensary doctors were required to act as medical officers of health for their districts. Not being obliged to possess special qualifications in Public Health, they were often unsuited for such appointments.

The uneven working of the 1878 Public Health Act and the carelessness of many health authorities gave infectious diseases every chance of spreading. Even in Dublin, where the sanitary system was reasonably good, infection could spread with great rapidity. Six cases of smallpox appeared in Dublin in 1902. On 23rd December a boy of nineteen was admitted to the Hardwicke Hospital suffering from erysipelas. On 9th January 1903 he developed smallpox, probably contracted from a sailor off a Liverpool boat. Several cases followed, including a nurse who travelled by tram from Baggot Street to the North Circular Road whilst in an infectious state. By the beginning of March cases were reported from all over the city, and at the end of the month a total of 72 had occurred. In April there were 61 cases; in May, 69; in June, 42; and in July, twelve.

In December 1902, Sir Charles Cameron foresaw the possibility of a serious outbreak, and appealed to the Municipal Council for extra fever accommodation. With commendable promptitude the Corporation gave possession of buildings near the Pigeon House Fort, then being transformed into a power station, to the Public Health Committee. A contract was made with Messrs McMahon's of London to erect within twenty-one days (!) a building to accommodate fifty patients. Staff were seconded from Cork Street Hospital, and on 4th March 1903 the Pigeon House Isolation Hospital received its first patient. This was a tramp from Liverpool removed from the North Dublin Union Workhouse. All the subsequent cases in this epidemic were treated in the new hospital. Later the buildings were converted into a sanatorium and are now destroyed. A full history of this epidemic was published by Sir Charles Cameron in the *Dublin Journal of Medical Science* for 1903. The cost to the city was over £6,000.

Apart from epidemics such as this, enteric and typhus fevers were constantly present throughout the country. Typhus, the dreaded prison fever, still claimed over one hundred lives per year, and in 1900 nearly four hundred fatal cases of typhoid were reported. It was an improvement on the seven hundred and fifty deaths of only thirty years previously, but much still remained to be done. It was not until 1937 that a complete year passed without a death from typhus and even after this there were sporadic outbreaks.

The fields open to the newly-qualified Irish doctor at the beginning of the century included the Army, Navy, or Indian Medical Services, Poor Law Medical Appointments, Assistancies in England, and private practice.

The Irish Poor Law Medical Service was still condemned on all sides. The conditions of work remained appalling and the pay niggardly, with no prospects of promotion or pension. In the *Derry Standard* of 15th September 1902, a meeting of the Donegal Board of Guardians was reported as follows:

An application from Dr R. H. Pope, late Medical Officer of the Workhouse, who recently tendered his resignation through failing health, for superannuation was considered. Mr Edward Melly proposed and Mr Philip

McGoldrick seconded: 'That Dr Pope be allowed no superannuation.' This was passed unanimously.

No reason for such a mean motion, one of many, was ever given. One of the gravest objections to the Poor Law Medical Service arose from the methods of appointment. Ability and experience counted for little. Influence, religion and politics were the criteria by which appointments were made. Unfortunately, a team spirit did not exist in the profession, and badly-paid posts were occasionally taken by those with private means, to the detriment of the demands of the majority.

About two-and-a-half million of the population were attended under the Poor Law Service. Most country doctors were responsible for districts spread over one hundred or more square miles with a scattered population of some four or five thousand. Many of the dispensary doctors were over seventy years of age, but unable to retire without a pension. Their pay was so niggardly that their savings were nil. The long-sought principle of promotion within the service had not yet been accepted by the authorities.

At the beginning of the century two important studies were made on behalf of the Irish and British Medical Associations. In 1903 and 1904 they requested Surgeon-General Evatt to investigate and report on the Irish Poor Law Medical Service. These reports led, in 1906, to the appointment of a Viceregal Commission to advise on Poor Law Reform in Ireland. The recommendations included the establishment of a State Medical Service. A Royal Commission on the Poor Laws for both Ireland and England was appointed. This was made an excuse for shelving the Viceregal Commission's recommendations. One small reform resulting from the Commission's activities was the separation of the workhouse and district hospitals. This effort to separate the care of the sick poor from close association with the Poor Law was the first move in the direction of reforms made effective by the Local Government Act of 1925.

In the autumn of 1906, one of the largest gatherings of medical men ever seen in Ireland met under the auspices of the Irish Medical Association. A ten-to-one majority voted in favour of the Viceregal Commission's recommendation for the establishment of a State Medical Service. After a prolonged discussion in the Academy of Medicine the proposal to establish such a service was adopted almost unanimously. Unfortunately, no improvements followed for many years.

In the summer of 1907, Lady Aberdeen, wife of the Lord Lieutenant, conceived the idea of holding a Tuberculosis Exhibition in connection with the Dublin Exhibition. Amongst the distinguished lecturers was Sir William Osler, who proposed the revolutionary expedient of building cheap sanatoria which could be burnt down every few years as a drastic sterilising method. While the Exhibition focussed public and professional attention on the disease for a while, its lasting effects were few, so that forty years later consumption still killed some four thousand people annually in Ireland, and the sanatorium accommodation was quite inadequate. One of the useful results of the Exhibition was the establishment of a nursing service for the tuberculous poor.

On 1st January 1908, an Education Act was passed in England. This provided for the establishment by local authorities of a school medical service. Owing to the neglect of the Irish Members of Parliament the Act was not extended to this country. In the words of a speaker at a meeting of the Academy of Medicine in the same year: 'The schools receive less attention than cow-sheds.' Even until recently the phrase was not too strong.

Lloyd George's National Insurance Bill of 1911 was vigorously condemned by British practitioners. In Ireland there was the added objection that the Bill had been drafted solely with an eye to conditions in industrial England, and that its provisions would be almost useless to the Irish agricultural labourer and his medical attendant. In most districts the Irish dispensary doctors' paying patients were farmers or small tradesmen. Under the proposed scheme these would become eligible for free treatment, with a capitation fee of a few shillings yearly their only contribution to the doctors' income. The following resolutions, amongst others, were unanimously adopted by a meeting of the Fellows and Licentiates of the Royal College of Surgeons in Ireland:

That an income limit of £2 per week be fixed for those entitled to medical benefit. That adequate medical remuneration be given. That payment of the doctor be made according to work done – or that the sum paid to the doctor shall be capable of adjustment to local conditions.

Similar resolutions were passed by the British Medical Association, and at the annual general meeting of the Irish Medical Association in Cork. This Bill led to close co-operation between the British and Irish Medical Associations. A Conjoint Committee was established. This became the Irish Medical Committee in 1913.

The Insurance Act came into force in July 1912, and at the beginning of 1913 an annual grant of £50,000 was made available for payment of certificates. The grant was regarded as inadequate by the profession and proposals made on the basis thereof were refused in the greater part of the country. A great bone of contention between the profession and Government was 'Clause 14' of the Insurance Act. This provided for medical benefits to insured persons and for three forms of contribution to the insurance funds, from (1) the employee, (2) the employer, (3) the State.

At the instigation of the Catholic Hierarchy, John Redmond pointed out that the scheme could not be applied to Ireland and that the country was too poor to maintain it. In Belfast and some other areas the proposals were temporarily accepted, and the 'panel' system worked satisfactorily for a while.

The Commissioners in charge of the scheme attempted to solve the problem in the rest of the country on a different principle. They appointed some 170 medical men as medical certifiers at a fixed salary. Their duties were not clear. It was generally understood that they were required to certify as to the health of all insured persons referred to them. But, in Dublin for instance, the Insurance Commissioners declared that the doctors were not appointed to assist insured persons, but to prevent fraudulent claims. This scheme collapsed at the beginning of 1916. A new scheme provided for the certification of patients by the doctor of their choice.

The first World War had an immediate effect on the Medical Schools and the profession generally. Shortly after the outbreak of war supplemental examinations were held by many licensing bodies. This speeded up the qualification of senior students who were thus facilitated in their passage to slaughter. Many of those who feared the war would soon be over abandoned medical studies and enlisted as combatants. As a result the supply of locumtenentes and assistants fell to a low level. Increased work for those remaining in civil practice resulted, and the commercial value of doctors was enhanced. Finally, the numbers removed from the register by death grew ever larger.

In August 1914 Trinity College offered a civilian unit to the British Red Cross Society. It was intended that this should operate 'somewhere in Belgium.' Before arrangements could be completed a similar unit from St Bartholomew's Hospital in London was captured by the Germans in Brussels. The staff were not uniformed and the Germans threatened to shoot them as *francs-tireurs*. As a result all similar units were disbanded, under orders from the War Office.

In June 1917 arrangements were made to work a hospital at Boulogne (88th General Hospital) by relays of medical men appointed for successive periods of some months. All were given temporary R.A.M.C. commissions. Sir William Taylor, then President of the College of Surgeons, played the most prominent part in establishing this highly successful hospital.

In the early months of 1913, the Government proposed to establish a separate Ministry of Health. This received the approval of the College of Physicians, provided they were consulted in drafting any scheme for this purpose. In the following year the redoubtable Dr Hennessy, then secretary of the Irish Branch of the B.M.A., read a paper on the proposed new Ministry to the Academy of Medicine.

An Irish Public Health Council, established in 1919 under the chairmanship of Dr (later Sir Edward) Coey Bigger, was composed of representatives of the Health Departments and other bodies interested in Public Health. This was a temporary council created to advise the new Ministry on steps to be taken for the improvement of the public health. The Chief Secretary acted as Minister for Health for Ireland. The Council drew up and presented to Parliament a report on the Public Health and Medical Services in Ireland recommending *inter alia* an improved co-ordination between the various health services. Unfortunately, the political unrest put a stop to these timid advances of Public Health, and all attention was focussed on the development of a new State.

The most disastrous medical effects of the disturbances were felt in the sphere of tuberculosis treatment. Some local authorities refused to recognise British rule, and were deprived of their grants. As a result great hardship was inflicted on all the sick poor. This was all the more severe in such a chronic illness as tuberculosis.

The profession remained badly organised, and in 1922 only a third of the 2,400 practising doctors in Ireland belonged to either the Irish or British Medical Associations. Despite the poor support, officials of the Associations visited over sixty Poor Law Unions between 1918 and 1921, and secured substantial salary increases for the doctors employed therein, some of whom were not members of either Association.

During the period 1916–1921 the profession was, like the rest of the country, divided on political matters. The Irish Republican Army maintained a medical service, some of whose members were employed by the very authorities whom they defied. Particularly during the guerrilla period from 1919 to 1921, orders were issued by the occupying authorities that all cases of bullet wounds should be reported to the police by the hospitals and doctors concerned. To their eternal credit the profession refused, almost without exception, to do so. In many cases wanted men were tended and hidden by doctors, who thereby ran a grave risk. In one Dublin hospital a dangerously-wounded Republican soldier was hidden in a lift between two floors whilst Black and Tans ransacked the building in a fruitless search. The defiant answer of a Dublin surgeon: 'I'm a doctor; not a detective!' was echoed throughout the country.

This ethical dilemma has once again become a very live matter for doctors both in hospital and general practice. All the doctor's training stresses the need for professional secrecy and when a patient is treated for wounds received during unlawful activities the doctor in charge must balance the several calls on his conscience. Not the least worrying factor is the anxiety lest silence should indirectly lead to other woundings or deaths when a suspected terrorist is discharged from medical care.

THE ARMY MEDICAL CORPS

On the occupation of military posts vacated by the British in February 1922 the existing I.R.A. Medical Service was maintained pending the establishment of a Regular Army equivalent. For a time Headquarters were at Beggars' Bush Barracks in the Dublin South suburbs, until George V Hospital, renamed St Bricin's, was handed over. Unfortunately the pay, promotion and pensions offered to Medical officers were very poor and the Irish Free State Medical union discouraged doctors from joining the Army. Medical students were advised not to become members of the University Volunteer units. Throughout the 1939–45 war period this ban was suspended so that many doctors joined the National Army and gave excellent service either as full time officers or with the various part-time defence services. After lengthy negotiations reasonable standards of employment were obtained and the ban on National Army service was eventually lifted.

The silver hand badge of the Army Medical Service (Corps since 1946) recalls the story of Nuadhat chief of the de Danann while the motto 'Comraind leighis' reminds us of the chivalry of Ferdiád and Cuchualainn who shared their medical supplies at the end of each day's battle as described in Chapter I.

MEDICAL REGISTRATION

In August 1925 the Executive Council of the Irish Free State decided to bring to an end the arrangement by which the profession in the Twenty-Six Counties enjoyed the privileges of the British Medical Register. The decision followed two years of discussion by the Government and the Licensing Bodies. The general feeling in the profession was against the proposed change on the grounds that if Irish doctors were not allowed to practise in England the profession here would be flooded where the potential medical wastage was only some thirty per year. The daily press was bombarded with vituperative articles whose bitterness against the proposed scheme was reminiscent of that raised by Lloyd George's Insurance Plan in 1911. A few letters in defence of the scheme were published.

Eventually an agreement was signed between Great Britain, the Free State and Northern Ireland which regularised the control and registration of doctors in the three areas. The result of this agreement was to allow doctors qualified in the Free State to practise in either part of the country or in England provided that their names appeared on the General Medical Register. Reciprocal facilities were given to those qualified in England or the North.

As a result of this agreement, the Medical Practitioners Act of 1927 was passed by the Oireachtas. An Irish Medical Registration Council was established with eleven members made up of:

(*a*)   Two nominated by the Executive Council.
(*b*)   One each nominated by University College, Dublin; University College, Cork; University College, Galway; Trinity College, Apothecaries' Hall, College of Surgeons and College of Physicians.
(*c*)   Two registered medical practitioners elected by the profession.

Except for the two last members of the Council did not have to be doctors though in practice they always were. One of the most important non-disciplinary functions of this Council was the establishment of a register containing the names of those entitled to practice medicine in this country. It is sometimes thought that the Medical Council is a sort of doctor's trade union. Nothing could be further from the truth. The whole function of the Council is to ensure that only properly trained people shall practise medicine and that those who do maintain high standards in their professional, public and even private lives. A serious crime with no medical implication and committed outside the jurisdiction of the Irish Courts could be grounds for removal from the Medical Register. Under the Medical Practitioners' Act of 1978 a new Council was established in July 1980 with terms of reference more relevant to the changing medical scene particularly in view of developments within the European Economic Community. This is a considerably larger body than its predecessor though its basic functions remain the same. An important routine part of the Council's work is visitation and assessment of hospitals giving employment to interns in their provisional registration year.

The type of problem never envisaged by the original Council was encountered in 1981 when two American surgeons put forward a proposal to build an International Hospital in Dublin staffed largely by doctors who had qualified elsewhere. To practise legally in this country they would require to be registered at least temporarily.

Despite considerable pressure from business and political interests the Council was adamant that registration could not be granted unless all the normal statutory requirements were fulfilled.

MEDICAL RESEARCH

As soon as the period of adjustment which followed the establishment of the Irish Free State was ended it became obvious that Irish research workers were gravely handicapped in their investigations by lack of funds. The teaching bodies were unable to endow research units. There were no Rockefellers or Carnegies in the country, and few, if any, workers had sufficient private means to carry on full-time non-remunerative investigations over long periods. After lengthy discussions between the Minister for Local Government and Public Health, the Sweepstakes Committee, the Hospitals' Commission, the Academy of Medicine, and the Medical Schools, the Medical Research Council was incorporated in January 1937 under the chairmanship of Professor R. P. Farnan. A sum of £10,000 was allocated to the Council out of Sweepstakes' funds. Fifteen grants were made to full-time and part-time workers during the first year.

In 1938 the annual grant was fixed at £5,000 per annum, guaranteed for five years. As a result the activities of the Council were gravely curtailed. In 1946, at a meeting of the newly-founded Society of Thoracic Surgeons, a speaker mentioned that the annual grant would not buy a house in a good-class Dublin suburb. One of the greatest disadvantages was that the research worker had no guarantee of security for longer than one year at a time. As a result, many who might otherwise have done good laboratory work were forced to go into practice or study elsewhere.

In May 1943, a special grant of £3,000 was voted by the Dáil for the purpose of research into the chemotherapy of tuberculosis. During the war years the Council gave valuable advice on wheat extraction, deterioration of drugs in storage, and substitute drugs. In June 1944 it acted as a controlling body for the distribution of the limited supplies of penicillin available.

With the end of the war in 1945 and the possibility of sending workers abroad, the Council's funds became even more inadequate. Once again the Annual Report stressed that the small and uncertain payments offered would not attract any workers, let alone the best, and that those who forwent financial security for research were deserving of the highest praise. A few small supplementary sums became available as bequests and as grants from firms interested in particular aspects of research.

As an example that the Council's work is not merely of academic importance, it is convenient to note here that in 1945 a committee reported to the Minister for Local Government as to the establishment of dietary standards suitable for the Irish population. Arrangements were later made to have field workers trained in the methods necessary for carrying out a survey. In 1946 the Minister for Local Government and Public Health informed the Council that its annual grant of £5,000 could only be guaranteed for a further two years. Consequently no long-term plans could be made.

For several years the Council's work was severely limited by financial restrictions but, despite this, work which was later to produce magnificent results was carried on. In 1944 a team had been set up to develop antituberculosis agents. Several active compounds were discovered but it was noted that one of these had properties suggesting that it might be effective against leprosy. Trials in Nigeria confirmed all the early forecasts and clofazimine is now a major anti-leprotic drug used throughout the world. The importance of this work was recognised when the UNESCO Science Prize for 1980 was presented to the four workers who had carried out the research. Doctors J. Belton, M. Conalty, J. O'Sullivan and D. Twomey.

From the early 1960's the Council received not alone more realistic Government support but also grants from commercial sources either for specific projects or to aid research generally. With an annual budget now around the two million pound mark the Council could make more realistic purchases in the suburban property market, even at present prices. Recent and current work has ranged over a very wide field. Cancer, Mental Health, Microbiology, Alcoholism, Brucellosis and many other conditions often with a major social implication have all come within the ambit of the Council's investigations.

Post War Developments

Just as during the earlier conflict, the World War of 1939–45 brought profound changes to the lives of Irish medical men. The rapid wastage of medical man-power in England provided a ready market for our doctors. Unfortunately, many of the posts offered were 'for the duration' with an uncertain future ahead. Nevertheless more Irish doctors than ever before went abroad to civilian and military posts often serving with great distinction.

When the present work was originally published, a distinguished colleague in Belfast criticised the author for failing to devote at least a chapter to the work of Irish doctors serving with the R.A.M.C. To have done so would have opened not one more chapter, but several more volumes for those who served in other allied armies and as civilians in many countries might reasonably claim that their field of activity would equally justify inclusion in the story of Irish medicine. Hopefully the definitive history of their work will someday be written by a researcher having the time and expertise to do so.

At home the shortage of building materials, petrol, drugs and equipment generally had severe repercussions on medical practice. Building and reconstruction of hospitals came to a standstill for all practical purposes. Restricted travel handicapped those who wished to study abroad. This was particularly awkward for the winners of scholarships in 1939–43. Most of these settled in practice, and, when transport became available, had to make a choice between abandoning growing practices for a year's foreign study, or foregoing their scholarships and consolidating their positions at home.

In the field of preventive medicine, progress came practically to a standstill until well after the end of fighting. In 1946, the Government announced that on 22nd January 1947 new Departments of Health and of Social Services would be established. A further Order altered the name of the Department of Local Government and Public Health to the Department of Local Government. Dr Séamus Ryan, formerly Minister for Agriculture, became the new Minister for Health and Social Services.

The Minister for Social Services would be responsible for Home Assistance, Children's Allowances, Food Allowances, Health Insurance, Unemployment Assurance, Widows', Orphans', Old Age and Blind Pensions.

In February 1947 Dr Ryan announced that a Consultative Council of Medical Practitioners would be set up to assist him in the development of new health schemes. The first meeting of this Council was held on 11th April. Four bodies were represented: the Medical Association of Eire, The Royal Academy of Medicine, The Medical Registration Council, and The Association of Medical Officers.

As a result of the developments in England and the many changes in Public Health administration here, grave fears were expressed that the profession would be nationalised or subjected to some measure of official direction. Dr Ryan, in a statement to the Dáil, said:

I don't think that a State Medical Service would be the best thing at all. I think the medical practitioner will have his practice and his own individual freedom much the same as he has now, but more State work will be put on to him as time goes on.

A White Paper on Health Services was issued in 1947. This reviewed the growth of the Public Health system and forecast future developments as well as listing the functions of the new Department of Health. The latter included all measures conducive to the health of the people, the prevention and cure of diseases, the care of persons suffering from mental and physical defects, the control and appointment of health officers, and the control of research, proprietary medicines, food, and vital statistics. Environmental services, such as water supply, drainage, bathing-places and burial-grounds were left in charge of the Minister for Local Government.

The Health Bill (1947) became law on 3rd July of that year. It was the most comprehensive measure ever enacted by an Irish Parliament. Under it, a general duty was imposed on the individual to take precautions against infecting others with communicable diseases. Defaulters were liable to a fine not exceeding £50. In the Act, the Minister had power to make regulations for the prevention of danger to the public health. This could be interpreted in the widest possible manner. In the course of debates on the Bill, exception was taken to compulsory powers given to authorities to examine school-children. These were alleged to conflict with the rights of parents to exclusive control of the health and education of their children.

When the Bill had been passed by both Houses, Deputy James Dillon requested the President to consult the Council of State and seek its advice as to submitting the Bill to the Supreme Court to ascertain whether Part III, which related to Mother and Child Services, was in fact repugnant to the Constitution. The President did not do this, and on his signature the Bill became law. In December 1947 Mr Dillon took the unprecedented step of issuing a summons against the then Minister for Health, Dr Ryan, in order to test the validity of the Act.

Two months later a Coalition Government, of which Mr Dillon was a member, came into power. Dr Noel Browne, the new Minister for Health, decided to re-consider the controversial sections, and the prospective summons was dropped. Later the offending sections were deleted. Shortly after assuming office, Dr Browne, in exercise of the powers vested in him by the Health Act, established a Health Council to advise him when necessary on matters of health. It included representatives of all bodies concerned in the public health. A Consultative Child Health Council was also formed in order to assist in lowering the very high rate of child mortality.

Dr Browne was young and enthusiastic, and had already tackled the then huge problem of tuberculosis energetically and effectively. His task was made easier by the discovery of streptomycin, the first drug to be effective against the tubercle bacillus. In fact the use of streptomycin precipitated one of many differences between doctors and the Minister of Health for the latter brought in an order limiting the drug to specified categories of doctor, believing that indiscriminate use of steptomycin could result in the development of resistent strains of T.B. As we now realise, this happened with many other antibiotics. The Irish Medical Association felt that this was an undue limitation on the doctors' right to prescribe and administer the drugs they felt to be most effective. After much bitter argument and the intervention of the Medical Research Council, the offending Order was rescinded but the Tuberculosis Advisory Council was abolished and relations between the Department and the I.M.A. deteriorated.

In 1950 every doctor received a document which has gone down to history as the 'Mother and Child' scheme. This contained 'tentative' proposals for the development of maternity and paediatric services. To some people it appeared that these proposals amounted to the socialisation of a large segment of medical practice. The most worrying aspect, to many doctors, was that almost all maternity, gynaecological and child care would be confined to District Medical Officers and area obstetrician – gynaecologists. The medical profession rejected the proposals by a hugh majority in a referendum held during November 1950. Following discussions with the then Taoiseach, Mr John Costello, the I.M.A. put forward counter proposals including the establishment of a voluntary health insurance scheme. These were rejected by the Minister of Health as impracticable and undesirable and a bitter, vicious bout of mud-slinging developed with its lowest point being reached when an anonymous pamphlet vilifying the whole medical profession was widely distributed.

The Taoiseach made a further effort to heal the breach and it became obvious that the Cabinet was divided on the matter. Dr Browne resigned, a bitterly disappointed idealist and Mr Costello took over the Health portfolio. He asked the I.M.A. to co-operate in developing a Health Scheme particularly in relation to maternity and child services. A joint committee with representatives of the Department of Health and the organised profession was set up and for several months worked hard to produce an acceptable scheme and real progress was made up to the Autumn of 1951 when a new Government came to power with Dr James Ryan as Minister of Health. One of his first actions was to withdraw the Departmental representatives from the joint committee leaving it powerless. A few months later he introduced a wide ranging 'Act to Amend and Extend the Health Act 1947 with certain other enactments', which gave rise to the reproduced *Dublin Opinion* cartoon. Some of the provisions of this Bill were actually desirable from the medical point of view, but there were sections giving rise to anxiety because of the wide powers of control which a Minister would have, extending even into post graduate education. At this time there were few days without some body of doctors holding discussions in the Customs' House. A number of improvements and concessions were obtained.

The idea of voluntary health insurance was now revived and largely owing to the diligence of Mr T. C. J. O'Connell a scheme was propounded and presented to the Minister and his Department who promptly turned it down, and just as promptly brought in a Ministerial Order implementing the new Act. Shortly afterwards this Fianna Fail administration was defeated in a general election. Mr T. F. O'Higgins, the new Minister of Health, introduced the 1954 Health Act, delaying the 1953 Act which allowed him and everyone else time for consideration and discussion. Eventually agreement was achieved on most points. Equally important legislation enabling a Voluntary Health Insurance Scheme to be developed was passed and signed hours before the Government went out of office.

Mr McEntee now took over control of the Department of Health. While he approved of and even encouraged the new V.H.I. scheme his relations with the doctors were appallingly bad. His refusal to meet the I.M.A. and his statement that it 'does not exist as a legal entity' led directly to the foundation of the Medical Union as described elsewhere in the present volume. For several years a guerilla war was carried on between the Department and the medical profession and apart from essential contacts for routine purposes few useful discussions could be held.

This unsatisfactory situation continued up to 1967 when the then Minister of Health Mr Sean Flanagan appointed a Consultative Council, with wide terms of reference to examine the position in regard to general hospital in-patient services and to make recommendations for their improvement. After only eight months of intensive work their conclusions, popularly called the 'Fitzgerald Report' after the Chairman, Professor P. A. Fitzgerald were published.

The recommendations, which were far reaching, may be summarised as follows,

1) Radical changes in organisation, staffing and operation would be required.
2) The system should be organised in three regions based on the three teaching centres, Dublin, Cork and Galway.
3) Acute care hospitals should be graded as Regional and General with a back up system of Health Centres and District Nursing Homes.

More detailed recommendations involved the regrading and sometimes abolition of many small hospitals. Inevitably this attempt at rationalisation led to vigourous local protests when a community facility was threatened.

The Council's recommendation was that a bed complement of 300 was the minimum for a General Hospital and that this should service a catchment population of 120,000 people. The Regional Hospital was to provide general services in its immediate vicinity with more specialised services for a wider area. Under the heading of implementation of recommendations it was stated that all the major changes outlined in the report should be accomplished by 1980. By 1983 this was still far from reality, but a further recommendation that a Consultant's Establishment Board be set up led to the foundation, in 1972, of Comhairle na n-Ospidéal which had the additional function of advising the Minister on hospital services generally.

The first meeting of An Comhairle was held under the Chairmanship of Professor Basil Chubb, in September 1972. After a period in temporary accomodation the new body leased accomodation in Fenian Street, calling their premises Corrigan House, in memory of the distinguished nineteenth century physician. The first report on An Comhairle was published in December 1975. In his prefatory letter Professor Chubb was highly critical of central authority delays in making decisions, and stated that these were having a demoralizing effect on hospital staffs, who had hoped that the administrative reforms and modernization plans of the early 1970's would be implemented with minimal delay. An important piece of ground work carried out by An Comhairle was the assessment of consultant medical man-power, available and required, throughout the country.

In this first report recommendations were made which aimed at rationalising hospital services and making the best use of available resources. Inevitably some of these led to local dissatisfaction and in the letter already quoted, Professor Chubb noted that the Minister, in making decisions would have to

take other considerations into account, not least political and local community pressures. These will sometimes lead to arguments that, from a strictly medical viewpoint, are neither the best nor the most economical. This may be inevitable, but let it be clear that a price *is* being paid.

But a further area of dissention and anxiety appeared with the publication of the proposals for a common selection procedure for appointment to advertised posts, leading to what became known as 'The Common Contract'. The stumbling blocks in this contract included the proposed maximum of 33 working hours per week to be eligible for payment as well as dissatisfaction with proposed pensions and retiral gratuities. But the dissenting voices which drew most attention were those of the Catholic hierarchy who had serious reservations on several grounds. These included, anxiety about the ethical content of the contract, the fact that they were not consulted and that the working party which drew up the contract had no members specifically representing the hospitals. Both the I.M.A. and Medical Union were represented by hospital doctors but they were nominees of these bodies and not of the hospitals. Towards the end of 1982 the Hierarchy proposed a modified contract with a firm ethical content, procedures for disciplinary action, an interpretation machinery for resolving disputed clauses and altered selection procedures giving the hospitals much more influence in the appointment of staff. These proposals were unacceptable to the Minister of Health, Mr Barry Desmond. Later the Department of Health approved what had come to be known as 'the Bishops' contract' and at the beginning of 1983 it was introduced for consultants in the ten Catholic Hospitals in Dublin.

The Medical Union now requested that the Labour Court should investigate 'the Bishops' Contract'. After submissions by both the Union and the Hospitals the Court rejected the disciplinary clause, recommended that the references to an ethical code should appear only as an annex to the main document and that the contract should be retrospective to 1981. Barely had this decision been handed down and digested when Mr Desmond called for a review of the original common contract which he described as 'not a particularly well documented contract that should be revised'.

At the same time as all these discussions about hospital matters were going on there were also changes in the general practice field, both politically and, as described in the account of the Royal College of General Practitioners, academically.

Under the Public Assistance Act of 1939 a general medical service had been made available to poor persons. For the purposes of the service the country had been divided into 586 dispensary districts usually in the charge of a single doctor giving the patient no freedom of choice.

In 1952 a White Paper, proposing improved and extended health services generally, was published. This envisaged a two-tier system of medical help giving total care to lower income patients with hospital and specialist services being provided for middle income patients a class which was to include all persons compulsorily insurable under the Social Welfare Act of 1952 together with farmers having a rateable valuation of less than £50. Legislation implementing this White Paper was brought in and various sections were made operable, often in the face of serious medical misgivings. Eventually, in April 1972, after lengthy and often acrimonious discussions, a General Medical Service supplanting the dispensary service came into being.

Under this scheme persons eligible for 'free' service are given authorisation cards. They select G.P.s who may accept them as patients and are then obliged to provide a 24-hour, 365 day service either personally or through a deputy. At first all medicines could be prescribed free of charge but in 1982 some 900 items previously available were withdrawn as an economy measure. At almost the same time a considerable number of people who had certain statutory pensions were made eligible despite the fact that many had very substantial means from sources other than their pensions. This Gilbertian situation only lasted a few months but must have made a considerable contribution to the soaring costs of the service which are currently about £2,000,000 per week. While this is a high figure it is only about eight per cent of the total health bill for a service giving primary and often total medical care to a third of the population of the Republic.

CHAPTER TWENTY

PROFESSIONAL SOCIETIES

The professional mind has always thrived on discussion. This is particularly so in medicine where several methods of treatment, all equally good – or bad – may be employed in similar cases. Indeed a discussion centre is now an essential unit of any school of medicine, hospital or research department.

THE DUBLIN PHILOSOPHICAL SOCIETY

The Dublin Philosophical Society was formed in 1683 by William Molyneux. The first chairman was Dr Charles Willoughby. The proceedings of this society were published with those of the Royal Society in London. According to a letter from William Molyneux, the secretary: 'we have very regular discourses concerning philosophical, medical and mathematical matters.' The early minute books of this society are preserved in the British Museum. Some scattered papers are also kept in the Library of Trinity College. The letters between the brothers Molyneux are fully reprinted in the *Dublin University Magazine* of 1841.

Thomas Molyneux, in 1669, offered on behalf of an anonymous gentleman £2,000 towards the maintenance of a lunatic asylum. Further letters of Molyneux to his brother in Holland refer to premises in Crow Street off Dame Street, to a botanical garden and to a laboratory built in 1664 to Dr Mullen's directions. The society became well known in scientific circles and the majority of its members attained considerable eminence both at home and abroad. Unfortunately, political and military commotion upset learning, and the meetings became few and irregular. The medical papers read from the foundation until 1687, when the society lapsed for some time, included:

Dr Allen Mullen – On the human and comparative Anatomy – Experiments on the Blood – On the Mineral Waters of Chapelizod – On Ague – On Ovarian Disease – Dissection of a Man who died of Consumption.

Mr W. Molyneux – On double Vision – On Circulation.

Mr St George Ashe – On Haemorrhage – On a Man in Galway who suckled his child and had Pendulous Mammae.

Mr Patterson – Various dissections of the human subject. – On Stone in the Bladder – On cohesion between the Liver and Diaphragm.

Dr Houlaghan – Description of a Human Kidney weighing 42 ounces. On dissection of a monstrous child with two heads, and three arms.

Dr (later Sir) Patrick Dun – On the Analysis of Mineral Waters. The several references to human dissection are of some interest, for, prior to the passage of the Anatomy Act a century and a half later, the dissector performed in secret and often in terror of mob violence.

From an entry in the diary of Archbishop Marsh it appears that the society was revived in 1693. The papers read have no direct medical interest, although medical men took a leading part in the society. The most notable of these was Sir Thomas Molyneux, Professor of the Practice of Physic in the University of Dublin and the first medical baronet created in Ireland. His communications to this society and other publications include: An essay on Giants – Stone in the Bladder – On the Influenza – On the Irish Elk – On Elephants' Teeth. He was not alone a man of great scientific and professional ability, but a classical scholar of the first order.

Medical papers were read to this society at infrequent intervals during the next quarter of a century. The principal of these and their authors were:

'An account of Spina Bifida' by Dr John Rutty (1720) and 'Mortification and Sloughing of the Shoulder Joint by Peter Derante, (1722). Derante was a surgeon practicing in Waterford.

In 1731 Dr Thomas Madden described two cases of poisoning from laurel water. In 1736 he detailed the dissection of a person who had died after taking two ounces of mercury. Madden was elected President of the College of Physicians in 1731. A letter of his, dealing with cataract, is preserved in the manuscript collection in T.C.D.

In 1739 John Ferguson, a surgeon, of Strabane, published an account of the removal of portion of the human spleen; surely a formidable operation in pre-anaesthetic days.

THE PHYSICO-HISTORICAL SOCIETY

The Physico-Historical Society of Ireland was founded on 14th April 1744. Its main objects were indicated by its name. Many doctors, however, were members and contributed papers of medical interest, as well as adding to the museum collection of the society. This body expired after only three years. Two of its medical members, Charles Smith and John Rutty, determined to continue some of its work. In 1756 they founded the Medico-Philosophical Society, with the pursuit of medical knowledge as a primary function.

The minutes of its meetings have been preserved in the Royal Irish Academy and in the College of Physicians. Most of the communications, from 1757 to 1784, are kept in a book called 'the Repository' in the handwriting of their authors. The last meeting of this society was held in 1784. Amongst the most active members of the Medico-Philosophical Society were Drs MacBride, Barry, Smith, Purcell and Rutty. David MacBride, apothecary, was without question the most able member of the group.

Shortly after the foundation, Dr Charles Smith read a paper on the advantages and necessity of such an organisation. At the suggestion and expense of the society, Smith later published Histories of Cork and Waterford. He subsequently read a paper on the composition of human, bovine and other milks. Most of the papers read to this society dealt with the application of chemistry to medicine. In the clinical papers full use was made of the limited biochemical methods of the day. In April 1765 Dr Rutty described the urine of a man suffering from diabetes as having the smell of burned sugar and a sweet taste. He does not seem to have recognised the presence of sugar in the urine in question. Rutty's favourite subject was mineral waters in the spas of Ireland and elsewhere. A very full account of the work of this society was published in the *Dublin Quarterly Journal of Medical Science* for August 1849.

In 1785 the society's meetings were continued under the altered name of the Medical Society. This functioned rather as a dining club than as a professional society. About 1831 Dr John Beatty, the secretary, died. He had held the post for twenty-five years and the society lapsed. In 1856 it was revived as a peripatetic dining club, sometimes jocularly referred to as the Philo-oesophageals. The revived society had such famous members as Wilde, Marsh, Stokes, Rynd, Adams and Crampton. Meetings were now conducted in a much more light-hearted vein than formerly. Gastronomic rather than medical topics were discussed. In 1862 the club obtained an album to hold portraits of members. This is still kept up to date, and is proudly displayed to visitors. The minutes of meetings held fifty years ago are read at meetings to-day. The Medico-Philosophical Society is one of the oldest medical dining clubs in existence.

THE ROYAL IRISH ACADEMY

The Antiquarian Society, known as The Palaeosophers, was established in T.C.D. in 1782. One year later the Neosophers were established by Robert Perceval, a member of the Medico-Philosophical Society, for the study of science and modern literature. From the union of these was born the Royal Irish Academy in April 1785. This body has always possessed a strong corps of medical members. The most distinguished names in Irish Medicine have contributed to its work. Some references to these appear in the chapter on Professional Publications and elsewhere in the present volume.

THE PHYSICO-CHIRURGICAL SOCIETY

In 1780 the Dublin surgeons made efforts to establish their profession more securely. To this end they founded the Dublin Society of Surgeons. After four years this became the College of Surgeons.

At the first meeting of the College of Surgeons in their own premises in 1790 a memorial was received from a number of members and licentiates of the Colleges of Physicians and Surgeons, stating their proposal to form a Physico-Chirurgical Society. They asked and were granted permission to meet in the Mercer Street buildings of the College. The books of this society formed the nucleus of the College's present collection. Until 1811 the President and Vice-President of the College of Surgeons were *ex-officio* holders of similar offices in the Society. In that year a rule was introduced by which a president and vice-president were elected from the society as well.

Few dentists have featured in these pages, but one at least deserves mention. Robert Blake, a Dublin dentist, published in Edinburgh in 1798 a thesis for the degree of M.D. His subject was the *Structure and Formation of the Teeth in Man and Various Animals*. The work was long regarded as a standard reference work. He was for many years Secretary of the Physico-Chirurgical Society. In 1816 the society became extinct and its library passed to the College of Surgeons. Blake had advanced £60 to pay a debt of the society to the bookseller. Fortunately the College repaid him.

A prominent member of the society was Edward Hamilton (1824–1899). At one meeting he read a paper on Hippo, in which he described 'hippo coryza,' from which he suffered, when exposed to powdered ipecacuanha. He advocated from a large experience the use of ipecacuanha emetic in Asiatic cholera.

In 1831 the Council of the College provided a room for meetings of the Surgical Society of Ireland. Its transactions were published in the *Dublin Medical Press* and in the *Dublin Journal of Medical Science*.

SOCIETIES IN THE ROYAL COLLEGE OF SURGEONS

In 1790 the College of Surgeons students formed their own medical society in association with the Physico-Chirurgical Society. Unfortunately, no records of this society exist except a memorial signed by twenty-four students requesting permission to meet as a professional society. The request was supported by William Hartigan, one of the Professors of Anatomy.

In August 1826 a committee was formed to enquire into the foundation of a medical, not a surgical, society in the College, but apparently nothing came of this.

In 1862 a group of College of Surgeons students met as the 'Junior Surgical Society of Ireland.' The guiding spirit was Charles Benson (1797–1880), destined to fill the Chair of Medicine and the Presidency of the College. The inaugural meeting was attended by prominent members of the profession in Dublin. The society had a highly successful career until 1870 when it lapsed. In the second session membership of the society was opened to all Dublin medical students. In 1873 an attempt was made to reform the society. This failed, and the College had no student medical society until 1931, when the Biological Society of the Royal Colleges of Physicians and Surgeons was founded by Drs J. Lewis and J. D. H. Widdess. On 16th February 1886, the Carmichael College Medical Science Association was inaugurated in the presence of a large gathering. The establishment of a scientific debating society in connection with an extra-mural school was a completely new venture.

SOCIETIES IN UNIVERSITY COLLEGE, DUBLIN

The Catholic University Medical School in Cecilia Street possessed a Scientific Society from an early date, but in 1901 it was felt that this did not give sufficient scope for those who wished to acquire fluency in speaking on non-technical subjects. Accordingly a debating society was formed in May of that year. The inaugural meeting was held in November when the Auditor, Mr P. J. Dwyer, read a paper on 'A Nation's Struggle for Existence.' Unfortunately, this society lapsed after two years.

In 1903 a Medical and Scientific Society was founded in Cecilia Street. Dr Anthony Roche read a paper and Dr Martin Dempsey took the chair. Though records of the early period of this society have been lost random recollections of members reveal that the society kept up to date and discussed current events, but names, dates and details of administration are missing. The president elected for each session was one of the professors of the school. The committee were all students.

In November 1909, control of the society was secured by a body of students whose interests were political rather than medical. At the general meeting in the following session a new committee was elected for the 'Medical Society of University College.' A new minute book was started to mark the change. The society now gave a forum for discussion to the newly graduated and junior staff members as well as to students. Unfortunately there was no medium for the publication of papers read to the society. This was remedied in later years, as papers of exceptional merit were published in the *Irish Journal of Medical Science*.

Until 1924, the President of University College, Dr Denis Coffey, was permanent president of the society. Each Michaelmas term saw the election of a student president and student committee. In this year, following the suggestion of Dr John Mowbray, a twofold change was made. Dr Coffey was appointed 'patron' of the society and a new president was chosen annually from the College graduates. The first occupant of this new post was Mr William Doolin. The society received a further much-needed stimulus when accommodation for meetings was found in the main College buildings.

SOCIETIES IN TRINITY COLLEGE

On 2nd May 1801 a society of medical students and graduates was given permission to meet in Trinity College. One of the few remaining records of this society is the address delivered by the vice-president, John Murray, in 1803, on the subject of Medical Ethics, which was published in the *Dublin Medical and Physical Essays*. Unfortunately, the prevailing unrest influenced the Board to withdraw its sanction in 1808. 'To guard against the introduction of any political and metaphysical discussions which had proved detrimental to another society in the same place.' In 1814, another society was founded but, even with the leadership of James Macartney, the celebrated Professor of Anatomy, permission to meet was withdrawn in 1822 for an unknown reason. Despite the ban the society struggled on until 1830.

In 1853 a Zoological Society was founded. Most of the members were graduates. Later the scope of the society was increased to include botany. The society failed after publication of a volume of proceedings in 1859.

In 1872 the Biological Club was founded in No 30 T.C.D. After three years it moved to quarters in Brunswick (now Pearse) Street, where it remained until 1881. Then it was accommodated in the College of Physicians in Kildare Street.

In 1874, a Biological Association was founded in Trinity. The similarity of names caused some annoyance to the older body and they suggested an alteration. Henry Mackintosh, secretary of the association, replied that the name was adopted after careful consideration and declined to make any alteration. Professor Macalister, the first president of the association, was a man of wide interests. Until his appointment to the Chair of Anatomy at Cambridge he was the driving force of the young society, contributed many papers and continually urged his students to record their original observations. So diverse were his interests that the article on palmistry in the *Encyclopaedia Britannica* came from his pen.

The first meeting of the Biological Association was addressed by Macalister on the work of a biological society. In addition, papers of zoological and medical interest were discussed and twenty members were elected. At the end of the year a volume of proceedings were published. During this period, 1874 to 1878, medical subjects were regarded as proper to the society, but did not predominate. From 1878 onwards, the society became more medical in nature. The subjects discussed included: 'Two cases of tuberculous meningitis.' 'Antiseptic surgery.' 'Tracheotomy.'
The paper on antiseptic surgery was read very shortly after Lister's first work with the carbolic spray. In March 1882 Koch announced his discovery of the tubercle bacillus. A few months later the record secretary of the Biological Association exhibited microscope slides in which the germ was demonstrated. About this time the society lost much of its vigour. The minutes of the period are missing, or may never have been written. The society was also in a bad way financially.

In 1894, matters improved and several important papers mainly on medical subjects were read. These included a description by Richard T. Smith of the first recorded case in Ireland of trans-sacral removal of the rectum for cancer. In 1894 Dr T. E. Gordon's presidential address on surgery of the prostate included a reference to the use of castration as a means of reducing the size of the gland. In 1897 on the motion of Dr T.P.C. Kirkpatrick, the society resolved:

That this Association views with concern the danger to public health arising from the prevalence of tuberculosis in dairy cattle in Dublin, and is of opinion that efforts should be made to stamp out the disease and to protect the community from this source of infection.

From this time onwards the papers read were almost exclusively medical. The presidential addresses dealt usually with the latest advances in the profession. Dr Robert Woods suggested during his presidency in 1897 that a library should be founded in connection with the society. He presented a book-case which still remains in the association's rooms.

An echo of the long-dead Robert Graves was heard in the association in October 1929, when quotations from his original notes were used by a student with telling effect to illustrate a discussion on thyroid diseases. In November of the same year, female medical students attending hospitals were admitted to meetings of the association with the limitation that they might not attend during private business, vote, introduce visitors or be eligible for office. In view of this restricted membership the remarks of a later speaker applauding the association's efforts to raise the status of women students seem over-enthusiastic. A few months later a motion 'That women be excluded from the annual dinner' was passed.

The first paper by a lady member did not appear until November 1934, when Miss Gore Grimes read a paper on 'Aphasia.' The ladies of the association justified their admission in 1938, when two of their number, Miss E. Rees and Miss P. Concannon, secured the Society's silver and bronze medals respectively, for their papers on 'The Accident Room' and 'Radium.' In February 1940 Miss M. B. Kelly read a paper on 'Women in the Medical Profession.' In the course of this, she castigated the association for its reactionary policy of refusing women the rights of full membership. In May 1941 women students were at last admitted to full membership of the association. In the following year Miss M. B. Kelly and Miss M. E. Rutherford were the first women to be elected to the council.

THE ROYAL ACADEMY OF MEDICINE IN IRELAND AND ITS FORERUNNERS

William Brooke (1760–1829) was born at Granard, where his father was rector. Like many others of his Irish contemporaries, he graduated M.D. Edinburgh in 1789, reading a thesis on acute rheumatism. In 1793 he was admitted a Licentiate of the King's and Queen's College of Physicians. In 1824 he received the double honour of an M.D. (*honoris causa*) of Dublin University and a Fellowship of the College of Physicians. In February 1826 he was elected to the Presidency of the College in place of James Leahy, who had resigned. On the following St Luke's Day he was re-elected for a complete session. He practised in North Cumberland Street, and for some time lectured on medicine at the Jervis Street Hospital School.

On 23rd October 1813 Brooke called a meeting of Licentiates of the

College of Physicians at his house. At this meeting a society was formed whose primary function seems to have been the protection of its members' professional interests. Discussions were held with the College of Physicians as to the desirability of establishing a Physicians' Hall as a joint meeting-place. In a resolution dated 10th June 1816, the College refused its support for the proposal as a corporate body, but promised the help of its Fellows as individuals. Notwithstanding this partial set-back, the Licentiates convened a meeting of themselves and the members of the College. On 3rd July 1816 the Association of Fellows and Licentiates of the King's and Queen's College of Physicians in Ireland was founded.

One of the most difficult matters for the young Association to overcome was the lack of a suitable meeting-house. The scheme for the foundation of a Physicians' Hall was a complete failure. For several years the society met in the back room of a bookseller's shop in College Green. A dining club was formed in 1830. The minute book of this club is preserved in the Library of the Royal College of Physicians. The club met regularly for ten years on the first Tuesday of each month from November to April.

Six volumes of the transactions of this society were published separately between 1817 and 1830. When the *Dublin Journal of Medical and Chemical Science* was started in 1832 it became the medium for publication of the association's transactions. At the end of the 1863–4 session the society was renamed The Medical Society of the College of Physicians. Further details of this society appear in the chapter on Professional Publications.

THE PATHOLOGICAL SOCIETY

Prior to 1838 the study and discussion of pathology in Dublin was a haphazard affair. In October of that year, the Pathological Society of Dublin was founded, having for its principal object the cultivation of pathological anatomy, particularly with reference to the diagnosis and treatment of disease. The places of meeting were the Anatomy Theatre of Trinity College, the Park Street Medical School and the Richmond Hospital Medical School. The society consisted of presidents, vice-presidents, other officers and ordinary members. The first presidents elected were Messrs Carmichael, Colles, and Crampton, Doctors Cusack, Graves, and Marsh.

Membership was originally confined to those who held the degree of a university or the licence of a College of Physicians or Surgeons. Students were permitted to attend as visitors. At the end of the first year apothecaries who held no medical or surgical degree were admitted to membership. In their first report the council of the society recommended the publication of a volume of transactions. This was done and proceedings of the society appeared irregularly from 1832 until 1855.

The society was a pioneer one and in the third report, published in 1840, it was proudly claimed that the Dublin Pathological Society had led to the formation of similar associations in London, Cork, Liverpool, Philadelphia and elsewhere. The honorary diploma of the society was conferred on distinguished foreign pathologists, including Sir Astley Cooper, Sir Benjamin Brodie, Richard Bright, J. Cruveillier, J. L. Schönlein, and Carl Rokitansky. Twenty-one Dublin hospitals were represented at meetings of the society.

A curious objection was raised that the work of the society would result in mutilated bodies being sent to the schools of anatomy. In fact the vast majority of specimens exhibited at the society's meetings were taken from 'claimed' bodies which would not have reached the schools in any case.

Although the society occasionally published its own proceedings, these were also reported in the *Dublin Quarterly Journal of Medical Science.* In 1862 a new series of the society's 'Transactions' appeared. Nine volumes of this series were published in the following twenty years. When the Pathological Society merged in 1882 with the Medical, Obstetrical and Surgical societies to form the Royal Academy of Medicine, the proceedings of the Pathological section were published in the *Transactions* of the Academy.

THE DUBLIN OBSTETRICAL SOCIETY

The Obstetrical Society was founded in 1835 by Evory Kennedy, then Master of the Rotunda. Sir William Wilde, Professor Richard Doherty of Galway, and John Ringland, all three then students, were the original members.

At first the society consisted almost exclusively of students attached to the Rotunda Hospital. The president was selected from prominent members of the staff. Later membership became a sought-after privilege amongst qualified men and the meeting-place was transferred to a hall in the College of Physicians.

In the early days the society was in chronic financial trouble. Samuel Little Hardy (1815–1868), who was treasurer from 1842 to 1847, paid some debts out of his own pocket. Without the zeal of a few staunch members the society would have perished within the first few years. The proceedings were regularly reported in the *Dublin Quarterly Journal of Medicine.* In addition several separate volumes of transactions were published between 1871 and 1881. These form a valuable contribution to our knowledge of midwifery in Dublin during the nineteenth century.

In 1862 the constitution of the society was altered. The existing presidents were named honorary presidents and provision was made for the annual election of a President from amongst the members. In 1882 the Society merged with the Medical, Pathological and Surgical Societies to form the Royal Academy of Medicine in Ireland.

THE SURGICAL SOCIETY OF IRELAND

The Surgical Society of Ireland was founded in 1831 in order to give a free forum of discussion for all practitioners on purely professional subjects. The first meeting was not held until 1833. Members of the College and Licentiates admitted to the College were ordinary members. Physicians and surgeons of other colleges were admitted as honorary members and students were admitted as visitors. At first no discussion of papers was permitted, but very shortly afterwards this rule was modified.

The society anticipated the Academy of Medicine in being divided into sections of Medicine and Surgery, Anatomy, Materia Medica, etc. The contributors to the proceedings of the society included most of the well-known practitioners. Amongst the important papers in the early years were 'Tubercles in the Brain' by Dr Charles Benson (1839) and 'Pressure Treatment of Aneurism' by Dr O'B. Bellingham (1843). In 1843, Dr Mitchell, of the South-Eastern Lying-In Hospital, exhibited a monster delivered in that institution. The subsequent discussion centred largely on whether ante-natal influences could affect the unborn child. Papers dealing with obstetrical matters appeared frequently, even after the foundation of the Obstetrical Society. In 1844 Sir James Murray opened a discussion on Marsh Miasmata. His theory was that damp air, being a good conductor of electricity, altered the electrical balance of the body so as to bring about malarial attacks. Joliffe Tufnell propounded a similar theory for the cause of Asiatic cholera. Richard Carmichael, during his term of office (1846), repeated his plea for union between the different branches of the profession and for a higher standard of professional education and ethics.

The society was continually concerned with matters outside the realm of surgery for, in 1847, during the Famine, Dr Power read a paper on 'Microscopical Observations of the Potato Disease.' A few months previously Dr Leeson and Professor Thomas Brady (1801–1864), Professor of Medical Jurisprudence in the Royal College of Physicians, published their findings in cases of starvation in County Leitrim. Papers on zoological subjects were read at intervals, notably by Professor Robert Harrison (1796–1858).

Although the society flourished it did not receive unanimous support from the profession, and in his presidential address (1849) Robert Harrison castigated those who would not support their own society. But William Hargreave (1797–1874), president in 1853–54, was able to report that during his year of office the membership and members' activity had been vastly increased and that papers by corresponding and foreign associate members had become of considerable importance to the meetings. These included two cases of aneurism treated according to the 'Dublin method' by Dr Sargint of Clonmel and Dr Jacob of Maryborough. This technique developed a considerable international reputation and in 1852 Professor Boeck, of Christiana, reported a case of aneurism treated by the Dublin method. Although the Obstetrical Society was quite active, gynaecological papers appeared at many of the Surgical Society's meetings. The obstetrician was not yet accepted as an operative specialist.

When Thomas Lewis Mackesy (1790–1869) read his inaugural address in December 1862, he expressed the opinion that a detailed history of the Surgical Society would be a great boon to the profession as a whole. Mackesy regarded his profession highly and rejoiced that the surgeon's status should have improved so markedly within a few years. He pointed out to the students present that a broad liberal education was essential for professional success.

In February 1868 Mr Henry Tyrrell (1833–1879), of the Mater Misericordiae Hospital, and Professor of Surgery in the Catholic University School, read a paper on the use of Lister's antiseptic methods in surgery. He mentioned cases in which the method had failed as well as those in which it was successful. Apparently the members were hesitant of adopting the new technique, as for several years afterwards there are references to operative and other wounds becoming septic. In 1876 Edward Hallaran Bennett, Professor of Surgery in Trinity College, read a much-discussed paper on the use of carbolic and salicylic acids in antiseptic surgery. George H. Kidd, who was president of the society and Master of the Coombe Hospital in 1876, referred to the tendency which still existed to regard obstetrics as a not-quite-respectable branch of medicine in some quarters. E. D. Mapother's paper on shock, read in 1879, is still of considerable clinical interest.

In 1858 the Medical Act put all practitioners on the same register and broke down many of the distinctions between them. The work of the four medical societies overlapped and there was agitation in favour of their amalgamation. In 1882 the 569 members of the societies were circularised on the matter.

Of the 292 replies, 275 were in favour of amalgamation. After long negotiations the first meeting of the Academy (Royal – since 1887) of Medicine in Ireland took place on 22nd November 1882. The Academy was originally divided into four sections: Medicine, Obstetrics, Pathology, and Surgery. In December of the same year sub-sections of State Medicine (Public Health) and Anatomy and Physiology were formed. In 1930 a section of Oto-Rhino-Laryngology was established and in 1946 a section of Anaesthesia was added. These sections meet in rotation in the Kildare Street premises of the College of Physicians.

When the Academy was founded, Sir Charles Cameron proposed that the Society of Metropolitan Officers of Health, of which he was president, should enter the union under the title of Section of Hygiene. The proposal was defeated. However, Cameron was elected chairman of the Sub-section of State Medicine when the original four sections were increased in 1882, anatomy and physiology being introduced under the supervision of the sections of Medicine and Surgery. Both were declared full sections in 1887 and Cameron became President of his group.

There was no further extension until 1930 when an E.N.T. section was formed. Since then practically every specialty has developed its own section as follows: Anaesthetics (1945), Paediatrics (1950), Odontology (1952), Dermatology (1952), Radiology (1955), History of Medicine (1955), Psychiatry (1968), Neurological Sciences (1969), Rheumatology (1973), Ophthalmology (1974), Medical Education (1975), and General Practice (1976).

These developments have placed a very considerable strain on the finances and accomodation available to the Academy. It is commonplace for two or more meetings to be held on the same night, and many a speaker arriving to present some abstruse paper must have been delighted to find a large crowd having tea before the meeting, only to be deflated as at least two thirds disappeared into other rooms, when the meeting bell was rung.

Fellowship of the Academy is open to individuals who are not medically qualified, but are interested in the science of medicine. There are now some 1,200 Fellows of the Academy with a dozen Honorary Fellows, whose number is limited to 25 at any one time. Amongst the well known foreign names which have appeared on the honorary roll, are those of Paget, Billroth, Pasteur, Lister, Koch, Cushing, both Mayos, Stroganoff, Munro-Kerr and most recently, Sir Richard Doll the distinguished epidemiologist.

Important events in the Academy's annual calender are the prize lectures. The Graves lecture is for original observations by candidates under forty years of age, a limit which also applies to the St Luke's lecture on the subject of cancer, which is jointly sponsored by

St Luke's hospital. The third lecture was founded to commemorate a distinguished Dublin Biochemist, Edward Conway, who was attached to U.C.D. for many years.

THE IRISH MEDICAL ASSOCIATION

The societies and associations just described were all concerned with the purely scientific aspect of medicine. Medico-political affairs were outside their scope and co-operation between different branches of the profession for their common support was non-existent. In order to remedy this the Irish Medical Association was founded in the College of Surgeons in 1839. This Association did much useful work, but it received insufficient publicity. Also the Association could not control or speak for the majority of the divided profession. The central council of the Association met regularly until 1846, when there was a lapse of several years. Many of the country branches continued to work actively, but without unified control. As a result the conditions of doctors working in the dispensaries established under the Medical Charities Act of 1852 were highly unsatisfactory.

On 7th June 1853 a congress was held in Dublin which formally re-established the association. Dr Charles Benson (1797–1886), Professor of Medicine in the College of Surgeons, was elected President. The newly-constituted Asssociation made provision for the privileges of reciprocal membership with the Provincial Medical and Surgical Association, the forerunner of the British Medical Association, but full reciprocity did not become established until 1936, eighty-three years later.

The Association concentrated on improving the dispensary doctor's lot. A minimum salary of £100 per year with pension was demanded. A Superannuation Act passed in 1865 gave Boards of Guardians power to allow pensions at their own discretion. It was not until 1919 that pensions were granted as a right rather than as an act of grace.

In 1882 the Association was incorporated with much the same objects as previously, notably:

To unite the members of the profession in Ireland and so form a body competent to exercise influence in sanitary and medical affairs for the public benefit and to protect and promote the interest of the medical profession.

In 1890, internal differences arose amongst the members. Archibald Jacob (1837–1901), a member of the council, submitted a scheme for the re-constitution of the Association. His proposals were passed. The President, Dr Anthony H. Corley (1840–1890), stated that he looked upon the passing of Dr Jacob's resolutions as a vote of censure and felt bound to resign. Twenty-five members of the council resigned from the Association shortly afterwards. The legal position was not clear for some time and members claimed that the amendments had no legal force. They were supported in this claim by counsel's opinion. Later the council of the Association proposed its own amendments, which were substantially the same as Dr Jacob's. These were passed and the Association settled down again to improving the doctor's lot under the presidency of Dr George I. Mackesy of Waterford.

In the new century the Irish Medical Association wakened to fresh activity. This was particularly noticeable in the country branches. In 1903 the annual meeting was held in Enniskillen. This experiment in decentralisation was successful and the principal of holding meetings outside of Dublin and the other University cities is now firmly established.

The Association worked in harmony with the British Medical Association and it became obvious that amalgamation between the two was desirable in order to avoid overlapping and wasted effort. The first attempts at amalgamation were made in 1919. As a result of this the B.M.A. went to considerable expense by altering its articles in order to permit of the affiliation. Unfortunately, the scheme fell into abeyance until 1932, when a proposal for a conference of the two associations was postponed until after the 1933 annual meeting of the B.M.A.

After long negotiations the Irish Free State Medical Union (I.M.A. and B.M.A.) was established as from the 1st January 1936 with 778 foundation members. The Union was governed by a central council, so constituted as to give representation to every interest in the profession. The Union was composed of divisions corresponding to county areas. For purposes of organisation the profession was divided into special groups for each of its various sections. Members of the Union going to England automatically became members of the B.M.A. Since its establishment the Union did valuable work in improving the conditions of Irish doctors. The Union was concerned with a wider field than the medico-political one. For example, in 1941 a Dietetic Council was established. This made valuable investigations of the country's nutrition during the war years. In the same year the name was changed again to the Irish Medical Association.

THE GENERAL MEDICAL PRACTITIONERS' ASSOCIATION

At a meeting of the General Council of the Apothecaries' Hall held in February 1854, it was unanimously resolved that an Association of General Medical Practitioners should be formed, having for its objects the welfare of the profession and the promotion of practical and scientific knowledge. Membership was open to qualified practitioners of Medicine and Pharmacy. At the period the term 'general practitioner' was virtually synonymous with 'apothecary.' Amongst the secondary objects of this association was the establishment of a benevolent fund for the relief of necessitous members or of their widows and orphans.

The society was formally constituted on 10th March 1854, with E. H. Bolland and W. J. Harrison as president and vice-president respectively. At one of the first meetings an ethical code was drawn up on the suggestion of Dr Charles Leet. Later a committee was set up to watch over the interests of the profession, particularly in the fields of education and qualification.

Much of the first year's work was devoted to organisation. A few papers were read, notably by Dr Long, on 'Scarlatina' and by Dr Leet on 'Functional Diseases of the Heart'. Leet was one of the most prominent members of the society. His name appeared in the minutes of nearly every meeting as taking an active part. In 1858 he received a piece of plate in token of gratitude for his services to the association. His son was the first winner (in 1857) of a prize presented by the association for a medical essay.

At the end of the first year the association was left with a credit balance of £5 11s. 7d. As no benevolent fund payments had been made the society was hardly in a sound financial state. At the first annual meeting J. W. Harrison was elected president, with Dr Owens as his deputy. The most notable event in his year of office occurred just before he vacated the chair for the last time. A lengthy discussion took place on the merits of the proposed Medical Bill. The association deplored the fact that the apothecaries had been excluded from the rights and privileges of other practitioners. The association protested against

such reckless legislation which evinces neither regard for constitutional rights nor concern for the public's health – and petition Parliament for the total rejection of the Bill as most unjust and dangerous.

A resolution to this effect was passed and sent to the press, as well as to the Members of Parliament supporting the Bill. The Bill failed to become law and a few months later the association sent a message of thanks to Lord Elcho, Mr Fitzroy, and Mr Hamilton for their recognition of the apothecaries' rights in a new Medical Bill.

When the College of Physicians issued a supplement to the

Pharmacopoeia in 1856 the association was instantly up in arms, claiming that such work was its alone. In a preface to the book the College made slighting remarks concerning the apothecaries generally. Later in the year the inspectors of apothecaries' shops made recommendations about the storage and sale of poisons.

In May 1857 daily meetings of the association were ordered so as to consider without delay Bills before Parliament which dealt with the regulation of the medical profession. The first of these, introduced by Sir William Heathcote, Mr Headlam and Mr Napier was denounced, as it confiscated the professional rights and privileges of the apothecaries. The Bill proposed by Lord Elcho was supported and all apothecaries were pressed to work for its passage with some modifications. In September 1857 negotiations were opened with the British Medical Association on the subject of the proposed Bills. Following all this activity a reaction set in, for the monthly meetings of February and March 1858 were attended by only two and three members, so that no business could be conducted. Only sixteen attended the fifth annual meeting when Dr William D. Moore was appointed president.

In January 1859 Dr Leet read a letter from the president of the Provincial (later British) Medical Association asking him to become a member thereof. He placed the letter before the Irish association with a view to bringing about an amalgamation.

THE BRITISH MEDICAL ASSOCIATION

At the last general meeting of the Irish Association of General Practitioners, held on St Patrick's Day 1859, it was unanimously resolved that a Dublin branch of the British Medical Association should be formed. The support for this became so strong that in 1867 the Association held its annual meeting in Dublin. William Stokes took the chair before four hundred delegates. His presidential address dealt with the necessity for a Public Health scheme. For the first time at a respresentative meeting a physician pleaded for prevention rather than cure.

In 1879 the Cork medical men invited the Association to hold its annual meeting in that city. The most notable paper was that read by William S. Savory, F.R.S., on 'The Prevention of Blood Poisoning in the Practice of Surgery.' Superficially his paper seemed reactionary, for he condemned Lister's methods, but it contained the germ of the aseptic method, for he believed that it was better to clean the hospitals and prevent dirt entering rather than to kill germs bred in ill-ventilated, dirty wards and operating theatres.

The first Irish branch of the British Medical Association had been founded by Dr McNaughton Jones in Cork in 1874. The Dublin branch was not founded until 1877 through the efforts of Dr George Duffey. The Belfast meeting of 1884 was marked by the establishment of a separate section of Pharmacology and Therapeutics following the active agitation of Sir William Whitla.

In 1887, the fourth Irish meeting was held in Dublin. The president was the Regius Professor of Physic, Sir John Banks (1816–1908). At this meeting an echo of William Stokes' address of 1867 was heard. Revd Samuel Haughton of Dublin University read a paper on 'Reflections on Death Rates with Special Reference to Dublin and its Suburbs.' He stated bluntly that Dublin's high death rate was due to the conditions in the slums, but that before new houses were provided the people should be taught how to live in them.

The 1909 meeting was held in Belfast. Sir William Whitla, speaking as President of the Association and of the newly-established Queen's University, criticised the medical curriculum and urged extension of the time given to clinical studies.

In 1933, the sixth annual meeting of the B.M.A. in Ireland was held, again in Dublin. Professor T. G. Moorhead, President of the Royal College of Physicians and Regius Professor of Physic in Trinity College, presided over this one hundred and first annual meeting of the B.M.A. There were now sixteen sections representing various branches of medicine. So many delegates attended that meetings were spread over four different premises, those of the Royal Dublin Society, the Mansion House, Trinity College and University College, Dublin.

The annual meetings of the Association were, of course, the highlights. In the years between an active campaign was waged, having for its object the improvement of conditions of doctors generally and particularly in the public services. Prior to 1891, the Irish Medical Association was the only body giving full-time attention to this question. In 1911, as a result of correspondence in the *British Medical Journal*, Mr Ernest Hart, then the editor, brought a memorandum on the Irish dispensary system before Members of Parliament. No results were achieved until 1898, when the right of doctors to holidays with pay was conceded by the Local Government Board.

In 1903, at the request of the Association, Surgeon-General Evatt issued an exhaustive report on the working of the Poor Law System. Following consultation with the Irish Medical Association, certain dispensary districts were boycotted by members. In 1905, an Irish Committee of the B.M.A. was established.

In 1914 an office was established in Dublin, with Dr Thomas Hennessy as a full-time secretary. He was also honorary secretary to the Irish Medical Committee, founded in 1913. His energy and activity were of immeasurable help in improving the status of the profession. With his long experience as a dispensary medical officer, Hennessy was particularly keen on improving and standardising conditions in the dispensary service.

Little by little, conditions of dispensary medical officers were improved. Salaries, pensions and methods of appointment were all bettered until at the annual meeting in 1933 the members could look with great satisfaction on their Association's work. At this meeting the question of amalgamation between the British and Irish medical associations came to a head. Professor Moorhead pointed out that their memberships were respectively 1,100 and 400 and that their rivalry, although amicable, resulted in much duplication and wasted effort. Prolonged negotiations resulted and on 1st January 1936, the I.M.A. and the branches of the B.M.A. in the then Irish Free State became one under the name of the Irish Free State Medical Union (later the Medical Association of Eire). Dr Hennessy died suddenly on the next day.

In 1937 the British Medical Association held its annual meeting at Belfast under the Presidency of Professor Robert J. Johnstone, Professor of Gynaecology in Queen's University. The main subject of his address was medical education before and after qualification. Over eleven hundred members attended.

THE POOR LAW MEDICAL OFFICERS' ASSOCIATION

Although the Irish Medical Association and the General Practitioners' Association had as their objects the improvement of professional status, the long-neglected Poor Law medical officers felt that their interests were insufficiently protected and in 1871 they formed an association of their own. Their first annual meeting was held on 5th June 1871, and a brief report was issued.

At the first meeting Dr Hanrahan of Queen's County took the chair. He observed that the Poor Law medical officers comprised 50 per cent of the profession, but they were precluded from membership of the Irish Medical Association Council. Subsequently speakers emphasised that the newly-formed body did not wish to antagonise the older associations and would join with them in pushing forward schemes for professional advancement. One of the suggestions made was that the Poor Law doctors should be paid by the central Government rather than by the local authorities and that salaries should increase with length of service, with promotion and superannuation allowances. An avowed object of the association was that medical officers should become, to a certain extent, a branch of the civil service.

In the association's second year Dominic Corrigan was elected to the Presidency.

Lord O'Hagan's Lunacy (Ireland) Bill as introduced in the House of Lords contained a clause requiring medical men to examine and certify lunatics when requested and to send to a central office a very elaborate report, within one week under a penalty of £10. Provision was made in the Bill for the payment of all concerned except the doctor. As a result of vigorous protest by the association, the obnoxious clause was dropped.

Unfortunately, like so many similar bodies, the association gradually became less active and records of its work have been lost.

The Medical Union

In 1957 relations between the Irish Medical Association and the Department of Health were at an appallingly low level. The Government of the day seemed to be making a deliberate effort to antagonise the medical profession both under cover of Parliamentry privilege and at public meetings. Doctors of all grades were lambasted as ultra-conservative incompetent money grabbers with the most virulent attacks made on the Dispensary medical officers who derived a considerable portion of their incomes from State sources.

It became impossible even to open discussions with the responsible Minister for he claimed that the I.M.A. not being a trade union or 'excepted body' had no authority to negotiate terms and conditions of service. A number of members of the I.M.A. were co-opted to a sub-committee for the purpose of discussing the desirability and feasibility of founding a trade union, so that the Minister would be forced to the negotiation table. While there was broad agreement on the neccessity for such a step there was less unanimity about what the Union would be. Three main proposals emerged: a) a Union which would be the I.M.A. under another name; b) a Union which would automatically grant membership to Association members, unless they for personal reasons opted out; and c) a completely independent body.

Eventually a referendum of I.M.A. members was held and a majority decided in favour of establishing a union. It was now pointed out that the £1000 lodgement required before registration of the Union could not be taken from I.M.A. funds because of its Articles of Association. However, fifty prospective members were keen enough to pay £20 each as an interest free loan and in June 1962 the certificate of registration was issued and the Union came into being under the Presidency of Dr John Cox who held office until the first General Meeting at Athlone on November 18th 1962.

At this meeting Dr Seaghan Ua Conchubair of Oranmore, Galway, was elected President.

During this period the infant Union had the use of premises at I.M.A. House together with secretarial help and, despite differences and reservations about methods, though not about aims, it appeared that both organisations would be able to work together towards a common end.

The then Minister of Health, Mr McEntee, now took a step which was to divide the profession for almost a quarter of a century. He recognised the danger of having a determined trade union as an opponent and offered a limited negotiating licence to the older body. On the face of it this seemed to be what had originally been sought, but closer examination revealed that not alone did the licence exclude industrial action it could also be arbitrarily revoked by the Minister or his successors. Unfortunately this licence was accepted by the I.M.A. and though peace makers in both organisations tried to promote unity there were hot-heads and extremists who refused even to consider the possibility of joint action. Not for the first time implementation of the maxim *divide et impera* had borne fruit. With a divided profession resistance to Ministerial manoeuvring was often ineffective.

The Union soon outgrew the cramped offices available from the I.M.A. and moved to rented premises at 72 Northumberland Road, where the first fulltime secretary, Mr John McLoughlin, was installed.

Since those early days the Union has grown steadily in strength and effectiveness as a representative body. Alone or in combination with the I.M.A., it influenced legislation affecting conditions of service for General Practitioners, temporary Dispensary Medical Officers, Junior Hospital Doctors, Specialists in many disciplines and the community in general.

But, no matter how vigourously points of view were presented a recalcitrant Minister, his officials or local authorities could always weaken an argument by emphasising that the Union or the Association did not necessarily represent the views of every doctor in the country. Sometimes trivial differences in the opinions expressed by the two medical bodies were misrepresented as evidence of deep division. Repeated efforts were made to achieve unity and at the time of going to publication (1983) it seems that this aim is on the verge of being achieved. Joint meetings have been held in several centres with, as might be expected, unity of objective but reservations about methods. The new body which will probably be called the Irish Medical Organisation will have the negotiating rights of a trade union, failure to secure which had led to decades of sterile squabbling and internecine conflict.

THE GUILD OF SS LUKE, COSMAS AND DAMIEN

Although the majority of medical associations founded in recent years had a common professional interest, in 1911 a society was founded whose bond was the unusual one of religion. In 1910, owing to the work of Surgeon-General Thomas Maunsell – an Irishman – the Guild of SS Luke, Cosmas and Damien was formed in England. Later an Irish branch was established.

In 1931 a separate Irish guild was founded under the mastership of Dr John Stafford Johnson. The headquarters were in Dublin, with branches in Cork and Belfast. In 1938 a new constitution reorganised the guild on a provincial basis. At first provincial branches were formed in Dublin, Cork and Galway.

Membership of the guild is of two kinds – full and associate. Those eligible for election to the first class are Catholic doctors and medical students. Catholic priests are eligible for election to the second class. The general purpose of the guild is to foster and spread the Catholic outlook and ethics in relation to medical problems.

In 1954 the Irish Guild hosted the Sixth International Congress of Catholic Doctors. The subjects discussed[9] from the ethical point of view, ranged from the genetic structure of populations to a discussion of the demographic problems consequent on atomic warfare. Some of the questions posed in the latter have been grimly answered by now.

Many other medical groups have been formed in this country for discussion or mutual assistance. The history of their work would be in large measure the history of medicine in Ireland. At the present day every medical school and many of the hospitals have their medical discussion groups. These fulfil an essential function in the development of students and doctors alike. At their meetings new techniques are discussed, different points of view are presented and erroneous conclusions corrected. For the practising physician and surgeon this is of prime importance. At the same time students benefit by hearing their seniors discuss problems, often more informally than is possible in lectures. In time the students learn to think clearly and analytically as well as to express their opinions convincingly.

Even nowadays the doctor's word carries great weight and there are still patients who will not dare ask a question let alone query a medical opinion. But there has always been great lay curiosity about medical matters and there have been writers who pandered to this by giving sometimes palpably false or slanted information about sickness, public health and medical discoveries. In 1975 the Health Education Bureau was set up to disseminate accurate health information and to co-ordinate the work of several bodies already operating in relation to specific matters. After a trial period of three years the Bureau was expanded with the task of advising the Minister of Health on health education priorities, drawing up national and local education programmes, helping other bodies financially and otherwise to carry out specific programmes, promotion and conduct of research, and to promote greater community awareness of health education.

In 1982 the Bureau adopted a life cycle model of Health Education which identified the key issues, phases and needs in health and illness throughout life and reflected the overall aim of the Bureau i.e. 'To provide means and opportunities for all vulnerable people to protect, maintain and improve their health as far as educational methods permit'. Amongst the topics dealt with by the Bureau have been, drugs', abuse, cigarette smoking, migraine, alcoholism, personal safety and maternity.

CHAPTER TWENTY ONE

PROFESSIONAL PUBLICATIONS

The professional mind has always thrived on discussion. The larger the audience and the more topical the subject of debate the greater the interest and keenness. The result of the need for an open forum and a means whereby new thoughts and discoveries can be transmitted, for approbation or for criticism, has resulted in the growth of the technical or trade journal.

The Irish medical men of the eighteenth century and earlier – Petty, Boate, Dun, Madden, Steevens, Proby – published their findings either as detached papers or in the *Philosophical Transactions* of the Royal Society in London.

Dr Allen Mullen (or Moulin) was the first medical man in this country to publish in the *Philosophical Transactions*. His original communication was an anatomical description of an elephant which was accidentally burned to death in Dublin in June 1681. The same volume contains a paper by him on 'New anatomical observations in the eyes of animals.'

Within the country the only means of expression of opinion were the publication of books or pamphlets. Being on specialised subjects these were unlikely to catch the attention of those not already interested.

In 1783 Richard Harris, a general practitioner in Clonmel Co. Tipperary, published what he hoped would be the first number of a regularly appearing medical journal, *Collectanea Hibernica Medica*. There were four essays in this pioneer effort all written by Harris: 'On the Pathology of General Disease', 'On the Acquired and Hereditary Right of Chronic Disposition', 'A deficiency of parts in the Foetus' and 'On the Chin-Cough'. In the Preface he expressed his hopes that others would contribute to further volumes which he intended to edit. If any in fact appeared they have been lost.

The *Transactions* (later *Proceedings*) of the Royal Irish Academy first appeared in 1787 and included medical subjects under the general heading of 'Science'. These were often highly technical and at no time did the authors seem to be 'writing down' to a lay audience. Unfortunately, there are no records of discussions following the papers. Possibly the lay members of the day had leisure to read up medical subjects and take part in technical debates.

The first medical paper to appear in these *Transactions* was by Stephen Dickson, Regius Professor of Physic and a Fellow of the College of Physicians. His subject was Pemphigus. The paper is of some interest as it gives an indication of the knowledge of fevers of the time. The first volume also contains a paper of James Cleghorn on what was probably a dermoid tumour of the ovary. The tumour, removed after the patient's death, contained hair, teeth and bones.

Joseph Clarke, Master of the Rotunda, published an account in 1789 of Nine-Day Fits which killed 17 per cent of the children born in the hospital. From his description of the disease it seems to have been an acute form of infantile gastro-enteritis. He lists the causes as being (i) Foul air, or a 'phlogisticated' atmosphere; (ii) neglect of keeping the children clean and dry; and (iii) drunken mothers. Clarke attributed most of the trouble to the foul air of the wards. Although he was probably right he made the error of considering asphyxia to be the prime cause of death. It is hardly likely that the air could be so bad as to kill children without causing serious discomfort or worse to the mothers.

In Vol. IV of the *Transactions* there is an account by Samuel Croker King (1728–1817) of a trephine invented by him. He claimed that this instrument made the operation of opening the skull easier and safer. In the same volume trephining is discussed by Sylvester O'Halloran (1728–1807) of Limerick and there are two papers by George Burrowes, on an enlarged spleen and on fistula of the stomach. Alexis St Martin is known to all medical students as the Canadian trapper with a permanent fistula into the stomach which enabled William Beaumont to study the digestive functions. Burrowes missed a chance of similar immortality. Whilst he was in charge of a ward in the House of Industry in 1792, a patient was admitted who had suffered from a gastric fistula for twenty-seven years. Burrowes intended to

expose aliments to the action of the succus gastricus alone to ascertain the effects of several medicines when confined to the stomach and of making experiments on narcotics.

Unfortunately, the patient left hospital without permission. When he returned after some months his condition was so weak that experimentation was impossible, and he died shortly afterwards. Burrowes preserved his patient's organs and exhibited them to the Academy.

Medical subjects were occasionally dealt with by lay authors. In

Vol. V (1793) the Revd Edward Kenny described a method of preparing a sulphurous medicinal water. He claimed that this was a cure for impurities of the blood, itch, herpes, head eruptions, scrofula, worms and chronic rheumatism. Conversely, medical authors dealt with non-medical subjects. Kenny's paper is followed by one from Robert Perceval, M.D., on the decomposition of lead by lime. In the same volume two Scottish doctors discussed such widely-divergent subjects as coal-mining and rain-gauges.

Although the role of the Academy as a forum of medical discussion has become less important since the establishment of professional societies the pages of its *Proceedings* still contain papers by medical men on various subjects.

It became obvious from the example of other countries that collections of medical papers published periodically would command a wider publicity at a lower cost.

THE DUBLIN MEDICAL AND PHYSICAL ESSAYS

In 1807 *The Dublin Medical and Physical Essays* was issued for the first time as a quarterly journal by four doctors, of whom three had studied in Edinburgh.

Hugh Ferguson (1768–1844) was born in Scotland. He entered Trinity College in 1783 when only fifteen years of age. After eight years he secured a B.A. In 1794 he graduated M.D. of Edinburgh, his graduation thesis being on the subject of pulmonary phthisis. He returned once more to Dublin where in 1802 he was admitted a Licentiate of the College of Physicians. In 1804 he was elected to a Fellowship and was President on four occasions, in 1819, 1827, 1831 and 1833. For some time he lectured at the Hardwicke School of Medicine.

Francis Barker (1773–1859) took his Edinburgh M.D. with a thesis on Galvani's work. When he returned to Dublin University he was appointed assistant to the Professor of Chemistry. He seems to have taken great interest in this work, for he was entrusted with College funds for the purchase of fossils in Paris and received a grant of £50 as a token of appreciation of his services. He became Professor in 1808. He was admitted L.K. & Q.C.P. in 1805 and elected a Fellow two years later. He was for many years secretary to the Board of Health and one of the physicians to Cork Street Fever Hospital.

Samuel Bell Labatt (d. 1849) was also an Edinburgh man. His subject for the M.D. thesis in 1797 was 'Gout.' From 1800 to 1803 he was Assistant Master at the Dublin Lying-In Hospital. He was elected Master for seven years in 1814.

Charles Hawkes Todd (1782–1826) might well claim more

recognition than is usually given him. His great contribution to surgical technique was the Dublin method of treating aneurisms by compression. In 1803 he passed the examinations of the Irish College of Surgeons and was elected a member in 1805. His principal appointments were as surgeon to the House of Industry Hospitals and Professor of Anatomy and Surgery in the College of Surgeons School. He was for many years Assistant Secretary to the College. Two of Todd's sons, James Henthorn and Robert Bentley, became famous in the fields of antiquarian research and anatomy respectively. The latter was appointed Professor of Anatomy and Physiology in King's College Hospital School at the age of twenty-seven.

The four editors, Ferguson, Barker, Labatt and Todd, decided to accept only articles signed by their authors and to reject papers dealing with the currently vigorous discussion on medical reform. They anticipated many of the present journals by printing digests of articles published elsewhere. However, medical politics were not as rigorously excluded as originally intended and the 'projected plan of reform' was favourably mentioned.

The first volume of these essays contained a description by Mr R. M. Peile (1763 ?–1858) of an improved method of performing lithotomy with instruments originally invented by George Daunt in 1750. Amongst other well-known contributors were Whitley Stokes, Sir Philip Crampton, and Richard Carmichael, as well as the editors. Material published was not confined to medical matters. For example, a paper by Sir Philip Crampton concerned the discovery of a new muscle in the eyes of birds. This paper was later presented to the Royal Society by Sir Humphrey Davy. In 1806 T. J. Mackey, Curator to the Trinity College Botanical Garden, published a catalogue of rare plants found in Ireland. Unfortunately, the *Dublin Medical and Physical Essays* only survived for six issues. The last number appeared in June 1808. No further medical journal was issued in Dublin until 1817.

THE DUBLIN HOSPITAL REPORTS

In 1815 John Cheyne, Edward Perceval (d. 1827), Abraham Colles and Charles Hawkes Todd decided to issue an annual volume of *Dublin Hospital Reports*. All four had reason to encourage such a publication. Cheyne and Perceval were endeavouring to establish a school of medicine and museum of pathology in connection with the House of Industry Hospitals. Colles was Professor of Anatomy and Surgery in the College of Surgeons. Todd had been one of the editors of the *Medical and Physical Essays*.

The first volume was issued in 1817. Most of the contributions came from the four founders. They included papers by Cheyne on 'A case of melaena,' 'Jaundice,' 'On the virtues of James's Powder in Apoplectic Diathesis,' and 'Report of Hardwicke Fever Hospital,'; by Colles 'On the cause of Trismus Nascentium'; by P. Crampton 'On Periostitis'; by Perceval on 'Epidemic Petechial Febricula,' and 'The Deleterious and Medicinal Effects of Green Tea'; and by Todd on cases of Ruptured Intestine and Hernia. Perceval left Dublin after the publication of the first volume and retired to Bath.

The second volume appeared in 1818. One of its most interesting papers was by Cheyne, describing a case of apoplexy in which the fleshy part of the heart was converted into fat. The third volume appeared in 1822. Richard Burgess recorded two cases of bronchotomy and Colles discussed the fatality of wounds received in the dissecting-room. The fourth volume appeared in 1827 and the surviving editors announced their intention of 'bringing the first part of this work to a close by publishing the present volume.' As both were engaged in active practice they may have felt unable to act efficiently as editors. Amongst the interesting papers is one by Cheyne on 'The simulated diseases of soldiers.'

The fifth volume was edited in 1830 by Robert Graves and contains several important papers. Amongst them are Graves, R. J., 'On the effects produced by posture on the frequency and character of the pulse'; Houston, John., 'Observations on the Mucous Membrane of the Rectum'; (this paper contained the original description of Houston's valves in the last portion of the intestine) and Evory Kennedy's 'Observations on the Utero-Placental circulation.'

The *Dublin Hospital Reports* were well produced and illustrated. The papers are sound and give a good idea of the state of medical knowledge in Ireland at the beginning of the nineteenth century. A sixth volume was promised for 1832, but instead there appeared the *Dublin Journal of Medical and Chemical Science* edited by Robert Kane.

THE *DUBLIN HOSPITAL GAZETTE*

In 1845 Drs Corrigan, O'Ferrall, Evans and Aldridge established the *Dublin Hospital Gazette*, a fortnightly periodical entirely devoted to matters of scientific import and unconnected with medical politics. The first number appeared on 15th February 1845. In No 30, for 1st May 1846, there was a notice that the proprietors intended to suspend publication indefinitely. On 1st February 1854 the *Gazette* resumed publication again as a fortnightly periodical. According to the 'Prospectus' which appeared in the first number, the *Gazette* was to be mainly devoted to the cultivation and improvement of practical medicine and surgery through the publication of carefully recorded cases. Politics and personal discussion were debarred. Contributors to the first number were representative of most of the city hospitals, including the Meath, St Vincent's, Jervis Street and the Rotunda.

Although the principal contributors were practising in Dublin, papers soon began to arrive from country practitioners. Amongst the subjects dealt with by these were 'Chloroform in Insanity' by H. Thompson of the Tyrone Infirmary; 'Fractures of the Arm' by Crofts Shinkwin of Cork and 'Stone in the Kidney' by Dillon Kelly of Mullingar.

Glascott Symes, one of the attending physicians to the Kingstown (Dun Laoghaire) Dispensary, recorded a case of tetanus successfully treated by chloroform inhalation. Later Robert Hannay of Lurgan reported a similar case.

The *Gazette* continued publication regularly until 1862. In later years it was renamed the *Dublin Hospital Gazette and Journal of Practical Pharmacy*, and considerable space was devoted to reprints of articles in other journals.

IRISH HOSPITAL GAZETTE

When the *Dublin Hospital Gazette* ceased publication it was felt that the gap could best be filled by a periodical which should act as a medium for the publication of papers from doctors throughout the country. Accordingly, the *Irish Hospital Gazette* first appeared on 1st January 1873. Like its predecessor it was strictly non-political in character. The principal contents were hospital reports; original communications and lectures; and abstracts from reports of societies and from foreign journals.

The *Gazette* must have been of good international standing, for the original communications included papers by Vald Ramussen of Copenhagen, and by Professor See of the Charité Hospital in Paris. Although as usual the majority of contributions came from Dublin doctors the *Gazette* published papers from practitioners in Carlow, Drogheda, Cork and Cashel amongst other Irish provincial towns.

The *Gazette* was published fortnightly for two and a half years. In the issue of 15th June 1875, there is a notice signed by George F. Duffey (1843–1903), the originator and editor, to the effect that the *Gazette* would for the future be amalgamated with the *Dublin Journal of Medical Science* as from the commencement of the sixtieth volume of the latter journal published on 1st July 1875.

The Medical Press and Circular, noting the *Gazette's* demise, mentioned that it was 'the third effort to supply some fancied want which a politico-scientific journal like the *Medical Press and Circular* is – upon unknown data – supposed to be incapable of satisfying.'

TRANSACTIONS OF THE ASSOCIATION OF THE COLLEGE OF PHYSICIANS

During this period the Association of Fellows and Licentiates of the King's and Queen's College of Physicians in Ireland was the most important medical society in the country. This body issued six volumes of its *Transactions* between 1817 and 1830. The preface to the first number proposed that the improvement of pathological science should be the object of chief importance, and members of the Association as well as country practitioners were encouraged to illustrate their papers with post-mortem reports. The papers published in the first number included: 'On the Use of Oxigen [*sic*] Gas in Angina Pectoris' by Robert Reid, M.D. and 'Dissections of Two Habitual Drunkards' by Samuel Black, M.D. as well as reports on the Fever and Lying-In Hospitals. Several papers written by surgeons were published, but it seems to have been the custom that these were read by a physician at meetings of the association. Most of the surgical cases recorded died of septic complications some time after operation.

In the second volume, John Milner Barry of Cork published a paper on 'The Origin of Intestinal Worms.' In this he repeated the then novel assertion that intestinal parasites might be traced to an external origin rather than to spontaneous internal generation. Bleeding and purgation are mentioned as remedies in the majority of the varied cases discussed. Unusual therapies include the use of emetics in haematemesis and rubbing with tartar emetic ointment in epilepsy.

Five volumes of the *Transactions* were published, in 1817, 1818, 1824, 1826 and 1828. In 1830 a new series appeared under the slightly altered title of '*Dublin Medical Transactions* – a Series of Papers by Members of the Association of the King's and Queen's College of Physicians in Ireland.'

When the *Dublin Journal of Medical and Chemical Science* appeared in 1832 financial reasons made it necessary for the association's *Transactions* to be published therein rather than in separate volumes.

In 1882 the association combined with the Obstetrical, Pathological and Surgical societies to found the Royal Academy of Medicine in Ireland. In 1883 the first volume of the Academy's *Transactions* appeared under the general editorship of William Thomson, F.R.C.S.I. (1843–1909). For a brief period in his youth

Thomson had been connected with the journalistic profession and was an active contributor to medical literature. He edited fourteen volumes of the *Transactions*. The first volume of these *Transactions* was notable for the fact that, for the first time, in Dublin, papers were illustrated by photographs instead of by drawings. These were published to illustrate Dr Theodore Stack's paper on the transplantation of teeth.

From 1897 until 1904 (Vols. XV to XXII), J. B. Story (1850–1926) occupied the editorial chair. He also had contributed extensively to medical literature, particularly in the field of ophthalmology. James Craig edited the *Transactions* from 1905 until 1910. His successor and the last editor was Professor John Scott. The *Transactions* for 1918 and 1919 (vols. XXXVI and XXXVII) were published as a single volume. In 1920 the *Dublin* (now *Irish*) *Journal of Medical Science* became the official organ of the Royal Academy of Medicine in Ireland.

THE DUBLIN JOURNAL OF MEDICAL AND CHEMICAL SCIENCE (1832–1836).
THE DUBLIN JOURNAL OF MEDICAL SCIENCE (1836–1846).
THE DUBLIN QUARTERLY JOURNAL OF MEDICAL SCIENCE (1846–1871).
THE DUBLIN JOURNAL OF MEDICAL SCIENCE (1872–1922).
THE IRISH JOURNAL OF MEDICAL SCIENCE (1922 to date).

Although Robert Kane's (1809–1890) name is not so familiar to the general public as those of his great contemporaries, his work for medicine in this country can scarcely be overestimated. He was the first editor of the *Dublin Journal of Medical and Chemical Science*. His father was the owner of a chemical factory which may have influenced the young man in his later interests in life. At seventeen years of age he started to study in the School of Physic and at the Meath Hospital under Graves and Stokes. His first medical qualification was L.A.H. in 1829. In the same year he was awarded the gold medal of the Meath Hospital Medical Society for a paper on the introduction of various animal and vegetable substances into the blood stream. A year later he won Graves' prize for an essay on typhus. After some time abroad he took the chair of chemistry in the Apothecaries' Hall in 1831. Amongst his many honours and appointments were the Professorship of Natural Philosophy at the R.D.S., 1834; a knighthood in 1846; F.R.S., 1849; and the Presidency of Queen's College, Cork, in 1849.

Originally Kane intended that the new *Journal* should concentrate on chemical subjects. In order to produce the medical section he asked for the assistance of Graves, Stokes and William Henry Porter (1790–1861), a surgeon of the Meath Hospital. The volume appeared every two months. Like its predecessor, it was divided into original communications, bibliographic notices and scientific intelligences. On his appointment to the Royal Dublin Society, Kane resigned in March 1835.

Arthur Jacob now became co-editor of the *Journal*, and articles therein, dealing with medical politics, have been attributed to him. In May 1836, the name of the publication was changed to *The Dublin Journal of Medical Science*.

In 1842 charge of the *Journal* was given to John Hamilton, a surgeon of the House of Industry, and Robert Lea MacDonnell. They held office for three years. In July 1845 William Wilde took over. When the year closed he completed the series with the publication of an index of 127 pages, compiled with his usual amazing gift for indexing and tabulation.

The first number of the *Dublin Quarterly Journal of Medical Science* appeared on 1st February 1846. The size of the volume was increased, but otherwise it retained the characteristics of its predecessors. Wilde's contributions formed a substantial portion of each issue until his resignation in 1849 in favour of John Moore Neligan (1815–1863), who guided the *Journal's* destinies without any great change until 1861.

George H. Kidd was the editor from 1861 until 1868, when James Little assumed office. In 1871, Little announced that as from January 1871 the *Dublin Journal of Medical Science* would appear every month. It was not always easy to secure sufficient articles, and in May 1874, when Sir William Moore was editor, only one original paper was submitted. This was a somewhat facetious contribution, entitled 'The History of a Bad Leg – A Lame Story.' The anonymous author was Fleetwood Churchill, an obstetrician. The only other articles were reports of societies and book reviews, including a withering criticism of a new book on surgery by Fourneaux Jordan, of Birmingham. Jordan was editor of the *Birmingham Medical Review*. In the following number of the *Review* he wrote:

The Dublin School is a quarter of a century behind the day; the *Dublin Medical Journal* is a quarter of a century beind the school; and the particular reviewer whom we feel it our duty to chastise, lags behind the general tone of even the least influential, the least capable and the least read of existing medical journals.

Although the *Journal* was not so poor as Jordan in his anger claimed, it did not rank highly among its fellows. In 1875, *The Irish Hospital Gazette* was incorporated and a feature known as 'The Periscope' was introduced. This latter was a careful review of the principal journals and articles wherever published. Moore held the editorial chair alone until 1907, when Dr Thomas Gillman Moorhead was associated with him as co-editor. Despite this, the *Journal* fell on evil days and the outbreak of a world-wide war accentuated by insurrection at home left the situation so grave that it seemed as if Dublin would be left without a journal. Messrs Fannin and Co were at this time the proprietors of the *Journal*. They suggested to the Academy of Medicine, who were in equally poor circumstances for the productions of their *Transactions*, that the publications should amalgamate. In March 1920 the 'Fourth Series' began under the editorship of Arnold K. Henry. Sir William Moore retired after forty-seven years.

In March 1922, the name was changed to *The Irish Journal of Medical Science* in the hope of attracting a wider audience. Messrs Cahill purchased the *Journal*, which became the official organ of the Academy of Medicine. On his appointment in 1925 to the Chair of Surgery in Cairo, Arnold Henry handed over editorial responsibility to Mr William Doolin, one of Ireland's most distinguished medico-literary figures. Under his control the *Journal* prospered and it is noticeable how many papers dealing with medico-historical matters were published during this period, reflecting Doolin's great interest in that subject.

Doolin occupied the editorial chair for thirty seven years including the difficult second World War period when an editor had to face not alone shortages of paper but also censorship for fear that an inadvertent comment could reveal national or international military information. When Doolin died Charles Dickson took over until 1970 when an editorial board representing a broad spectrum of the profession was appointed. From this period the *Journal* attracted many more contributors from abroad and the two latest editors R. P. Towers (1972–1980) and J. F. Murphy (1981– to date) have the help of the Editorial Board in assessing the value of papers submitted on an ever increasing range of specialised subjects.

THE DUBLIN MEDICAL PRESS

The *Dublin Medical Press* appeared for the first time on 9th January 1839. Unlike the other journals, its primary function was

. . . to rouse the slumbering energies of the Irish practitioner; to preserve the respectability of the professional character; to instil honourable principles, and foster kind feelings in the breast of the student; and to protect the institutions of the country against the attacks of those interested in their destruction.

The founder and first editor was Arthur Jacob (1790–1874), third member of a family of able surgeons. He became L.R.C.S.I. in 1813 and M.D. Edinburgh a year later. Immediately afterwards he walked from the latter city to Paris, except for the Channel crossing. He settled in Dublin in 1816 as an ophthalmologist. At intervals he held Professorships of Anatomy, Surgery and Physiology in the Royal College of Surgeons. He was twice President of that College in 1837 and 1864.

Jacob's most important discovery was the layer of 'rods and cones' in the eye which are concerned with vision in poor light. He was also the first to describe 'Jacob's ulcer,' a chronic condition of the eyelid. In 1852 he played a part in the foundation of the City of Dublin Hospital in Baggot Street.

As we have already seen, Arthur Jacob had been a co-editor of the *Dublin Journal of Medical Science*. His editorials were so violent that he was asked to resign. Following this he founded the *Dublin Medical Press* to give free expression to his opinions. Another Professor of the College of Surgeons, Henry Maunsell (1806–1879) was co-founder and co-editor of the *Press*. Maunsell's interests were wide. He was M.D. Glasgow and M.R.C.S.I. He held the Chair of Midwifery and later of Hygiene, and took a prominent part in medical politics. Gradually his medical interests waned. In 1844, when a member of Dublin Corporation, he moved a resolution that Queen Victoria should hold a parliament in Dublin every three years. In 1860, he bought the *Dublin Evening Mail*, which he owned and conducted up to his death, when it was bought by Francis B. Quinlan (1834–1900) of St Vincent's Hospital.

From the earliest days the *Dublin Medical Press* fought for an improved status of medical practitioners. It attacked those both inside and outside the profession who lowered the dignity or the temporal rewards of medical men. During the Famine of 1847, it criticised bitterly the bungling, incompetent authorities who paid the doctors five shillings per day for the most hazardous and nauseating work in the 'fever sheds' where dead, living and moribund patients were crowded as tightly as space would allow.

In 1850 the Medical Charities Bill was introduced in the House of Commons. In 1858 Cowper introduced his Medical Bill to legalise the status of the profession. Both these received due and unfavourable notice from the *Medical Press*. Unfortunately, personalities became so mixed with bona fide comment that many were prejudiced who would otherwise have supported the *Press*. In particular it resented the improved status given to the Apothecaries.

In 1860 Jacob resigned the editorship in favour of his son, Archibald Hamilton. The elder Jacob was then in his seventieth year.

Nevertheless he continued to hold the Chair of Anatomy and Physiology until 1867.

A second series of the *Dublin Medical Press* was started in 1860. Except for an increase in size and some minor changes the policy and appearance remained as formerly. With the change of editors the tone of the leading articles became less truculent, a feature which was noted approvingly in other medical journals.

The younger Jacob (1837–1901) also adopted ophthalmology as a speciality and published numerous articles on that subject. His most outstanding effort in this field was the foundation of the Dublin Eye and Ear Infirmary, which existed from 1872 until 1875. In 1876 he prepared an Irish medical directory. His editorship of the *Press* did not lead to any very startling developments except for occasional tiffs with its future partner, *The Medical Circular*. The standard of the paper remained high and some of the clinical material therein is still of considerable interest.

In 1865, the word 'Dublin' was dropped. At the end of the year the incorporation of the *Medical Press* and *Medical Circular* was announced. The intention was to enable a freer exchange of ideas between Ireland and Great Britain without relegating the Irish medical school to a secondary place. There were to be separate editorial staffs for both countries as well as for Scotland.

The *Medical Circular* was founded in 1852 by James Yearsley (1809–1869), an aural surgeon practising in London. Like Jacob, his opposite number in Dublin, he enjoyed a fight but often spoilt his arguments by his violence.

George Ross (1815–1875) was associated with the *Circular* from its earliest days. Prior to this he had been a contributor to the *Medical Times* and the *Lancet*, as well as to lay magazines. Probably he did most of the editorial work for the *Circular*. The first number appeared under the title of *The Medical Circular and General Medical Advertiser* as a fortnightly journal, priced threepence. Its main function was to act as a digest of current medical events. Despite a promise to avoid controversial subjects the *Circular* soon indulged in as vigorous mud-slinging as any of its contemporaries. There were many battles with the *Lancet* and its editor, of whom the *Circular* said in 1853:

We need hardly say that this notice is characterised by the usual grossness of that editor's invective, and that its mendacity is only rivalled by the artfulness with which it is designed and concealed. There are some animals that are never so happy as when rolling in slime and it is obvious that the editor of this literary kennel has qualities in common with the porcine family.

In 1855, the *Circular* was enlarged; it appeared weekly and devoted considerable space to original clinical articles. In 1865 it announced, jointly with the *Medical Press*, the amalgamation of the two journals.

The first number of the combined journal appeared on 6th January 1866, under the title of *The Dublin Medical Press and Circular*. The publisher's address was given as Dublin and it was stated that the combined journal was 'printed in Ireland − published in Ireland − edited in Ireland by Irish men and devoting itself to Irish interests.' There is no doubt that Jacob was the editor-in-chief. The word 'Dublin' in the title disappeared in 1867.

In 1868 the printing of the journal was transferred to England and the Irish predominance gradually lessened, although, even after the younger Jacob's death in 1901, prominence was given to Irish affairs. An Irish office, was continued until 1935, when the merging of the Irish Medical Association in the Irish Free State Medical Union terminated a connection of nearly one hundred years between *the Medical Press* and the Association.

Journals of the Irish Medical Association

The *Journal of the Irish Medical Association* was first published as a supplement to the *Medical Press and Circular* in December 1867. Its principal contents were to be 'matters of interest to the Poor-Law Medical Officers of Ireland.' Editors of provincial papers were invited to forward copies of their journals containing items of local medical interest.

This *Journal* appeared weekly until December 1871. At first all articles dealt with Poor-Law Reform, the wretched working conditions of dispensary doctors and the possibility of some change for the better. In January 1870 brief clinical notes were first included. These were subsequently enlarged and reports of clinical material published throughout the world were regularly printed. At the same time the title was changed to: *The Irish Medical Journal, being the Journal of the Irish Medical Association*.

In March 1871 the Postal Authorities claimed that this supplement constituted a separate journal and surcharged all copies of the *Medical Press and Circular* containing it. Accordingly the *Journal* now became the *Supplement to the Medical Press and Circular − Irish Poor Law Intelligence*. The following week (29th March 1871) the title was again altered, this time to *Irish Poor Law Intelligence under Authority of the Irish Medical Association*.

In August 1871 the editor of the *Supplement* proposed a scheme of weekly plebiscites to ascertain the feelings of the profession on matters of interest to them. This came to nothing and no reports of such plebiscites were published up to the time that the *Supplement* expired as a separate entity at the end of 1871.

In 1901 the Association entered on its sixty-second year with a record high (about 900) membership of doctors throughout the country. Unfortunately, many of the country members felt themselves divorced from the main body of the organisation centred in Dublin. With the niggardly salaries given by most Boards of Guardians few of the doctors in remote districts could even afford to attend the annual meetings.

To remedy this state of affairs the *Journal of the Irish Medical Association* was founded to serve as a link between all parts of the country. Its circulation was confined to members of the Association at the low annual subscription of half a guinea. Further proof of a desire to include country practitioners in the proceedings of the Association was given by the new practice of holding the annual meetings in towns other than Dublin.

Dr Langford Symes of 74 Merrion Square was appointed editor of the *Journal*, which appeared monthly. Unfortunately the rank and file of the Association gave little assistance to the editor and in November 1902, Symes reported to the Association the he could not continue to edit the *Journal*. Various suggestions were made for the improvement of the *Journal*, including one that it should be printed and issued by the *Medical Press and Circular*.

Some months later Dr Symes was succeeded as editor by Dr Thomas Donnelly of Rutland (now Parnell) Square. The *Journal* was enlarged and vigorous efforts were made to secure regular co-operation from country members. Unfortunately, the Association itself suffered from many internal weaknesses and full support was not available. Prior to July 1903, papers on the science and practice of medicine and surgery had been invited, but from that date the *Journal* was exclusively devoted to objects of the Irish Medical Association.

With the publication of the sixth volume in 1906 this rule was modified and reports of scientific societies were once more published. A notice inserted in this volume called on all medical men to resist vigorously the proposed tax on motor cars in so far as it affected them.

In July 1908 the editor was empowered to publish articles in Irish. Papers published under this ruling included 'An Troid i n-aghaidh na hEitinne' (The Campaign against Tuberculosis) in December 1908, and 'An Eitinn i gConnamara' (Tuberculosis in Connemara) in January 1909. In 1911 a specimen copy of the *Journal* was sent to every doctor in Ireland not already a member of the Association. This resulted in an influx of 122 new members.

In January 1914 the Council of the Irish Medical Association arranged that publication of the *Journal* should be suspended and its place taken by the *Medical Press and Circular*. The measure was adopted despite strong opposition, and Irish doctors remained without a business organ until July 1937, when a new *Journal* devoted to their professional interests appeared. This was the organ of the Irish Free State Medical Union (later the *Journal of the Medical Association of Eire*).

In its first editorial the new *Journal* laid down its objects. Briefly they were those of the Union. That is, the promotion of the interests of the medical and allied professions. A subsidiary function was to keep members informed of work which had already been done for them and to offer a forum for free discussion of medico-political problems. Arrangements were made so that members of the Union might receive the *British Medical Journal*. By this means the Irish journal's pages were left freer for discussion of local problems, while the members of the Irish Union had the benefit of a weekly bulletin on clinical subjects. One of the first measures to call for censure by this *Journal* was the action of the Government of Northern Ireland in excluding for all practical purposes practitioners educated in Southern Ireland from participation in the Dispensary and Public Health services in the Province.

The *Journal* was to undergo further alterations of format and name, the latter to some extent reflecting political changes. In 1951 it became the *Journal of the Irish Medical Association* and Mr William Doolin was appointed editor. Under his control, which lasted for eleven years, so many authors sought publication that it was necessary to increase the *Journal's* appearance to fortnightly. On Doolins death Dr H. Counihan assumed editorial responsibility until 1983 when he left Ireland to take an appointment in the Middle East. He was succeeded by Dr Hugh Staunton.

On New Year's Day 1967 a new kind of medical periodical appeared in Ireland, under the title of the *Irish Medical Times*. With a format similar to the popular tabloids it covers practically all aspects of the Irish medical scene and undoubtedly gives a forum for expression and discussion to many whose approach to subjects might not prove attractive to the editors of more conservative medical journals. There is nearly always at least one tongue-in-cheek or humourous article and over the years hundreds of medico-historical features have appeared. For the first year the *I.M.T.* appeared monthly, in the second year fortnightly, and now even its critics look forward to its weekly appearance with comments on medical affairs which not uncommonly start controversies and discussions.

Though occasional articles and letters in the Irish language were published in the journals there was little real opportunity for a doctor writing in this medium to appear in print. Acadamh na Lianna, a group of medical Irish language enthusiasts had been founded in 1968 to promote the use of Irish in the profession. Regular meetings were held and efforts were made to standardise Gaelic professional terminology. In June 1983 this group launched the first medical periodical in Irish, *Acta Medica Gaedelica*, to be published annually. The first issue carried articles on multiple sclerosis, Irish medical manuscripts and cytology, attracting contributors from both sides of the Border.

CHAPTER TWENTY TWO

WHAT OF THE FUTURE?

The views expressed in this chapter are the author's own, except where otherwise stated. They do not necessarily coincide with those of the publisher or of any other medical practitioner.

When it was decided to republish this book it was obvious that a good deal of revision would be necessary to cover the many changes which have taken place in over thirty years. Some of the problems of those days have been solved, but one of the basic ones is still largely unsolved. Who is to get into a medical school and how does one select the would-be-student? It is axiomatic in any manufacturing process that a good product can only come from the proper treatment of good raw material. I feel that too often we reject potentially good material and do not always treat what is selected in the most effective way.

What methods of student selection are available? They fall into three broad categories with variations.

A) Open admission of all students with evidence of a good standard of education to a common University first year in a Science or Arts Faculty after which, subject to examination, Faculty selection may be made.

B) An extra school year followed by a University entrance examination on subjects of the student's choice.

C) A more extensive use of an interview and assessment system.

The points system is administratively easy and that concludes the arguement in its favour. Academic brilliance does not correlate with medical ability and I am quite sure that many potentially good or even great doctors are denied entry to medical school because their school results were mediocre. It has been claimed that this is an independent assessment from outside the medical school but it is still an assessment of something which is not necessarily relevant to medicine. It could even be argued that this system tests not the pupil's ability but the school's adeptness at preparing students for academic examinations as distinct from education. Thus the scales are loaded against those with a broadly based curriculum encouraging interests and activities aimed at making a whole person rather than a good performer at examinations.

Open access to the University with Faculty selection after the first year has been tried but resulted in serious overcrowding of facilities, ruthless competition for places in the medical school and a sense of down grading of non-medical Faculties to which alleged second-raters would gravitate. If an extra school year with emphasis on science subjects is instituted then care must be taken that the resultant examination does not simply become another form of the points system. An interview no matter how searching cannot hope adequately to survey all of a candidate's abilities and aspirations but I feel must be a part of any future admission policy.

So far my comments have been largely critical and so I feel obliged to put forward three constructive suggestions. The first is that membership of a medical family should carry some weight in the selection of students. This is not a plea for a closed shop or for officially endorsed nepotism. It is a cold blooded practical suggestion with no special pleading. It is only common sense to recognise that young people brought up in a medical milieu will have a better understanding of what being a doctor entails than those brought up otherwise. They will know that 'Dr Kildare,'' Emergency Ward 10' and 'St Swithin's Hospital' are light years removed from the everyday practice of medicine with its hard, often unpleasant, aspects.

I recognise of course that many excellent students and doctors have come from a non-medical background and my second suggestion is that we should all be prepared to help such youngsters. With this in mind I propose what I have called the 'foster parent scheme.' Under this any young person wanting to enter a medical school would have to be vouched for by a doctor of at least ten years standing. This would ensure that before making a final decision a potential student would have had some discussion with someone who had been through the mill. But the sponsor's responsibility should not stop there. He or she should be kept informed of the student's progress and be available in any situation, academic or otherwise, in which mature advice and discussion would help. I am sure that, like me, most of my readers know where students have got into minor trouble which has escalated because they did not want to go to their parents or to anyone in authority in their College or Hospital and had no one to whom to turn.

My third suggestion if that if we are to introduce an extra school or pre-medical University year then an extra subject should be introduced at the earliest possible opportunity and this is advanced

First Aid. How often have we seen medical students and even our qualified colleagues helpless in a sudden emergency because they had not all their equipment with them? But there would be two extra benefits to be secured by first aid training. The student's approach to a medical situation could be assessed at an early stage and the student himself would feel, at a time when his enthusiasm for doctoring was at its strongest, that he was being taught some 'real' medicine not just pre-clinical subjects whose relevance is not always obvious to him.

Student satisfaction with the medical curriculum is, I feel, a subject which has been inadequately studied. A survey by members of the East of Ireland Faculty of the Royal College of General Practitioners in 1977 indicated an alarmingly high dissatisfaction rate amongst Dublin students particularly in relation to general practice teaching and experience. This dissatisfaction reached peaks in the pre-clinical and final years which could be interpreted as indicating disappointment at not coming into contact with patients early on and realizing, coming up to the final examinations, that some of what had been taught was irrelevant.

In relation to these points another question comes to mind. 'How many who teach students have learned how to impart knowledge?.' To communicate well requires both natural ability and training. A Diploma in Medical Education is an extra qualification we might well consider establishing.

In theory the present pre-clinical and clinical curricula would be adequately covered if we only had enough time. To extend the medical course to ten or more years would be quite impractical from several points of view, not least the financial. No matter where I suggest pruning I am going to be shot at by someone, but I do feel that a great deal of the pre-clinical laboratory work could be eliminated with no disadvantage. In the field of pathology, emphasis should be placed on the interpretation of pathological reports in relation to clinical findings, rather than on the personal carrying out of tests and examinations of gross or microscopic specimens by the student.

In hospital, patients fall broadly into two categories surgical and medical. In surgery the principles of surgical techniques, asepsis and anaesthesia can be demonstrated quite effectively on minor cases. With the heavy pressure on their time I feel that students could be better employed than attending, or assisting at, lengthy operations for uncommon conditions, interesting though these may be. Some of the time saved here could be well employed in the follow up of cases in their own homes where the impracticality of attempting an ideal dietary or other regime is often obvious to the patient, his family and his G.P., but not to the student who has only seen the victim in the artificial hospital environment.

The original closing paragraphs of this chapter are still very relevant to-day, so much so that I make no apology for reprinting them without alteration.

The question may now be raised. Has Ireland a future as a medical centre? Can she with her small population, limited finances, and limited clinical material hope to vie with other countries? I think the answer is 'yes.'

Ireland has always bred doctors who were primarily clinicians; men and women who saw the patient as a whole. They have carried this reputation with them elsewhere. If we concentrate on this aspect of medicine there is every reason why the Irish profession should develop as honoured a name as in any other country. But let us not forget that our primary duty is to relieve pain and anxiety rather than gain laurels for ourselves in abstract fields of research, even though such work may eventually be applied clinically.

Every patient has a complete anatomical museum in his body. His disease is an entity. A well-thought-out scheme of diagnosis and treatment in a single instance may be worth more than years of laboratory experience away from the bedside. Don't imagine that I scorn the laboratory worker. Far from it. Don't imagine that I scorn the man who can collect hundreds of cases of an uncommon disease with the population of a continent as his field of study. Far from it again. But I do say, that with out small population every case must be treated as if it were the only one of its kind and discussion between all those who can each collect one or two similar cases will eventually build up an imposing wealth of information.

At a meeting of the Medical Society of University College Dublin, whilst still an undergraduate, I pleaded for the publication of single interesting cases. The then President disagreed strongly with my views. A distinguished speaker, later a President of the Royal College of Surgeons, supported me and reinforced my request. He said: 'In such a small country as this few of us can hope to study more than one or two cases of the rarer diseases. But, the multiplication of these one or two cases by ten or twelve students may give us a sufficient body of material to draw fresh conclusions, make new discoveries, find more successful cures,'

We have come a long way since Diancecht founded the Irish Medical profession. Witchcraft and religion, reason and superstition, prejudice and magnanimity have all played their part in making us what we are to-day. But these were only influences. The big thing in any community is the people who make it up. The lesser are just as important as the greater. And so it is to-day.

This closing paragraph was written on a brilliant day in August in St Stephen's Green, Dublin. All around that Green are monuments to our medical past: the College of Surgeons, the houses of medical men, the old Catholic University, Mercer's and St Vincent's hospitals, the last two both founded by non-medical women.

These buildings stand because the men and women who worked in them had faith and courage. Let us make that faith and that courage our own, going forward to the future with hope, with joy, with resolution.

A Thighearna, cuirim an saothar so fá choimirce Do Chroidhe Ro-Naomhtha agus bheirim suas Duit é i gcomphoirt le D'chuid saothar mhorluaigh féin.

Thirty two years have passed since the above words were written. The interim changes in the field of medicine have been vast. Formerly lethal diseases, such as small pox, have disappeared. Diphtheria and typhoid are now rarities in this country. Tuberculosis requires months of effective treatment rather than years of often ineffectual bedrest. Pneumonia with a pre-antibiotic death rate of twenty per cent may respond within hours to the appropriate drug.

But, on the debit side there are entries too. Premature and deformed babies now survive to pose major social, economic and personal questions for their parents, their families and the community at large. Old people are maintained, sometimes in a state little better than death, because the facilities for doing so are now available and our whole instinct as doctors is to fight the Grim Reaper for as long as possible. New and sinister variants of pathology appear occasionally. Who had ever heard of Green Monkey disease or Legionaires' disease thirty years ago?. Were they in fact present, unrecognised as clinical entities in their own right?.

In the field of psychiatry a whole new literature, nomenclature and concept of treatment is still growing. Frontal lobotomy was gaining ground as a treatment in 1951. Now it is as outdated as the bromides and tight custodial care which were its predecessors. Centuries ago travellers from abroad were sometimes kept in quarantine for fear that they would import exotic diseases and foreign animals are still subject to this provision. In theory human beings are protected by vaccination and other prophylactic measures. Are these adequate and effective? Recently cholera appeared in the Mediterranean littoral after years of absence and more than one doctor in these islands, facing an exceptionally severe flu-like illness has suddenly realised that the case is in fact one of malaria.

Thirty years ago the importation of contraceptives was illegal for all and sinful for many, while a question about the possibility of pregnancy in an unmarried woman had to be put with the greatest tact. Drug addiction was rare and many doctors must have ended their working days without ever encountering the condition. Tragically, cases were seen amongst those who had access to narcotics. Doctors, nurses, pharmacists, dentists and veterinary surgeons were all at risk but at medical exhibitions samples of barbiturate drugs were available on request even to medical students without the necessity for a doctor's signature.

Many of the problems presented to the doctor of today have an ethical content which was undreamt of thirty years ago. These often involve the care of terminal cases, particularly those on a life support regime, mechanical or otherwise. The decision to switch off the ventilator may be more dramatic than the decision to withold antibiotics in a terminally ill patient developing an intercurrent infection but in each case a decision has to be made by the doctor in charge. He or she may consult colleagues, ask for legal and clerical advice or discuss with relatives but the ultimate decision rests firmly on his or her shoulders. It is a very lonely and awesome position in which to be.

When I started practice in 1941 some of the drugs and treatments I had learned were identical with those prescribed by my grandfather who qualified in 1871. Within a few years many of these were to disappear for ever and some of their successors are already forgotten. Unfortunately some of those successors are remembered only too well not for their therapeutic benefits but for their disastrous side effects. Maybe we should think very hard before we race to discard the old and adopt the new. Many of the old remedies gave comfort rather than cure but sometimes that is just what the patient needs, symptomatic relief, either combined with effective therapy or while waiting for Nature to get on very effectively with one of the basic physiological reactions, healing damaged tissue.

Unlike the original finish of this chapter these closing words were not written on a park bench in the sunshine but in my study with the sounds of family life faintly in the background, though the thoughts are much the same. We have much to be proud of in our chosen profession in Ireland. We may differ amongst ourselves in religion, in politics, in national allegiances and in our treatment of patients but in relation to the last we carry on a centuries old tradition of caring for our fellow men when they come to us for help. Perhaps our philosophy is best summed up in the Grace of the Royal College of General Practitioners:

> God be praised for food and friends
> Inspire our skills
> Kindle our compassion.
> Amen

CHRONOLOGICAL TABLE

Circa

B.C.

4000. Neolithic Period. First habitation of Ireland.

1000. Battles of Moytura. Diancecht treats wounded.

460. Birth of Hippocrates.

300. References to 'Hospital' of Princess Macha.

137. Josina, King of Scotland, studied medicine in Ireland.

A.D.

140. Dublin (Eblana) mentioned by Ptolmey.

432. St Patrick lands in Ireland.

634. Battle of Moira. St Bricin trephines wounded.

675. Monastic records of smallpox.

794. First Norse raids.

1014. Battle of Clontarf.

1101. *Regimen Sanitatis* published.

1204. Plague in Dublin.

1314. First (Latin) edition of *Rosa Anglica*.

1446. Barbers' Guild receives Charter of Henry VI.

1460. Irish translation of *Rosa Anglica*.

1479. Plague in Dublin.

1492. Discovery of America.

1496. European pandemic of syphilis begins.

1505. Royal College of Surgeons, Edinburgh, founded.

1577. Dublin Barber Surgeons receive Queen Elizabeth's Charter.

1591. Pandemic plague. Trinity College founded.

1594. Trinity College opened.

1626. Charles I authorises foundation of College of Physicians.

1641. Rebellion.

1654. Foundation of College of Physicians as Fraternity of Physicians.

1661. Boyle defines chemical elements.

1667. College of Physicians receives Charter of Charles II.

1683. Dublin Philosophical Society founded.

1692. College of Physicians receives Charter of William and Mary.

1711. Medical School of T.C.D. founded.

1718. Cook Street Surgical Hospital opened.

1733. Steevens' Hospital opened.

329

1744. Incurables' Hospital opened. Cork Charitable Infirmary founded.
1745. Original Rotunda Hospital opened.
       Constitution of a separate Apothecaries' Guild.
1755. Original Lock Hospital opened.
1756. Meath Hospital opened.
1765. Establishment of County Infirmaries' Board.
1780. Dublin Society of Surgeons founded.
1784. Incorporation of Royal College of Surgeons in Ireland.
1785. First School of Physic Act.
1791. Irish Apothecaries' Act.
1794. Belfast Lying-In Hospital opened.
1797. Birth of Robert Graves.
1798. United Irishmen's Rebellion.
       Cork Lying-In Hospital founded.
1800. School of Physic Act and Act of Union passed.
1804. Dublin Cow-Pock Institution opened.
       Cork Street Fever Hospital opened.
1805. Present building of R.C.S.I. occupied. The first building of R.C.S.I. was opened in 1810, the present (enlarged) building was completed 1825.
1806. Dublin Hospitals obliged to submit to Government inspection.
1815. Grangegorman Mental Hospital opened.
1821. Act for Insane Persons.
       Institution for Sick Children founded at 9 Pitt Street.
1826. Coombe Hospital opened.
1829. Catholic Emancipation Act.
1831. Surgical Society of Ireland founded.
1832. The Anatomy Act.
       'Corrigan's Pulse' described.
1834. St Vincent's Hospital opened.
1837. Colles' Law defined.
1838. Irish Poor Relief Act.
       Kennedy founds Dublin Obstetrical Society.
1839. *Dublin Medical Press* and Medical Association of Ireland founded.
1844. First use of hypodermic medication by Rynd.
1845. Queen's Colleges founded.
1847. Potato famine. First use of ether anaesthesia in Dublin.
1850. Queen's University founded.
1851. Establishment of Dispensary system.
1854. Foundation of the Catholic University.
1855. Foundation of the Catholic University Medical School.

1857. Mercy Hospital opened in Cork.
1858. First Medical Act established G.M.C.
1862. Mater Hospital founded in Dublin.
1867. Lister introduces antisepsis.
1876. Register opened to women.
St Michael's Hospital, Dun Laoghaire, founded.
1877. L.R.C.P.I. first granted to a woman.
1878. Public Health (Ireland) Act.
1879. Royal University founded.
1882. Queen's University dissolved.
Royal Academy of Medicine founded.
1884. National Maternity Hospital opened.
1886. Establishment of Conjoint Diploma.
1889. Amalgamation of R.C.S.I., Ledwich and Carmichael Schools.
1890. Queen Victoria's Charter to R.C.P.I.
1895. Röntgen discovers X-rays.
1898. Local Government (Ireland) Act.
1909. National University and Queen's University, Belfast, founded.
1916. Easter Rebellion.
1919. First Dáil.
1920. Abolition of Poorhouses.
1921. Establishment of Irish Free State.
1925. Local Government Act.
1928. Schools' Medical Service begun.
1933. Royal Maternity Hospital, Belfast, opened.
1937. New Constitution of Ireland.
Journal of Irish Free State Medical Union founded.
1945. Mental Treatment Act passed.
1947. Public Health Bill introduced and passed in the Dáil.
Foundation of Department of Social Services.
Public Health and Local Government separated.
1948. Dr N. Browne appointed Minister of Health.
1949. Declaration of Republic of Ireland.
1950. Dr Browne resigns.
1952. Foundation of R.C.G.P.
1953. Re-Opening of Drogheda International Missionary Hospital.
1954. Voluntary Health Insurance Scheme inaugurated.
1962. Irish Medical Union Founded.
1967. Fitzgerald report on Hospital services.
U.C.D. transferred to Belfield.
1972. General Medical Services established
Comhairle na n-Ospidéal founded.

1975. Health Education Bureau opened.
      Irish Institute of General Practice formed.
1980. New Medical Registration Council.
1981. Smallpox declared extinct.
1983. Mercers Hospital closed.
      Amalgamation of I.M.A. and I.M.U.,

BIBLIOGRAPHY

ABBREVIATIONS

B.J.O.:	*British Journal of Ophthalmology.*
B.M.J.:	*British Medical Journal.*
B.S.I.:	*Bibliographical Society of Ireland Journal.*
D.(Q.)J.M.S.:	*Dublin (Quarterly) Journal of Medical Science.*
D.H.R.:	*Dublin Historical Record.*
I.J.M.S.:	*Irish Journal of Medical Science.*
J.I.F.S.M.U.:	*Journal of the Irish Free State Medical Union.*
J.I.M.A.:	*Journal of the Irish Medical Association.*
J.M.A.E.:	*Journal of the Medical Association of Eire.*
J.R.S.A.I.:	*Journal of the Royal Society of Antiquaries of Ireland.*
M.P. & C.:	*Medical Press and Circular.*
P.R.I.A.:	*Proceedings of the Royal Irish Academy.*
U.M.J.:	*Ulster Medical Journal.*

GENERAL AND COMPARATIVE

Allison, R.S. Aspects of Medical History. U.M.J., (1941)

Baas, J.H. *Outlines of Medicine* (Harrison's translation) New York, 1889.

Bankoff, G. *Milestones in Medicine.* Museum Press, 1961.

Bulletin of the History of Medicine Johns Hopkins U.P., Baltimore. 1933 in progress.

Calwell, H.G. Development of Neurology in Belfast. *U.J.M.*, (1979).

Castiglione, A. *History of Medicine* (trans. E.B. Krumbhaar) New York, 1941.

Glendening, L. *Source Book of Medical History.* Hoeber, 1942.

Cohen, R.A. History of Dentistry with Special Reference to Irish Practitioners. *I.J.M.S.*, (1952).

Cole, F.J. *A History of Comparitive Anatomy.* Macmillan, 1949.

Comrie, John D. *History of Scottish Medicine to 1860* Bailliere Tindall, 1927.

Cooke, J.G. Landmarks in the History of Medicine. *U.M.J.*, (1932).

Cumston, C.G. *Introduction to the History of Medicine.* London, 1926.

333

Current Work in the History of Medicine Wellcome Foundation, London, 1954 in progress.

Davidson, G.R. *Medicine through the Ages*. Methuen, 1968.

Dawson, B. *The History of Medicine: A Short Synopsis*. Lewis 1931.

Doolin, W. *Wayfarers in Medicine*. Heinemann, 1947. The Arrest of Haemorrhage. *J.I.M.A.*, (1956). The Conquest of Pain. *J.I.M.A.*, (1956). The Conquest of Sepsis. *J.I.M.A.*, (1957).

Doolin. W. and Fitzgerald O. *What's Past is Prologue*. Monument Press, 1952.

Elliott, J. The Rod and the Staff. *U.M.J.*, (1979).

Fearon, W.R. The Commonwealth of Medicine. *I.J.M.S.*, (1936).

Fleming, J.B. Folklore Fact and Legend. (Obstetrics) *I.J.M.S.*, (1953).

Freind, J. *History of Physick from Galen to the XVI Century*. London, 1726.

Fulton, J. Through the Artist's Eyes (Medical Art). *U.M.J.*, (1982).

Garrison, F.H. *Introduction to the History of Medicine*. Philadelphia and London, 1929.

Garrison, F.H. and Morton, L.F. *A Medical Biography*. Grafton, 1943.

Gibson, G.B. Caesarean Birth. *U.M.J., (1962)*.

Guthrie, D. A History of Medicine. Nelson, 1945.

Hamilton, C.S.P. Landmarks in the History of Medicine. *J.I.M.A.*, (1955). History of Medicine in Russia *J.I.M.A.*, (1960).

Hayward, J. *The Romance of Medicine*. Routledge, London, 1945.

Illich, Ivan. *Medical Nemesis*. Calder and Boyers 1974.

Inglis, B. *Revolution in Medicine*. Hutchinson, 1958. *A History of Medicine*. Weidenfeld and Nicholson, 1965.

Journal of the History of Medicine and Allied Services. Yale U.P. 1946 in progress.

Kernohan, R.J. Primitive Medicine. *U.M.J.*, (1961).

Kiely, J. The Golden Age of Surgery. *J.I.M.A.*, 1974.

Landmarks in Medicine; Laity Lectures of the New York Academy of Medicine. Appleton-Century, 1939.

Laurence, C. The Healing Serpent. *U.M.J.*, (1978).

Lewis, J.T. Peaks of Clinical Medicine. *U.M.J.*, (1939).

Livingstone, R.H. History of Nursing in Belfast. *U.M.J.*, (1981).

Lloyd Wyndam, E.B. *A Hundred Years of Medicine*. Duckworth, 1939.

Lyons, J.B. The Advent of Neurophysiology. *J.I.M.A.*, (1963).

McCormick, J. *The Doctor: Father Figure or Plumber?* Croom Helm, 1979.

McKenzie, D. *The Infancy of Medicine*. Macmillan, 1927.

Medical History. London, 1957 in progress

Montgomery, F.P. Some Aspects of Medicine and Literature. *U.M.J.*, (1938).

Moore, Norman. *History of Medicine in the British Isles*. London, 1926.

Nelson, M.G. Science and the Progress of Medicine. *U.M.J.*, (1961).

Neuburger, M. *Essays in Medical History*. New York, 1932. History of Medicine (trans. Playfair) London and Oxford. (*Vol. I*, 1910; *Vol II,* 1925).

Ogilvie, W.H. Fashions in Surgery. *J.I.M.A.*, (1962).

O'Rahilly, Ronan. Three and a half Centuries of Histology. *J.I.M.S.*, (1958).

Osler, W. *Evolution of Modern Medicine*. New Haven, 1921.

Pastour, L.J. *Guide to the Study of Medical History*. London, 1931.

Philips, E.D. Beginnings of Medical and Biological Science among the Greeks, *I.J.M.S.*, (1957). The Brain in Hippocratic Writing *I.J.M.S.*, (1957). Asklepios, God of Healing. *I.J.M.S.*, (1957).

Pinkerton, J.H.M. Foetal Auscultation. Its History. *J.I.M.A.*, (1976).

Raftery, H. Anaesthesia. *I.J.M.S.*, (1968).

Rodgers, J. Whither Medicine? *U.M.J.*, (1960).

Singer, C.J. *Short History of Medicine*. Oxford, 1928.

Starobinski, J. *A History of Medicine*. Leisure Arts, 1964.

Stern, Bernhard J. *Society and Medical Progress*. Scientific Book Club, 1941.

Stokes, *et al. Medicine in Modern Times*. MacMillan, 1869.

Stubbs, S.G.B. and Bligh, E.W. *Sixty Centuries of Health and Physick*. Sampson-Low, 1931.

Towers, R.P. *et al.* Clinical Pathology. An Historical Review. *J.I.M.A.*, (1958).

Turkington, S.I. Students of Medicine. *U.M.J.*, (1937).

Walsh, J.J. *Makers of Modern Medicine*. New York, 1907.

Wheeler, J.R. Three Generations (1846–1963). *U.M.J.*, (1963).

William, H. *Masters of Medicine*. (Pioneers). Pan, 1954.

Withington, E.T. *Medical History*. London, 1894.

GENERAL IRISH

Bell, W.R. Dermatology a Century Ago. *J.I.M.A.*, (1953).

Browne, H.J. A Century of Peptic Ulcer Surgery. *J.I.M.A.*, (1979).

Callan, B. Sown in Tears Reaped in Joy (St John of God Order in Ireland) A.D.C. 1981.

Cameron, Sir Charles. *History of the College of Surgeons in Ireland*. Fannin, 1916.

Colles, W.R.F. *State of Medicine in Ireland.* Parkside, 1944.

Connell, K.H. *Irish Peasant Society.* Clarendon Press, 1968.

Cummins, R.C. Medical History of Cork. *J.I.M.A.*, (1950).

Doolin, W. and Fitzgerald, O. *What's Past is Prologue.* Monument Press, 1952.

Fleetwood, J.F. An Irish Field Ambulance in the Franco Prussian War. *Irish Sword.* Co. Meath's place in Medical History. *J.I.M.A.*, (1962).

Fraser, I. The Campbell Heritage Lives on. *U.M.J.*, (1973).

Gallagher, H.W. Medical Aspects of the First Recorded Celtic Invasion of Ulster. *U.M.J.*, (1978).

Gilbert, J.F. *Calender of Ancient Records of Dublin.* 19 volumes Dublin, 1889–1944.

Harris, W. *History of Antiquities of the City of Dublin.* Dublin, 1766.

Hennessy, T. Organisation of the Medical Profession. *I.J.M.S.*, (1922).

Hickey, E.M. Background of Medicine in Ireland. *U.M.J.*, (1932).

Irish Times. B.M.A. Supplement – July 1933. Irish Times, 1933.

Johnston, J.A.L. Medical History of Derry and Londonderry. *U.M.J.*, (1960).

Joly collection of pamphlets in the National Library, Dublin.

Kirkpatrick, T.P.C. Index to Biographical Papers. *D.J.M.S.*, (1916). Index to Historical Papers. *ibid.*

Leeson, M.A. *Reminiscences of the Franco Irish Ambulance 1870–71.* M'glashan and Gill, 1873.

Logan, J. Folk Medicine. *J.I.M.A.*, (1957).

Logan, P. *Irish Country Cures.* Appletree Press, 1981.

Lyons, J.B. Irish Head Injuries in the 18th Century. *I.J.M.S.*, (1959).

Macnamara, D.W. A Century of Practice. *J.I.M.A.*, (1966). Folk medicine in Clare. *J.I.M.A.*, (1963). A Medical Ramble in the 19th Century. *J.I.M.A.* (1963). Memories of 1918 and 'the flu'. *J.I.M.A.*, (1951).

Magennis, J.B. Medicine. *I.F.S. Hospital Year Book*, (1937).

Maloney, Michael. *Irish Ethno-Botany.* Gill, 1919.

Martin, E.A. Irish Neurological Books (1724–1894). *I.J.M.A.*, (1966).

Medical Research Council *Reports.*

Moore, Norman. Essay on History of Medicine in Ireland. *J.I.M.A.*, (1909).

Moorhead, T.G. A sketch of the History of Medicine in Ireland. *D.J.M.S.*, (1908).

Nicks, Rowan. Irish Surgeons and Australian History. *U.M.J.*, (1978).

O'Brien, E. *et al. A Portrait of Irish Medicine* – Ward River Press – in preparation.

O'Connell, C.D. Birth of a specialty. (E.N.T.) *I.J.M.S.*, (1959).

O'Connell, T.C.J. Something Old Something New. (19th Century Surgery). *I.J.M.S.*, (1960).

O'Sullivan, J.F. Highlights of Obstetrics in Ireland. *U.M.J.*, (1980).

Thorpe collection of pamphlets in the National Library, Dublin.

Widdess, J.D.H. Beginnings of Medical Microscopy in Ireland. *I.J.M.S.*, (1948).

Early Irish Opthalmology. *J.I.M.A.*, (1961).

Wilde, Lady. *Ancient Cures of Ireland.* London, 1890.

Wilde, W.R. *Irish Census: Report* (1841). Dublin, 1841. *ibid* (1851). Dublin, 1851.

Woods, Oliver. History of Medicine in Ireland. *U.M.J.*, (1981).

BIOGRAPHIES

(LISTED BY SUBJECTS ALPHABETICALLY)

Adair, Robert:— Widdess, J.D.H. *I.J.M.S.*, (1948).

Adams, Robert:— *Medical Classics, Vol. III.* William—Wilkins, 1938. O'Brien G.T. *I.J.M.S.* , (1949).

Alcock, Benjamin:— O'Rahilly, R. *I.J.M.S.*, (1947).

Andrews, Thomas:— Hunter, R.H. *U.M.J.*, (1933).

Athill, Lombe:— Recollections. *B.M.J.*, (1910).

Barry, Sir Edward:— Kirkpatrick, T.P.C. *D.J.M.S.*, (1909).

Bellingham, O'Bryen:— Mulcahy, R. *J.I.M.A.*, (1957).

Bennett, Edward H.:— O'Rahilly, R. *I.J.M.S.*, (1948).

Bermingham, Ambrose:— Hooper, A.C. *I.J.M.S.*, (1971).

Bird, Frederick:— Fleming, J.B. *I.J.M.S.*, (1959).

Cameron, C.A.:— *Reminiscences.* Dublin and London, 1913.

Campbvell, R:— Campbell, W.S. *U.M.J.*, (1963).

Carnworth, Thomas:— Elwood, J.H. *U.M.J.*, (1982).

Casey, M:— Fifty years of G.P. *J.I.M.A.*, (1981).

Cheyne, M:— *Pettigrew's Medical Portraits.* London, 1886. *Medical Classics, Vol. III.* Williams—Wilkins, 1938.

Coffey, Denis J:— O'Sullivan, J.M. *Studies* (1945).

Colles, Abraham:— Doolin W. *J.I.M.A.*, (1955). *Medical Classics, Vol. IV.* Williams—Wilkins, 1939. Hunter, R.H. *U.M.J.*, (1933). Lyons, J.B. *J.I.M.A.*, (1973). McDonnell, R. New Sydenham Society, London, 1881.

Colles, R:— *To be a Pilgrim.* – Autobiography Secker and Warburg.

Connor, Bernard:— Knott, J. *D.J.M.S.*, (1907). le Fanu, W.R. *I.J.M.S.*, (1964).

Corrigan, Sir D.:— *Medical Classics, Vol. I.* Williams—Wilkins, 1936. Dixon, F.E. *D.H.R.*, (1946). Hunter R.H. *U.M.J.*, (1933). Neuburger, M. *I.J.M.S.*, (1948). O'Brien, E. Glendale Press, 1983.Rolleston, Sir H. *I.J.M.S.*, (1932). Widdess, J.D.H. *I.J.M.S.*, (1967). Windle, B. *Twelve Catholic Men of Science.* London, 1912.

Crampton, Sir P:— Goldberg, A.H. *J.I.M.A.*, (1959).

Crawford, Thomas:— Eakin, W.A. *U.M.J.*, (1982).

Cuming, James:— Hunter, R.H. *U.M.J.* (1933).

Cunningham, D.J.:— Little, J. *D.J.M.S.*, (1912)

Doolin, W.:— Freeman, E.T. In memoriam. *I.J.M.S.*, (1962). Kiely, J. Memorial Lecture. *J.I.M.A.*, (1974). O'Connell, T.C.J. Memorial Lecture. *J.I.M.A.*, (1964). O'Connell, T.C.J. Memories of W. Doolin. *I.J.M.S.*, (1964).

Dowling, J.:— A Country Doctor Looks Back. *J.I.M.A.*, (1952).

Dun, Sir Patrick:— Anon (?William Wilde) *D. (Q). J.M.S.*, (1846). Belcher, T.W. *ibid*, (1866).

Emmett, Thomas:— McCabe, A.M.E. Medical Connection of . . . *I.J.M.S.*, (1963).

Ferguson, John C:— Pinkerton, J.M.H. *U.M.J.*, (1981).

Gaddesden, John of:— Cholemely, H.P. Clarendon Press. 1912.

Gogarty, O. St. J.:— Lyons J.B. *I.J.M.S.*, (1962).

Goldsmith, Oliver:— Lyons J.B. *I.J.M.S.*(1962).

Gordon, Alex:— Hunter, R.H. *U.M.J.*, (1933). Esler, R. *Transactions of the Ulster Medical Society*, (1877).

Drury, M.I. Graves Disease 1861–1961. *J.I.M.A.*, (1961). *Medical Classics Vol. V*-Williams-Wilkins, 1941. Stokes, W.–*Studies in Physology and Medicine* (containing life and labours of Graves)–London, 1863. Hunter, R.H. *U.M.J.*, (1933). Neuburger, M. *I.J.M.S.*, (1948).

Greatrakes, V:— Anon. *Dublin Penny Journal*, 1833.

Hamilton, C.S.P.:— Events in a Doctor's Life. (autobiography) *J.I.M.A.*, (1958).

Henle, Jacob:— Breathnach, C.S. *J.I.M.A.*, (1962).

Hippocrates:— Doolin, W. *J.I.M.A.*, (1960).

Houston, John:— Anon. *D. (Q.) J.M.S.* (1846).

Jacob, Arthur:— Sommerville-Large, L,B. *B.J.O.,* (1948). Lyons, J.B. *J.I.M.A.*, (1974). Widdess, J.D.H. *J.I.M.A.*, (1961).

Joyce, James:— Joyce's Miltonic affliction. *I.J.M.S.*, (1968).

Kirkpatrick, T.P.C.:— Obituary and list of published works. Doolin, W. *I.J.M.S.*, (1954).

Labatt, Samuel B.:— McCabe, A.M.E. *I.J.M.S.*, (1962).

Little, Robert:— Froggatt, P. *U.M.J.*, (1979). Froggatt, P. and Wheeler, W.G. *U.M.J.*, (1983).

McCormac, Henry:— Hunter, R.H. *U.M.J.*, (1933). Burden. H. *Trans. U.M.S.*, (1887). 'The open window'. Marshall, R. *U.M.J.*, (1948).

McCormac, William:— Hunter, R.H. *U.M.J.*, (1933).

Mac Cormac, H&W:— Frazer, Sir Ian, *U.M.J.*, (1968).

McDonnall, James:— Sims, S. The Founder of the Belfast Medical School. *U.M.J.*, (1932).

McDonnell, R:— Widdess, J.D.H. *I.J.M.S.*, (1952).

MacDonnell, J:— Froggatt, P. *U.M.J.*, (1976).

McDonnell, Ephraim:— *Medical Classics, Vol. II.* Williams-Wilkins, 1937.

Madden, R.R.:— *Reminiscences 1798–1886.* London, 1891.

Malcolm, Andrew:— Hunter, R.H. *U.M.J.*, (1933).

Malcolmson, A:— Calwell, H.G. Brough, Cox and Dunn, 1977.

Mosse, Bartholomew:— Anon. *D.(Q) J.M.S.* (1844). Fleming, J.B. *I.J.M.S.*, (1962). MacLochlainn, A. *J.A.M.I.* (1958).

O'Beirn, Séamus:— O'Brien, G.T. *I.J.M.S.*, (1949).

O'Glacan, Neill:— Sims. S. *U.M.J.*, (1935).

O'Halloran, S:— Lyons, J.B. *J.I.M.A.*, (1961). *I.J.M.S.*, (1963).

O'Meara, D&E:— Logan, P. *J.I.M.A.*, (1958). Le Fanu, W.R. *I.J.M.S.*, (1964).

Osborne, Jonathan:— Kirkpatrick, T.P.C. *I.J.M.S.*, (1915). Little, J. *ibid.*

Purdon, Thomas H:— Ross, R. *Transactions of the Ulster Medical Society*, 1877.

Quin, Henry:— Kirkpatrick, T.P.C. University Press, 1919.

O'Scanlon, J:— Inoculation of Small Pox. Logan, P. *J.I.M.A.*, (1964).

O'Shiel, Owen:— Logan, J. *J.I.M.A.*, (1957).

Quinlan, James:— Curtin, J. Mc A. Surgeon General to the Tzar. *I.J.M.S.*, (1967).

Sloane, Hans:— Thomson, W.W.D. *U.M.J.*, (1938).

Smyth, William:— How, F. *A Hero of Donegal.* London, 1902. Memorial Window. *Transactions of the Ulster Medical Society.* 1902.

Solomons, B:— *One Doctor in his time.* Johnston, 1956.

Stevenson, Walter:— O'Brien, G.T. *I.J.M.S.*, (1949).

Stokes, G:— Breathnach, C.S. on Haemoglobin. *I.J.M.S.*, (1966).

Stokes, William:— Acland, H. New Sydenham Society, 1882. Hunter, R.H. *U.M.J.*, (1933). Neuburger, M. *I.J.M.S.*, (1948). Stokes, W. *Wm. Stokes, his life and work.* London, 1898.

Swift, Jonathan:— Brain, W.R. *I.J.M.S.*, (1952).

Thompson, Francis:— Breathnach, C.S. *J.I.M.A.*, (1959).
Thomson, Samuel S:— Stewart, R. *U.M.J.*, (1963).
Thomson, W:— Gallagher, H.W. *U.M.J.*, (1973).
Tweedy Family:— Tweedy, O. Valentine Mitchell, 1957.
Wadding, Luke:— Logan, P. The Medical History of . . .*J.I.M.A.*, (1957).
Wakley, T:— Froggatt, P. 1979. *Journal of the Society of Occupational Medicine*, (1979).
Whitla, Sir William:— Mitchell, A.B. An Appreciation. *U.M.J.*, (1934). Kidd, C.W. *U.M.J.*, (1962).
Widdess, J.D.H.:— *Essays in Honour of J.D.H. Widdess*. Cityview Press, 1978.
Wilde, Sir William:— Wilson, T.G. *Victorian Doctor*. Fischer, 1946.
Froggatt, P. The Demographic Work of . . .*I.J.M.S.*, (1965) Centenary appreciation, Froggatt, P. *P.R.I.A.*, (1977).
Willoughby, Charles:— Kirkpatrick, T.P.C. *P.R.I.A.*, Vol 36.
Wilson, H:— Curtin, J McA. *I.J.M.S.*, (1969).
Woodroffe, J:— Cummins, N.M. A Cork Pioneer. *J.I.M.A.*, (1959).

The weekly issues of the *Irish Medical Times* usually include short biographies of both Irish and foreign doctors.

COLLECTED BIOGRAPHICAL WORKS

Cosgrave, E. MacD. and Pike, W.J. *Dublin in the 20th Century*. (brief accounts of contemporary doctors). Pike, 1908.
Doolin, W. The Pathfinders, (19th Century Clinicians). *I.J.M.S.*, (1945). Dublin's Surgeon Anatomists. *Annals R.C.S.E.* (1951).
Fleetwood, J. Some Lesser Known Irish Physicians. *Medical History*, (1972).
Gibson, G.A. Ireland and the Study of Circulation. (19th Century Clinicians). *D.J.M.S.*, (1907).
Gilborne, John. *The Medical Review—A poem*. Dublin, 1775.
Gleeson, M.E. Limerick Doctors. *Limerick Leader*, 1946.
Hayes, Richard. Some Notable Limerick Doctors. *North Munster Antiquarian Journal*, (1938).
Kirkpatrick, T.P.C. Index to Biographical notices in the *D.J.M.S.* *D.J.M.S.*, (1916). Irish Medical Obituraries. *I.J.M.S.*, (1952).
Lyons, J.B. Hall of Fame, (twelve Immortals) *J.I.M.A.*, (1978). *Brief Lives of Irish Doctors (1600–1965)*. Blackwater Press, 1978.
Madden, R.R. Irish Mesmerists. *D.(Q). J.M.S.*, (1847).
Mapother, E. Essays, (19th Century Clinicians). *Irish Monthly*, (1878). Lessons from Lives of Irish Surgeons. *D.J.M.S.*, (1873).

Meenan, F.O.C. Georgian Squares of Dublin and their Doctors. *I.J.M.S.*, (1966). Victorian Doctors of Dublin. *I.J.M.S.*, (1968).

Montgomery, D. Dublin's Contribution to Surgery. *Practitioner*, (1968).

Mulcahy, R. 19th Century Irish Cardiologists. *I.J.M.S.*, (1963).

Murphy, E.L. The Saints of Medicine. *J.I.M.A.*, (1958).

O'Brien, E. (Ed.) *Essays in Honour of J.D.H. Widdess.* Cityview Press, 1978.

Schmid, L. Irish Doctors in Bohemia. *I.J.M.S.*, (1968).

Whitla, William Biographical Sketches of Belfast Practitioners. *Transactions of the Ulster Medical Society*, (1901).

Widdess, J.D.H. Index to Biographical Papers and Notices in the *I.J.M.S.* 1916–1954 – *I.J.M.S.*, (1954). 1955–1959 – *I.J.M.S.*, (1959).

Wilson, D. J. Napoleon's Doctors on S. Helena. *I.J.M.S.*, (1971).

PRE-CHRISTIAN PERIOD

The Ancient Laws of Ireland. Dublin, 1865–1901.

Buckley, J. An ancient Hot-Air Bath House. *Journal of the Cork Historical Society*, (1913).

Hickey, E.M. Background of Medicine in Ireland. *U.M.J.*, (1939).

Joyce, P.W. *Irish Names of Irish Places.* Dublin, 1903. *Social History of Ancient Ireland.* London,1903.

Kirkpatrick, T.C.P. *Care of the insane in Ireland.* University Press, 1931. Medical Organisation in Ancient Ireland.*J.I.F.S.M.U.*, (1939).

MacManus, S. *The Story of the Irish Race.* Dublin, 1930.

MacNeill, E. *Early Irish Laws and Institutions.* London, Burns Oates, 1935.

Maloney, M. *Irish Ethno-Botany.* Dublin, Gill, 1919.

Martin, C.P. *Prehistoric Man in Ireland.* London, Macmillan, 1935.

Meyer, K. *Todd Lecture Series.* Dublin, Royal Irish Academy, 1906.

O'Curry, E. *Lectures on the Manuscript Materials of Ancient Irish History.* Dublin, 1861.

Stokes, W. Extracts from the *Book of Leinster. Revue Celtique*, Vol. III.

Wellcome, Sir H. *Medicine in Antient Ireland.* Burroughs Wellcome, 1909.

Wilde, Sir W. *Lough Corrib.* Dublin, 1867.

MEDIEVAL AND RENAISSANCE PERIODS

Archdall, M. *Montasticon*. Dublin 1873.

Boyle, R. *Medicinal Experiments*. London, 1692.

Calendar of State Papers of Ireland. London, 1874–1908.

Cardwell, M.G. *Helping the Sick*. Dublin, 1946.

Childers, E.S.E. *The Story of the Royal Hospital, Kilmainham*. Hutchinson, 1921.

Cholmeley, H.P. *John of Gaddesden*. Clarendon Press, 1912.

Cummins, R.C. Epidemics of the Middle Ages *J.I.M.A.* (1958).

Dunlevy, A.J. Notes on Ancient Gaelic Medicine. *J.M.A.E.*, (1948).

Friend, T. *History of Physick from Galen to the XVI Century*. London, 1726.

Gilbert, J.T. *Calendar of Ancient Records of Dublin*. Dublin and London, 1889–1944.

Cregg, George. Medicine at the Time of the Crusades. *U.M.J.*, (1963).

Harris, W. *The Whole Works of Sir J. Ware concerning Ireland*. Dublin, 1739.

Healy, Most Rev. J. *Insula Sanctorum et Doctorum*. Dublin and London, 1890.

Hinch, J. de W. Notes on Boates' Naturall History of Ireland 1652. *B.S.I.*, Vol. III.

Hunter, R. H. The Medieval Physician. *U.M.J.*, (1935). *Irish Builder*. Vol. 37 (1895).

Irish Manuscripts in British Library; Bodleian Library; King's Inns, Dublin; Royal Irish Academy; Trinity College, Dublin.

Joyce, P.W. *Social History of Ancient Ireland*. London, 1903.

McNeill, C. Hospital of St. John Without the New Gate. *J.R.S.A.I.*, (1925).

Moore, N. *History of Study of Medicine in the British Isles*. Clarendon Press, 1908.

O'Ceithearnaigh, Séamus. *Regimen na Slainte (I–III)*. Thom, 1942.

O'Curry, E. *Manners and Customs of the Ancient Irish*. Dublin, 1873.

O'Grady, S.H. *Catalogue of Irish MSS in the British Museum*.

Petty, Sir W. *Dublin Bills of Mortality*. London, 1683.

Ronan, Rev. M.V. Hospitals of Ancient Ireland. *Irish Independent*. (1950).

Simms, S. Neill O'Glacan of Donegal. *U.M.J.*, (1935).

Stokes, W. and Strachan, J. *Thesauras Palaeohiberniae*. Cambridge, 1903.

Walmsley, T. A Trephined Irish Skull. *Man.* (1923), No. 113.

Walsh, *Medieval Medicine.* 1920.

Walsh, Paul. *Gleanings from the Irish Manuscripts (Lilium Medicinde).* Three Candles, Dublin, 1933.

Wilde, Sir W. *Census Reports,* 1841–51.

Wulff, Winifred. *Rosa Anglica.* Irish Texts Society, Vol. XXV, 1923.

DUBLIN UNIVERSITY AND
THE COLLEGE OF PHYSICIANS

Bailey, K.C. *A History of T.C.D. (1892–1945).* Dublin University Press, 1947.

Belcher, T.W. *Records of K. & Q.C.P. in Ireland.* Hodges Smith, 1866. Memoirs of John Stearne *D. (Q.) J.M.S.,* (1865).

Bolton, R. *Translation of the Charter and Statutes of T.C.D.* Dublin 1784.

Gatenby, J.B. History of Zoology in T.C.D. *I.J.M.S.,* (1960).

Hill, E. *Address to the Students of Physic.* Dublin, 1803. *Address to the President and Fellows of K. & Q.C.P.I.* Dublin, 1805.

Kirkpatrick, T.P.C. Centenary Address. *I.J.M.S.,* (1926). *History of Medical School in T.C.D.* Hanna and Neale, 1912. Short History of the Medical School of T.C.D. *Hermathena,* (1941).

McDonnell, H.H.G. *T.C.D. Statutes.* Dublin, 1844 and 1898.

Mahaffy, J.P. *An Epoch in Irish History.* London, 1903.

Maxwell, C. *History of T.C.D. (1591–1892).* Dublin University Press, 1946.

Perceval, R. *Account of the Bequest of Sir P.Dunn.* Dublin, 1804.

Register of T.C.D. MS in T.C.D. Library.

Report of Commissioners on University of Dublin. H.M.S.O., 1853.

Rolleston, Sir H. Links Between the Colleges of Physicians of Ireland and London. *I.J.M.S.,* (1925).

School of Physic Act 1800 and amending Acts 1867.

Smith, A. History of the College of Physicians. *D.(Q.)J.M.S.,* (1849).

Shaw, G.F. *T.C.D. Statutes.* Dublin, 1898.

Stubbs, J.W. *History of University of Dublin to 1800.* Dublin, 1889.

Taylor, W.B.S. *History of University of Dublin.* Dublin, 1848.

Transactions of the Association of Fellows and Licentiates of R.C.P.I. Dublin, 1817–28.

Widdess, J.D.H. *A History of the R.C.P.I. 1654–1963.* Churchill Livingstone, 1963.

THE HOSPITALS

Annual *Reports* of the individual Hospitals.
Belcher, T.W. Notes on the Leper Hospitals of Ireland. *D.(Q.)J.M.S.*, (1868).
Belfast Hospital for Sick Children. *U.M.J.*, (1937).
Bell, M. On the Move (Belfast City Hospital). *U.M.J.*, (1979).
Benn Ulster Eye, Ear and Throat Hospital. *U.M.J.*, (1937).
Brady, C. *Dublin Hospital for Incurables.* Hodges Smith, 1865.
Calwell, H.G. *The Life and Times of a Voluntary Hospital.* (Royal Belfast Children) Brough, Cox and Dunn, 1973. The Royal Belfast Hospital for Sick Children. *U.M.J.*, (1969).
Canavan, Rev. J.E. *The Irish Sisters of Charity.* Dublin, 1941.
Campbell, W.S. The Samaritan Hospital Belfast. *U.M.J.*, (1963).
Casement, Rory. The Mater Infirmorum. (Belfast). *U.M.J.*, (1969).
A Century of Service. St Vincents Hospital. Browne and Nolan, 1934.
Corcoran, J. Dublin Hospitals – Voluntary or State? *I.J.M.S.*, (1948).
Cosgrave, E. MacD. History of Drumcondra Hospital. *D.J.M.S.*, (1916).
Cummins, N.H. The Cork Fever Hospital. *J.I.M.A.*, (1953).
Dalton, R. Hospitals; Their Origin and Development. *D.J.M.S.*, (1900).
Doolin, W. Then and Now. (St Vincents) *J.I.M.A.*, (1974).
Down Co. Infirmary Bicentenary. Morecambe, 1967.
Dublin Hospitals Commission *Report.* Dublin, 1887.
Evans, E.H. *The British Voluntary Hospital Movement.* Hutchinson, 1930. History of Dublin Hospitals 1188–1897. *Irish Builder*, (1896–7).
Feeney, J.K. The Coombe Hospital 1828–1976. *J.I.M.A.*, (1977).
Foster, E. *An Essay on Hospitals.* Dublin, 1768.
Gleeson, M.E. Barrington's Hospital. *Limerick Leader* (1945).
Hospitals' Commission's *Report.* Dublin, annually.
Howard, John. *On Lazarettos.* London, 1791.
Hunter, R.H. The Royal Maternity Hospital, Belfast. *U.M.J.*, (1937).
Hunter, R.H. The Belfast Hospital for Sick Children. *U.M.J.*
Irish Hospitals Year Book. Dublin 1937 in progress.
Johnston, R.J. Frederick Street. (Royal Victoria Hospital, Belfast) *U.M.J.*, (1940).
Johnson, Z. The Provincial Hospitals of Ireland. *D.J.M.S.*, (1891).

Keatings, R.H. Extracts from Mercer's Hospital Minute Book. *I.J.M.S.*, (1935).

Kelly, K.N.M. *The Story of the Ulster Hospital 1952–1973.* Brough, Cox and Dunn, 1973.

Kirkpatrick, T.P.C. Coombe Hospital The. *M.P.& C.*, (1944). History of Mercer's Hospital, *I.J.M.S.*, (1935). *Steevens' Hospital.* University Press, 1924. *A Calendar of Anniversaries.* Dublin, 1913. Origin of Some Dublin Hospitals. *D.J.M.S.*, (1914).

Kirkpatrick, T.P.C. and Jellett, H. *The Book of the Rotunda Hospital.* Adlard, 1913.

Leaves from the Annals of the Sisters of Mercy. New York, 1881.

Lumsden, Sir. J. Reminiscences of Mercer's Hospital. *I.J.M.S.*, (1935).

Lyons, J.B. Mercer's Hospital 1734–1972. *J.I.M.A.*, (1972). *St Michaels Hospital, Dun Laoghaire, 1876–1976.* Systems Printing, 1976.

McCreary, A. *One Hundred Years of Caring.* (Royal Belfast – Children). Brough, Cox and Dunn, 1973.

MacNamara, D.W. The Coombe in 1916. *J.I.M.A.*, (1966). The Mater, (Dublin) *J.I.M.A.*, (1961).

McNeill, Charles. History of St John Without the New Gate. *J.R.S.A.I.*, (1925).

Malcolm, A.G. History of the General Hospital Belfast. *U.M.J.*, (1851).

Mapother, E. *Dublin Hospitals.* Fannin, 1869.

Marshall, R. The Royal Victoria Hospital, Belfast. *U.M.J.*, (1936). *The Story of the Ulster Hospital.* Brough, Cox and Dunn, 1973. *The Royal Victoria Hospital Belfast.* Belfast, 1953.

Martin, L.S. *A Visual Tour of Dublin Hospitals.* Dublin, 1975.

Meenan, P.N. Modern Hospital Legislation in Ireland. *J.M.A.E.*, (1945).

Moorhead, T.G. Newcastle Sanatorium. *I.J.M.S.*, (1943). *Sir Patrick Dun's Hospital.* Hodges Figgis, 1942.

Moore, H. *et al.* Irish Hospitals and the Public. *I.J.M.S.*, (1935).

Moore, J.W. Private Hospitals or Home Hospitals? *D.J.M.S.*, (1895).

Nixon, Sir C. A General Hospital's Work. (Mater Dublin). *D.J.M.S.*, (1904).

O'Donel Browne, T.D. *The Rotunda Hospital.* Livingstone, 1947.

Ormsby, Sir L.H. *Medical History of the Meath Hospital.* Dublin 1892.

Osborne, Jonathan. *Annals of Sir Patrick Dun's Hospital.* Dublin, 1831.

Outline of the Hospital System. Report of the Consultative Council on Hospital Services. Stationary Office, Dublin, 1968.

Parkinson, R.E. *The Bicentenary of the Down Co. Infirmary.* Morecambe Bay Publishers, 1967.

Pollock, J.H. Richmond Reminiscences 1916. *J.I.M.A.,* (1958).

Quane, M. A Dublin Hospital in 1788–89. (Clarendon St) *J.I.M.A.,* (1965).

Ronan, Rev. M.V. St Stephen's Hospital. *D.H.R., (1941–2).*

Rowlette, R.J. *The Irish Hospital System, in Irish Hospital Year Book,* 1937. The Problems of the Dublin Voluntary Hospitals. *D.J.M.S.,* (1920).

St Laurence General Hospital Act 1943.

St Luke's General Hospital Act 1947.

Somerville-Large, L.B. Dublin's Eye Hospitals *I.J.M.S.,* (1944).

Stoker, Sir Thronley. Hospitals of the House of Industry. *D.J.M.S.,* (1885).

Townsend, H. *History of Mercer's Hospital. I.J.M.S.,* (1935).

Widdess, J.D.H. *The Charitable Infirmary, Jervis Street.* Hely Thom, 1968.

Wright, G.N. *A Historical Guide to the City of Dublin.* London, 1825 (Reprinted, Four Courts Press, Dublin, 1980).

THE APOTHECARIES

Donovan, M. *Letter to the Apothecaries of Ireland.* Dublin, 1833.

Haydn, F.F. *The Medical Mentor.* London and Dublin, 1822.

Keogh, J. *Botanologia Universalis Hibernica.* Dublin, 1735.

Kerr, J.J. Pharmacy in Old Dublin. *D.H.R.,* (1941–2).

Lucas, C. *Pharmacomaster.* Dublin, 1741.

McWalter, J.C. *History of the Worshipful Company of Apothecaries of the City of Dublin.* Ponsonby, 1916.

Moore, W.D. History of Pharmacy in Ireland. *D.(Q.)J.M.S.,* (1948).

The Pharmacy Acts, 1875 and 1890.

Year Books of the Apothecaries' Hall, Dublin.

THE DUBLIN SCHOOL OF MIDWIFERY

Brenan, J. *Reflections upon Oil of Turpentine.* Dublin, 1817.

Browne, O'Donel. *The Rotunda Hospital (1745–1945).* Livingstone, 1947.

Curran, C.P. *The Rotunda Hospital, its Architects and Craftsmen.* Dublin, 1945.

Davidson, A.H. The Dublin Maternity Hospitals. *Irish Hospital Year Book*,1938.

Doolin, W. The Coombe Hospital. *I.J.M.S.*, (1926).

Essen-Moeller, E. An Ancient Irish Book of Midwifery. *I.J.M.S.*, (1932).

Greer, H.L.H. Epochs in the History of Obstetrics. *U.M.J.*, (1935).

Kirkpatrick, T.C.P. The Coombe Hospital. *M.P. & C.*, (1935). and Jellet, H. *The Book of the Rotunda Hospital*. Adlard, 1913. Proceedings of the Dublin Obstretrical Society (1838–82) in *D.(Q.).J.M.S.* and separately.

Ringland, J. *Annals of Midwifery in Ireland*. Dublin, 1870.

Smyly, Sir W. Recollections of the Rotunda Hospital. *I.J.M.S.*, (1930).

Tweedy, E.H. Obstretrical Recollections. *I.J.M.S.*, (1932).

THE NATIONAL UNIVERSITY MEDICAL SCHOOLS AND THEIR PREDECESSORS

Atlantis. The Organ of the Catholic University. Dublin, 1858–63.

Cairnes, J.E. *University Education in Ireland*. Dublin, 1866.

Calendars of the University Colleges. 1909 in progress.

Cameron, Sir C. *History of the R.C.S.I*. Dublin, 1916.

Catholic University *Calendar*. Dublin, 1869.

Catholic University *Constitution*.

Catholic University *Gazette*. Dublin, 1854–6.

Comhthrom Feinne (National Student). The U.C.D. Magazine. 1931 in progress.

Cork University Record. Cork University Press. 1944 in progress.

Cummins, R.C. Hogans Skull. (Cork School) *J.I.M.A.*, (1960).

Doolin, W. Newman and his Medical School. *J.I.M.A.*, (1953).

D.W.M. *Cecilia Street. A Retrospect*. (Poem) *J.I.M.A.*, (1953).

Curran, C.P. *Nos. 95–86 St Stephen's Green*. Dublin, 1939.

Fitzgerald, D.P. The Cork Schools of Medicine. *Cork University Record*, (1945).

Haughton, Rev. S. *University Education in Ireland*. Dublin, 1868.

Irisleabhair Ollscoil na Gaillimhe. Galway, 1930 in progress.

Meenan, F.O.C. The Catholic University School of Medicine (1860–1880) *Studies*, (1977). The Catholic University School of Medicine (1880–1909) *Studies*, (1981). Cecilia Street (1909–1932), in preparation.

Molloy, Rt. Rev. G. The Catholic University School of Medicine. *Irish Ecclesiastical Record*, (1902).

Mulcahy, R. U.C.D. and its teaching Hospitals *J.I.M.A.*, (1955).

National Student, The. (U.C.D. Student Magazine.) Dublin, 1910–21.

National University Handbook, Dublin, 1932. *National University Handbook, Supplement.* Dublin, 1939.

Nixon, Sir C. *Scientific Teaching in Medicine.* Dublin, 1893.

O'Raghallaigh, D. *Sir Robert Kane.* Cork. 1942.

O'Rahilly, R. *A History of the Cork Medical School,* Cork University Press, 1949. Benjamin Alcock, Anatomist. *I.J.M.S.*, (1947). The Pre-Collegiate Medical Schools in Cork. *I.J.M.S.*, (1948).

O'Sullivan, J.M. Dr Denis F. Coffey. *Studies*, (1945).

Pollock, J.H. Medical Novitiate (U.C.D.). *J.I.M.A.*, (1959).

Quarryman, The. The Magazine of U.C.C. Cork, 1929 in progress.

Report of. Queen's Colleges Commission. Dublin, 1858.

St Stephen's. (A Record of the Catholic University,) Dublin 1901–5.

Sullivan, W.K. *University Education in Ireland.* Dublin, 1866.

Taylor, M. *Sir Bertram Windle: A memoir.* Longmans, 1932.

University College, Cork, Official Gazette. Cork 1911–1918.

University College, Dublin, a page of Irish History. Talbot, 1930.

U.C.D. Its building Plans. Browne and Nolan, 1959.

Walsh, W.J. *The Irish University Question.* Dublin, 1897.

Wheeler, T.S. *Sir Robert Kane: His Life and Work.* Life and Work of William K. Sullivan. *Studies.* (1945).

Whittle, J.L. *Freedom of Education–What it means.* Dublin, 1866.

THE BELFAST SCHOOL

Allison, R.S. *The Seeds of time.* Brough, Cox and Dunn. 1972. *The Very Faculties.* (Eye and ENT) Baird, 1969.

The Belfast Book. Carswell, 1929.

Cuming, James. Address to Ulster Medical Society. *D.(Q.) J.M.S.*, (1868).

Esler, Robert. Early History of Medicine in Belfast. *D.J.M.S.*, (1885). The Ulster Medical Society and its Presidents. *D.J.M.S.* (1886).

Frazer, Ian. The first three Professors of surgery. *U.M.J.*, (1976).

Froggatt, P. The foundation of the 'Inst' *U.M.J.*, (1976). The first Medical School in Belfast. *Medical History*, (1978).

Hickey, E.M. Medicine and Surgery in Belfast 50 years ago. *U.M.J.*, (1935).

Hunter, R.H. The Royal Maternity Hospital. *U.M.J.*, (1937). The Belfast Medical School. *U.M.J.*, (1937).

Johnston, R.J. Frederick Street, (Royal Victoria Hospital, Belfast). *U.M.J.*, (1940).

Kennedy, D. *Towards a University*. Baird, 1946.

Leman, R.M. Fifty years. A Radiographic Retrospect. *U.M.J.*, (1966).

Livingstone R.H. History of Nursing in Belfast *U.M.J.*, (1981).

Lyle, W. The Dispensary Doctor . *U.M.J.*, (1983).

Macafee, G.H.G. The Belfast School of Obstetrics. *U.M.J.*, (1942).

McCreary, A. *Survivors*. Century Books, 1976, 1983.

Malcolm. A.G. *History of the General Hospital, Belfast*. Belfast, 1851.

Marshall, R. Address to Royal Victoria Hospital Belfast. *U.M.J.*, (1936). *Book of Belfast* (B.M.A. Meeting Souvenir). Belfast, 1937.

Russell, M. The Dispensary System in Ulster. *U.M.J.*, (1983).

Simms, S. Curious Advertisements of old Ulster Physicians. *U.M.J.*, (1933).

Strain, R.W.M. The History and associations of the Belfast Charitable Society. *U.M.J.*, (1953). The History of the Ulster Medical Society. *U.M.J.*, (1967).

Ulster Medical Society Transactions. 1877–1932.

Wheeler, J.R. The Belfast School of Ophthalmology. *U.M.J.*, (1944).

Whitla Medical Institution, Foundation. *Belfast News Letter* (April, 1902).

ADMINISTRATION AND PUBLIC HEALTH

Barr, A. Tuberculosis in Ireland 1850–1900. *I.J.M.S.*, (1956).

Cameron, Sir C.A. Reports on Public Health. *D.(Q.) J.M.S.*, (1869–1906).

Civics Institute of Ireland. *Public Administration in Ireland*. Parkside, 1944.

Clarke, J.J. *Local Government of the United Kingdom*. Pitman, 1929.

Clery and McWalter. *The P.H. Admendment Act of 1907*. Ponsonby, 1908.

Crowe, Morgan. Origin and Development of P.H. Services in Ireland. *I.J.M.S.*, (1948).

Dewhurst, K. The Genesis of State Medicine in Ireland. *I.J.M.S.*, (1956).

Falkiner, N.M. The Evolution of the Diploma in Public Health. *I.J.M.S.*, (1924).

Finnane, M. *Insanity and the Insane in Post-Famine Ireland.* Croome Helm, 1981.

Handbook of Saorstát Eireann. Irish Free State. Talbot Press, 1932.

Health Services Act 1947. Northern Ireland Official Publications.

Hennessy, T. Ireland and a Ministry of Health. *D.J.M.S.,* (1918).

Kirkpatrick, T.P.C. *Care of the Insane in Ireland.* University Press, 1931.

Knight, C. *Public Health Acts.* Knight, 1937.

Logan, P. The Census in Ireland. Petty to Wilde. *J.I.M.A.,* (1975).

McDonnell, R.P. *Manual of Sanitary Law.* Powell, 1945.

Meenan, P.N. Modern Hospital Legislation in Ireland. *J.M.A.E.,* (1945).

Moore, Sir J.W. Epidemiology in Ireland: Past and Present. *I.J.M.S.,* (1928). Hindrances to Public Health Work in Ireland. *D.J.M.S.,* (1921).

Musgrave, J.A. History of Public Health Services. *Irish Medical Directory,* 1939.

O'Brien, W.P. *The Great Famine.* Downey, 1896.

Public Assistance Orders, Various. Government Publications. *Report of the Commission on the Relief of the Sick and Destitute poor including the Insane poor, 1928,* Government Publications, Dublin.

Review of the above report. Eason, 1928.

Reports (annual) of the Departments of local Government and Public Health and Social Services. Government Publications.

Reports (annual) of the County medical Officers of Health.

Rowletter, R.J. Medical Reform in Ireland. *D.J.M.S.,* (1921).

Shanley, J.P. The State and Medicine. *I.J.M.S.,* (1929).

Story, J.B. The National Insurance Bill. *D.J.M.S.,* (1911).

White Paper on Health Services. Government Publications, 1947.

Year Books of the Departments of Local Government and Public Health. *ibid.*

MEDICAL EDUCATION

Bailey, J.B. *Diary of a Resurrectionist.* Sonnenshein, 1896.

Ball, J.M. *The Sack-em-up-Men.* Oliver and Boyd, 1928.

Breathnach, C.S. The Advancement of Learning. *J.I.M.A.,* (1962).

Colles, W.R.F. *State of Medicine in Ireland.* Parkside, 1944. Medical Education in Ireland. *I.J.M.S.,* (1954).

Cameron, C.A. *History of the R.C.S.I.* Fannin, 1916.

Counihan, T. and Gatenby, P. The Dublin School of Medicine. *J.I.M.A.,* (1961).

Doolin, W. Medical Education in Ireland. *Studies*, (1925). Dublin's Medical Schools. Burroughs Wellcome, 1952.

Doyle, E. The Dublin School of Medicine. *J.I.M.A.*, (1961).

Duff, F.A. The making of a Doctor *J.I.M.A.*, (1976).

Fitzgerald, P.A. Medicine and Education. *J.M.A.E.*, (1945–6).

Fleetwood, J.F. Dublin's Private Medical Schools. *I.J.M.S.*, (1948). The Future of Medical Education. *J.M.A.E.*, (1943).

Fleetwood, J. and Coggin, J. A Survey of Medical Student Opinion in Dublin. *J.I.M.A.*, (1977).

Holland, T.S. *The Irish School of Medicine as it is and as it ought to be.* Cork, 1853.

Kelly, D.A. *et al.* Medical Graduates of the Seventies – *Supplement* to *I.J.M.S.*, (1982).

Kirkpatrick, T.P.C. Diary of a Medical Student 1831–7. *D.J.M.S.*, (1913). Schools of Medicine in Dublin in the 19th Century. *B.M.J.*, (1933).

Langdon-Browne, W. The Origin and Purport of Universities. *I.J.M.S.*, (1940).

Lavelle, P.A. Liberal Education for the Medical Student. *J.I.M.A.*, (1953).

Lowry, W.S.B. Medical Education in the U.S. *U.M.J.*, (1964).

McCormack, J.S. What is wrong with Medical Education? *I.J.M.S.*, (1980).

MacNamara D.W. Student Life in the 19th Century. *J.I.M.A.*, (1961).

Medical Students' Guide. Fannin, 1855.

Moore, H. Relations of Hospitals to Schools, Profession and Public *I.J.M.S.*, (1935).

Moore, J.W. Medical Education in 1887 (Carmichael College). *D.J.M.S.*, (1888).

Newman, C. The Evolution of Medical Education in the 19th Century. *J.I.M.A.*, (1971).

Newman, J.H. *Discourses on University Education.* Duffy, 1852. *Idea of a University.* Pickering, 1881.

O'Rahilly, R. The pre-Collegiate Medical Schools in Cork. *I.J.M.S.*, (1948). *A History of the Cork Medical School 1849–1949.* Cork U.P., 1949.

Prospectuses and Advertisements of the Schools and Colleges.

Reports of Medical Education Investigation Committee. Dublin, 1945.

Storey, W.L. Undergraduate Days. (Belfast). *Transactions of the Ulster Medical Society,* (1904).

Symposium on Medical Education. *I.J.M.S.,* (1926).

Tunbridge, R.E. Clinical Apprenticeship. *J.I.M.A.*, (1971).

Turkington, S.I. The Resident Pupil System. *U.M.J.*, (1938). Students of Medicine. *U.M.J.*, (1937).

Westwood, James. Medical Education in Ireland. *Sunday Independent*, (1946).

THE ROYAL COLLEGE OF SURGEONS

Anaesthetists' Faculty Foundation. *I.J.M.S.*, (1959).

Berry, H.F. The Ancient Corporation of Barber Surgeons Dublin. *J.R.S.A.I.*, xxxiii, (1903).

Cameron, Sir C.A. *History of the R.C.S.I.* Fannin, 1916.

Charters of the College.

Doolin, W. Dublin Surgery 100 Years Ago. *I.J.M.S.*, (1949).

Dwyer, F. Conway. The R.C.S.I. and the War. *D.J.M.S.*, (1915).

Flanagan, H. Twenty years a Growing: The R.C.S.I. 1961–1981. *J.I.C.P. & S.*, (1981).

Mapother, E. The Founders of the College of Surgeons. *Irish Monthly*, (1887).

Moore, W.D. Records of the Barber Surgeons of Dublin. *I.J.M.S.*, (1849).

Thorpe collection of pamphlets in the National Library, Dublin.

Wall, Cecil. *History of the Surgeons' Company*. Hutchinson, 1937.

Webb, J.J. *The Guilds of Dublin*. Three Candles Press, 1929.

Widdess, J.D.H. Catalogue of Books in R.C.S.I. *I.J.M.S.*, (1948). *An Account of the Schools of Surgery-Royal College of Surgeons, Dublin*. Livingstone, 1949. The R.C.S.I. in 1916. *J.I.M.A.*, (1960). *The R.C.S.I. and its Medical School 1784–1984*. R.C.S.I. Publications, 1983.

SOCIETIES AND PUBLICATIONS

Browne, A.D.H. The Role of the Royal Academy of Medicine in Ireland. *I.J.M.S.*, (1976).

Burke, M.P. The Dublin Surgical Society. *I.J.M.S.*, (1954).

Cameron, R.C. Selections from *Trans. of Cork Medical Society* 1854–63. *I.J.M.S.*, (1936).

Counihan, H.E. The Medical Association of Ireland. *J.I.M.A.*, (1978).

Cox, Alfred. *Among the Doctors*. Johnson, 1956.

Doolin, W. Recollections of the Medical Society U.C.D. *National Student*, (1944).

Foot, A.W. *Reminiscences of the Biological Club*. Dublin 1892.

Froggat, P. and Thos. Wakley. *The Lancet* and the Surgeons. *Journal Irish College of Physicians and Surgeons.*

Garrison, F.H. and Morton, L.F. *A Medical Bibliography.* Grafton, 1943.

Hennessy, T. Organisation of the Irish Medical Profession. *D.J.M.S.*, (1922).

Hunter, R.H. History of the Ulster Medical Society. *U.M.J.*, (1936).

Hurry, J.B. *History of the Reading Pathological Society.* London, 1909.

Irish Medical Union. *Medical Monthly* (1982).

Irish Poor Law Medical Officers' Association *Reports.* Dublin 1871, *et seq.*

Kirkpatrick, T.P.C. The Dublin Medical Journals. *I.J.M.S.*, (1932). Irish Medical Periodicals. *D.J.M.S.*, (1915). Wm. Kingsley and the Royal Medical Benevolent Fund. *J.M.A.E.*, (1942). The Royal Academy of Medicine In Ireland *M.P. & C.*, (1937). The Periodical Publications of Science in Ireland. *B.S.I.*, (1922).

Le Fanu, W.R. *British Periodicals of Medicine.* Baltimore, 1938.

Little, E.M. *History of the B.M.A. 1832–1932.* London, 1932.

Medical Societies and Journals in Ireland. *I.J.M.S.*, (1968).

Montgomery, D.A.D. The Ulster Medical Society. *U.M.J.*, (1976).

Moore, J.W. Medical Education in 1887. *D.J.M.S.*, (1888).

Moorehead, T.G. Presidential Address to 101st Annual Meeting of B.M.A. *B.M.J.*, (1933) and *I.J.M.S.*, (1933). First Ten Years of the Medical Association of Ireland. *J.M.A.E.*, (1946).

Power, Sir D'Arcy. British Medical Societies. *M.P. & C.*, (1939).

Reid, S.P.J. D.U. Biological Society and D.U. Medico- Chirurgical Society. *I.J.M.S.*, (1974).

Rowlette, R.J. *The Medical Press and Circular. M.P. & C.*, (1939). Medical Organisation in Ireland, 1839–1939. *J.I.F.S.M.U.*, (1939).

Royal Academy of Medicine in Ireland (Centenary) *I.J.M.S.*, (1983).

Sachs, S.B. Dublin University Biological Association 1801–1900 *I.J.M.S.*, (1936).

Shanley, J.P. Origin and Foundation of the I.F.S. Medical Union. *J.M.A.E.*, (1946).

Ulster Medical Society List of Past Presidents and Members. *U.M.J.S.*, (1932).

Vaughan, Paul. *Doctor's Commons.* Heinemann, 1959.

Ware, J. *History of Writers of Ireland.* Dublin, 1764.

Wilde, W. Periodic Medical Literature in Ireland. *D.(Q.) J.M.S.*, (1846).

Widdess, J.D.H. *Collectanea Hibernica Medica. I.J.M.S.*, (1955).

THE ROYAL COLLEGE OF GENERAL PRACTITIONERS

Files of the College *Newsletter* and *Journal.*
Fry, J. *et al. A History of the R.C.G.P.* M.T.P. Press, 1983.
Gilliland, I. The Renaissance of General Practice. *J.I.M.A.*, (1972).
Moran, I.B. Progress of R.C.G.P. in N.I. *U.M.J.,* (1979).
Waine, C. *et al. The R.C.G.P. members Reference Book.* Sabrecrown, 1982.
Woods, O. A History of Medicine in Ireland. *U.M.J.*, (1982).

Index

355